CW01497459

Porcupine in a Python's Throat

Porcupine in a Python's Throat

The Ambazonia Story in West Central Africa

Edited by Fonkem Achankeng

LEXINGTON BOOKS

Lanham • Boulder • New York • London

Published by Lexington Books
An imprint of The Rowman & Littlefield Publishing Group, Inc.
4501 Forbes Boulevard, Suite 200, Lanham, Maryland 20706
www.rowman.com

86-90 Paul Street, London EC2A 4NE

British Library Cataloguing in Publication Information Available

Library of Congress Cataloging-in-Publication Data

Names: Achankeng, Fuankem, editor.
Title: Porcupine in a python's throat : the Ambazonia story in West Central Africa / edited by Fonkem Achankeng.
Description: Lanham, Maryland : Lexington Books, 2023. | Includes bibliographical references and index.
Identifiers: LCCN 2023028477 (print) | LCCN 2023028478 (ebook) | ISBN 9781793632289 (cloth) | ISBN 9781793632296 (ebook)
Subjects: LCSH: Self-determination, National—Cameroon—West Cameroon. | West Cameroon (Cameroon)—History—Autonomy and independence movements. | West Cameroon (Cameroon)—Politics and government.
Classification: LCC DT581.W4 P67 2023 (print) | LCC DT581.W4 (ebook) | DDC 967.11—dc23/eng/20230620
LC record available at https://lccn.loc.gov/2023028477
LC ebook record available at https://lccn.loc.gov/2023028478

This book is dedicated to the memory of
Mr. M. G. Thomson, MP representing Dundee,
East Constituency in the British House in 1961

Contents

Preface

The first reason for choosing to work on this book is the democratic need to understand any group of people from their own perspectives. The people of ex-British Cameroons in postcolonial British West Africa are not known, studied, and understood as a disappearing people. Compelled by the United Kingdom and the United Nations to accede to independence by joining in October 1961, the British Southern Cameroons, a UN Class B Trust Territory under UK administration, soon found itself annexed and re-colonized by Republique du Cameroun, another Class B Trust Territory under the French. This book is a unique opportunity to understand the people, who because of their colonial plight and the increasing numbers seeking asylum across the world finally found themselves in a genocidal war to restore independence. Until we listen to the people themselves on how and why they engaged in a war of self-defense in the British Southern Cameroons territory missing in the political map of postcolonial Africa, we may never have a complete picture of the re-colonized lives of the people. This book is written because of the need to understand the uniqueness of the unending colonial experiences and situations involving the British Southern Cameroons and its people.

Above all, the idea to work on this book began in my mind many years ago when I first read Stanley Nzefeh's piece titled "The Anglophone Problem in the Cameroons: The Real and Disturbing Dimensions" in *Cameroon Review*, Vol. 1, pp. 6–7 in 1994. When Nzefeh wrote his piece, it was an un-named crime in *Republique du Cameroun* punishable possibly by disappearance to use the name "British Southern Cameroons," the name of the West African UN Trust Territory of the Cameroons under the UK administration. For strange reasons, the people of this territory were compelled at independence by the UK (trustee) and the UN (trustor) to accede to "independence by joining" one of two neighbors. The territory joined *Republique du Camer-oun* on October 1, 1961 (UNGA Res. 1608). The verb "join" is used here in quotation marks because the people of British Southern Cameroons argue that the 1961 joining in the UN-recommended "Independence by Joining" concept did not legally take place even if "independence by joining" did not make/does not make any sense from the standpoint of freedom as intended by nationalism scholars. However, when Nzefeh wrote his piece, the people and their territory had become known as "Anglophones." This new name aka label also corresponded to "West Cameroon" (1961–1972), "Northwest and Southwest Provinces" (1972–2000), and later "Northwest and Southwest Regions" or worse still "NOSO" in a nutshell. These different names of British Southern Cameroons are used in this book, and all refer to the same territory. The different names or labels are only a pointer to the many and varied colonial experiences of the people and the territory under the British (1858–1885), the Germans (1885–1816), the British again (1916–1961), Nigerians (1922—1960), and *Republique du Cameroun* (1961–Present).

Why was it taboo to use the name of the people and territory after "joining?" Colonial theory informs its students that taking away one's name is a way to deprive one of one's identity. And when once that is done, one is lost. The intention of depriving the people of the name of their territory from the time of "joining" was part of a planned agenda to take the territory away from itself and its people, and from the political map of Africa. It was intended to completely assimilate the people into French Cameroon in French Equatorial Africa. The president of *Republique du Cameroun* thinking he completed the assimilationist agenda in 1984, unilaterally changed the name of the country back to *Republique du Cameroun*, the name French Cameroon gained her independence from France on January 1, 1960. That president was to affirm this fact at the November 2019 Paris Peace Conference in an interview with Mo Ibrahim.

The idea of the book kept roaming behind my mind until Nfor Ngala Nfor, a leading British Southern Cameroons' nationalist leader and National Chairman of the Southern Cameroons National Council (SCNC), approached me for assistance with publishing a book manuscript he had on the British Southern Cameroons. As I read through his manuscript, a section stood out so eloquently that I decided (with the author's permission) to extract it from that book. That extract from Nfor Ngala Nfor's book and Stanley Nzefeh's 1994 article formed the basis for this book. With the two foundation stones in my mind, this book evolved as a series of separate essays, and I cannot claim for it the virtues of any systematic organization. Each chapter in the book is an essay, and each essay is a self-contained argument. Nevertheless, the book as one whole has a single point of reference and a single argument. The reference point is the Southern Cameroons' independence and sovereignty question in British West Africa. Although repressed for many decades through the manipulation of discourse, the suppression of history, the manipulation of the educational system, and many other methods, the Southern Cameroons' independence and sovereignty question remained persistent among the people of the territory, hence the analogy of a "porcupine in the throat of a python" that tried to swallow the porcupine. That legendary porcupine remained stuck in the python's throat—unable to be swallowed. The prescription from this book is for the services of a skillful surgeon to save the lives of both the porcupine and the python. That skillful surgeon remains the UN, the organization formed after the Second World War to ensure international peace and security and promote international cooperation.

From the different chapters in this book, it is clear that in the case of ex-British Southern Cameroons' independence question, the UK and the UN can be said to be at the origin of the problem they created in 1961. As I worked on this book, the problem remained as clear as it was in 1961. It only got further compounded by colonial annexation and war. In a House of Commons debate in August 1961 reported in the *Hansard* (vol 645 cc1332-51), G. M. Thomson of Dundee East stated:

Normally, the point of reaching independence is a matter for congratulation and celebration, but I think that it must be frankly said that in this case the Southern Cameroons is approaching conditions of full independence in circumstances of singular obscurity and considerable peril.

He added,

The problem of uniting these two territories would in any event be difficult. They are two territories of completely different cultures, with different political systems, the one English-speaking and the other French-speaking in the language of its administration. There are extremely complex problems in bringing these two countries together within one national State.

The warning was very clear "for the welfare of the inhabitants of the territory, for which the United Kingdom Government had been responsible ever since the First World War and whose wishes the United Kingdom had the responsibility to see fulfilled."

Porcupine in a Python's Throat provides a glimpse into the lives of the people of ex-British Southern Cameroons after 1959 when they were the first people in Africa to organize free, fair, and transparent multiparty elections and to democratically and peacefully transfer power from one administration to another. A subject of International Law from the First World War, the British Southern Cameroons was self-governing from 1954 following the developments after the 1953 London Conference from 30 July to 22 August. This book contributes to the story of these people and their territory in colonial bondage since 1846, why they fight for freedom and why the people finally found the energy to tell the world they would fight until their freedom comes.

The reason for this book I must mention again is that the Southern Cameroons' restoration of sovereignty question has remained seriously debated for decades within and among political and intellectual allies and opponents alike in many circles. Dag Hammarksjold, UN Secretary General (1953–1961), for example, pointed out that "Uniting the Southern Cameroons to the Cameroun Republique is like forcing a balloon under the sea. One day, it will come out." Clement J. Zabloiski of the United States (D-WI) also argued at the UN that "the results of a hurried choice imposed on the population of the Trust Territory would be catastrophic for their political future" (1959). On November 30, 2018, President Paul Biya of *Republique du Cameroun* declared war on the people of the territory claiming to defend a "one and indivisible Cameroon."

The questions on the minds of the people of the territory always were and remained, how do people with a homeland, a history of successful and democratic self-governance with known, recognized, and marked international boundaries continue to disappear from the map of Africa and the world? How does a territory with a history in International Law dating as far back as 1846 when the British signed treaties with Ambazonian Coastal Chiefs from Bimbia disappear from history and descend from a self-governing people to a tribe and to nothing? How could a people be shifted by transfer from an advanced existence where the difference was debated dialogically to one where dialogue became replaced by state terror and genocide? Above all, and in the age of a BREXIT generation, the question increasingly being asked is, who gives any people the right to determine what other people become or do not become? These questions demand answers and an understanding of this *Porcupine in a Python's Throat*, aka an understanding of the persistence of the independence and sovereignty question of the former British Southern Cameroons in ex-British West Africa.

Acknowledgments

Let me now acknowledge the different authors of the chapters in this volume for the interest and time they took to put together the different contributions. I am most thankful to many of them who were very encouraging as the idea of this book developed. Many of the different contributors shared my viewpoint about persisting colonial relationships within nation-states in a world said to be postcolonial. Amid the 21st-century rhetoric on freedoms and human and people's rights, many of the contributing authors have brought the invisible realities of a people in colonial bondage to the forefront. These contributors who are scholars from ex-British Southern Cameroons, a territory expected to be independent from October 1, 1961, but currently still within the borders of the Republic of Cameroon, make the important contributions that represent the voices of the colonized in the 21st century.

I owe a debt of gratitude to all the friends and colleagues with whom I have had conversations on the lived experiences of the people of ex-British Southern Cameroons aka Ambazonia as we grew our ideas on this book. As indicated earlier, I also owe a very special debt of gratitude to Stanley Nzefeh and Nfor Ngala Nfor for their academic contributions to the independence struggle of the ex-British Southern Cameroons, which formed the mindset for this book. I also want to thank particularly Professor Carlson Anyangwe, one of the pioneers of the freedom struggle of ex-British Southern Cameroons, who never wavered in his vision for and passion about the freedom of the territory and her people. Similarly, I remain indebted to all the contributors to this volume. They continue to believe strongly that any meaningful peace must be based on justice. I do not leave out Becca Rohde Beurer of Rowman and Littlefield, who saw the merit in this book.

To my family, I express my profound gratitude for all the love, encouragement, and support over the years as I reflected on the plight of the people of ex-British Southern Cameroons (Ambazonia) and worked on this book and other intellectual projects. Finally, my debt of gratitude goes to God Almighty for my mother's health. God kept her alive for many years but finally took her home as I was completing work on this book manuscript. Thank you, God, for taking her home and for the independence and sense of direction I continued to notice in one of my children as she looked forward to beginning her university education with over 30 Credits and a full scholarship for four years.

Introduction

This book presents one example of the reality that sovereignty and social conflict remain alive and a subject of debate to this day not just in supposedly postcolonial states but even in empires of old with the example of Scotland's desire to break free from Great Britain. The difference with the story of ex-British Southern Cameroons aka Ambazonia is that whereas the issues across the globe are debated dialogically in the 21st century, in the case of ex-British Southern Cameroons (Ambazonia), the people are killed like flies (Dias, 2019) in a genocidal war for daring to demand to restore their sovereignty rights as a people on a basis of history and International Law.

International Law theory indicated that when a colonial power established a presence along the coast, the hinterland of that area also belonged to that colonial power by virtue of the hinterland doctrine. That theory only changed at the Berlin Conference of 1884–1885 to one of effective occupation. A glimpse of more than one century and a half of Southern Cameroons' aka Ambazonia's colonial experience under many different colonial masters and notably the nearly 60 years of annexation and colonial occupation by the Cameroon Republic in Central Africa is the concept Karl Mannheim referred to as the "social document." The social document is the narration of lives and/or events that, through their fullness, elegance, and clarity, embody a more comprehensive pattern of events and perspectives. The "social document" is the approach in *Porcupine in a Python's Throat: The Ambazonia Story in West Central Africa*. This book is an account of some 60 years of life and society in ex-British Southern Cameroons (Ambazonia) in ex-British West Africa and beginning on October 1, 1961, in Cameroon Republic (in ex-French Equatorial Africa).

From the accounts of the people, the Southern Cameroons (Ambazonia) restoration of sovereignty conflict has its own unique context. Compared with other similar conflicts, it is not a minority conflict as some people may want to depict it. It is not a religious conflict. It is not an ethnic conflict as we find in the literature. It is also not a conflict over any disputed territory or even a disputed natural resource like a waterway. Unlike many other intractable conflicts, the Southern Cameroons' freedom conflict is not even an ideological struggle. Rather, it is singularly about the freedom and rights of a people. It is primarily a case of a self-governing people, with recognized international boundaries in history, who were cheated out of their right to independence in 1961 and have since found their territory annexed and re-colonized. The native population has been involved in a struggle to restore the statehood and independence of its homeland in accordance with the UN principles: the UN Charter in its Article 76 (B), the UN Trusteeship Agreement, and the 1960 UNGA Declaration on Colonial Countries and Peoples. It is the case of a people who assert their fundamental right to be masters of their own future, based on their history and on International Law.

The sovereign independence of any people with a territory recognized under International Law is an inherent and inalienable right, not a privilege. This understanding of human rights and the reliance on the concept of human rights establish the basis on which the restoration of statehood struggle was and/or is founded. The reality, however, was and/or is at considerable variance. The application of that concept in the case of the ex-British Southern Cameroons was not what the people had envisioned in the freedom struggle. The people found it difficult to understand why the issue of their "human rights" did not appear to be acknowledged in the West, principally in the UK and the UN. These powerful actors do not seem to perceive the restoration of statehood struggle as founded on human and people's rights principles; from a Western perspective, human rights refer mainly to the rights of individuals rather than to groups and peoples.

The outside world appears to experience life in Cameroon without the knowledge that there were two Cameroons, one of which was considered "expendable" by the UK and compelled to accede to "independence by joining." It is very unclear whatever "independence by joining" concept really meant to the UK, trustee of the people and territory of British Cameroons and the UN as trustor. For life among the ordinary people of the former UN Trust Territory of the Cameroons under UK administration, *Porcupine in a Python's Throat* offers a gripping perception of history and change in the destiny of the people of British Southern Cameroons in colonial British West Africa who, after a century and a half of colonial subjugation, consider themselves as invincible. The people's perception as invincible is an anti-colonial message to a world community that preaches freedom and democratization and yet sacrifices a people practicing freedom and democracy to an endless colonial experience. Tired of the colonial experience in which the UK (trustee) and the UN (trustor) plunge them in 1961, the people of the territory rose in 2016 against fear and cowardice to restore freedom and determine their lives. Acts of fear and cowardice in the face of a state of Cameroon's terror are balanced by acts of courage and the ability to raise awareness and resist the new desperate circumstances of the lives of an otherwise very trusting people of the territory. A people forced to endure a genocidal war and mass suffering resulting from political, historical, and other circumstances, which they neither sought nor created, but which they understood and wanted to change in accordance with the Charter of the UN Article 76(b) and many UN principles, including UN General Assembly Resolution 1514 (XV) that "All peoples have the right to self-determination; by virtue of that right they freely determine their political status and freely pursue their economic, social and cultural development."

The debates on the political future of ex-British Cameroons always constituted a central theme in family conversations and within circles of friends and colleagues in the Cameroons, West-Central Africa. Over the decades, these debates continued to be very animated, as the ex-British Cameroons' struggle to restore statehood status increased in intensity. In an article in the *East Oregonian* of June 6, 2010, Harriet Isom, US ambassador to Cameroon from 1993 to 1996, asserted that "the dichotomy between the former British colonial part of Cameroon and the larger, dominant, former French colonial Cameroon still exists." The dichotomy and the political tensions that go with it resulted in massive refugee flows from Cameroon into a genocidal war in 2017.

Understanding the basis of these debates among the people of British Southern Cameroons (Ambazonia) on new subjects by "unionists with Cameroun," "federalists," and "independentists" amid cynically selected and manipulated opinions in the territory is the reason for this book. It argues that understanding a people living in a situation of political, social, psychological, and economic despair as well as hopelessness from over a century of colonial subjugation may be useful in grasping and rationalizing some of the choices the people can make to find any iota of dignity to their lives. This may be more important when the people have great memories of who they once were and how well they ran their lives before "the pitch darkness and plunder fell upon them" (Anyangwe, 2011, p. 3) through the colonial decisions of other nations and human beings on others. There are many Southern Cameroons' (Ambazonia) people like this author who doubted the effectiveness of armed struggle, yet they do not know what else they and their people could do again to draw the attention of the world community to their plight after decades of struggling nonviolently via the "force of argument not the argument of force" slogan to persuade an irrational world community to the plight of the people and the territory known in ex-British West Africa as British Southern Cameroons.

Through narrating politics and everyday life in British Southern Cameroons renamed Ambazonia as experienced by the population in general and the youths in particular in over half a century of "independence by joining" *Republique du Cameroun, Porcupine in a Python's Throat* makes an invaluable contribution to understanding the choices and constraints facing both Southern Cameroons' (Ambazonia) people and the people of *Republique du Cameroun* as the people of Southern Cameroons (Ambazonia) seek alternatives to the cycles of repression and state terrorism turned into reprisal, retaliation, and a genocidal war from 2016.

As I have indicated before in an earlier book *Nationalism and Intra-State Conflicts in the Postcolonial World,* Lexington Books (2015), this book challenges the authorities over delimited territories and their inhabitants in states arbitrarily put together and held together by external power and control. The perspective of the contributors to this book is that the Westphalian sovereignty of authority as indivisible in postcolonial and other settings is unworkable and does not last very long in plural societies put together and sustained with the use of force. It was from this standpoint that I challenged those who included Crimea and other Russian-speaking peoples in the making of Ukraine and those who divided the Kurds into four different countries (Syria, Turkey, Iraq, and Iran). Considering the ensuing conflicts, violence, and wars in Southern Cameroons (Ambazonia) as in other similar settings, including in Ukraine, the one question staring us in the face is whether the world community has the will to change the current view of the untouchability of Westphalian sovereign states. From the *Porcupine in a Python's Throat* image of this book, the risk is that the python will not be able to swallow the porcupine, and neither is vomiting it out an easy task. In the interest of justice and peace, we will need the services of a very skillful surgeon failing which both the porcupine and the python may die.

The target audience in this book includes undergraduates, graduates, scholars, and professionals in politics, governance, cultural studies, sociology, conflict and peace studies, social justice, anthropology, law, international studies, and other related fields of study.

Chapter 1

Change and History in the Destiny of the British Southern Cameroons

Nfor Ngala Nfor

We of the late second millennium who have entered the third are living in a predictably fast-changing world. It seems everything else has refused to be stagnant. In this fast-changing world, there are agents of change. Those who impact the world, those who are a force to reckon with, and those who are masters of their destiny. Such agents of change reflect on issues and without accepting anything as a given, question and analyze every given situation until they have an answer. With an identified problem they do not give up whatever may be the hurdles and challenges, the goal being the driving force. Such freedom of thought, of experimentation, of research, the freedom to question everything without fear of being reprimanded or arrested and detained exists unhindered in the leading democracies of the world. As free societies, democracies are dynamic and promote human freedom as an instrument of development.

This is to say that those whose destiny has been confiscated and are subjected to foreign rule, those whose fortunes and land are controlled, managed, and exploited by foreigners, those whose inalienable right to self-determination has been denied them, those who have surrendered to the servitude of foreign rule and foreign domination are not partners in the architectural design of this fast-changing world. These victims exist in the backwoods of their foreign rulers who have imposed on them their laws and their rule. Those who are part of the fast-changing world are actors and contributors and not passive observers. Passive observers, those who wait to be told, can never contribute to shaping the world. Their ordained space in the scheme of things has been occupied by their oppressors.

As each people, by the infinite wisdom of the creator, have an inheritance to properly manage not only for self but also for posterity, so do each people have a definite role to play in the shaping of a better future for their descendants. Each people must preserve for their descendants a legacy and a heritage to be proud of.

Those held in chains must look back and look inward to understand where they came from and what has put them in chains in this fast-changing world of the free. This introspection is necessary for it is by understanding the nature of things surrounding them that the people can have a clearer vision of what must be done to get rid of the chains so the people can be where they rightly belong. As no man is an island, so is no human community, indeed, no society. We all belong to the humankind family, irrespective of cultural background, religion, and political ideology.

The 21st century, though still in its infancy, promises to go down in recorded history as one of great human development and achievement. But we must accept that achievers are those who conceive and act to translate their dreams into measurable and verifiable results. Achievers are not wishful thinkers and dreamers. Achievers are those who believe they are entitled to live in a better society and by dint of hardwork and sacrifice, go for it. They are people who never sit to be told; they confront, they challenge the status quo, they are never contented with the back seat; they are determined to be part of something, to be involved, to be doers not just hearers. Those who shape their society abhor dependence and domination of any kind. They are action-oriented and proactive. They believe in their self-worth and deliberately take the driver's seat in their determined effort to be at the center where they rightfully belong. This center is where free people decide for themselves and for posterity.

Those who believe in human equality and human dignity cannot at the same time surrender their place in history to others. They cannot surrender their inherent right to rule themselves to be ruled by foreigners. People who believe and defend human equality and dignity must be masters of their own destiny and must be ruled by people freely elected from among them. The rulers and the ruled must be sharers in one history, one cultural heritage, one language, one political system, and one vision and must be the ordained custodians of one territory recognized under International Law. And proud of their history and culture, they must believe that to surrender their land and destiny into the hands of foreigners is slavery pure and simple from cradle to the grave.

A people recognized under International Law as a people cannot and must not abandon their cherished system of government to become slaves of a foreign system. They cannot surrender their land and natural wealth to be exploited for the good of their impostors while they wallow in misery and abject poverty. They cannot take refuge under foreign laws and foreign rule and expect to command respect and recognition in the council of free men and women. They must not wait on their knees subserviently for an archangel to come from celestial space and convert their oppressor to change and be nice to them. History has taught us a very hard lesson that imperialists and annexationists are interested in their prestige and grandeur: they care not about the feelings and legitimate ambitions of their victims.

If by accident of history a people have been dispossessed of their land, they must repossess the land, their God-given inheritance by physically and concretely dispossessing the aggressor for they are the rightful and legitimate owners of the land. Colonialism is like a smoked fish which no matter for how long you soak in water, it remains dry and bent and can never become straight and smooth again. Annexation and colonial occupation can never be reformed. We must not forget that even a tamed tiger in the zoo when starved will transform its attendant into its breakfast. People under foreign rule are dehumanized and must never compromise. They must work for the change they most need to assume their rightful place in the history of humanity.

Changes that impact the world and that are acclaimed are not just physical. No. To be of benefit to humanity, these changes must equally be ethically, spiritually, and intellectually sound if they must enhance human dignity. Wars, violence, injustice, oppression, foreign domination, poverty, and exploitation are as old to humans as recorded history is concerned. They are evil. The bane of conflicts and strife are provoked by greed, the endless search for wealth, prestige, and grandeur by few dictators who see power not to serve but for self-aggrandizement.

But the irreconcilable paradox is that those who subject others to their rule will not accept to be so treated as the footstool of others. It is now universally accepted that for world peace to reign, democracy and justice must be promoted in all corners of the globe considering that the reign of injustice anywhere is a threat to peace and justice everywhere. This inevitably implies that the will of the people, the right to freely choose without foreign interference and manipulation, and the right to self-determination must be respected at all cost for all peoples irrespective of cultural background or religious and ideological differences. Above all, it is therefore an imperative that no people with a recognized territory, history, and culture should be subjected to foreign domination and alien rule. In defense of their inherent and inalienable right to self-exist in dignity, they must not surrender to annexation and colonialism in whatever form and manifestation. This situation equally makes it imperative that any evil colonialism left in its trail at the dawn of de-colonization and any imperfections in the de-colonization process should be put right in conformity with the UN Charter and UNGA Resolution 1514 of 1960.

The mission and abiding role of the UN is to foster and defend the inherent inalienable and unquestionable right to self-determination of all peoples. This UN mission is the surest means of building world democracy and peace based on justice for all humanity. And to achieve this goal and end all wars, as its founding mission declares, the UN and the international system must stop listening to tyrants committed to expansionism on flimsy and unfounded excuses and listen to victims of foreign aggression and domination. As Archbishop Desmond Tutu put it,

> If you are neutral in situations of injustice, you have chosen to side with the oppressor. If an elephant has its foot on the tail of a mouse and you say you are neutral, the mouse will not appreciate your neutrality.

Greed is the manifestation of the lack of love and compassion for one another. Injustice is the lack of equal respect for a fellow human being. Oppression results from a feeling of superiority and spitefully looking low on a fellow human being. But religious teachings in every culture and civilization demand that we should do unto others what we would want done to us. Among many people where there is dedication to a shared life, communal life, to the concerns and needs of others, there is bound to be faith in common humanity whereby the urge to cheat, to exploit the weak, to oppress the helpless, and self-satisfaction derived therefrom, will be far less, if not non-existent. To build world democracy and peace, we must aim to build a world communal spirit, where shared life, feeling for one another, respect for the truth, and commitment to working for a just and fairer world will be a moral, spiritual, and intellectual obligation.

With courage, honor, and ingenuity, duty calls on every human being to rise to the challenge of his or her time and place. It is by positive response that we can reach great heights of human endeavor. Challenges are not against humanity; they are for humanity to assail. Challenges stimulate and nourish the human potential and the spiritual will power to rise. Without challenges matched by a determination to overcome, there will be no record of achievement; there will be no human progress. Challenges inspire humanity to rise above lower nature to godly nature. That is the natural ascendance of humanity's true being. Challenges should produce conquerors, not those who retreat or those who escape from responsibility. Challenges should inspire not create the spirit of despair. They should encourage not dispirit. And challenges that face each generation are never more than the capacity with which that generation is endowed. It is only by surrendering or retreating to the back seat that a generation fails in the mission of its age. Such a generation, the generation that passes on the buck to the next generation, and a generation of self-seekers, is never forgiven by history and by posterity.

With courage, honor, and ingenuity, we must build a society in which each and every one is at his best for the common good. Our mission is to raise the British Southern Cameroons from the ashes of foreign domination and alien rule to a nation firmly at its best on its own feet, not a threat to any other neighbor, but a fair partner in the search for global democracy, peace, and justice and human progress.

Reference to "the good old days" is not a call for us to retreat into our past, or for us, like the tortoise, to coil back into an old existing shell. That is far from it! It is a call for us to remember our noble past and courageously ask ourselves how it is that a lion has given birth to a toothless bulldog. It is an inspirational wake-up call. It is a clarion WAKE-UP CALL to sons and daughters of the British Southern Cameroons to assert themselves and be masters of their destiny, to know and defend the truth and in solidarity set themselves free from foreign domination and foreign rule.

And recalling that modern African nations are the colonies and trust territories of yesterday based on colonial boundaries, the people of the British Southern Cameroons in their legitimate struggle for freedom and independence anchored on legality must seek to understand many things. They must seek to understand by what instrument of International Law the United Kingdom as the Administering Authority in her policy of administrative convenience split British Cameroon into north and south and worked hard to sink each unit into its colony of Nigeria contrary to the mandate of the sacred trust enshrined in the Trusteeship Agreement. The destiny of the people bound together by the colonial boundaries of 1916 and affirmed by the Versailles Peace Treaty was shattered by the British Order in Council of June 26, 1923, when British Cameroon was, for British administrative convenience, divided into British Southern Cameroons and British Northern Cameroons. While the British Southern Cameroons was administered as part of the group of Southern Provinces of Nigeria, the British Northern Cameroons, which was noncontiguous, was further fragmented into three units and administered as integral parts of the Northern Nigeria provinces of Benue, Adamawa, and Bornu. This fragmentation, to my mind, was the greatest injustice ever done to a territory and a people under international obligation. That the UN Trusteeship Council bowed to the will of the United Kingdom as the Trustee for British Cameroon and allowed this evil machination remains the root cause of the botched de-colonization problem of the British Cameroons in 1961.

Thus, as people of one house (Trust Territory) turned apart and forced under strangers, in the 1961 debacle, the fate of one or the other cannot be effectively discussed, analyzed, and properly appreciated without going back to the origin and the house in which this one people found their abode and hope under British influence. The question is what was responsible for this diabolic machination of 1923 compounded by "independence by joining" in 1961? Both the machination of 1923 and the "independence by joining" in 1961 went completely contrary to the spirit and letter of the UN Charter and Trusteeship Agreement as the destiny of the people of the British Cameroons was dictated by foreigners under unholy circumstances manipulated by the Administering Authority.

It is a fact of history that the primitive man was at peace in his cave. The peace of the primitive man is not the kind of peace the modern man craves for. The modern man will not be happy with the peace of the graveyard. The modern man vehemently rejects this kind of peace, including the security of the slave behind the slave master's house without a choice and a right. We live in a fast-changing world, and humanity remains the agent of that change. I am referring to positive change, which enhances the dignity and equality of all human beings.

What is emphasized here is that human freedom underlies the flowering of human potentialities for development. It is a truism that people in chains, people subjected to foreign domination and foreign rule no matter how "benevolent" it may be, exist at the pleasure of their oppressor in the dark backwoods of the oppressor. In bondage their talents never see the light of day to bloom, let alone blossom. People under foreign domination and foreign rule are subjected to the rule of impunities: they are dehumanized, dispossessed, and denied their rightful place in history.

On this reality, to redeem their battered image and become shapers of their destiny and to be part of the free humanity, slaves rebelled and fought against their slave masters to regain their freedom, and colonies rose against the metropolitan colonial powers for their independence. And since the 1990s, annexed and occupied territories began to rise, one after the other, against annexationist regimes to restore their sovereign statehood. This situation has not only increased the number of sovereign nations at the UN, the world is being transformed into a fairer, more competitive, and peaceful world. The inherent right of every people and nation under international instruments is the unquestionable right to self-exist as an equal to other nations.

Each time people are challenged and threatened, that is when they strengthen their bonds of solidarity and prove their worth and ignite their hidden talents. The people of the British Southern Cameroons faced such a challenge in 1953. And they did not surrender. They did not shrink into a shell like the proverbial tortoise. No. On the contrary, they summoned courage, and in solidarity they answered the national call. They rose to the challenge. Like one man they defended their identity, the Southern Cameroons' identity. And they came out victorious.

Yes, times have changed. They have changed for good. But the fact remains that the very trump card, namely, the International Law that the Endeleys and Fonchas used is still there to the credit of the people. With experiences gathered from other peoples under similar circumstances, the people of the British Southern Cameroons should work triumphantly for their freedom and independence. What is more, the unstoppability of the right to self-determination of victims of foreign domination and foreign rule and the victorious records set by other peoples and nations who yesterday were in the abyss of annexation and colonial occupation such as Namibia, Eritrea, Estonia, East Timor, to name only a few, are concrete evidence and logical torch bearers of the new age of the unstoppability of the right to self-determination. The victorious records set by these nations and peoples point to the equality of all nations, large and small, and the right to freedom for all peoples irrespective of race and culture.

Change is the agent of history. Change constructs and reconstructs history. And in all this, humans are the engine and promoter of this change. For a nation, it is the people who, acting in solidarity for their common good, create the material content of their national and progressive history. These are a people in control of their destiny, shaping their destiny for their collective good and for posterity. These are people who by dint of their action contribute to human progress and by their collective positive action deservedly occupy their station within the world family of sovereign nations.

In this fast-changing world, it pays for each people to look back and remind themselves where they came from and where they stand in the order of things vis-à-vis other peoples in similar circumstances. We must remember we live in a competitive world. And it is the nature of this competitiveness at a very high level that makes the world a fast-changing place. Those who excel are those endowed with the capacity to compete fairly, not those in the backwoods of others. Those with the capacity to compete fairly are those endowed with a vision, and those with a vision are those who have firmly answered the question "Who are we?" and "Who is not us?"

Yes, the people of the British Southern Cameroons cannot rewrite the history of 1961 or change it. However, by a careful analysis of the past errors they can reorder and reshape the future in line and in keeping with their legitimate aspirations. To be part of the free world, they must graduate with a bachelor's degree, that is "Begin Again."

If we must tomorrow be the winners,
We must today be the beginners
Those who fear to begin
To confront evil head-on
Never triumph
In cowardice they allow
Tyranny and injustice triumph
For in the land the irresponsible
Seek comfort and contentment in the backwoods
And the irresponsible are traitors
Who for a crown wear IMPOSSIBILITY!

No! Impossibility is a cowardly fiction of a feeble mind. As every human product has, embedded from within, its expiration date, annexation, and

colonial occupation, indeed neo-apartheid in the British Southern Cameroons imposed by la Republique du Cameroun must end as apartheid ended
in South Africa. In our land, annexation and colonial occupation must end
and, and as in South Africa, give birth to popular and plural democracy, the
triumph of human dignity and decency. There is no fate that can overcome
the resolve of a determined people to heal the wounds inflicted on their bodies, souls, and consciences by injustice and brutal annexation, for the God of
justice never forsakes the oppressed.

The people in solidarity must like one man rise against this reigning mon-
ster, foreign rule, and foreign domination. History challenges the people of
the British Southern Cameroons to do no less for the future, for those who
are masters of their own destiny, those who have refused to bend their backs
for others to ride on, and those who have stood up tall to be counted among
the free people of the world.

REFERENCE

Brown, R. M. (1984). *Unexpected News: Reading the Bible with Third World Eyes.*
   Westminster: John Knox Press

Chapter 2

Decoding UNGA Res 1608 (XV) of April 21, 1961

Carlson Anyangwe

The Southern Cameroons (indigenous name, Ambazonia) has an international boundary with Nigeria to the west and with Cameroun Republic to the east. The boundaries are well-defined and delimited by boundary treaties. The boundary with the Cameroun Republic is in fact demarcated. During the period of international administration, the Southern Cameroons had international status and a degree of international personality. By 1958 it was firmly on the path of sovereign statehood. It achieved self-government status in 1954 and became a state *in status nascendi* in 1958. Preparatory to independence, it was endowed in 1960 with a Westminster-modeled independence Constitution, *The Southern Cameroons (Constitution) Order-in-Council*. The country enjoyed a congener of statehood. Its national sovereignty was in abeyance waiting to revive and rest on the new state at the moment of its independence.

BACKGROUND

Decolonization of the Third World occupied a major part of the activities of the UN during the first three decades of its existence. The UN decolonization agenda derived from two sources: Chapters XI, XII, and XIII of the UN Charter devoted to the interests of dependent peoples and two distinct but interrelated rights under International Law, namely, the equal rights of peoples and the right of self-determination of peoples. Since 1960, the UN has also been guided in its decolonization efforts by the Declaration on the Granting of Independence to Colonial Countries and Peoples. In that binding instrument, UN Member States proclaim the necessity of bringing a speedy end to colonialism in all its form.

Some colonial territories achieved independence consensually, others through armed struggle. In cases of consensual decolonization, sovereignty was simply transferred to the new state. The departing colonial power concluded devolution agreements with the new state providing for inheritance of certain treaties. In rare instances, the plebiscite procedure was used to ascertain the wishes of the dependent people on the question of independence. Sometimes the UN also uses that procedure to ascertain the freely expressed wishes of a given population when satisfied that the population in question constitutes *a people* within the meaning of the legal right to self-determination. It appears therefore that the plebiscite was considered a legitimate method of decolonization, provided of course that at the plebiscite all the political status options are proffered to the people concerned to choose from.

In terms of UNGA Resolutions 648, 742, 1541 (XV) of 1960, and 2625 (XXV) of 1970, termination of colonial status may result in any of the following political status options: independence, internal autonomy within a freely formed association, integration in an independent state, or emergence into any other political status *freely* determined by the people concerned. Therefore, to be meaningful and legitimate a self-determination plebiscite must make available to the people concerned all those four political status options to choose from. A free and informed choice made from those four options would be a full exercise of the right of self-determination and would result in complete decolonization. Dependent political status (annexation, occupation, absorption, incorporation, integration, re-colonization, etc.) cannot possibly be a permissible outcome of implementation of the right to self-determination. If a colonial territory is transferred to another state, the territory in question cannot by any stretch of the imagination be said to have been decolonized. The termination of colonial status, even where it results in integration with an independent state, must at the very minimum result in autonomy or internal self-government for the territory in question.

The excuse for the incomplete decolonization of the British Southern Cameroons was the self-serving "reason" given by Britain that the territory would not be economically viable to stand on its own as a sovereign state. This "reason" clearly had no merit. It was a red herring. If indeed it was a real issue, the UN would have on its own dispatched an expert mission to the Southern Cameroons to ascertain the issue of economic viability. The mission would then have carried out its duties in cooperation with the Government of the Southern Cameroons and the Administering Authority. The object of the mission would then have been to determine the implications of economic non-viability for the independence of the Southern Cameroons and to recommend corrective measures. That did not happen. In fact, the UN has never carried out such an exercise in any territory set to be decolonized because no purpose stood to be served by any such exercise. The question of economic viability is irrelevant to the matter of decolonization.

The real reason for the incomplete decolonization of the Southern Cameroons was not the economic non-viability of the territory, which was in fact false; it was Britain's longstanding policy of sinking the territory of the Southern Cameroons into Nigeria. Britain considered the Southern Cameroons as mere material for infilling on Nigeria's south-eastern border. On the matter of decolonization, it is clear that economic self-sufficiency is irrelevant to the question of independence. Economic viability may be used to support a claim to independence, but it cannot be used to deny entitlement to independence. The Declaration on the Grating of Independence puts the matter beyond any shadow of doubt when it emphatically states that "Inadequacy of political, economic, social or educational preparedness should never serve as a pretext for delaying independence."

The UN stampeded the Southern Cameroons into a plebiscite for which the people were not mentally and politically ready. The political leadership of the Southern Cameroons requested deferment of the plebiscite to 1962. It also requested deferment to October 26, 1962, the termination of trusteeship in accordance with Article 76b of the UN Charter.

This is the humble request made by the Southern Cameroons political leadership to the United Nations (UN Doc. A/C.4/414. GOR. 14th Session, 1959. Annexes. Agenda Item 41), contained in the document – 'Agreed Statement by Mr. J.N. Foncha, Premier of the Southern Cameroons, and Mr. E.M.L. Endeley, Leader of Opposition in the Southern Cameroons House of Assembly.'

[Coming back to the United Nations after six months, we, the elected leaders of the Government and political parties in the Southern Cameroons House of Assembly, have been greatly encouraged, as we were at the thirteenth session, by the friendly interest of delegations and their concern for the welfare of our people. We for our part are anxious, by reaching agreement among ourselves as to the next step to be taken, to help the work of the Fourth Committee and still more important to promote the future well-being of our people.

We have had the advantage of discussions with the representatives of African Member States in the United Nations, whose sympathy and help we greatly appreciate, and with our colleagues in the United Kingdom delegation, who share with us the task of interpreting to the United Nations the wishes and aspirations of the people of the Southern Cameroons.

We are both of us of course anxious that the Southern Cameroons should attain independence as early as circumstances permit in the form most suitable to its circumstances and the wishes of the people. But, since the parties represented in the House of Assembly were not able to agree during recent discussion in the Southern Cameroons on the arrangements for a plebiscite in 1960, we think that it would be wiser to defer consultation with the people for the time being.

Subject therefore to the agreement of the General Assembly, we are agreed as follows.

1. There should be no plebiscite in the Southern Cameroons in 1960.
2. Pending settlement of its future the Southern Cameroons should continue to be administered under the present Trusteeship Agreement, but separately from Nigeria. We understand that the United Kingdom Government would be prepared to continue to administer it on this basis.
3. The separation of the administration of the Southern Cameroons from that of the Federation of Nigeria should be completed not later than the date on which the Federation of Nigeria becomes independent.
4. The Administering Authority in consultation with the Government and Legislature of the Southern Cameroons, should take steps to complete the separation of the administration of the Southern Cameroons from that of the Federation of Nigeria not later than 1 October 1960, the date on which the Federation of Nigeria becomes independent.
5. The Administering Authority, in co-operation with the Government and people of the Southern Cameroons, should work towards the achievement of the objectives of the Trusteeship System in accordance with Article 76 b of the United Nations Charter.
6. In the light of the above we suggest that the General Assembly should decide to consider this question not later than its sixteenth session with a view to ascertaining the wishes of the people of the Territory in 1962 as to their future.
7. We would be agreeable if the General Assembly should recommend that, in agreement with the Administering Authority, the Trusteeship Agreement should be terminated not later than 26 October 1962, in accordance with Article 76 of the United Nations Charter.]

Deploringly, the UN denied this simple and sensible request for the deferment of the plebiscite to 1962. The UN went ahead to impose a plebiscite to be concluded "not later than March 1961." This *diktat* deprived the people of the Southern Cameroons of much-needed breathing space. It also deprived them of time for cogitation on a very serious matter affecting their future. The Southern Cameroons was not drowning. The plebiscite was not a God-ordained life jacket for rescuing the territory from a British-perceived perdition. If, as it seemed, the UK was unwilling for reasons of costs to continue its administration of the Southern Cameroons up to October 1962, the UN could have taken direct administration of the territory for a year or so pending a well informed and mature decision on its future.

Had the plebiscite been deferred just to 1962, as the political leadership of the territory had requested, there would certainly have been the third option of separate independence as provided in the 1960 Declaration on Decolonization. The vote would undoubtedly have gone in favor of that option. The refusal to defer the plebiscite was compounded by other acts of misfeasance by the UN. The UN refused to proffer the fundamental political status option of independence. The UN used woolly and deceptive language ("independence by joining") in framing the plebiscite questions. In 1953 the Southern Cameroons advisedly declined to continue to participate in Nigerian politics, and on October 1, 1960, it was separated from that country. How could going back to Nigeria to be permanently federated to that country be politically correct? Associating with Cameroun Republic was an even worse option. That country was a foreign country and *terra incognita* in relation to the Southern Cameroons. It was in the throes of a bitter civil war, awash with blood, literally in flames, anarchical, and disorganized. The UN had a duty to safeguard the welfare and interest of the people of the Southern Cameroons. It beats the imagination how it made "joining" Cameroun Republic a well-meaning alternative, even if the suggestion came from some quarters.

The purported decolonization of the Southern Cameroons was deeply flawed procedurally and substantively. It resulted in the re-colonization of the territory, this time by the adjacent foreign state of Cameroun Republic. The so-called "two alternatives" were not alternative political status options. They were simply two alternative countries to choose from in the context of one political status option, the option of continuing dependent status. The people of the Southern Cameroons were in effect required to choose between becoming a dependency of Nigeria or a dependency of Cameroun Republic.

The imposition of that Hobson choice willy-nilly meant that the people of the Southern Cameroons were in fact not allowed to decide *freely* what their wishes were as to their future. The whole plebiscite was a cynical public relations exercise. It was designed to make the world at large to believe that the people of the Southern Cameroons were being given freedom of choice, whereas in fact the only choice they really wanted, that of sovereign statehood, was denied to them. The plebiscite was unnecessary and thus redundant. The UN should simply have decolonized the territory in consultation with the Administering Authority as happened, for example, in the case of Tanganyika, Ruanda-Urundi, and French Cameroon. There was therefore no credible issue for the UN to resolve by imposing a Hobson choice that was demonstrably not in the interest of the people and territory of the Southern Cameroons.

CHRONOLOGY OF EVENTS LEADING TO
THE ADOPTION OF RES 1608 (XV)

The German protectorate of Kamerun (*Schutzgebiet von Kamerun*) lasted thirty years, from 1884 to 1914. In the First World War, Germany was utterly defeated in Kamerun. The territory was completely overrun by British-led forces advancing from neighboring Nigeria and Franco-Belgian-led forces advancing from French Equatorial Africa. Following its *debellatio*, Germany renounced under the Treaty of Versailles 1919 and in favor of the victorious powers its rights and claims to all its colonial territories. By 1919 Kamerun was already under Anglo-French wartime occupation but provisionally divided into two unequal parts in March 1916 along what was called the Simon-Milner Line. The British sphere was a small strip of territory on the eastern border of Nigeria from Lake Chad down to the Atlantic Ocean. The division was formalized by an Anglo-French Declaration of 1919, became permanent when it was confirmed under the Treaty of Versailles, 1919, accepted by the League of Nations in 1922, reconfirmed by another boundary treaty in 1931, and further reconfirmed by the UN in 1946.

The international administration of the Southern Cameroons began in 1922. But before then, by the end of August 1914, German colonial apparatus in the British conquered and occupied area collapsed following its destruction. Rather than leave the area in a state of international no-man's-land, Britain assumed sovereignty over it and annexed it to its protectorate of Nigeria. The Versailles Peace Conference frowned on wartime annexation. It decided that conquered German colonial territories be placed under international tutelage. Accordingly, in 1922 the British Cameroons became a League of Nations mandated territory, divided into the Southern Cameroons and the Northern Cameroons. From that date up to October 1, 1960, the Southern Cameroons was practically administered as an integral part of Eastern Nigeria. This in effect meant the territory was administered as a dependency of Nigeria. It was administered from Nigeria rather than directly from London. By so doing, Britain created an environment that eventually eclipsed the issue of separate independence for the Southern Cameroons. Consequently, much of the political struggle of the Southern Cameroons at that time focused on extricating itself from Nigeria. Had there been no forced administrative union with Nigeria, the issue of outright independence would have been the primary focus of politicians of the Southern Cameroons. The question of "joining" Nigeria or Cameroun Republic would hardly have arisen.

The chronological thematic approach below is based on event analysis that marks the turning point in the history of the Southern Cameroons decolonization debacle from 1959 to 1961. The salient events leading to the adoption of Resolution 1608 (XV) of April 21, 1961, began in 1958, the year of the

Centenary Celebration of the founding of the British Settled Colony of Victoria, in the Southern Cameroons.

January 1952

The British consul-general in Brazzaville, member of the UK delegation to the UN, articulated the British policy on the question of self-government or independence for the Southern Cameroons:

> The British view is that . . . the progressive development of the inhabitants of [the Southern Cameroons] towards self-government or independence must . . . be promoted in association with the socially advanced protectorate of Nigeria. The British delegation has impressed this view with consistent firmness and frankness upon the Trusteeship Council and the Council has been obliged to accept it grudgingly . . . qualified by a natural and legitimate anxiety that our policy should be accompanied by adequate measures to preserve the identity of the Trust Territory.

June 1957

Mr. Alan Lennox-Boyd, the British secretary of state for the Colonies, echoing the British position stated five years earlier by the UK delegation to the UN, told a Southern Cameroons delegation to London that "Many of the best friends of the Southern Cameroons do not foresee a destiny more likely to promote her happiness and prosperity than in continued association with Nigeria."

June 27, 1958

Britain submitted to the General Assembly Memorandum T.1393 in which it informed the UN that the Southern Cameroons, like Nigeria, had not been delayed in its political evolution toward full autonomy and independence.

February 25, 1959

At the 849th Session of the Fourth Committee of the UN, French Cameroun Premier, Ahmadou Ahidjo, declared that his country was not annexationist. He gave the undertaking that his country would not annex the Southern Cameroons should it vote "to join" it. He further declared that both countries would associate on a footing of complete equality. "We are not annexationists. . . . If our brothers of the British Cameroons wish to unite with independent Cameroon, we are ready to discuss the matter with them, but we will do so on a footing of equality."

March 13, 1959

The UNGA adopted Resolution 1350 (XIII). The resolution recommended, *inter alia*, that the Administering Authority should take steps to organize separate plebiscites in the northern and southern parts of the British Cameroons in consultation with the UN Plebiscite Commissioner for the British Cameroons and under the supervision of the UN. The purpose of the plebiscites was to ascertain the wishes of the inhabitants of the territory concerning their future.

August 10–11, 1959

At the very representative Mamfe Conference, the Paramount Chief (*Fon*) of Bafut expressed the sentiment of the day when he declared that the people of the Southern Cameroons removed Dr. Endeley as Premier by voting against him because he wanted to take the Southern Cameroons to Nigeria, and that should Mr. Foncha the incumbent Premier try to take the Southern Cameroons to French Cameroun the people would also remove him from power as Premier. He famously declared: "French Cameroon is an inferno; Nigeria is the sea." By that turn of phrase, he meant that voting to associate with French Cameroon would be death by burning at the stake and voting to remain part of Nigeria would be death by drowning. He concluded by stating that he supported "secession from Nigeria" but "without unification with French Cameroon"; in other words, he stood for sovereign independence for the Southern Cameroons.

The conference was in complete agreement with that profound and sagacious assessment and stated position. It accordingly resolved that the question to be put at the plebiscite should be this: Integration with Nigeria or Secession from Nigeria. To understand conference's formulation of the question in this manner, it is well to bear in mind that in 1959 the Southern Cameroons was still administered as an integral part of Nigeria. "Integration with Nigeria" meant permanent incorporation with Nigeria; "secession from Nigeria" meant exit from Nigeria. It was clearly understood that secession from Nigeria entailed achieving independence as a sovereign state.

The UN ignored the resolution of the Mamfe Conference thanks to wheeling and dealing at the UN by the Administering Authority. It arm-twisted Premier Foncha to accept the alternative of "joining" French Cameroon as the second plebiscite question in exchange for a short period of continued trusteeship. The calculation of the Administering Authority was that the horror of the armed violence taking place in French Cameroon would drive the people of the Southern Cameroons to vote for joinder with Nigeria, the outcome desired by Britain.

October 1959

A controversial report by Sir Phillipson on the economic viability of an independent Southern Cameroons concluded that the territory would not be economically viable to stand on its own. The report was commissioned by the British Government. In the same month, Sir Andrew Cohen, the UK Ambassador to the UN, simply repeated to the UN the dubious conclusion by Sir Phillipson that "An independent Southern Cameroons would not be economically viable."

October 7, 1959

The Fourth Committee of the General Assembly discussed the fake question of economic viability of the Southern Cameroons. Miss Angie Brooks (Liberia) who chaired the meeting closed it by declaring that paragraph 2 of the proposed draft resolution of the Committee to be forwarded to the General Assembly would be framed in such a way as "to allay any apprehension that the Southern Cameroons might become independent as a separate entity, an eventuality which all were agreed should be ruled out in view of the territory's limited economic potential."

October 16, 1959

The General Assembly adopted Resolution 1352 (XIV) in which it (i) decided that arrangements for the plebiscite had to begin on September 30, 1960, and the plebiscite concluded not later than March 1961; (ii) recommended that the two questions to be put at the plebiscite should be: "(a) Do you wish to achieve independence by joining the independent Federation of Nigeria?" "(b) Do you wish to achieve independence by joining the independent Republic of Cameroun?"; and (iii) recommended that "only persons born in the Southern Cameroons or one of whose parents was born in the Southern Cameroons should vote in the plebiscite."

January 1960

Lord Perth, British minister of state at the Colonial Office, shamefully recorded in a secret memo that "The Southern Cameroons and its inhabitants are expendable."

June 1960

Mr. Boothby of the British Foreign Office wrote in a secret memo to his colleagues as follows: "We are no attracted to the idea of an independent Southern Cameroons. . . . We cannot expect to get any advantage from being foster mother to an independent Southern Cameroons and it is clear that it would have to be fostered by somebody. . . . In fact, the sooner we can . . . wash our hands off the Southern Cameroons, the more pleased we shall be."

June 1960

Sir Andrew Cohen, UK's ambassador to the UN, sent a secret dispatch to the Commissioner of the Southern Cameroons in which he wrote as follows:

> I believe a firm attitude on this now may save us a great deal of trouble later and I think that Her Majesty's Government position should be made abundantly clear to Foncha [the Premier of the Southern Cameroons] in an effort to scotch tendencies towards the third question on sovereign independence. . . . The policy of Her Majesty's Government is to discourage any tendency towards a third question very strongly.

June 1960

Foncha sent an outline of his constitutional proposal to Ahidjo and suggested that an early opportunity be found to discuss it.

July 15–17, 1960

Foncha and Ahidjo, together with certain members of their respective governments, held discussions on the outline of the constitutional proposal by Foncha. At the end of the discussions a communiqué was issued stating that the two sides "unanimously adopted" a resolution by which they, *inter alia*, "agreed to unification on a federal basis adapted to the conditions peculiar to all sections of *Kamerun*."

August 1960

Further discussions were held between the two sides regarding outline proposals for a federal constitution. The proposals were submitted by the Southern Cameroons.

Early October 1960

Talks were held in London between the UK and the Southern Cameroons on the meaning and implications of "achieving independence by joining Republic of Cameroun." Speaking through its Secretary of State for the Colonies, Ian Macleod, the UK Government, claimed that the UN in adopting the resolution on the plebiscite ruled out a period of continued trusteeship and also ruled out separate independence for the Southern Cameroons. Macleod went on to declare that if the plebiscite went in favor of joining Republic of Cameroun, arrangements would be made "for the early termination of trusteeship and the *transfer of sovereignty to Cameroon*." The UK Government further stated that a vote for attaining independence by joining Cameroun Republic would mean that "the Southern Cameroons and Cameroun Republic would *unite in a Federal United Cameroun Republic*." He went on to state further that "arrangements would be worked out after the plebiscite by *a conference consisting of representative delegations of equal status* from the Republic and the Southern Cameroons. *The United Nations and the United Kingdom would also be associated with this conference.*" The Southern Cameroons delegation was satisfied with this explanation. The formula by Macleod was presented to and accepted by Cameroun Republic as consistent with the meaning of the second plebiscite question.

October 10–13, 1960

A third meeting took place between the Southern Cameroons and Cameroun Republic. It ended with the adoption of two documents, a Communiqué and a Joint Declaration. The *Communiqué* stated that "the implementation of unification on the federal basis adaptable to conditions peculiar to all sections of the Cameroons cannot be automatic but gradual." It further stated that the political leadership of both countries have examined and adopted the broad outlines of the constitution which they will implement in the event of the plebiscite vote being favorable to them. The *Joint Declaration* contained the "Outline Proposals for a Draft Constitution for a Federal United Kamerun Republic." It declared inter alia that the two sides "wish to create a federal State," that "nationals of the federated states will enjoy Cameroon nationality," that "the Federal Legislature will consist of a Federal Assembly and a Federal Senate," that federal laws will only be enacted in such a way that no measures contrary to the interests of one state will be imposed upon it by the majority, that the Federation will be created by the Southern Cameroons and Cameroun Republic, and that if the vote went in favor of federating with Cameroun Republic those entrusted with the affairs of the unified Cameroon would put the federal constitution to the people to pronounce themselves on it. These two documents were signed by John Ngu Foncha, Premier of the Southern Cameroons, on the one part, and by Ahmadou Ahidjo and Charles Assalé, respectively president and prime minister of Cameroun Republic, on the other part.

December 1–3, 1960

The Southern Cameroons and Cameroun Republic held a final pre-plebiscite meeting which ended with a signed *Joint Communiqué* confirming the contents of the October Communiqué and Joint Declaration. It is noteworthy that the pre-plebiscite agreement was framed not in facultative terms. It was framed in the phraseology of legal obligations. The rights and the status of the Southern Cameroons thereunder did not depend upon the permission and pleasure of Cameroun Republic. Any suggestion that the agreement was not legally binding and that therefore Cameroun Republic was not bound to implement and to respect the federation agreement would, by parity of reasoning, mean that the Southern Cameroons was also not bound to federate with Cameroun Republic. If the agreement was ineffectual, then it was so as regards each of the parties. A party cannot approbate and reprobate.

December 24, 1960

Cameroun Republic sent the following *note verbale* to the UK Government through its Embassy at Yaoundé, confirming "as an expression of its official views" its "desire for unification" with the Southern Cameroons "on the basis of a federation."

The Minister of Foreign Affairs presents its compliments to the British Embassy to Cameroon at Yaoundé and with reference to its *note verbale* No. F.M. 68 (1041/60) dated December 16, 1960, has the honor to state that, following the conversations which have just taken place in Douala between the president of the Republic of Cameroun and Mr. Foncha, the Premier of the Southern Cameroons, it has been decided that, in connection with the plebiscite organized in the Southern Cameroons on the question of whether that country should join the Federal Republic of Nigeria or the Republic of Cameroun, the Government of the Republic of Cameroun has announced that it adheres to the spirit of the attached joint communiqués, which indicates its desire for unification with the Cameroons under British administration on the basis of a federation. The Government of the Republic of Cameroun requests the British Embassy to consider the attached communiqués as an expression of the official views of the Republic and further requests that they be published for the purposes prescribed by Trusteeship Council Resolution 2013 (XXVI), referred to in its note verbale quoted above.

Attached to this *note verbale* were the French texts of the Communiqué, the Joint Declaration, and the Joint Communiqé. The contents of these three documents formed the basis of an expected political association between the Southern Cameroons and Cameroun Republic. The documents provided inter alia for (i) a federation of two states, equal in status; (ii) a post-plebiscite conference consisting of representative delegations of equal status from the two countries; (iii) the association of the UN and the UK with the post-plebiscite Conference; and (iv) the transfer of sovereign powers to *an organization* representing the future federation.

The Southern Cameroons and Cameroun Republic thus committed to creating a federal political association. The statement contained in the *note verbale* and publicized in *The Two Alternatives* evidenced a clear intention on the part of Cameroun Republic to be bound by the contents of the three instruments attached thereto and to accept binding legal obligations vis-à-vis the Southern Cameroons. In International Law, such a *note verbale* constitutes a unilateral act of a heteronormative character. It gives rise to an international legal obligation. In the *Eastern Greenland Case* (1933) PCIJ, Ser. A/B, No. 53, p. 71, the court declared that a statement of that nature, including even a unilateral oral declaration in the nature of a promise, given by a foreign minister, in reply to a request by the diplomatic agent of a foreign power in regard to a question falling within his province is binding upon the state to which the minister belongs. In the *Nuclear Test Case (Australia v France)*, Judgment, ICJ Rep. 1974, 253, the ICJ stated that a declaration may be made by way of a unilateral act by a state concerning a legal or factual situation and under such circumstances as to have the effect of creating a legal obligation on that state. The statements contained in Cameroun's *note verbale* were taken by the UN and the UK as constituting the binding undertaken given by that country on the question of "joining" Cameroun Republic.

January 27, 1961

The UK Government produced a booklet entitled *The Two Alternatives* for use in the plebiscite enlightenment campaign. The document reproduced Nigeria's constitutional offer to the Southern Cameroons. The offer is that of regional status for the Southern Cameroons within the Nigerian Federation. *The Two Alternatives* also reproduced the Communiqué and Joint Declarations by the Southern Cameroons and Cameroun Republic agreeing on the creation of a federation of two states, equal in status. The production of the booklet marked the official launch of the campaign, a mere two weeks to the plebiscite. The Communiqué, the Joint Declaration, the *Note Verbale*, and *The Two Alternatives* were all made available to the UN.

February 11, 1961

The plebiscite took place. The vote went in favor of federating with Cameroun Republic. This decision was in reality indicative of a negative vote against Nigeria due to fears of Nigerian domination rather than of a positive desire for political association with Cameroun Republic.

March 1961

The Colonial Office informed the British Commonwealth that "Nigeria was kept fully informed of every move in the discussion of *the hand-over* of the Southern Cameroons to the Cameroun Republic."

April 11, 1961

Plebiscite Commissioner presented his Report to the General Assembly.

April 13, 1961

The Fourth Committee met and considered the Report of the UN Plebiscite Commissioner (UN Doc. A/4727) and also the Report of the Trusteeship Council (UN Doc. A/4726). It granted oral hearings to seven petitioners from the Southern Cameroons who expressed dissatisfaction with the plebiscite results and urged the UN to partition the territory conformable with the results for each division. The seven petitioners were: E. M. L. Endeley, Sam Endeley, Nerius Mbile, S Andoh Seh, Chief Sakwe, Ajebe Sone, and Chief Molongo. These seven petitioners were echoing a signed resolution of the Victoria Divisional Council and that of the Nkambe Divisional Council, both expressing dissatisfaction with the plebiscite results and vowing to remain part of Nigeria. These petitions were heard but rejected as lacking in substance.

Bad faith characterized the handling of the Southern Cameroons Question at the UN in April 1961.

April 15, 1961

Ten French-speaking African countries sponsored and submitted a draft resolution to the Fourth Committee proposing a six-member commission elected by the General Assembly to visit the Northern and Southern British Cameroons to ascertain in particular whether the basic objectives of the trusteeship system could be regarded as achieved throughout the British Cameroons.

April 17, 1961

The draft resolution as presented by those ten countries was revised at the instigation of France and Cameroun Republic. The revised draft required the proposed commission to ascertain only whether the separation of the administration of the Northern British Cameroons from Nigeria had been effectively carried out as the UN had ordained in 1959. France and Cameroun Republic were content that the Southern Cameroons already voted to federate with

Cameroun Republic. Their strategy was simply to work to prize the Northern Cameroons away from Nigeria which the former had opted to "join." If the commission, as proposed by the ten French-speaking countries, were to be given the broad mandate as proposed, the whole question of British steward-ship in the entire British Cameroons would be opened up with the very real possibility of the Southern Cameroons having second thoughts on federating with Cameroun Republic.

April 18, 1961

Another draft resolution, UN Doc. A/C.4/L.685, was presented by Ethiopia, India, Iran, Ireland, Jordan, Libya, Morocco, Nepal, New Zealand, Pakistan, Saudi Arabia, and Sudan. Malaya and Liberia joined as co-sponsors. The Fourth Committee adopted this draft by a roll-call vote of fifty-nine to two with nine abstentions. It then recommended it to the General Assembly for adoption.

The draft resolution adopted by the Fourth Committee contained two criti-cal paragraphs, 5 and 6. Numbered paragraph 5 invited

> the Administering Authority, the Government of the Southern Cameroons, and the Republic of Cameroun to initiate urgent discussions with a view to formaliz-ing, before 1 October 1961, the arrangements by which the agreed and declared policies of the concerned parties for a union of the Southern Cameroons with the Republic of Cameroun into a Federal United Cameroun Republic will be implemented.

The same recommended draft resolution provided in numbered paragraph 6 for the appointment, by the General Assembly, of "a commission of three constitutional and administrative experts to be nominated one each by three Member States designated by the General Assembly to assist at the request of the parties concerned in the discussions" "on a union of the Southern Cameroons with the Republic of Cameroun into a Federal United Cameroun Republic."

The adoption and implementation of the recommended resolution were to entail a petty financial expenditure (mainly for hiring of the three constitu-tional and administrative experts) estimated at a mere $46,000. It was clear that the draft resolution had financial implications. The Fourth Committee was fully alive to this fact.

April 20, 1961

In its report to the General Assembly on this matter, the Committee pointed out that the adoption of the recommended draft resolution "would give rise to additional expenditures of some US$ 46,000 which would be included in the supplementary estimates for 1961 to be submitted to the General Assembly at its 16th session." On the same day, the UN Secretary-General Dag Hammarskjold noted that

> Should the draft resolution as recommended by the Fourth Committee be adopted by the General Assembly, financial commitments up to $46 000 will have to be made for which no budgetary provision is included in the 1961 budget. In that event the Secretary General would propose to meet these requirements as unforeseen expenses for the financial year 1961 and will submit supplementary estimates to the General Assembly in its sixteenth session in this regard.

April 21, 1961

The UNGA adopted Resolution 1608 (XV) on "The Future of the Trust Territory of the Cameroons under United Kingdom Administration." Separate votes were taken on "independence," "joining," termination of trusteeship on October 1, 1961, and on the resolution as a whole. In each case, there was an overwhelming majority "Yes" vote. But the resolution was a dangerously watered-down version of the resolution recommended by the Fourth Committee for adoption by the General Assembly. In the adopted resolution, no mention is made of the appointment of the three constitutional and administrative experts. No mention is made of "a union of the Southern Cameroons with the Republic of Cameroun into a Federal United Cameroun Republic." The removal of those matters was highly prejudicial to the interest of the Southern Cameroons. Aided by France and supported by Member States of the French-speaking *Union Africaine et Malagache*, Cameroun Republic successfully opposed the inclusion of those words in the final resolution. These French-speaking countries argued that the UN cannot "impose" federation on an independent sovereign state. And yet, there was nothing new in that process. In 1952, the UN in its Resolution 390(A) favored federation as the form of the Eritrean-Ethiopian union and actually appointed a Commissioner, Mr. Eduardo Anze Matienzo, to frame a federal constitution to that effect, which he did and was unanimously approved by the General Assembly. Curiously, even after the removal of the group of words it objected to, Republic of Cameroun still went on to vote against adoption of Resolution 1608 (XV). In sharp contrast, to the support Cameroun Republic got from France and other French-speaking countries, every initiative in the interest of the Southern Cameroons was vigorously opposed and killed by Britain's autocratic UN Representative, Sir Andrew Cohen, whose inexplicable demonstrated antipathy toward the Southern Cameroons bordered on the pathological.

It is extraordinary that the UN pleaded financial constraints for leaving out those matters which it knew, or must be taken to have known, were very critical for safeguarding the status, dignity, and self-determination of the people of the Southern Cameroons within the "joining" into which the UN had forced the Southern Cameroons. The UN refused, for claimed financial reasons, to provide the territory with much-needed constitutional and administrative experts to assist in constitutional talks with Cameroun Republic which already enjoyed the unalloyed assistance of the French in this regard. The provision of such expertise by the UN would have been nothing new. As already noted, only ten years earlier it had done so in constitutional talks between Eritrea and Ethiopia leading to the Eritrean/Ethiopian Federation.

Once more, the money factor plagued the Southern Cameroons decolonization saga. Claimed economic non-viability of the territory was the excuse conveniently invoked in 1959 by the UN for ruling out separate independence for the Southern Cameroons. In April 1961, when it came to the effective implementation of the result of the very plebiscite the UN had imposed on the people of the territory, economic considerations again entered the calculus in working out the future of the territory and its people. The UN considered the paltry sum of $46,000 too large an amount to spend in order to secure and safeguard the Southern Cameroons and the dignity and worth of its people. One wonders what happened to the much-vaunted UN principle of human dignity and worth, and the principle of equality of all peoples and nations, small and large. In the eyes of the UN, the Southern Cameroons and its people were not worth spending $46,000 on! And yet when it imposed a plebiscite, unnecessary and costly, on the Southern Cameroons the UN did not apply its mind to the question of cost.

Had the UN provided the much-needed constitutional and administrative experts, the Southern Cameroons would have at least been an internationally guaranteed independent self-governing state within an overarching federal system. It would have applied for and be admitted to membership of the UN. It would today not be the dependent territory it is, under the colonial yoke of Cameroun Republic.

The Adoption of Resolution 1608 (XV) of April 21, 1961

On April 21, 1961, at its 994th plenary meeting, the UNGA adopted Resolution 1608 (XV) on the future of the Trust Territory of the Cameroons under UK administration. The four paragraphs of the resolution's preamble recall a number of matters: the General Assembly's recommendation for two separate plebiscites to be organized in the northern and southern parts of the trust territory, the questions to be put at the plebiscite, the period within which the plebiscites were to be organized, and the General Assembly's examination of the Plebiscite Commissioner's report on the conduct of the two plebiscites, the one in the Southern Cameroons on February 11, 1961, and the other in the Northern Cameroons on February 12, 1961.

The operative part of the resolution reads:

- 1. *Expresses* its high appreciation of the work of the United Nations Plebiscite Commissioner for the Cameroons under United Kingdom Administration and his staff;

Endorses the results of the plebiscites that:

The people of the Northern Cameroons have, by a substantial majority, decided to achieve independence by joining the independent Federation of Nigeria;

The people of the Southern Cameroons have similarly decided to achieve independence by joining the independent Republic of Cameroun;

Considers that, the people of the two parts of the Trust Territory having freely and secretly expressed their wishes with regard to their respective futures in accordance with General Assembly resolutions 1352 (XIV) and 1473 (XIV), the decision made by them through democratic processes under the supervision of the United Nations should be immediately implemented;

Decides that, the plebiscites having been taken separately with differing results, the Trusteeship Agreement of 13 December 1946 concerning the Cameroons under United Kingdom administration shall be terminated, in accordance with article 76 b of the Charter of the United Nations and in agreement with the Administering Authority, in the following manner:

With respect to the Northern Cameroons, on 1 June 1961, upon its joining the Federation of Nigeria as a separate province of the Northern Region of Nigeria;

With respect to the Southern Cameroons, on 1 October 1961, upon its joining the Republic of Cameroun;

Invites the Administering Authority, the Government of the Southern Cameroons and the Republic of Cameroun to initiate urgent discussions with a view to finalizing, before 1 October 1961, the arrangements by which the agreed and declared policies of the parties concerned will be implemented.

UN membership at the time of adoption of Resolution 1608 (XV) of April 21, 1961, stood at 100. This resolution was adopted by an overwhelming majority of sixty-four votes for and twenty-three votes against (sixteen of the twenty-three negative votes were cast by French-speaking countries rallied by France). Sixty-four states *voted in favor*: Afghanistan, Albania, Australia, Austria, Bolivia, Bulgaria, Burma, Byelorussia, Canada, Ceylon, Chile, Costa Rica, Cuba, Cyprus, Czechoslovakia, Demark, Dominican Republic, Ecuador, Ethiopia, Federation of Malaya, Finland, Ghana, Guinea, Honduras, Hungary, Iceland, India, Indonesia, Iran, Iraq, Ireland, Japan, Jordan, Laos, Lebanon,

Liberia, Libya, Mali, Mexico, Morocco, Nepal, Netherlands, New Zealand, Nigeria, Norway, Pakistan, Philippines, Poland, Romania, Saudi Arabia, South Africa, Sudan, Sweden, Thailand, Tunisia, Turkey, Ukraine, USSR, United Arab Republic, UK, USA, Venezuela, Yemen, and Yugoslavia. The states that *voted against* were twenty-three: Argentina, Belgium, Brazil, Cambodia, Cameroon, Central African Republic, Chad, China, Congo-Brazzaville, Congo-Leopoldville, Dahomey, France, Gabon, Greece, Israel, Ivory Coast, Luxembourg, Madagascar, Niger, Paraguay, Senegal, Upper Volta, and Uruguay. Ten states *abstained*: Colombia, El Salvador, Guatemala, Haiti, Italy, Panama, Peru, Portugal, Spain, and Togo. Two states were *absent* during the voting: Nicaragua and Somalia. It does not seem that Myanmar attended the session of the UNGA at which the vote on Resolution 1608 was taken.

By Resolution 1608 (XV) of April 21, 1961, the General Assembly: (i) endorsed the decision of the people of the Southern Cameroons to achieve independence by "joining" Cameroun Republic; (ii) approved the decision to terminate the Trusteeship Agreement on October 1, 1961, in accordance with Article 76(b) of the Charter of the UN, *upon* the Southern Cameroons "joining" Cameroun Republic; and (iii) prescribed finalization of the method by which the declared agreement between the Southern Cameroons and Republic of Cameroun on federal political association would be implemented.

FRAMING OF THE RESOLUTION

The manner in which the resolution was framed and the key terms used in it ("independence," "joining") give an indication of the thinking of the General Assembly.

Content of the Resolution

The resolution is couched in five numbered paragraphs. The General Assembly is the subject performing the action of the opening verb—expresses, endorses, considers, decides, and invites—in each of those five paragraphs.

Paragraph 1 "expresses" high appreciation of the work of the UN Plebiscite Commissioner and his staff. *Paragraph 2* "endorses" the results of the plebiscite that the people of the Southern Cameroons have by a substantial majority decided to achieve independence by "joining" the independent Republic of Cameroun.

Clearly, the plebiscite was not simply about "joining," as Cameroun Republic and some commentators erroneously claim. The plebiscite was primarily about achieving independence in conformity with the International Law of self-determination and the decolonization agenda of the UN.

"Joining" was a secondary matter. That is why the first thing the UNGA did was to endorse the decision of the people of the Southern Cameroons to achieve independence. The decision to achieve independence was taken by the people of the Southern Cameroons, and by no one else. The UNGA simply endorsed that decision. To endorse means to give approval or support. The decision to achieve independence was taken on February 11, 1961, by the substantial vote to that effect. However, the effective date of that independence was postponed to the happening of a future event—federating.

On October 1, 1961, independence was effectively achieved *by* (and not *after*) federating with Cameroun Republic. "Independence by federating" connotes contemporaneity of two separate and distinct occurrences—the Southern Cameroons becoming independence and the emergence of the Federation created by and constituted from the territories of the Southern Cameroons and Cameroun Republic, both events happening at the same time. At the moment of federating on October 1, 1961, independence voted for nine months earlier on February 11, 1961, took effect.

What kind of independence was contemplated by Resolution 1608 (XV)? French Cameroon became an independent sovereign state on January 1, 1960, under the name and style of Cameroun Republic. Analytically, by creating a federation together with Cameroun Republic, the Southern Cameroons automatically became a sovereign state as well since one of two federating entities cannot be an independent territory and the other a dependent territory. After October 1961, the political association with Cameroun Republic became so destructive of the interests of the Southern Cameroons that it could no longer be endured. That negative condition imposed on the Southern Cameroons the absolute necessity to opted out, as it finally did in October 2017. The exit simply resulted in the re-emergence or restoration of the statehood of the Southern Cameroons, notwithstanding the colonial occupation and the expansionist claim to the territory by Cameroun Republic. All that is needed, in the face of the occupation and claim by Cameroun Republic, is to assert that statehood and make it effective. Any contention that by dint of that exit the Southern Cameroons lacks statehood and simply reverted to its pre-1961 status of a colonial territory would be fallacious.

The Cameroon Federation had to be, and was, constituted from two distinct territories, the territory of the Southern Cameroons and the territory of Cameroun Republic, each being an independent state. Strictly speaking, a confederation rather than a federation is what was contemplated and conveyed by the concept of "independence by joining" (read: "independence by federating"). That was in fact the openly ventilated position of the Southern Cameroons even though it spoke in terms of a federation. Cameroun Republic was hardly enthusiastic about even a federation. It had all along been nursing the wild ambition of "grabbing" the territory of the Southern Cameroons through the subterfuge of an absorptive federation. The legal effect of "independence" by joining the *"independent* Republic of Cameroun" came to it as a surprise. In order to avoid a confederation, Cameroun Republic decided to become extinct and to adopt the downgraded political status of a federated state in an overarching federation within which it set out to impose itself on and control the Southern Cameroons.

The sovereign statehood of the Southern Cameroons was not by the will of Republic of Cameroun. It came about as a result of the two plebiscite questions (formulated in UNGA Resolution 1352 (XV) of October 16, 1959) on the basis of which the people of the Southern Cameroons made a decision, a decision solemnly endorsed by the UN General Assembly. On October 1, 1961, then, and in contemplation of law, the emergent Cameroon Federation was constituted from the territory of two sovereign independent states. At the same time, the two states voluntarily submerged their respective status as sovereign states and accepted to be the federated states of "West Cameroon" and "East Cameroon" within a new jointly created subject of International Law, the Federal Republic of Cameroun. The Federation was constitutionally established, although the constitutional document suffered from certain procedural and substantive infirmities. The Federation was the state successor to the two federating countries which disappeared as subjects of International Law and partially lost their respective independence.

In International Law, when two or more independent states enter into a federal state, they transfer a part of their sovereignty to the Federal State and become thereby part sovereign states. Also, when a state ceases to be an international person it ceases to exist. It becomes extinct. By voluntarily merging into the Federal State, the two merging countries became mere parts of that state. The newly independent Southern Cameroons forbore to assert its sovereign statehood. Cameroun Republic, a thirty-one-month-old independent sovereign state, became extinct and voluntarily accepted the lesser political status of a federated state. Through its instrumentalist "reunification" rhetoric, Cameroun Republic labored over the years to present the Federation as the absorption of the Southern Cameroons by Cameroun Republic in circumstances where the former simply disappeared and the latter continued, albeit with increased territory and population. This was false. Equally false is the propaganda that Cameroun Republic, having become extinct in October 1961, re-emerged as state successor to the "Federal Republic of Cameroun" and the "United Republic of Cameroun" but with a larger territory and population.

Paragraph 3 "considers" that the people of the Southern Cameroons having *"freely"* and secretly expressed their wishes with regard to their future in accordance with General Assembly Resolution 1352 (XIV) of October 16, 1959, the decision made by them through democratic process under the supervision of the UN should be immediately implemented. The reference in this paragraph to Resolution 1352 is an acknowledgment that the wishes of the people of the Southern Cameroons were expressed in the context of the imposed limited options that deliberately excluded independence as a stand-alone state. The wishes of the people of the Southern Cameroons as to their future could not therefore be said to have been freely expressed. The plebiscite options were truncated or limited since the independence of the Southern Cameroons had, perforce, to be enjoyed in the context of association with another independent country. There is a further point. Trusteeship Council Resolution 2013 (XXXVI) of March 31, 1960, invited Nigeria and Cameroun Republic to each state the constitutional terms and conditions under which each expected the Southern Cameroons to "join" it. What this meant was that the destiny of the people of the Southern Cameroons was not allowed to remain exclusively in the hands of the people of the territory themselves and to be taken by them alone, as ought to have been the case. The destiny of the people of the Southern Cameroons was determined in a decisive way by the UN, the UK, and the territory's two adjacent neighbors. In the result, there was no determination by the *self* but determination by others. All the international political status options were not put on the table and a free choice made after a full consideration of all of them. It follows that the people of the Southern Cameroons did not freely and exclusively determine their own future and the destiny of their territory.

Paragraph 4 "decides" that the Trusteeship Agreement shall be terminated, in accordance with Article 76(b) of the UN Charter and in agreement with the Administering Authority, on October 1, 1961, *upon* the Southern Cameroons "joining" Cameroun Republic. This is the only paragraph of Resolution 1608 in which the UNGA took a decision with respect to any of the matters covered in the resolution. The decision it took concerned the termination of trusteeship on a specified date, October 1, 1961. There was no date explicitly stated on which the Southern Cameroons was to federate with Cameroun Republic. The clause "*upon* the Southern Cameroons joining the Republic of Cameroun" denoted the General Assembly's assumption that the Southern Cameroons having voted to federate with Cameroun Republic, the federation was bound to emerge as well on the date of termination of trusteeship. Perhaps this assumption was informed by the need to avoid a situation where, even for just a matter of days, the Southern Cameroons would be without any clear-cut political status under International Law. However, making that assumption was not the same thing as deciding that termination of trusteeship and the act of "joining" had to take place on the same date. If the General Assembly wanted that to be the case, it could have done so by appropriately formulating paragraph 4. For example, it could have said: "decides that the Trusteeship Agreement shall be terminated, in accordance with Article 76 b of the UN Charter and in agreement with the Administering Authority, on October 1, 1961; and further decides that the Southern Cameroons shall "join" Cameroun Republic on that same date."

It is declared in paragraph 4 that the Trusteeship Agreement shall be terminated in accordance with Article 76(b) of the UN Charter. But that Charter provision does not provide for the manner of termination of trusteeship. It simply sets out one of the core basic objectives of the trusteeship system. It was generally taken that attainment of that objective would entail termination of trusteeship. The sensible implication of referring to Article 76(b) in this paragraph could only be that the General Assembly was satisfied that the objective of "self-government or independence" had been attained in the Southern Cameroons. Logically, therefore, a plebiscite was redundant, and the Southern Cameroons ought to have achieved independence as a sovereign state.

On September 25, 1961, five months after Resolution 1608 was adopted, the British Queen proclaimed and declared Britain's agreement to the termination of the Trusteeship Agreement with respect to the Southern Cameroons on the first day of October, 1961, upon the Southern Cameroons "joining" Republic of Cameroun. Her Britannic Majesty signified that as from that date Britain would cease to be responsible for the administration of the Southern Cameroons. But she did not say who was thenceforth going to be responsible. The British notification of termination of Trusteeship was followed two days later, on September 27, 1961, by a British diplomatic note to the Government of Cameroun Republic recalling that as stipulated in Resolution 1608 UK trusteeship over the Southern Cameroons would terminate at midnight of September 30, 1961, *upon* (i.e., contemporaneously with) the Southern Cameroons "joining" Cameroun Republic. Three days later, on September 30, 1961, Her Britannic Majesty addressed a message "on the occasion of the ending of UK trusteeship in the Southern Cameroons." Curiously, the message was not addressed to the prime minister of the British Trust Territory purportedly being decolonized. The message was instead addressed to the president of a foreign state, Cameroun Republic, which was never under British rule. The Queen's message made no mention of the prime minister of the Southern Cameroons. It made no mention of the Southern Cameroons, the territory under British administration for almost half a century. It was as if the ending of British rule was not in respect of the Southern Cameroons but in respect of Cameroun Republic.

Paragraph 5 "invites" the Administering Authority, the government of the Southern Cameroons, and the Republic of Cameroun to initiate urgent discussions with a view to finalizing before October 1, 1961, the arrangements by which the agreed and declared policies of the concerned parties will be implemented. The use of weak language in this paragraph is puzzling.

Why did the General Assembly not use stronger and mandatory language? It could have used terms like "decides" or "calls on." The invitation contained in this paragraph was addressed to the three parties named in it. Being such, it imposed no obligation on the parties to initiate urgent discussions and no obligation, even if they initiated discussions, to finalize them before October 1, 1961. Nevertheless, it appeared to have been the reasonable assumption that the parties would act responsibly and in good faith. They had five long months within which to accomplish the task they were invited to perform. The subject-matter of the discussions was clearly indicated in the paragraph: the "arrangements by which the agreed and declared policies" of the concerned parties were to be implemented. The "agreed and declared policies" of the Southern Cameroons and Cameroun Republic on the matter at hand referred to a union of the two countries on the basis of an agreed federation of two states, equal in status. This was agreed on and declared in written documents (Joint Declaration and Joint Communiqué) put out in the second half of 1960, confirmed in a *Note Verbale* by Cameroun Republic, made available to the UN, and included in the plebiscite enlightenment campaign pamphlet known as *The Two Alternatives* issued by the UK government. The political obligation to finalize the agreed and declared policies of the Southern Cameroons and Cameroun Republic was not carried out. An inconclusive tripartite meeting was held in Buea in May 1961. There are unsubstantiated claims that another tripartite meeting was held in Yaounde in August. But a thousand tripartite meetings without even a document attesting to the outcome of each such meeting could not and cannot amount to *finalization*. There had to be a detailed and approved final document on the subject. Resolution 1608(XV) was silent on what was to happen in the event where discussions on finalization collapsed, or failed to take place. The UN simply assumed, without any basis for doing so, that finalization would take place.

Resolution 1608 failed to prescribe due diligence measures aimed at ensuring the effective and complete decolonization of the Southern Cameroons. There should have been at least three more paragraphs in that resolution. In one additional paragraph, the General Assembly would have decided that the UN shall remain seized of the question of the decolonization of the Southern Cameroons. In a second additional paragraph, the General Assembly would have requested the Secretary-General of the UN to prepare for the General Assembly at its next session a report on the implementation of Resolution 1608 (XV). In a third additional paragraph, the General Assembly would have requested the Administering Authority to present to the Trusteeship Council, at its next session, information on the measures already taken or planned by the Administering Authority to ensure the implementation of Resolution 1608 (XV), including the transfer of powers to the government of the Southern Cameroons, consistent with the UN 1960 Declaration on the Granting of Independence to Colonial Countries and Peoples.

Unfortunately, after adopting Resolution 1608 (XV) on April 21, 1961, the UN in effect declared itself *functus officio* with regard to the Southern Cameroons decolonization question even though the Trusteeship Agreement still had about six months to run. The UN never concerned itself again with the Southern Cameroons but maintained and promoted the fiction that the territory had been completely decolonized. Termination of trusteeship did not mean that the Southern Cameroons *ip*so facto became completely decolonized. The purported decolonization of the Southern Cameroons resulted in the re-colonization of the territory, this time by the adjacent foreign state of Cameroun Republic.

MEANING OF THE KEY TERMS: "JOINING," "ACHIEVE INDEPENDENCE"

The two expressions "achieve independence" and "joining" must be understood in the context of what was advertised by the UN as the decolonization of the British Trust Territory of the Southern Cameroons. They concerned two separate matters that required a decision on each, yet expressed in one voting exercise. The outcome of the vote was to give rise to two distinct processes. "Achieving independence" was the basic and foremost matter. "Joining" was a secondary matter which was to take place only upon achievement of independence. "Joining" was not feasible without prior or contemporaneous achievement of independence. In contemplation of law, the Southern Cameroons had to achieve independence, even if just for a matter of minutes, before "joining" Cameroun Republic.

"Joining"

A colonial territory may choose to unite with another colonial territory to form one country and to achieve independence as one state. For example, the Trust Territory of Togoland under UK administration united with the Gold Coast also under British rule, in May 1956. Ten months later, in March 1957, the united entity achieved independence under the name Republic of Ghana. The Australian administered territory of Papua and the former German territory of New Guinea seized by Australia during the First World War became the Territory of Papua and New Guinea from 1949. On September 16, 1975, the conjoined entity achieved independence as Papua New Guinea. But how does a colonial territory achieved independence by "joining" an independent sovereign state? Is there any such concept as "independence by dependence"? Where a colonial territory opts for integration into its *parent state* the effect of that option is simply to confirm the *status quo* followed by constitutional adjustments to accommodate the formal incorporation. That is what happened when the miniscule Cocos-Keeling Island (8 sq. km and about 650 habitants) voted in 1984 for integration with Australia. That is what happened to the Northern Cameroons when it opted to "join" (read: to integrate with) Nigeria. And that is what would have happened to the Southern Cameroons had it opted to "join" (read: to integrate with) Nigeria.

Arguably, when a colonial territory integrates with an independent state, it becomes ipso facto independent. Independence rubs off on the colonial territory, as it were. Presumably, the colonial territory thereby becomes automatically invested with the quality of independence derived from the political status of an independent state which the state it is integrating with has. But this argument has only a superficial attraction and is hardly persuasive. When a dependent territory integrates with an independent state, it does so from a position of legal inequality in political status, a position of subordination. It retains that dependent status within the independent state. It does not, whether in law or in fact, become independent because all matters in relation to the territory, internal and external, are outside its control. Besides, when a colonial territory joins an independent state without proper self-government safeguards, the territory becomes merely additional territory for that independent state. When that happens, the colonial territory in question could perhaps technically be described, in an abuse of language, as having become "independent" by dint of its absorption by the independent state.

Yet, it is beyond doubt that the dependent status of the absorbed territory remains unchanged. In strict legal terms, there has simply been succession to territory: the independent state has succeeded to the territory of the dependent entity. In fact, such a situation is indistinguishable from that of transfer of colonial territory. The only difference is that the classic transfer case is a unilateral act of the colonial power whereas here the act has a veneer of "consent" by the inhabitants of the colonial territory. That is why some jurists used to argue, but without conviction or authority, that the plebiscitary formula may be used as a method of transfer of territory as happened in some cases of transfer of territory in Europe (e.g., the transfer of Savoy and Nice from Italy to France in 1859). In one situation, however, that of free association, a dependent territory achieving independence by freely associating with an independent state ipso facto becomes an independent sovereign state and is eligible for UN membership. A classic example is that of the trust territory of Micronesia and of the Marshall Islands which opted in 1990 to become fully self-governing in free association with the USA and were each admitted in 1991 to membership of the UN.

In the Southern Cameroons case, the agreed meaning of "joining" was "federating." By October 1960 the Southern Cameroons, Cameroun Republic, and Britain agreed (the UN being so informed) that the plebiscite alternative of "joining" Cameroun Republic meant federating with that country. There has to be a federation of two states, equal in status. The constituent federated states would be the Southern Cameroons and Cameroun Republic. The federation was going to be underpinned by either a treaty establishing the federation or a federal constitution which would be the fruit of common bargain between the two countries and submitted for approval either by the parliament of each country or by the people of each country.

"Independence"

Ordinarily a territory achieves independence when it is politically free or emancipated. It achieves independence when it is no longer politically dependent on or controlled by some other country. It becomes its own master. It becomes responsible for its own internal and external affairs. It takes its destiny into its own hands. When a country becomes independent, it is sometimes described as "independent and sovereign." The word sovereign emphasizes supreme authority. It means that the state, subject to the confines laid down by International Law has full liberty to act within its four walls and to act beyond its borders in the intercourse with other states. The word independence signifies that the state is subject to no other earthly authority. Practically, independence and sovereignty mean one and the same thing because both concepts exclude dependence upon any other authority, in particular from the authority of another state.

The primary purpose of the trusteeship system was "to promote the *political, economic, social and educational advancement of the inhabitants of the trust territories.*" In Article 3 of the Trusteeship Agreement for the British Cameroons the Administering Authority undertook to administer the Territory in such a manner as to achieve the basic objectives of the international trusteeship system as laid down in Article 76 of the Charter. Article 76 recognizes as one of the objectives of the trusteeship system the promotion of the progressive development of the trust territories "*towards self-government or independence* as may be appropriate to the particular circumstances of each territory and its peoples and the freely expressed wishes of the people concerned." The Trusteeship Agreement for the British Cameroons also contained provisions obliging the Administering Authority to promote the development of free political institutions suited to the Territory and to give the inhabitants a progressively increasing share in the government of the country with a view to their political advancement to self-government and eventual independence in accordance with Article 76(b) of the Charter. The idea of encouraging respect for human rights and fundamental freedoms for all is expressly adopted as one of the objects of the trusteeship system. Fundamental human freedoms include the eventual right of every human being to a share in the political independence of his country. Fundamental freedoms include, ultimately, freedom from government imposed by another state or nation.

The plebiscite in the Southern Cameroons was conducted in virtue of the inalienable right to self-determination. Self-determination may not necessarily involve solely and exclusively an absolute right to elect for autonomous statehood. It may involve also an option to choose integration with another country. But the choice of autonomous statehood or integration is always a matter for decision by the people concerned and no one else. Neither the Administering Authority nor the UN could legitimately make that choice in the place of the people. Yet, both manipulated the process leading to the making of that decision by the people of the Southern Cameroons.

The term "achieve independence," as used in formulating the plebiscite questions and also as used in Resolution 1608, did not mean *autonomous* or stand-alone statehood. It meant being free from British administration under the international tutelage system. When a colonial territory achieves independence, it achieves freedom to make laws or decisions without being governed or controlled by another country. When a country gains independence, it has its own government and is not ruled by another country. Achieving independence entails at the very minimum self-government and self-identity because self-determination has to do with self-preservation and not self-destruction or extinction. On the good authority of Professor Philips Cadbury of the University of London, speaking in November 1960, federating with Cameroun Republic

> does not connote absorption or loss of identity but . . . something more like the Ghana-Guinea Union . . . In the absence of a third option, the second option offered in the plebiscite in February will win a substantial majority. But this will not be a mandate for absorption, but for negotiation of equal terms. (*The Guardian Newspaper*, London, November 25, 1960)

The Southern Cameroons could not before and after the plebiscite have negotiated with Cameroun Republic on equal terms and then proceeded to federate with that country as an unequal party. Unequal parties cannot conclude a valid contract.

The Southern Cameroons did not vote and could not have voted for the destruction of its personality, identity and dignity, for the transfer of its territory to Cameroun Republic, and for its citizens to become stateless persons and a people of a lesser order. That would not be self-determination but self-destruction. There is nothing the Southern Cameroons stood to gain by such a tragic vote which would have been an act of collective political suicide. Achieving independence entails at the very minimum self-government and self-identity because self-determination has to do with self-preservation and not self-destruction or extinction.

The UN endorsement of the decision of the people of the Southern Cameroons to achieve independence signified that it endorsed their decision to be free from British tutelary rule with effect from October 1, 1961. On that date, the trusteeship ended and Britain ceased to have responsibility for the Southern Cameroons and left the territory. The independence of the Southern Cameroons did not derive from, and was not granted by, Cameroun Republic which, in any case, does not have and has never had such capacity or status. The independence of the Southern Cameroons was achieved by act, by vote at the plebiscite, of the people of the Southern Cameroons in accordance with Article 76(b) of the UN Charter. It is thus not the federating with Cameroun Republic that gave the Southern Cameroons independence. The independence of the Southern Cameroons was direct and not derivative. Cameroun Republic has no sovereign right over the Southern Cameroons and therefore could not, on October 1, 1961, have granted it independence or extended its independence (necessarily confined only within its territorial boundaries) to the Southern Cameroons. Of course, legally and politically, achieving independence is one thing, exercising that independence is another thing. The Southern Cameroons could not exercise the independence it had just achieved because that independence was suppressed by the conjunction of two events: (i) Cameroun Republic's assertion of its illegal annexationist claim to the territory of the Southern Cameroons and its illegal assumption of constituent and other legislative powers over the territory even before the termination of trusteeship; and (ii) Britain's factual transfer of powers, by conduct, to Cameroun Republic which then took over, de facto, as successor colonial authority responsible for the overall oversight and administration of the territory.

SALIENT DEVELOPMENTS AFTER
ADOPTION OF THE RESOLUTION

In October 1960, the UK government assured the Southern Cameroons delegation at the London talks that after the plebiscite, arrangements for a "Federal United Cameroun Republic" would be worked out by "a conference consisting of representative delegations of equal status from Cameroun Republic and the Southern Cameroons, and that the United Nations and the United Kingdom would also be associated with this conference." No arrangement for any such conference was ever worked out. And when the Southern Cameroons and Cameroun Republic met in Foumban in July 1961 for discussions on a proposed constitution for the would-be federation, neither the UN nor the UK bothered to attend the conference. This was surprising because the UK was still responsible for the defense and external relations of the Southern Cameroons, and British trusteeship had not yet been terminated.

In breach of the International Law principle of territoriality, Cameroun Republic unilaterally drafted, enacted, signed, and promulgated on September 1, 1961, a so-called "federal constitution" and foists it on the people of the Southern Cameroons. The document in question was in reality an annexation law thinly disguised as an amending constitutional statute. In that document, Cameroun Republic claimed the territory of the Southern Cameroons as its territory returned to it, presumably by Britain and the UN. In mid-September 1961 Cameroun Republic made good this claim when its French-led troops marched into the defenseless territory of the Southern Cameroons, occupied it, and started visiting the people with all kinds of cruel abuses, including atrocious torture, killings, and other forms of violent oppression and terrorization. These happenings, together with the extraterritorial legislation by Cameroun Republic, took place even while the Southern Cameroons was still a UN Trust Territory under British administration. Neither Britain nor the UN lifted a finger.

Then on the 30th of that same month, the British Government purportedly transferred "sovereignty" over the Southern Cameroons to Cameroun Republic. The Southern Cameroons once again found itself under foreign occupation, rule, and oppression. In 1975 when Spain acted in a similar indecent manner by transferring the Western Sahara to Morocco and Mauritania, the UNGA refused to recognize the transfer, rejected it, and decided that the Western Sahara remained a colonial territory still to be decolonized. The Southern Cameroons was a UN Trust Territory. It was not a British territory, colony, or protectorate. Britain was the Administering Authority, not the owner. It had no plenitude of powers over the territory. Sovereignty ultimately vests in the people of the territory, not in Britain. The term "trust" is wholly incompatible with any exclusiveness of rights of sovereignty. Admittedly, the *exercise* of sovereignty vested with the Administering Authority. But that was subject to supervision by and accountability to the UN. It is fundamental that a Trust Territory does not form part of the territory of the Administering Authority. The British delegation to the 1946 UNGA session that approved the Trusteeship Agreement for the British Cameroons stated that the retention of the words "as an integral part" in the Trusteeship Agreement for Togoland and the Cameroons under British administration "did not involve administration as an integral part of the United Kingdom itself and did not imply British sovereignty in these areas."

The Administering Authority could not therefore validly cede or otherwise alter the status of the trust territory, except with the approval of the UN in which the residuary sovereignty was vested. Accordingly, Britain could not lawfully have transferred the Southern Cameroons to a third party. Britain could not give what it did not have. Its purported transfer, by conduct or verbally or in writing, of the Southern Cameroons to Cameroun Republic was therefore illegal, null and void, and of no effect whatsoever. Britain could not even have validly transferred the power of administration it had. It was a departing Administering Authority and did not have any power of administration left to transfer as of the night of September 30, 1961. When Spain, the departing colonial authority over the Western Sahara, transferred administration of the territory to Morocco and Mauritania, the UN refused to recognize it and considered the territory still as under colonial subjugation. The system of international administration of trust territories was not created to facilitate re-colonization, annexation, or some other form of dependent status. There is no alternative to decolonization. A colonial territory is either completely decolonized or it is not.

The Southern Cameroons was a defenseless territory due to British neglect. The furtherance of international peace and security is a provision which appeared first in the enumeration of the aims of the trusteeship system. This signaled the intention of the UN to abandon the drastic limitation which the Covenant of the League of Nations had imposed upon the mandatory powers in respect of recruiting in and fortification of the mandated territories. Undesirably, the general policy of Britain in the trust territory of the Southern Cameroons was not consistent with the general purpose of promoting international peace and security. Britain took no steps to ensure that the Southern Cameroons played its part in the maintenance of international peace and security. It adopted no measures for the defense of the Southern Cameroons. It raised no military or police force in the Southern Cameroons. It counted on deploying such forces from its adjacent colonial territory of Nigeria rather than stationing Britain's own forces in the Southern Cameroons or raising a military force in the territory. It established no naval, military, and air bases, and erected no fortification anywhere in the territory. Furthermore, the British policy of forcing the Southern Cameroons as material for infilling at the border of Nigeria was clearly not such as to promote international peace and security in that part of the world. Finally, the transfer of "sovereignty" to Cameroun Republic negated the promotion of peace and security in the Gulf of Guinea and resulted in Cameroun Republic's colonial imperialism in the Southern Cameroons. Colonial imperialism is widely considered as inimical to international peace. The ongoing war imposed since 2017 on the people of the Southern Cameroons by Cameroun Republic is a direct result of that British act of recklessness in transferring power not to the government of the Southern Cameroons, of which it was the trustee power, but to a foreign and violence-addicted state, to wit, Cameroun Republic. These actions by Britain were retrogressive steps. They were not in the interests of the inhabitants of the trust territory. They were not consistent with the purpose of the trusteeship system.

At the inception of the de facto federation, the Southern Cameroons was renamed "West Cameroon" and Cameroun Republic "East Cameroon." No proclamation was made then or afterward defining the boundary between the two territories because the Anglo-French boundary treaties of 1919 and 1931 already defined and delimited that boundary, making it redundant to do so again. During and after the de facto federation, therefore, that boundary alignment separating the Southern Cameroons from Cameroun Republic simply had the *appearance* of an internal boundary. Moreover, voting against Resolution 1608, Cameroun Republic continued the international boundary alignment with the Southern Cameroons as unchanged in legal character. Furthermore, the confirmation ipso facto of that boundary alignment as an international boundary is also evidenced by the February 1984 revival of Cameroun Republic which was extinct in October 1961.

During the Federation, the Southern Cameroons limited its sovereignty and submerged its international personality. Its external relations with other states were absorbed entirely by the Federal Government. However, as a Federated State, it enjoyed internal government status within an overarching two-state federal arrangement. It had legal personality under municipal law. It exercised such measure of territorial competence within the Federated State and sovereignty over such matters as conceded by the de facto federal constitution. It controlled much of its internal affairs. It had authority over, and the allegiance of, its citizens. It had a constitution with provisions on the various facets of government. There was in Buea, capital of the Federated State, a Head of Government who was the Prime Minister, and an Executive Council or Cabinet as the principal instrument of policy in the state. There was a bicameral legislature: the House of Assembly as the lower house, and the House of Chiefs as the upper house with powers similar to those of the House of Lords in Britain. Parliament had power to make law for the peace, order, and good government of the Southern Cameroons. There was a police force with responsibility for maintaining and securing public safety and order, internal peace, and security. There was furthermore a Judiciary responsible for the administration of justice, and a State Prosecuting Department headed by the Attorney General; a Public Service Commission headed by a chairman; and a vibrant Parliamentary Opposition and civil society holding the Government in check. Arguably, the Southern Cameroons continued to enjoy a congener of sovereign statehood.

Still, the Southern Cameroons was, to all intents and purposes, under the imperium of Cameroun Republic on account of the latter's larger size and population, its monopoly of political and economic power, and its unbearable domination. Cameroun Republic troops were in occupation of the Federated State. Its appointed governor to the state, known as *Inspecteur d'Administration*, stepped into the shoes of the departed British Commissioner of the Southern Cameroons. With the forcible takeover of the Southern Cameroons, it effectively and officially became an occupied territory and a dependency of Cameroun Republic.

The foundation of the political association between the Southern Cameroons and Cameroun Republic was destroyed when the Federation was abolished by Cameroun Republic in May 1972. The Southern Cameroons as a state was destroyed. And so too all its state institutions, structures, and agencies. The territory was then officially decreed a dependency of Cameroun Republic. The despotic abolition of the federation completely removed any obligation on the part of the people of the Southern Cameroons to continue to be connected in any form or shape with Cameroun Republic. The latter cannot claim any rights from the illegal termination of the Federation that existed for eleven years. Legal rights cannot derive from an illegal situation. The federal constitution could not legally be used to destroy the federal form of state entrenched by that constitution. A constitution is an instrument for construction and cooperation. It is not an instrument for destruction, confrontation, and contestation. One cannot destroy what one purports to amend or modify and still call that process one of amending or modifying the constitution. The despotic abolition of the Federation portended a future armed conflict between the Southern Cameroons and Cameroun Republic. In February 1984, President Biya proclaimed the revival of Cameroun Republic and the resumption of its former status as a separate independent sovereign state, but with territorial claim to the territory of the Southern Cameroons. He was not able to state the basis of such a claim.

In retrospect, it is the case that Cameroun Republic succeeded in colonizing the Southern Cameroons through a long process of clever deceit, falsehood, and political maneuvering; a process of soft colonization variously camouflaged as so-called "reunification," "unification," "national integration," and "national unity." When Cameroun Republic took over from Britain as successor colonial authority in the Southern Cameroons, that colonialism was disguised as "federation." Colonialism is the process whereby one country establishes and maintains its dominance of another. It is the policy or practice of taking political control, fully or partially, over another country, occupying it and exploiting it economically. The characteristics of colonialism include political and legal domination over another country, relations of economic and political dependence, and spoliation of the resources of the colonized country.

NOTEWORTHY EVENTS BETWEEN
JULY AND SEPTEMBER 1961

July 17–21, 1961

Foumban meeting of both the Southern Cameroons and Cameroun Republic to discuss the constitution of the future federation. The meeting ended inconclusively and was not reconvened.

September 1, 1961

Cameroun Republic unilaterally framed, passed, signed, and promulgated a "federal constitution" and declared it to be binding on the Southern Cameroons as from October 1, 1961.

September 25, 1961

The British Queen proclaimed and declared the UK's agreement to the termination of the Trusteeship Agreement with respect to the Southern Cameroons on the first day of October 1961, upon its "joining" Cameroun Republic. Her Britannic Majesty went on to signify that as from that date the UK would cease to be responsible for the administration of the Southern Cameroons. She did not say who was going to be responsible, the Southern Cameroons itself or Cameroun Republic.

September 27, 1961

The UK Government sent a diplomatic note through its Ambassador in Yaounde, Mr. C. E. King, to the Government of Republic of Cameroun recalling that as stipulated in UNGA Resolution 1608 (XV) of April 21, 1961, UK trusteeship over the Southern Cameroons would terminate at midnight of September 30, 1961, *upon* the Southern Cameroons "joining" Cameroun Republic.

September 30, 1961

The UK Government invited a foreign Prince, President Ahidjo of Cameroun Republic, to the Southern Cameroons and purportedly "transferred the Southern Cameroons" to him, according to the confession of Hugh Fraser, the British Under-Secretary of State for the Colonies. Addressing the House of Commons on October 1, 1961, he informed the House that as he was speaking, "the Southern Cameroons has already been transferred to Mr. Ahidjo of Cameroun Republic."

September 30, 1961

Her Britannic Majesty addressed a message "on the occasion of the ending of UK trusteeship in the Southern Cameroons." The message was addressed not to the prime minister of the British territory purportedly being decolonized, but to the president of another country, Cameroun Republic, which was never under British rule. The Queen's message "express[ed] sincere good wishes for the future of the united territories." The prime minister of the Southern Cameroons, the territory which was for almost half a century under British rule, was completely ignored in this message.

CONCLUSION

The result of the plebiscite vote was not a mandate for incorporation, absorption, integration, or assimilation by Cameroun Republic. It was not a mandate for transfer of the territory of the Southern Cameroons to Cameroun Republic. It was a mandate to achieve independence and to federate with Cameroun Republic. To accept the view that the Southern Cameroons did not achieve independence would mean the plebiscite was a pretended decolonization exercise and that the Southern Cameroons continues to be a classic colonial territory still to be decolonized. It would also mean that there was a big conspiracy at the UN to play a confidence trick on the hapless people of the Southern Cameroons. It would further mean the plebiscite was a gigantic political swindle by the UN. If the whole plebiscite exercise was a charade and a fraud, then the plebiscite poll was a complete nullity.

The more likely thesis is that the Southern Cameroons achieved independence though not as a separate state, since that eventuality was questionably ruled out by the UN and also given its de facto federal political association with Cameroun Republic. The UN itself maintains that the Southern Cameroons achieved independence in accordance with Article 76(b) of the Charter of the UN and also in accordance with its decolonization agenda as evidenced by the valid termination of trusteeship. *De jure*, the Southern Cameroons-Cameroun Republic federation was billed as a political association of two independent states. De facto, however, Cameroun Republic contrived to annex the Southern Cameroons by adopting measures designed to achieve over time its objectives of colonial rule and territorial aggrandizement. A number of actions taken in September 1961 by the Administering Authority emboldened Cameroun Republic to launch out on this adventure of territorial aggrandizement via annexation.

Republic of Cameroun's negative vote had important legal implications. It meant that Cameroun Republic: (i) refused to recognize the independence of the Southern Cameroons voted by the people of the territory and endorsed by the General Assembly; (ii) rejected the decision of the UN that the Southern Cameroons federates as an independent country with it; (iii) rejected the UN directive for finalization of the arrangements by which the agreed and published policies of the parties concerned were to be implemented; and (iv) continued the international boundary between itself and the Southern Cameroons as unchanged in character, despite appearances to the contrary. Republic of Cameroun's negative vote credibly explains its subsequent annexation project targeting the Southern Cameroons.

The frontier alignment between the Southern Cameroons and Cameroun Republic has always been, de jure, an international boundary, notwithstanding the de facto federation and the illegal assumption by Cameroun Republic of a colonial sovereignty over the Southern Cameroons. During the de facto federation, that alignment simply had the *appearance* of an internal boundary. The revival in February 1984 by President Biya of the hitherto extinct polity of Cameroun Republic ipso facto confirmed the frontier alignment as an international boundary. The confirmation of the international character of that alignment is further evidenced by the fact that Cameroun Republic has always maintained along the frontier its military, gendarmerie, police, and customs barriers erected since before its independence. These barriers exist to control the movement of persons, goods and services between the two countries. Up to the 1970s any citizen of the Southern Cameroons intending to travel to Cameroun Republic needed a laissez-passer to be able to enter that country.

What political status did the Southern Cameroons emerge into as from October 1, 1961? Incredibly, this all-important question did not exercise the mind of the UK or the UN. But arguably, and as a matter of law, on October 1, 1961, the Southern Cameroons became an independent half-sovereign state (on account of its internal independence) and a qualified subject of International Law. By politically associating with Cameroun Republic in a de facto federal set up, the Southern Cameroons voluntarily limited its sovereignty and submerged its international personality. Its external relations with other states were absorbed entirely by the Federal Government. But being a federated state, it enjoyed internal self-government status within an overarching two-state federal arrangement. It had legal personality under municipal law. It exercised such measure of territorial competence within the federated state and sovereignty over such matters as conceded by the de facto Federal Constitution. It controlled much of its internal affairs. It had authority over, and the allegiance of, its citizens.

The very basis of the political association between the Southern Cameroons and Cameroun Republic was destroyed when the Federation was overthrown by President Ahidjo, native of Cameroun Republic, in May 1972. The overthrow breached the federal-form-of-state undertaking by Cameroun Republic. With the forcible dissolution of the Federation and the takeover of the Southern Cameroons, the latter effectively and officially became an occupied territory and a dependency of Cameroun Republic. The destruction of the federation, the condition *sine qua non* of political association with Cameroun Republic, removed entirely any obligation on the part of the people of the Southern Cameroons to remain in any form of connection with Cameroun Republic. *Clausula rebus sic stantibus.*

Chapter 3

Cameroun's Presence in Ambazonia Has No Proper Basis in History, Politics, Law, or in Any Other Respect

Carlson Anyangwe

Cameroun blows hot air that Ambazonia is part of its territory.[1] This fiction has a familiar ring. It is a déjà vu. France claimed Algeria as part of France. "L'Algérie est française." So the French repeatedly shouted until they were forced to accept reality and to exit Algeria. Portugal claimed that its African colonies are part of Portugal separated from the motherland by accident of geography. Imperial Ethiopia claimed Eritrea as part of its territory. Indonesia claimed East Timor as part of the territory of Indonesia that was excised therefrom by Dutch-Portuguese colonialism. Morocco claimed Western Sahara as part of Morocco going back to precolonial times. Britain claimed Ireland as part of Britain by dint of English invasion and occupation. South Africa occupied Namibia and was on the verge of annexing it as a province of South Africa by reason of geographical propinquity and of having seized it from Germany in 1915. The specious claim in each of these cases was rejected by the peoples concerned. In each case the implausible claim imposed on the dependent people the necessity of a war of independence to vindicate the right of self-determination and end colonial presence. The same scenario is playing out with regard to Cameroun and Ambazonia. Pushed by and aping France, Cameroun chases the tragic illusion that "l'Ambazonie est Camerounaise."

The incontrovertible fact is that Ambazonia and Cameroun are, and have always been, two separate and distinct countries with distinct identities and firmly established international boundaries. In relation to Ambazonia, Cameroun is by any characterization a foreign colonizing state occupying Ambazonia. When Cameroun achieved independence from France, it succeeded by operation of law to the Anglo-French boundary treaties (of 1916, confirmed in 1919 and reconfirmed in 1931) establishing the international boundary between Ambazonia and Cameroun. The occupation of Ambazonia by Cameroun is aggression and colonization with the set objective of bringing about territorial change. That conduct is in breach of International Law. It violates the right of the people of Ambazonia to self-determination, dignity, humanity, and the integrity of their territory. It also violates the principle *uti possidetis juris* and the legal obligation to respect borders existing on the date of independence. There is no International Law instrument that Cameroun can plead in justification of its colonial occupation of Ambazonia.

Colonialism is a practice of domination whereby one people subjugates another, controlling them politically and economically through various techniques. A colonized people have no control over their own governance and socioeconomic situation. They are under the imperium of a foreign sovereign exercising illegitimate control over their homeland. Colonial rule, white or black or any other color, is *ipso facto* foreign domination and inherently brutal. Colonialism is an appalling human tragedy which has earned universal opprobrium, prompting international commitment to stamp it out. The UN Declaration on the Granting of Independence to Colonial Countries and Peoples, 1960, proclaims the need to unconditionally end colonialism in all its forms and manifestations. It calls on colonial authorities to transfer all powers to colonized peoples without any delay or conditions. It clarifies that the continued existence of colonialism impedes the social, cultural, and economic development of dependent peoples and militates against the UN ideal of universal peace. The African Union likewise commits itself to eradicate from Africa all forms of colonialism and neo-colonialism.

In the lines that follow I demonstrate that there is no basis whatsoever for Cameroun's presence in Ambazonia and that Cameroun is under obligation to end its presence in Ambazonia. To this end, I marshal three lines of argument.

First, I argue that historically Ambazonia and Cameroun are two separate and distinct countries; that the latter is in colonial occupation of the former since October 1961; that contrary to appearances and uninformed views there has never been a union of Ambazonia and Cameroun; and that eleven years into its colonial occupation of Ambazonia Cameroun formally annexed Ambazonia using force and fraudulent maneuvers.

Second, I contend that the presence of Cameroun in Ambazonia lacks even a political basis. I point out and explain that the plebiscite vote was never a vote for Ambazonia to be extinct and to become part of the territory of Cameroun. I further point out that the type of federation agreed on in 1960 during talks between the two countries failed to materialize; that Britain unlawfully transferred powers in respect of Ambazonia to Cameroun; and that despite appearances to the contrary Ambazonia's international boundary with Cameroun has never changed in character.

Third, I indicate a number of International Law principles that point to the illegality of Cameroun's presence in Ambazonia: the separate and distinct status of a dependent territory vis-à-vis the territory of the colonial occupier; the international legal obligation on colonial authorities to decolonize; the legal position that sovereignty concerning a dependent territory lies with the people of the territory, its true owners; the principle of obligatory non-recognition of invalid territorial changes; and the principle *uti possidetis juris*.

From these lines of argument, I draw the informed conclusion that the continued presence of Cameroun in Ambazonia is illegal and that Cameroun is under an obligation to withdraw its administration and military from, and end its occupation of, Ambazonia.

FIRST LINE OF ARGUMENT: NO HISTORICAL BASIS FOR CAMEROUN'S PRESENCE

Ambazonia's precolonial and colonial history differs from that of Cameroun. The year 2023 marks 177 years of unbroken alien domination of Ambazonia: British presence and sphere of influence from 1846 to 1887, a contested and precarious short-lived German rule from 1887 to 1914, British rule again from 1914 to 1961, and Cameroun rule from 1961 to date. Ambazonia was a mandated territory of the League of Nations from 1922 to 1945, and a Trust Territory of the UN from 1945 to 1961. As a separate and distinct territory, Ambazonia progressively pursued its developmental path and political advancement toward independence before it fell under Cameroun colonial rule and brutal oppression.

When in October 1961 Cameroun succeeded Britain as the new colonial authority in Ambazonia, it could not profess that Ambazonia is part of its territory. It carried on in the de facto capacity of an occupying colonial authority. Cameroun's administration of Ambazonia has always been through a network of imperious *"administrateurs civils"* who work only in French, enforce everything French, and have the backing of a ubiquitous Cameroun army of occupation. In 1972, consequent upon the formal annexation of Ambazonia through a combination of force and fraud, the territory was dismembered into two and declared appurtenances of Cameroun territory. To this day, Ambazonia remains dismembered. It does not enjoy even a modicum of self-government, which is additional proof positive that it has not been decolonized. Decolonization entails at the very least self-government. Cameroun vandalized and destroyed Ambazonia's state institutions. It embarked on spoliation of the natural resources of Ambazonia, and this has been going on for the past sixty years. It has continued with its ruthless onslaught on Ambazonia's legal, educational, and administrative system and on its official language which is

English. Sixty years on, the people of Ambazonia continue to experience the severe trauma of Cameroun's colonial rule and very harsh occupation.

The pretended "referendum" staged by Cameroun in 1972 advertises the fiction of "annexation by consent." That "referendum" served as an expedient for the annexation of Ambazonia in a Nazi-type Austro-German Anschluss. Cameroun thereafter explicitly asserted an implausible claim to the territory of Ambazonia, alleging that it falls within its territorial integrity. This specious claim continues to be roundly and repeatedly rejected by the people of Ambazonia, all the more so as annexation is not a valid mode of acquisition of territory under contemporary International Law. There is therefore no historical support for Cameroun's presence in Ambazonia.

SECOND LINE OF ARGUMENT: NO POLITICAL BASIS FOR CAMEROUN'S PRESENCE

The plebiscite in Ambazonia on February 11, 1961, was legally erroneous, factually unnecessary, and politically indefensible. It was based on the uninformed and invalid premise of lack of economic viability. It left out the status option of sovereign independence. The territory was unwarrantedly denied its legitimate right to sovereign statehood and, because of the unwarranted suppression of that all-important option, Ambazonia is still under colonial bondage to this day. It is important to clarify that the plebiscite vote was primarily a vote to achieve independence. The vote was also, but as a secondary matter, for free political association with Cameroun in the form of an aggregative federation, informed by the basic principle that a federation involves a dovetailing rather than a supersession of legal orders. The envisaged aggregative federation did not materialize as no instrument was executed by both countries evidencing the creation of such a federation. In other words, no treaty was concluded and signed by both parties attesting to the creation of a federal "union" of Ambazonia and Cameroun. Contrary to uninformed views, there was no union of the territory of Ambazonia with the territory of Cameroun. Rather, there was a colonial takeover of Ambazonia by Cameroun, a takeover disguised by Cameroun using the euphemistic language of so-called "reunification"/"unification." A valid "union" of countries does not take place casually or informally. A valid "union" of countries has to be, and is always, underpinned by a legal instrument consistent with International Law and signed by the "uniting" countries. The plebiscite vote cannot therefore be pleaded in justification of Cameroun's presence in and control of Ambazonia.

That vote was never, and could not have been, a vote for the territory of Ambazonia to become part of the territory of Cameroun and a license for colonial occupation. There is nothing Ambazonia stood to gain by voting to be absorbed or occupied by Cameroun. Ambazonia did not vote and could not have voted for a detrimental change in its political status as a self-governing country enjoying a large measure of economic, social, political, and cultural well-being. Any such action by any country would be totally against nature and the human instinct of dignity, self-preservation, and perpetual striving for improvement of the human condition. A country cannot voluntarily decide to become extinct. Nor can a people voluntarily decide to come under the domination and subjugation of another people. That would be national suicide, an act unknown in history. Britain's indecent flight from Ambazonia and the attendant illegal handover of the Trust Territory to Cameroun resulted in re-colonization of Ambazonia. This new situation of colonization revivified the inalienable right of the people of Ambazonia to self-determination.

On the eve of October 1, 1961, Britain questionably transferred power to Cameroun rather than to Ambazonia, making that country the colonial state successor to Ambazonia. The effect of this purported transfer was the supersession of British colonial rule by Cameroun colonial rule, resulting in re-colonization rather than decolonization of Ambazonia. Cameroun assumed the dubious distinction of successor colonial authority in Ambazonia: a black colonial authority replaced the departed white colonial power. Britain's conduct violated its obligation under the UN Charter to lead Ambazonia to self-government or independence. Britain's Charter obligation was not to lead Ambazonia to "join" or be transferred to another country. As a result of what Britain did, the end of trusteeship on October 1, 1961 (based on a mere announcement in April 1961) did not entail the disappearance of the dependent status of Ambazonia as should have been the case. Britain had, and exercised, only delegated and limited authority in the Trust Territory of Ambazonia. It did not enjoy an unrestricted plenitude of power and thus could not, for example, transfer or otherwise dispose of Ambazonia whether gratuitously or for value. Britain exercised no more than colonial authority in Ambazonia. So, what Britain purportedly transferred to Cameroun could only have been colonial authority (*nemo dat non quod habet*), making Cameroun the de facto successor colonial authority in Ambazonia. The illegality of Britain's transfer of power invalidates Cameroun's presence and exercise of authority in Ambazonia. Furthermore, the illegal transfer of Ambazonia to Cameroun did not have, and could not have had, any incidence on Ambazonia's national sovereignty. That sovereignty did not cease to belong to the people of Ambazonia. For the time being, it continues to be in abeyance until the moment of sovereign independence. Only the people of Ambazonia themselves can be owners of the territory of Ambazonia, and only in them does sovereignty lie.

In May 1972, Cameroun staged a pretended referendum under which it claimed to have received a mandate to decree out of existence Ambazonia as a state and a polity and to formally annex Ambazonia. *République du Cameroun* had declared itself extinct under its September 1, 1961, unilaterally framed, adopted, signed, and promulgated "constitution de la république fédérale du Cameroun." Twelve and a half years later, on February 4, 1984, Cameroun acted out another political event in which it resuscitated *République du Cameroun* as a legal and political expression. This by necessary implication entailed the resumption of its former status as a state shorn of its indefensible colonial pretensions. This fact makes Cameroun's presence in Ambazonia illegal because by asserting its pre-October 1961 political identity, Cameroun by necessary legal and political implications advertises severance of its colonial and any other kind of link with Ambazonia.

A critical matter often overlooked is that Ambazonia's international boundary with Cameroun has never legally changed in character. It continues as unchanged in character for the simple reason that an international boundary established by treaty endures even if the treaty establishing it ceases to exist. Besides, by voting against the adoption of UNGA Resolution 1608 (XV) of April 21, 1961, Cameroun thereby continued its international boundary with Ambazonia unchanged in character. The boundary alignment between Ambazonia and Cameroun has always been de jure an international boundary. This is so notwithstanding the de facto annexationist "federation" that existed from October 1961 to May 1972 and notwithstanding Cameroun's assumption and exercise of colonial authority in Ambazonia since October 1961. When Cameroun took control of Ambazonia as a successor colonial authority, the international boundary between the two countries merely had the *appearance* of an internal boundary. Furthermore, the so-called "federal republic" and "united republic" which Cameroun unilaterally created were not consensual, genuine, and enduring constitutional arrangements. They were stratagems and spurious contraptions designed to whitewash Cameroun's colonial occupation of Ambazonia. That being the case, the international boundary between both countries never legally acquired an internal character. Again, the revival of *République du Cameroun* as a legal and political expression confirmed Cameroun's frontier line with Ambazonia as unchanged. Finally, Cameroun has always maintained along the frontier line between the two countries the military, police, and customs barriers existing before independence to control the movement of persons, goods, and services between the two countries. Cameroun thereby also confirms the international character of the boundary alignment. These statements of the true state of affairs as to the international boundary between Ambazonia and Cameroun give the lie to the self-serving French misinformed view that on October 1, 1961, Cameroun moved its southwest border westward to share a common border with Nigeria and thereby enveloped the entire 45,000 sq. km territory of Ambazonia as Cameroun territory. In an abuse of legal language, France calls this purported unilateral shifting of the border a "border adjustment." International boundaries are never moved unilaterally. That would amount to an invalid territorial change. Such a purported massive shift would not qualify in International Law as a mere border adjustment. France is unable to supply the legal basis and raison d'être for the purported "border adjustment" which, in International Law, would be a territorial issue and not a mere border issue. This French view is so fanciful as not to merit any further comment.

THIRD LINE OF ARGUMENT: NO LEGAL BASIS FOR CAMEROUN'S PRESENCE

The status of a dependent territory (like Ambazonia) is separate and distinct from the territory of the colonial authority controlling it (like Cameroun controlling Ambazonia). It exists until the people of the dependent territory have exercised their right of self-determination. Like other peoples, dependent peoples have an inalienable right to complete freedom, exercise their sovereignty, and respect the integrity of their national territory. Colonial authorities are under an international legal obligation to decolonize. Force may not be used against dependent peoples to deprive them of their right to self-determination, a norm of jus cogens in International Law. Nor may force be used to deprive dependent peoples of their national identity or of their right to freedom and independence. The use of such force constitutes a violation of the inalienable rights of dependent peoples.

Cameroun's subjection of the people of Ambazonia to colonial control, domination, and exploitation constitutes a violation of the principle of equality and equal rights of people, a denial of fundamental human rights, and is contrary to the UN Charter. The inhabitants of Ambazonia unquestionably constitute a people within the meaning of International Law. They have a deep sense of common belonging, aspiration, and destiny. They have a distinctive history, linguistic and cultural identity, as well as a state culture that devolved on them. Like all other peoples, they have the right to existence and to freedom from domination. Cameroun's colonial occupation is a travesty of these fundamental rights. Cameroun is therefore under international obligation to end its colonial presence in Ambazonia.

Territorial changes are invalid if obtained in breach of International Law such as through war, coercion, fraud, subterfuge, or other illegal means, or in any other way inconsistent with the purposes of the UN. This follows from a general rule of International Law imposing a duty of non-recognition of invalid territorial changes. In Europe, for example, territories occupied or annexed between 1933 and 1940 were considered invalid and restored to states from which they had been taken by force. France was thus able to get back Alsace-Lorraine which Germany had seized.

In *Legal Consequences for States of the Continued Presence of South Africa in Namibia (South West Africa) Notwithstanding Security Council Resolution 276 of 1971*, ICJ Rep 1977, the International Court of Justice articulated the principle of obligatory non-recognition of invalid territorial changes in relation to the situation prevailing in Namibia at the time. The Court ruled that the continued presence of South Africa in Namibia was illegal. The illegality arose from South Africa's refusal to submit to the supervision of UN organs. Since it refused to submit to UN supervision, South Africa was under an obligation not only to withdraw its administration from Namibia but also to end its occupation of that territory. UN Members, the court further ruled, were under an obligation not to recognize the legality of South Africa's presence in Namibia. They were furthermore to refrain from any acts and any dealings with the South African government implying recognition of the legality of or lending support or assistance to such presence and administration. The validity or effects of any relations entered into by any state with South Africa concerning Namibia were not to be recognized by the UN or any of its members.

The principle of obligatory non-recognition is settled in International Law. The UN Security Council tends to include in resolutions binding on all UN Members an express prohibition of recognition of territorial changes brought about by the use of force or other illegal means. Examples include UNSC resolutions on the Turkish Republic of Northern Cyprus and on the four homelands or Bantustans created and granted "independence" in 1976 by Apartheid South Africa. However, the Security Council made no explicit call for the non-recognition of the annexation of East Timor by Indonesia in 1975, the occupation of Western Sahara by Morocco in 1976, and the colonial occupation of Ambazonia by Cameroun in October 1961. The fact that the Council did not make any explicit call for the non-recognition of the territorial changes in those three cases does not mean that those changes were valid. The territorial change in each case was brought about in violation of International Law. Indonesia's stubborn fanciful claim to East Timor impelled East Timor to launch a war of independence which ended with the achievement of sovereign independence in 2004. Morocco is still in illegal occupation of the Western Sahara. But the AU and a number of countries recognize the Western Sahara's sovereign independence proclaimed in 1975. Moreover, the question of Morocco's occupation of the Western Sahara is actively on the agenda of the UN. That leaves only the Ambazonian case which continues to invite urgent attention by the UN as a matter of law and justice. This is important because of the necessity to restore the people of the territory to their dignity and humanity.

The people of Ambazonia have never accepted to come under the sovereignty of Cameroun or for their territory to be part of Cameroun territory. Sovereignty in respect of territory is based only on legal title and nothing else. Flowing from its previous capacity as a Trust Territory and self-governing status up to 1972, Ambazonia has legal personality and constitutes a subject of law, possessing national sovereignty though lacking the exercise thereof. That sovereignty does not cease to belong to the people of Ambazonia in whom legal title unquestionably vests. Sovereignty is, for the time being, simply rendered inarticulate and deprived of freedom of expression. It is in abeyance until the people of Ambazonia obtain recognition as an independent state. Cameroun has no sovereignty title to the territory of Ambazonia. This fact makes its presence in Ambazonia and its claim to the territory of Ambazonia illegal.

The principle of territorial integrity often abusively invoked by Cameroun is a norm that protects a state's lawful territory. The territorial boundaries which have to be respected under that principle may derive from international frontiers which divide the then colonial territory of one state from the then colonial territory of another such as the frontiers dividing the then Trust Territory of the British Southern Camerouns from the then Trust Territory of French Cameroun. It may also derive from international frontiers which divide a colonial territory such as the Trust Territory of the then British Southern Camerouns from the territory of an independent state such as République du Cameroun which became independent on January 1, 1960, when Ambazonia was still a Trust Territory. Cameroun's territorial limit does not extend an inch beyond its boundaries as obtained on the date of its independence from France on January 1, 1960. That country's territorial limit has never, does not, and will never include the territory of Ambazonia.

The point is worth making that the principle of territorial integrity is confined to the sphere of relations between states. It does not apply to peoples. It is irrelevant to cases of exercise of the right of self-determination against colonial rule. Cameroun cannot therefore set up the principle of territorial integrity against the legitimate entitlement of the people of Ambazonia to self-determination. Also worthy of recall is the fact that the norm of respect for territorial integrity is secured by a series of consequential rules, including the rule of obligatory non-recognition of territorial changes brought about in breach of International Law and the rule imposing respect for international boundaries as they were on the date of independence. The obligation to respect pre-existing international boundaries in the context of state succession derives from a general rule of International Law sometimes expressed as the principle *uti possidetis juris* which sanctifies succession to colonial boundaries as they stood on the date of independence. It accords pre-eminence to legal title to territory, as defined by frontiers, over effective occupation as a basis for sovereignty. It rejects any sovereignty claim based on such purely political expression as history, or purely moral expression as personal allegiance, or purely emotional expression as "reunification"/"unification."

Cameroun's international boundaries did not disappear when it was decolonized, and it succeeded to the Trust Territory of French Cameroun. Cameroun may not therefore change the colonially inherited status quo by extending its boundaries or by grabbing adjacent territories. It is under international obligation to respect its pre-existing international boundary with Ambazonia. The boundary between Ambazonia and Cameroun is established by treaties and achieves a permanence which those treaties themselves do not necessarily enjoy because a boundary treaty can cease to be in force without in any way affecting the continuance of the boundary. Succession takes place not so much in the boundary treaty but rather in the boundary as established by that treaty. Cameroun's colonial occupation of Ambazonia violates the international obligation to respect pre-existing international boundaries. The territory of Ambazonia is outside, and not within, Cameroun's international boundaries. In the absence of a treaty showing subsequent new boundary arrangements between the two countries, Cameroun's claim to the territory of Ambazonia is expansionist, colonialist, and internationally wrongful.

CLOSING STATEMENT

By keeping Ambazonia in colonial bondage, Cameroun violates the UN Charter principle of equal rights and self-determination of peoples. Cameroun's colonial presence in Ambazonia is also illegal on that count because colonialism is dated and is inconsistent with International Law. Cameroun's conduct in annexing and occupying Ambazonia is an unlawful use of force or other egregious violation of norms of International Law. Cameroun is therefore under international obligation to peacefully and unconditionally withdraw from Ambazonia without further delay. It is obliged under International Law to respect the frontier between itself and Ambazonia.

Many countries have withdrawn from territories they once illegally claimed and occupied. Those countries did so without losing an inch of their rightful territory. Israel withdrew from the Gaza Strip in Palestine, Indonesia from East Timor, Ethiopian from Eritrea, South Africa from Namibia including Walvis Bay, Nigeria from the Ambazonian territory of the Bakassi Peninsula, Libya from the Aouzou Strip in Chad, and Somalia from the Ogaden and Haud regions of Ethiopia and the Northeast region of Kenya. Cameroun would do well to follow these good examples. They are consistent with UN fundamental purposes such as the maintenance of international peace and security, the development of friendly relations and co-operation between nations, and good neighborliness between countries.

NOTE

1. The former UN Trust Territory of the British Southern Camerouns is generally known by its abbreviated name "the Southern Camerouns," but its indigenous appellation is Ambazonia, which means the zone on Ambaas Bay and the hinterland of that Bay. The separate UN Trust Territory of French Cameroun achieved independence under the name and style of 'la République du Cameroun.' Here also I use its abbreviated appellation, Cameroun, in the French orthography rather than in the translated English form, Cameroun.

Chapter 4

From Words to War

Representation, Discourse, and Conflict in the Cameroons

Thomas Ayeh Jing

Cameroon is currently involved in an armed struggle in which Republique du Cameroun (French Cameroon, Francophones, and Republic of Cameroon) is pitted against British Southern Cameroons (Ambazonia, Southern Cameroons, English-speaking Cameroon, West Cameroon, and Anglophones), the two national components that came together in 1961 to form a federation (Chem-Langhee, 1976; Fonkem, 2014; Litumbe, 2010; Awasom, 2000). The conflagration had long been smoldering, with numerous historical developments helping to stoke the fire. At the heart of them all, was an unwritten national policy of deceit and the non-respect of laws by the leaders. Thus, it is still very common practice in Cameroon for government officials to state one thing in public while behind the scenes they do quite the opposite. "*Si vous voulez les beaux discours, allez au Cameroun!*" Omar Bongo, the late Gabonese president, once remarked. He was simply being sarcastic, for in English his statement could easily translate into "If you want those who only run their mouths, go to Cameroon!" The declaration captured the essence of a country where presidential and other official speeches are always embellished with discourses such as "*la rigueur et la moralisation*" (rigor and moralization), "*unité nationale*" (national unity) "*démocratie avancée*" (advanced democracy), and, in more recent times, "*les grandes réalisations nationales*" (great national achievements).

High sounding as these utterances may appear, a cursory survey shows that even when they come from Paul Biya, the country's current head of state, they often belie the conduct of a man whose administration, ever since he came to power more than three and half decades ago, has increasingly assumed the complexion of a tribal mafia. His predecessor, Ahmadou Ahidjo,

a Northerner who made *"integration nationale"* (national integration) a pil-
lar of his administration, once revealed by way of a pleasantry that some of
his subjects often referred to CNU—the acronym by which his one-party
political machinery of Cameroon National Union was widely known—as
Cameroon Northerners Union. The uneasy laughter that followed his revelation concealed the sad truth that it was indeed not quite a joke. So, when
Ahidjo stated that *"L'Union nationale camerounaise n'est pas un parti de
propagande demagogique, mais un parti missionaire"* (Cameroon National
Union is not a party of propaganda and demagoguery, but a party with a mission) (Kuoh, 1991, p. 37), he knew that he was being insincere. The culture
to betray the public is so entrenched that even when it is visibly eroding the
very foundation of the nation from which those in power only take and take
and give nothing in return, they are too blind to see.

The problems which have tipped Cameroon overboard are cumulative and
could provide enough material for a complete set of encyclopedia on the
tenets of a failing state. Over the years, they have been amply documented
by various news organs as well as national and international watchdog organizations such as Cameroon Human Rights Commission, Cameroon Network
of Human Rights Organizations (RECODH), *Réseau des Défenseurs des
Droits Humains en Afrique Centrale* (Network of Human Rights Defenders
in Central Africa), Amnesty International, FIFA, Transparency International,
Human Rights Watch, and so on. French-speaking Cameroonians opposed
to Ambazonia's ongoing struggle for self-determination have argued that, in
varying degrees, the country's overall mismanagement and culture of deceit,
theft, and impunity (Mukong, 1992; Kuoh, 1992) have adversely affected all
the different national communities. While acknowledging this observation as
a valid point, the people of Southern Cameroons, as Hon. Joseph Wirba, MP
for Jakiri Constituency, clearly articulated in 2017 at the National Assembly,
Cameroon's parliament, still maintains that there have been some practices,
by and large discriminatory in nature and anchored to their linguistic and
cultural specificity, to which only they have been subjected. These practices,
they argue, have cleverly been sustained over the years through various forms
of discourses and representation designed in the main to strip them of their
sense of dignity and national belonging (Dibussi, 2009; Mukong, 1992) as
well as prevent them from ever achieving collective economic independence
and development.

This chapter focuses mainly on those discourses and representation and
shows how they have culminated in French Cameroonian power monopoly
that in no small way has ignited and fuelled the ongoing crisis. It describes
how the quest for peace and stability has been terribly compromised through
various forms of discourses and representation. What, then, is representation
and discourse?

REPRESENTATION AND DISCOURSE
ANALYSIS: DEFINITIONS

Representation

Representation means using language to say something meaningful about, or to represent, the world meaningfully, to other people. Language in this sense transcends the spoken and written words; sounds, words, musical notes, gestures, expressions, dances constitute different forms of language, for their importance to language is not what they are but what they do, their function. Any sound, word, image, or object which functions as a sign and is organized with other signs into a system which is capable of carrying and expressing meaning is, from this point of view, "a language." Representation is an essential part of the process by which meaning is produced and exchanged between members of a culture, but also across cultures (Hall, 2013).

Young (2001) has noted that the study of representation is as much interested in what is not said as in what is said (p. 391). Soyinka (2012) calls this situation "revision by omission." Malcolm X (1966), slain African American leader, takes up the argument of omission by basing his analysis on his own personal experience at school as a black pupil.

> I remember we came to the textbook section on Negro history. It was exactly one page long. Mr. Williams laughed through it practically in a single breath, reading aloud how the Negroes had been slaves and then were freed, and how they were usually lazy and dumb and shiftless (p. 29).

From his account, black history in America, a field which spans four continents and had lasted for more than three centuries, a history replete with monumental historical figures, such as Harriet Tubman, Matthew Henson, Robert Rillieux, Sojourner Truth, Frederick Douglass, Booker T. Washington, C. J. Walker, Du Bois, and many others, and which comprises huge contributions in arts, music, sports, science, inventions and in every American struggle (Bennett, Jr., 2000, pp. 721–758; Hughes, 1986, pp. 221–272; J. W. Johnson, 1969; Cruse, 1984; Osofsky, 1971), is summed up in a single page. In Cameroon, similar forms of representation of its English-speaking population have been identified when they are often only associated with negative things.

Seen from the light of what to include or exclude, representation, as Shay (2006) argues, is a form of power. The scholar sees representation as a form of power which involves political, social, and economic factors. He maintains that how a community is to be represented, particularly in its appearance to the outside world, depends largely on who has the power. In *Orientalism* (1994), Said argued that

> The real issue is whether indeed there can be a true representation of anything, or whether any and all representations, because they are representations, are embedded first in the language and then in the culture, institutions, and political ambience of the representer (p. 272).

To him, methodologically, representations should be viewed as inhabiting a common field of play defined for them, not by some inherent common subject matter alone, but by some common history, tradition, and universe of discourse (pp. 272–273).

Hall (2013) identified three theories of representation: reflective, intentional or mimetic, and constructionist, the one which concerns us in this discussion. The constructionist approach comprises two variants: the semiotic (the study of signs) approach, influenced by Saussure (1966); and the discursive, by French philosopher, Michel Foucault (Hall, 1997). "Foucault himself identified as a historian of thought and often his own texts highlight how a particular discourse, or a way of knowing, evolved over time" (Markula & Silk, 2011, p. 128). Barker (2003) agrees with the argument, noting that Foucault "is determinedly historical in his insistence that language develops and generates meaning under specific material and historical conditions" (p. 101). The constructionist approach does not deny the existence of the material world; rather it argues that things do not construct their own meanings. The approach recognizes the public and social character of language and acknowledges that "neither things in themselves nor the individual users of language can fix meaning in language" (Hall, 2013, p. 11) and proposes a complex and mediated relationship between things in the world, our concept in thought and language. Saussure (1966) has argued that even when the relationship between "signifier" (the word) and "signified" (its mental conception) is fixed by cultural codes, this is not permanent; thus, words shift their meanings as the mental concepts (signifieds) revolve with historical and social trends and evolutions. For example, the term "wicked," in its current usage, especially in North America, sometimes has a positive ring to it. Asante (1998) demonstrates shifts in meaning by drawing on black history. "Words do change and have different appeals at different times. For example, 'Negro,' 'Black,' 'African American,' and 'African' have had their impact at various times" (p. 44). This same argument applies to the people of Southern Cameroons who have been described using derogatory terms such as "Biafrans," "Anglofools," "les Nigerians," and, in more recent times, "ton Bamenda," "les secessionists," and "*les terroristes.*"

These shifts of concepts open "representation to constant 'play' or slippage of meaning, to the constant production of new meanings, new interpretations" (Hall, 2013, p. 17). Thus, "in representation, constructionists argue, we use signs, organized into languages of different kinds, to communicate meaningfully with others" (p. 14). Foucault did not analyze particular texts and representations, as the semioticians did; but rather, he was more inclined to analyze the whole discursive formation to which a text or practice belongs. Expanding on the semiotic ideas of Saussure, Foucault saw the production of "knowledge" (rather than just meaning) through what he called "discourse" (rather than just language). Hall (2013) states that "Saussure's focus on language may have been too exclusive," and that

> the attention to its formal aspects did divert attention away from the more interactive and dialogic features of language . . ., questions of power in language between speakers of different status and positions" (p. 19).

DISCOURSE ANALYSIS

Discourse analysis, especially Foucauldian, is central in this discussion. Barker (2003) argues that "discourse constructs, defines and produces the objects of knowledge in an intelligible way while excluding other forms of reasoning as unintelligible" (p. 101). What then is discourse analysis? Howarth et al. (2000) state that discourse analysis

> refers to the practice of analyzing empirical raw materials and information as discursive forms. This means that discourse analysts treat a wide range of linguistic and non-linguistic data—speeches, . . . historical events, interviews, policies, ideas . . .—as "texts" or "writings" . . . (p. 4).

As tool for analysis, discourse has been extended to the colonial field, the "*colonial discourse analysis* . . . that examines the ways in which a special kind of discourse was developed in order to describe and administer the colonial arena" (Young, 2001, p. 392). Young argues that *colonial discourse analysis* "derived from Foucault via Said is not concerned with language as such, but rather with a discursive regime of knowledge" (p. 385). According to this "discursive regime of knowledge," Europeans positioned themselves as "superior," a feeling that led them to create a kind of "binary opposition" with the rest of the world which they considered as the "Other" (Said, 1994) and as "inferior." Africa, thus, came to be described as "Dark" and "backward" and its people as "savages" without history or any civilization worthy of the name (Crowder, 1967, p. 2). Similarly, for a long time, especially in the heyday of Cameroonian soccer, French-speaking Cameroonian often referred to teams from Southern Cameroons as "*les equipes de la brousse* (teams from the bush or backward regions)"

Stokes (2013) has pointed out that discourse analysis is a method which requires you to take close analysis of texts, visual and verbal; and she also adds that it "integrates several methods including textual analysis, interviews, fieldwork and historical and archive research" (p. 89). In discourse analysis researchers analyze the structures of discourse, and Yang (2000) identifies two kinds of structures, namely, *surface structures* and *underlying structures*. Of surface structures, he states that they "refer to the forms of language that can be seen or heard, such as sounds, intonations, gestures" whereas "underlying structures refer to discursive meaning and action or interaction" (p. 33). Hall (2013) has argued that when Foucault talked of discourse, he meant a group of statements which provide a language for talking about—a way of representing the knowledge about—a particular topic or a particular historical moment. These statements, Foucault believed, were building blocks of discourses (Markula & Pringle, 2006, p. 28). In *The Archeology of Knowledge* (2010), Foucault attempted to clarify his concept of discourse. According to him, "we shall call discourse a group of statements in so far as they belong to the same discursive formation" (p. 117); and he used the term "discourse" in three prime ways: "Treating it sometimes as the general domain of all statements, sometimes as an individualizable group of statements, and sometimes as a regulated practice that account for a certain number of statements" (p. 80).

Discourses are about the production of knowledge through language. They are made up of discursive practices which Foucault (2010) describes as a body of anonymous, historical rules, always determined in the time and space that have defined a given period, and for a given social, economic, geographical, or linguistic area, the conditions of operation of the enunciative function (p.117).

Seen through the lens of Foucault, discourses are ways of knowing and everyone using language is involved in the circulation and creation of these knowledges (Foucault, 1990). Markula and Silk (2011) maintained that "Foucauldian discourse analysis aims to detect what knowledges dominate particular fields, where they come from and how they have become dominant" (p. 130). Discourse governs the way a topic can meaningfully be talked about and reasoned about. It also influences how ideas can be put into practice and used to regulate the conduct of others (Hall, 2013, p. 29). For Foucault, "discourse is very much entwined with power and with ideological hegemony" (Stokes, 2013, p. 143).

DAVID AND GOLIATH: THE UNFOLDING NATIONAL CONFLICT

On November 30, 2017, Paul Biya declared war on Ambazonia. "Ambazonia" is a new entry into the lexicon of nations. Etymologically, the term derives from the geographical landmark of Ambas Bay (Anyangwe, 2014) and, according to Ambazonian Governing Council Chairman Cho Ayaba, in his 2019 Dublin Declaration, it was coined by Fongum Gorji-Dinka, Southern Cameroons' lawyer and civil rights activist, to designate the territory once referred to as British Southern Cameroons. Before assuming its new identity, since its independence and union with Republique du Cameroun, the territory had evolved under different labels, the last of which French Cameroonian colonial interest had it parcelled and incorporated into its fold as the Northwest and Southwest regions. As an identity marker, the appellation "Ambazonia" rapidly gained currency in the wake of the nationalist upsurge that witnessed the rise, collectively, of the people of the territory in a peaceful demonstration that culminated in the restoration of the independence of their territory on October 1, 2017. The restoration caught Republique du Cameroun napping; and when it was jolted out of that state, its leadership, ever crude, barbaric, myopic, and long accustomed to seeing every problem as a nail since it wields a heavy military hammer, thought of no other solution to bring an end to the crisis in the territory than the use of overwhelming force. Thus, began the current drama. Columns of trucks ferrying soldiers and war equipment were hastily dispatched to Ambazonia to help beef up local policemen and women as well as the gendarmes in their efforts to nip the crisis in the bud. Scores of villages were set ablaze, and hundreds of civilians, for the most part the elderly and children, were rounded up and summarily executed while an even larger group estimated at hundreds of thousands fled to other parts of the country as Internally Displaced Persons or to neighboring Nigeria as refugees and asylum seekers. Properties worth billions of francs were destroyed, stolen, or confiscated. In a report, Amnesty International (2018) writes:

> People in Cameroon's Anglophone regions are in the grip of a deadly cycle of violence. Security forces have indiscriminately killed, arrested and tortured people during military operations which have also displaced thousands of civilians.

The crisis marked the culmination of countless abuses, legal improprieties, and constitutional violations which have prevented the people of Ambazonia from exercising control over their land, their resources, their economy, their culture, and ultimately their lives. In the midst of the growing anarchy and atrocities in which the country now finds itself, the leaders of Cameroon continue to use propaganda in a bid to garner world sympathy and support. Its mouthpieces, stalwarts, and panhandlers, such as Banda Kani, Ernest Obama, Owona Nguini, Masanga Nyambing, and a host of others, took to the media in a futile attempt to brand the action in Ambazonia as "secession" or "terrorism." Both labels have failed to gain any traction, for they are clearly mischaracterizations whose falsehood a mere glance at the tortuous history of the union of the two countries can easily dispel (Anyangwe, 2014, pp. 1–12). Maurice Kamto, beleaguered and jailed National Chairman of the Cameroon Renaissance Movement, has provided an opening to explore the dark recesses of that history when, in his 2016 *End of Year Message* to the nation, he categorically rejected "secession" as an option for the English-speaking territory and appealed to Ambazonia to return to the fold because, in his assessment, "they cannot win the war." For the legalist that he is, his call is not a lapsus, for it translates a big stick colonial mindset typical of the bulk of Republique du Cameroun, irrespective of their gender, their level of educa-tion, their ethnicity, their social station, and their political affiliation. Raised on a national discourse in which Ambazonia is represented as no more than a territory whose resources should be exploited for their own betterment, they attribute no human value to its inhabitants. Achankeng (2014) shows how among intellectuals of Republique du Cameroun, this propensity often takes the form of obscurantism when it comes to discussion on matters relating to Southern Cameroons:

> there may be the need to indicate that some accounts by scholars of Cameroon republic origin already exist and many tend to view the Southern Cameroons' nationalism conflict mainly from the standpoint of the political leadership of the Cameroon Republic in strict colonialist tradition. Such scholars do not only refuse to recognize the existence of the conflict, but those of them who write about it at all mainly cast it in negative light as a cry of a handful of greedy individuals who seek to take away the oil wealth of Cameroon. Some of the scholars, are also either dismissive of aspects of the British Southern Camer-oons' history while others reproduce fictional aspects of the territory's history, including those who persist in writing about a "reunification" that never took place (pp. vii–viii).

Given this attitude, discourses such as "dogs," "rats," "*Ton Bamenda*" (Your Bamenda), "*les Anglofools*" (Anglofools), "*Anglofous*" (Crazy Anglos), and numerous others are the daily lot of the people of Ambazonia. However, an even more evil form of representation is to ignore their existence while at the same time doing everything to kill their dreams and aspirations. The upcom-ing anecdote clearly demonstrates this point.

It is 1992. In the heat of the presidential election campaign in Cameroon, Bouba Bello called on his peer opposition leader Ni John Fru Ndi of the Social Democratic Front (SDF), the Bamenda-based political party which, against all odds, fought for multiparty democracy in Cameroon (Achankeng, 2012), to abandon his ambitions to become president and join force with National Union for Democracy and Progress, the political outfit he had just hijacked from Samuel Eboua. In return, he promised Fru Ndi that he would be considered for a ministerial position should he, Bello, become the nation's president. This insult is deeply rooted in the country's history of Anglophobia and discrimination. Somehow, Ahidjo's mysterious rise from a postman to a president has embedded in the psyche of his Cameroonian Fulani compatriots (Bello comes from this group) a sense of narcissism and political entitlement which is way out of proportion to their national contributions. Veiled in Bello's appeal was a hint that Fru Ndi could never be the country's president. The question is why? Did Bello make a similar proposal to other party heads from Republique du Cameroun? Bello Bouba, the truth be told, is a political spoiler. He burst onto the 1992 political scene like a strand of hair in a bowl of soup.

After his implication in the failed coup plot hatched by Northerners to unseat Paul Biya in 1984, he was a step ahead of the law when he slipped across the border into Nigeria where he melted into the local population. He only surfaced from his hideout when the cult of fear and brutal political repression in Cameroon that his tribesmen had entrenched had receded in the face of democratic advances. Yet, the miasma of his unsavory past did not prevent him from seeing himself as a worthy contender for the presidency; and even worse, he went as far as questioning, most certainly by virtue of geographical origin and cultural belonging, the man whose audacity and courageous action had precipitated the political upheavals and changes that had paved the way for his return to the country. In this brief narrative, an apostate and political exile, a man who once held top government positions and served as the country's prime minister and who oversaw in no small way the extreme violence that came close to exterminating the Bamilekes, still had the effrontery to deny Fru Ndi a feeling of national belonging.

Unfortunately, Bouba Bello in 1992 was just an open wound to a festering national sore, for the bulk of his Republique du Cameroun compatriots share his attitude toward Ambazonia. Even though two and half decades and different ethnic identities separate Bello from Kamto, the two political figures, either deliberately or unconsciously, have embarked on forms of representation akin to Said's (1979) Us against "Others." It is in this context that Kamto's declarations should be analyzed. He talks down; and even though he comes across as an affable man reaching out, his attitude displays numerous colonial reflexes. Overall, Kamto's attitude depicts a binary opposition between Ambazonia and Republique du Cameroun, a hierarchy based on top and bottom, superior and inferior, a metropolis and a colony, a center and a periphery. Maurice Kamto thus inadvertently let the cat out of the bag by clinging onto a vision which views Ambazonia as an annexed territory whose people should be kept in check, if necessary, by violence. But where did all of this begin?

A QUICK GLANCE AT HISTORY

Anyangwe (2014) cites "1858 as the onset of foreign control over the Southern Cameroons (Ambazonia)" (p. 2) when the coastal City of Victoria on Ambas Bay was founded by certain British missionaries who named the settlement after the Queen of England (p. 1). Following the Berlin Colonial Conference of 1884, in which Africa was partitioned among different European powers, Germany proclaimed Kamerun as its protectorate in 1884 after signing the Germano-Douala Treaty of July 12, 1884, with King Ndoumbe Lobe Bell and King Akwa of Cameroons Rivers (Wouri People, Douala) (Ndoumbe III, 2012; Rudins, 2013); and then from this initial location, the Germans extended their imperial control to the contiguous territory that became Southern Cameroons in 1888 (Anyangwe, 2014). At the end of First World War, in which Germany was defeated in Cameroon by Britain and France, the two victorious powers signed the Treaty of London in May 1916 partitioning Cameroon between them.

The outcome of the 1916 Treaty of London was upheld in 1922 by the League of Nations under whose mandate former German colonies were placed (Ngoh, 1979). Their status as Mandates of League of Nations lasted until 1946 when it changed to that of Trust Territories of the UN (Awasom, 2000). Britain's share of the war booty comprised one-fifth while France kept the lion's share. Britain's share of the territory was further divided into Northern and Southern Cameroons and ruled as part of its larger colony of Nigeria. Southern Cameroons was administratively attached to Eastern Nigeria, but during the 1953 London Constitutional Conference, Endeley, head of Kamerun National Convention (KNC), did not hesitate to ask for the unconditional withdrawal of the Southern Cameroons from the Eastern region of Nigeria in order for it to become a separate region of its own. The request was eventually granted, and it made the Southern Cameroons a quasi-autonomous region of the Nigeria Federation (Awasom, 2000) by 1954, with its own House of Assembly and an Executive Council at Buea, its headquarters, and Endeley as the Leader of Government Business.

In 1959, Endeley's KNC ruling party lost to the opposition Kamerun National Democratic Party led by John Ngu Foncha. On October 1, 1960, Nigeria became independent as a Federal Republic and the fate of British Cameroons was hanging in the balance. From February 11 to 12, 1961, the UN conducted a plebiscite in Northern and Southern Cameroons, leaving them with only the choice of either integrating with Nigeria or forming a federal union with Cameroon. Chem-Langhee (1976) is of the opinion that the plebiscite conducted in Northern Cameroons was manipulated by the British and the UN and did not quite reflect the true will of the people of the region. Whatever might have been the case, the territory ended up being integrated into Nigeria and officially became part of that country on June 1, 1961. Southern Cameroons, already a self-governing people with a homeland, a defined territory and fully functional democracy, were compelled by the UN and Britain to achieve independence either by joining one of its two neighbors, the Federal Republic of Nigeria to the west or the Republique du Cameroun to the East, and on attaining independence on October 1, 1961, it agreed to form a federation with La Republique du Cameroun through a UN-sponsored referendum. Terms such as "plebiscite" or "referendum" should not obfuscate the real issue. According to Achankeng (2014), Britain simply transferred the territory to Republique du Cameroun as "a little gift from her Majesty the Queen of England to General Charles de Gaulle." Carlson Anyangwe (2014) sums up the transfer as "a country decolonised becomes coloniser" (p. 1). To give teeth to Anyangwe's (2014) assessment, over the years Cameroon has gone from Federal Republic of Cameroon in 1961 to the United Republic of Cameroon in 1972 and then to the Republic of Cameroon in 1984. It should be pointed out that Republic of Cameroon was the name of French Cameroon before it went into a federal union with Southern Cameroons.

The restoration of statehood war marks the climax of various acts of political perfidy and machinations that destroyed a federal union imposed on two different independent countries that should have gone their separate ways. Supposedly considered to be a union of equal partners, the federal arrangement of Southern Cameroons and Republique du Cameroun, from its very inception, bore all the hallmarks of "a sleeping volcano" (Mentan, 2014). A 1986 CIA Report on Cameroon had foreseen and warned against this danger.

The Anglophone—who constitute some 20 percent of the population of nearly 10 million—fear their gradual assimilation into the dominant Francophone community. Although they currently lack the leadership and unity to effectively challenge Biya's rule, we believe the Anglophone minority is a potential timebomb, and should the central government fail to respect their cultural and linguistic traditions, the two-million strong community may view armed confrontation as their only alternative.

How could the CIA have gone wrong! The two nations emerged from two totally different colonial traditions, housed a multitude of disparate ethnic groups, and were significantly lopsided in their demographic composition and even land areas to be used as an experimental laboratory for political neophytes. "The Republic of Cameroon was ten times the area of British Southern Cameroons, had four times its population," pointed out Nicodemus Awasom (2000), an eminent Ambazonian historian. All of these factors did not augur well for any kind of union, yet without sufficient guarantees and safeguards to prevent constitutional and power abuse and the erosion of the rights of the smaller partner of the union, the UN, with the complicity of Britain and France, the administering Western colonial powers into whose hands the destiny of the territories lay, went ahead with the union in October 1961 even though there were many important unanswered questions. Smith (1999) views decolonization as "a process which engages with imperialism and colonization at multiple levels" (p. 20). Did those who came to power in Cameroon seek to rid the country of those colonial fetters that could have obstructed such a union? Did they have the genuine interest of their people at heart; and did they work tirelessly to give the fledgling federation a chance to succeed? After all, the 1960s provided a proper context for political experimentation in Africa. The atmosphere then was suffused with Pan-Africanist rhetoric and Garvey's philosophy; and coming straight out of centuries of the slave trade and colonial exploitation, most African countries were in desperate need of union and solidarity to face up to the myriad problems they were confronting (Nkrumah, 1974). Besides, many ordinary citizens were not schooled and sophisticated and could have easily been steered in whichever direction politicians wanted them to go. This enormous political capital was squandered in schemes designed to entrench one-man rule and ethnic power. Albert Mukong (1992) points this out in the case of Cameroon when he states that in the days of Ahidjo "a Northerner who became convinced that you were a serious threat to the regime would not hesitate to put an end to your life" and that under Biya (a Beti) "the Betis had stepped into the Northern shoe and were learning to walk the same path" (p. 52). One of the direct outcomes of such ethnocentric power monopoly and abuse is the ongoing crisis between Ambazonia and Republique du Cameroun.

TOWARD COLONIAL REPRESENTATION
AND DISCOURSES

What took place in October 1961 was in reality not a federation of two states but rather a recolonization of Southern Cameroons by Republique du Cameroun with the tacit approval of Britain, France, and the UN. Achankeng (2014) has described the decolonization of Southern Cameroons as one "effected with little or no regard for the interests of the territory and its people" and thus the territory ended up "undergoing a new colonial experience in a postcolonial setting under a sister country" (p. 1).

Territorial annexation, irrespective of the kind, is about subjugation, dispossession, exploitation, and humiliation. To subjugate and dispossess the people of Southern Cameroons of their humanity, their resources and their culture, Yaounde sought to have total control over their territory. Gendarmes, a vestige of French colonialism made up of uniformed thugs trained to control the population and impose French imperial designs through violence, were hastily dispatched to every nook and cranny of Southern Cameroons.

Concerning the introduction of this corps in Southern Cameroons, Nkwi (2014) states:

> When the Cameroons under the British and French Trusteeship united in October 1961 and became the Federal Republic of Cameroon, Article 5 of the Federal Constitution supported the introduction of the Gendarmes, which had become a federal affair (p. 55).

People of the territory woke up to this new and painful reality when their peaceful life was shattered almost overnight by the influx of this horde with red caps. Almost immediately, the gendarmes began by impressing upon the populace what citizens of Republique du Cameroun knew just too well that "the fear of gendarmes is the beginning of wisdom." Anyangwe (2014) provides details of the activities of the gendarmes, noting that these activities were aimed at "the terrorisation of the people by an occupying force with licence to abduct, imprison, rape, torture, plunder and kill as a means of securing submission and maintenance of the colonial occupation" (p. 4). This savage conduct produced the required outcome as Nkwi (2014) outlined: "the Gendarmes were strongly abhorred by most West Cameroonians, because of their activities on the civilian population, police and custom officers," adding that even though "there were security functions embedded in the Gendarmerie Corps, it turned out to be more an insecure force to the population . . . than anticipated." People were stopped on the road, addressed in French, and slapped for not understanding the language. Bribery and other forms of extortions, hitherto uncommon, became the new currency with which to do business with the government. As if the violence unleashed on the population was not bad enough, the gendarmes instituted *calé calé*, a practice which Gorji-Dinka (2017) expatiated upon with vehemence in his interview with Ghana State Radio. Entire neighborhoods were surrounded in the wee hour of the morning, all its inhabitants rounded up at gunpoint and marched to an open area where they were beaten, forced to roll in mud, and ordered to produce their laissez-passer, a document analogous to the pass instituted in South Africa during apartheid. These acts of savagery were just one strand in the grand scheme of things Yaounde had in store for the territory.

Another strand witnessed cultural superimposition when gradually French began replacing English as the official language in this region. This was the first step toward cultural substitution and imperialism, "the process of a dominant group's norms and culture becoming defined as the norm" (Dubrosky & Young, 2013, p. 207). A third strand entailed the adoption of policies aimed at "the purposeful impoverishment of the territory and its people so that the people are unable to challenge the colonisers or fight back" (Anyangwe, 2014, p. 4). This aspect of the occupation targeted the economy and involved the destruction of local industries that had so far helped in reducing the problem of unemployment. Powercam, Southern Cameroons' state-owned electricity company, was instantly dismantled; so was the Wum Area Development Authority, an agro-industrial complex in the Mentchum Valley. Santa Coffee Estate and others followed suite. Those organizations that had been spared, such as the Cameroon Bank and the Produce Marketing Board, had their headquarters moved to Yaounde and Douala respectively where they came under the control and corrupt spell of officials of Republique Cameroun. Result: they ended up bankrupt. Now with their economic safety net and means of livelihood taken away, widespread unemployment and hardship forced many young people of Southern Cameroons to move to Republique du Cameroun in search of work. It was here that they would begin to endure a lot of the psychological trauma as colonized citizens of the country they considered theirs. In terms of representation and discourse "Anglo," the label with which they were tagged, became a sign of contempt and sometimes hate.

Pratt (2004) has exposed how the West and its modernity project have come under assault of anticolonial and antiimperial thinkers; and she advances four tropes as counter-narratives to the story of diffusion (the idea that knowledge was a one-way traffic from Europe to the Other): interruption, digestion, substitution, and reversal (p. 445). Cabral (1974), slain African nationalist from Guinea Bissau, maintained that interruption entailed "the negation of the historical process of the dominated people, by means of violently usurping the free operation of the process of development of the productive forces." Anyangwe (2014) agrees, noting with regard to Southern Cameroons, that the people "cannot exercise the right to their economic, social and cultural development" (p. 10). It certainly was with this mechanism in mind that leaders of Republique du Cameroun dismantled industries in Southern Cameroons. As for substitution, local models were substituted and replaced with those of Republique du Cameroun. For example, French replaced English, gendarmes, the mobile wing police, and, more recently, civil law replaced the common law practised in Southern Cameroons. The education system was not left out. The Anglo-Saxon education system in the territory was progressively being eroded: City and Guild were replaced with CAPS and BACCs, and the grading system in percentages was replaced with the French system of grading on 20.

REPRESENTATION, DISCOURSE, AND THE PEOPLE OF SOUTHERN CAMEROONS

In "The Danger of the Single Story," a lecture delivered by renowned Nigerian writer Chimamanda Ngozi Adichie, she recounts the beginning of the telling of the African stories in the West when she cites John Locke, a London merchant who traveled to Africa in 1561. In filling his log, the Londoner wrote this of Africans: "Beasts who have no houses, they are people without heads, having their mouth and eyes in their breasts." Adichie reads relationship based on power in this portrayal and defines power as "the ability not just to tell the story of another person but to make it a definite story." In Cameroon, that "single story" through which the people of Southern Cameroons (Ambazonia) are represented has revolved around one word: Anglo (short for Anglophone)! In the hands of the people of Republique du Cameroun, the term has magic and has been used to conjure up and propagate the overwhelming majority of discourses used in these representations: "*les anglofools!*" (foolish Anglos!), "*les anglos sont gauches!*" (Anglos are clumsy), "*les anglofous!*" (crazy Anglos!), "*les anglos ne sont jamais satisfaits!*" (Anglos are never satisfied!), "*ce morceau est trop gros pour un anglo!*" (this piece is too juicy for an Anglo to have!), "*s'habiller comme un anglo!*" (to dress up like an Anglo!), "*j'ai toujours dit que je deteste les anglophones!*" (I have often stated that I hate Anglophones!), "*j'ai vu un anglo avec les chaussures comme un cosmonaute!*" (I saw an Anglo with shoes like those of a cosmonaut!), "*les anglo-bamis!*" (Anglos and Bamilekes!), "*Les ennemis dans la maison*" (enemies in the house), and so on. The purpose of this exercise is not to compile an exhaustive lexicon of discourses which have been used over the years in the representation in Republique du Cameroun of the people of Ambazonia. I only wish to demonstrate the obsession the elite and people of Republique du Cameroun have with the term "Anglo" or "Anglophone" and to plumb the full depth of the Machiavellian intentions behind the various meanings and how this representation accounts in some ways for the current genocidal crisis in the country.

In Africa, the term "Anglo," especially as in "Anglo-America," the company which virtually owns South Africa, should elicit pride and not shame and embarrassment. Moreover, it is an Anglo-Saxon world we live in! Even in Cameroon, the Anglos are known as hard workers, people who get themselves dirty to take care of business (representing more the 60 percent in professions such as auto-mechanics, carpenters, masons, plantation laborers, farm workers, plumbers, etc.). Talking about plantation workers in Southern Cameroons as far back as 1955, Ardener and Warmington (1960) noted that "the three Bamenda Plateau Divisions (Bamenda, Wum and Nkambe) supplied 32.8 per cent of all workers, approximately the same as the proportion supplied by Nigeria" (p. 27). Known for openly challenging unfair government practices and decisions and advocating what is in the best interest of the country (Niba, 2016), they are viewed by many of their compatriots as courageous, more honest, and trustworthy. During his last official visit to Bamenda in 2010, Paul Biya declared in his speech that the Bamenda Region is "*remarkable for its economic dynamism, patriotic population*" and that its *"sons and daughters have been in the forefront of our political history."* When the salaries of Cameroonian civil servants were slashed by about 70 percent in 1993, the first question some French Cameroonians were rumored to have asked was: *"Est-ce que les gens de Bamenda vont accepter ca?"* (Will the people of Bamenda accept this?). So, why then does the term generate so much bad blood in Republique du Cameroun?

Swiss linguist Ferdinand de Saussure (1966) argues that words shift their meanings as the mental concepts revolve with historical and social trends and evolutions. In agreement with De Saussure, Hall (2013) maintained that these shifts of concepts open "representation to constant 'play' or slippage of meaning, to the constant production of new meanings, new interpretation" (p. 17). The positive aspects of the word outlined fall within the realm of "denotation," the simple basic descriptive level, where consensus is wild and most people would agree on the meaning.

The second level of understanding the word, especially in the context of conflict in Republique du Cameroun, is that of "connotation" which requires a knowledge of local culture to decode the meanings (Ibid, p. 23). For example, the word "cat" denotes an animal, but in the mouth of Louis Armstrong during a jazz session, the same term has nothing to do with any member of the feline family. Similarly, the term "Kaffir" is an Arabic word for a nonbeliever of Islam, but in South Africa it is a pejorative way of referring to black people. This is because the relationship between the "signifier" and the "signified" tends to be arbitrarily fixed (Hall, 2013; Saussure, 1966) and therefore is not permanent. Interpretations and meanings associated with the term "Anglo" continue to vary, for meaning has the potential to proliferate to eternity.

In Republique du Cameroun, various representations of the term "Anglo" fall under "colonial discourses" which to Young (2001) are "derived from Foucault via Said" and which "is concerned with discursive regime of knowledge" (p. 392). Foucault is concerned with the production of knowledge and meaning through discourse (Hall, 2013, p. 35). He is determinedly historical in his insistence that language develops and generates meaning under specific material and historical conditions. He is concerned with exploring the particular and determinate conditions under which statements are combined and regulated, how meanings are temporarily stabilized or regulated into discourse.

This ordering of meaning is achieved through the operation of power in social practice. Foucault was concerned with how knowledge was produced and put to work through discursive practice in specific institutional settings, such as schools, prison, and so on to regulate the conduct of others. He focused on the relationship between knowledge and power because he was concerned that many social problems arose from the imposition of particular way of knowing the self and others. For example, the "knowledge" that whites are superior to other races helped to produce the problem of racism. Foucault argued that what we think we "know" in a particular period, say, Anglos in the case of the two Cameroons, has a bearing on the discrimination to which the people of Southern Cameroons are subjected. Power/knowledge has produced a certain conception of them as "inferior, parasites, rats, and dogs."

The very first thing the term "Anglo" does is to create a binary opposition. Discourses do not reflect "reality" or innocently designate object (Hall, 2013). In representation, sometimes meanings depend on the differences between opposites: boy versus girl, man versus woman, and so on. Ancient Chinese philosopher Lao Tzu points this out when he stated that "as soon as the world regards something as beautiful, ugliness simultaneously becomes apparent" and that "difficult and easy define each other" (Hua-Ching, 1989, p. 2). Consequently, the term "Anglo" is opposed to "Francophone" and as Derrida (as cited in Hall, 2013) argues, there is always a relation of power between the poles of binary opposition. This argument has been clearly demonstrated by Said (1979) in *Orientalism*; and by Hall (2013) in the concept of "inter-textuality," where an image depends for its meaning on being "read" in relation to a number of other similar images (pp. 222–223). Thus, "Anglo" is a setup which gives squabbling elite and people of Republique du Cameroun the opportunity to connect with discourses such as *"ce morceau est trop gros pour un anglo"* each time a juicy position comes up in the government which requires someone to fill. It is this opposition which has been used to strip the people of Southern Cameroons of a sense of national belonging in Republique du Cameroun by calling them *"les ennemis dans la maison"* (enemies in the house) and identifying them with foreign nationals such as *"les Biafrais"* (Biafrans), *"les Nigérians"* (Nigerians), as well as to deny them their fair share of the national cake. To keep the fire of the divide glowing, since Ahidjo and Biya, the two persons who have served as head of state in Cameroon in over sixty years of independence, built their political survival on how much division they could sow among the country's population, they were very creative with the "Anglo" question. Behind the scenes, they were responsible for stoking the fire of hate and Anglophobia through unpatriotic policies and insensitive discourses.

A common thread which ran through the entire Ahidjo administration was to represent Anglos as beggars, as parasites. In interviews, the likes of Sardou Daoudou and Maikano Abdoulaye, both of whom come from the North and were former ministers under Ahidjo, hinted that the people of Ambazonia ought to be grateful for what they get from Cameroon because they were not invited to join Republique du Cameroun; and, besides, they came to the federal union table with nothing. In his *Biographie succinte d'Eldridge*

Mohammdou (2011), Seignobos wrote: "*La réunification fut réalisée par Foncha, Ahidjo n'était pas demandeur (Reunification was the achievement of Foncha; Ahidjo did not ask for it).*" Similar views were pointed out by Awasom (2000) who noted that:

> One influential opinion, championed by Charles Assale (the first Prime Minister of the Federated State of East Cameroon), and popularized in *le Temoin, le Patriote*, and the Cameroon Radio Television (CRTV), held that reunification was essentially an Anglophone affair. Ahmadou ahidjo was never interested in reunification.

It is from such regime of "truth" that Ahmadu Ali, former Minister of Justice under Biya, took his cue, as Joseph Wirba stated in his declaration at the National Assembly in 2017. When the MP confronted the Government Minister concerning the brutalities of gendarmes in Southern Cameroons, he responded by declaring that "*Mr. Wirba, it is your people who chose to come here.*"

Northerners live in a glass house as it were, so if they choose to throw stones, let us see what happens. It is shocking that it is from them that discourses "of bringing nothing to the table" should come. Even today, and for a people who held power in Cameroon for twenty-five years to boot, how many lawyers, engineers, economists, bankers, writers, journalists, doctors, nurses, pilots, scientists, and university professors are from the north? What is the region's rate of poverty, literacy, calorific intake, and other indexes through which the World Bank and other organizations measure development? A heavily populated and backward region with more than its fair share of troubles (heat, dust, high rate of illiteracy, highway robbers, religious zealots, high incidence of a vast gamut of diseases, from river blindness through meningitis to malnutrition) is not a contribution. What was Ahidjo's level of education when the French imposed him as the president of Cameroon; or that of a noisemaker like Sardou Daoudou when he was appointed by his "Nordiste brother" as Minister of Defense?

Ex-British Southern Cameroons (Ambazonia) came to the table with Tamajong Ndumu, Cameroon's first engineer, Bernard Fonlon, an Oxford-Sorbonne graduate and first person in the country to obtain a PhD, Nfon Victor Mukete, a Cambridge graduate in Botany who owns the largest private plantation in Cameroon today. Mukete made it clear in *My Odyssey* (2013), his autobiography, that he was not the only person who saw agriculture as a lucrative and noble profession. "There were in several Bafaw villages such eminent farmers as Bernard Sona of Mambanda who acquired a brand-new Mercedes-Benz lorry . . . Andreas Epie of Ikiliwindi . . . Chief Isaac Epie of Kurume . . .," he wrote (p. 61). In the same work, he said this of S. T. Muna, the one-time vice president of the Federal Republic of Cameroon and prime minister of West Cameroon: "I arrived in London in October 1948" when "Muna had completed his studies in London University and was getting ready to return to Cameroon." In other spheres, there were Simon C. Tamajong, an Ibadan-Oxford graduate in Forestry, businessmen such as Nangah and Che, honest politicians and individuals with integrity such as John Ngu Foncha, Emmanuel Endeley, Augustine Ngom Jua, and so on. In what year did Mola Njoh Litumbe become a Chartered Accountant? I have only skimmed the surface of the cream of the Ambazonian crop to dispel the myth that this community came to the table with nothing. Apart from human resources, they came with a region whose vast plantations, very rich subsoil, and huge forests account to this day for more than 70 percent of Cameroon's GDP.

In addition, they brought institutions such as the Cameroon Bank and Producing Marketing Board as well as a hardworking and dynamic population (Biya, 2017). Their farmers feed Cameroon and the rest of Central Africa by supplying cattle, pigs, goats, and poultry, as well as foodstuffs such as fresh vegetables, rice, corn, potatoes, peanuts, beans, and so on. They contribute to export earnings by growing large amounts of crops such as cocoa, both types of coffee (Robusta and Arabica), rubber, bananas, palm oil, and so on. "Oil, timber, gas, gold, diamond, bauxite, iron and other minerals and cash crop resources are taken from the Southern Cameroons for the almost exclusive development of Republique du Cameroun," notes Anyangwe (2014).

In terms of ideas, they brought a democratic tradition, the force of argument and not the argument of force, a sense of fair play, basic notions of hygiene, concepts still foreign to the inhabitants of Republique du Cameroun to this day. And what did the people of Republique du Cameroun bring: a dangerous epicurean leaning of consuming foreign items, such as champagne, cigars, perfumes, designer suits, cars, and so forth? This tendency only ended up producing "bag carriers" for the French that Francophones shamelessly describe as "bringing something to the table." Such baseless claims directed against the people of Ambazonia should not come as a surprise since in colonial discourse it is the truth of the colonizer that is dominant. In this case, Foucault (2000) refers to modes of objectification, the second of which he termed "dividing practices." Markula and Pringle (2006) pointed out similarly that these practices are "more broadly speaking, the socially constructed division between the abnormal and normal. The knowledge that helps create the divisions simultaneously justifies the confinement, isolation and control of certain groups of people" (p. 26). Here, we are confronted with an aspect of Foucault's conception of power.

To further alienate Ambazonians from "chop" (lucrative positions), since in Cameroon that is the site of power, the discourse of them as "unpatriotic" was hatched. When the SDF was launched in Bamenda on May 26, 1990, in a communique broadcast during the 1:00 p.m. radio and 7:30 p.m. bilingual

TV newscasts on May 27, 1990, some demonstrations at the University of Yaounde were attributed to a handful of misguided students from the Northwest Province who had gone on the rampage after being confronted by a larger group of patriotic students made up of individuals from all ten provinces of Cameroon. The broadcast went further to describe the individuals as "vandals" who had committed the most treasonable act by singing the national anthem of a neighboring country (Dibussi, 2009).

When it comes to patriotism and the love of country, the elite and people of Republique du Cameroun ought to shut up and listen, for they have no moral authority whatsoever to lecture anyone. A mere glance at the Cooperation Agreement signed between Ahmadou Ahidjo and France in 1959, which virtually handed over the entire country of Republique du Cameroun to the French, says it all. In Republique du Cameroun streets, schools, and institutions are still named after colonizers such as De Gaulle (Avenue Charles De Gaulle), LeClerc (Lycée Leclerc), Jamot (Centre Jamot) while the names of their nationalist heroes who fought and died for their country's independence, such as Ruben Um Nyobe, Félix-Roland Moumié, Ossende Afana, and Ernest Ouandié do not even exist in the very history books read by their own children. Take a look at the way they run their own country, like babies for whom everything goes straight into the mouth. See the amount of money that Mebe Ngo'o and his wife, a modern-day Louis XVI and Marie Antoinette, embezzled. The truth is very glaring when one visits their hospitals, looks at the classrooms where their children study, the state of roads in the country, the filth and squalor swallowing up Yaounde, the capital city!

The history of "postcolonial" Cameroon, which they have led, is one of the bloody massacres and decapitation, political repression of the most brutal kind, the non-respect of the constitution and other laws of the land, the worst forms of embezzlements, bribery, and corruption, an indolent and irresponsible head of state who spends the bulk of his time and the country's money idling in Swiss hotels, a nation incapable of organizing something as simple as the African Nations Cup, and so on (Kuoh, 1991, 1992; Deltombe et al., 2011; Mukong, 1992; Terretta, 2014). From such a band of rogues emanates a Fame Ndongo who once tried to lecture Cardinal Tumi on patriotism. Patriotism indeed!

According to Stokes (2013), Foucault's discourse is very much entwined with power and with ideological hegemony (p. 143). Talking about the West and "Others," Said (1979) has captured the ultimate purpose of discourses of difference, such as the one existing between Anglos and Francophones in Cameroon, when he describes the relationship between the Occident and Orient as one of power, of domination, of varying degrees of a complex hegemony (p. 8). Hall (2013) points out that hegemony is "a form of power based on leadership by a group in many fields of activities at once, so that its ascendancy commands widespread consent and appears natural and inevitable" (p. 248). Such domination operates in Cameroon where the Francophone comes first and the Anglophone, second; where only a Francophone, as my earlier anecdote with Bouba Bello illustrates, can be the president of the country; and where the English-speaking region provides the resources used to develop its French-speaking counterpart. Such practices advance ideological assumptions that legitimize certain ways of thinking and acting (Vissicaro, 2004, p. 85), and so it comes as no surprise that some individuals believe that the Francophone and his own colonial heritage are "superior" to the Anglophone and his.

Nothing is more potent a force for national disintegration in Africa than practices which put some groups above others. Most African countries are a mere patchwork of ethnic groups forcibly lumped together by Western colonial interests. While they struggle to cohere into nations, actions, and discourses which seek to legitimize the "superiority" of one group over another only help to widen fault lines among the various ethnic components of a state. In Cameroon, this destructive tendency has extended to the manner in which leadership approached the country's policy of bilingualism. Recently, perhaps in a desperate effort to calm the flaring tempers that is responsible for the ongoing bloodletting, Cavaye Djibril, the Speaker of the National Assembly, ventured to address the august body over which he presides in English. He is unable to see that the root of the current crisis plunges deeper than language is typical. And yet, his own statement to Hon. Joseph Wirba, the opposition MP for Jakiri, that the Anglophones constitute just two cubes of sugar that will eventually melt in a basin of water, provides a perfect instrument to plumb the depth of the problems facing the two national communities.

Bernard Fonlon was a spearhead of Cameroon's bilingual policy and a reading of his principle of individual and early bilingualism reveals that it was based on the quest for national integration and economic considerations (Yeriwa, 1998). Even though the policy was designed to foster inclusion, it was clearly a double-edged sword in that it also served as a bulwark against any form of assimilation. In line with Cameroonian leadership's mentality of winners-take-all, the policy gradually drifted to one of assimilation as Wancha Titus Neba (1998) has noted. Bilingualism is a mere slogan, he declared, adding that it is not a secret that monolingual top civil servants—Presidents, Ministers, Secretary-Generals, Directors, Governors, Prefect—still litter the Cameroonian landscape in their majority. Hence, he points out how flag-bearers of bilingualism are sidelined to the advantage of monolinguals who encourage social bitterness with utterances such as *"Je ne comprends pas votre anglais-là!"* (I do not understand your English!). This is mild when compared with the outburst of Mongo Soo, Ahidjo's Minister of Education: *"J'ai toujours dit que je deteste les Anglophones"* [Transl. I have always stated that I hate Anglophones], he once declared. He was never punished for making the statement, a clear hint that his boss tacitly endorsed the conduct. David Abouem A. Tchoyi (2017), a member of the recently formed National Commission on Bilingualism and Multiculturalism, a former governor of the Northwest and Southwest Regions and a government minister, unveiled the hypocrisy surrounding Cameroon's bilingualism in an interview with Dipita Tongo on Spectrum TV.

STANCHING THE HEMORRHAGE

Attempts at the deliberate and forcible assimilation of the people of Southern Cameroons into the predominantly French Cameroonian culture, as was expressed by English-speaking lawyers and teachers in their peaceful demonstrations in Buea in 2016, were the last straw that broke the camel's back. *"Does the president of the country know that the governors, the Divisional Officers (D.Os) and all the administrators sent to West Cameroon are out there behaving exactly like an army of occupation,"* Wirba asked the National Assembly before making a dark prediction which gradually turned out to be true: *"The problem we have in West Cameroon is the problem that will bring down Cameroon. If you do not handle it well, you will not know Cameroon in a few months or a few years."* All these problems recently dredged to the surface are an eye-opener to those observers who always maintained that Cameroon is an island of peace and tranquility in a sea of war.

The conflict which escalated in 2016 has clearly demonstrated that the government of the country misled and completely deceived the observers over the years. Obviously, the CIA did not see the terrible degree of corruption and mismanagement coming when it boldly stated in 1986 that "Cameroon remains one of Africa's economic bright spots." Things started to take a turn for the worse when the New Deal Administration of Paul Biya began to have a grip on power. "Political development during the Second Cameroon Republic, particularly in the 1990s under President Paul Biya, seems to suggest that reunification was an undesirable and unfortunate occurrence" (Awasom, 2000). The government's obsession to destroy the Anglo-Saxon and African legacy that Southern Cameroons brought to the table of the federal union seemed to have completely diverted its attention away from encroaching economic and administrative malpractices. The malpractices reached their peak with Mebe Ngo'o, yet another cabinet minister in Biya's administration, who was dragged to Kondengui Prison along with his sobbing wife, for stealing astronomical sums of money from state coffers, even in the midst of serious political crisis and numerous other scandals tied to CAF's (Africa's soccer governing body) decision to withdraw the rights to host the African Nations

Cup from Cameroon. The Mebe Ngo'o saga serves as a perfect barometer to measure the degree of the country's moral decay. In the face of all of these problems, orchestrated mainly by a man who has been in power for more than five decades and who recently stole yet another election victory that would have helped in sustaining him in power for the rest of his life, French Cameroonians are still to muster the courage to call collectively for an end to his administration.

When Biya declared war on the people of Ambazonia, using the excuse that "Cameroon is one and indivisible," most of his Francophone subjects sided with him. Ever since, they have used discourses such as "*les secessionistes*" [secessionists] and "*les terroristes*" [terrorists] in representing Ambazonians who took up arms only in self-defense in the face of the genocide being visited upon them by the army. This fact shows the complicity of the people of *Republique du Cameroun* with their government when it comes to the annexation and colonial occupation of Southern Cameroons.

The loyalty induces a high level of insensitivity, a condition which prevents them from seeing anything wrong in the conduct of the state. They have come to normalize innocent people being massacred and their villages razed to the ground, women being raped and killed or buried alive, and properties being destroyed as well as other forms of atrocities being committed. Those of them who are remotely interested in the ongoing conflict have been repeating official lines that for the government to recall its troops, Ambazonian rebels must drop their weapons. This is an idea that *Amba Warriors*, the name by which these rebels have gone into popular lore, have derided, even as the head of state made some cosmetic changes such as decreeing a National Commission on Bilingualism and Multiculturalism. An insignificant concession such as implementing the ten-region decentralization plan, which is even enshrined in the 1996 Constitution, was ignored by the country's leaders. Even worse, the conflict did not feature on the agenda of the National Assembly or the Senate by the end of 2019. All these developments were indications that both sides remained miles apart, especially as the government continued to pay a deaf ear to appeals from the international community for an unconditional and all-inclusive dialogue. Bole Butake (2016), the late Ambazonian playwright, stated in an interview that "*Paul Biya has never said a word about the Anglophone problem. Never. Never. He just ignores the problem and thinks that it is going to go away.*"

Given the sheer scale of destruction and killings that have taken place in Ambazonia, nothing short of outright independence will cause its fighters to drop their weapons. The best deal the government and people of *Republique du Cameroun* may ever obtain, that is, after sweetening it with numerous additional concessions to provide effective and lasting protective cover, is a return to the two-state federation. Even that possibility seemed dashed with the Southern Cameroons General Conference which took place recently in Washington, DC from March 29 to 31, 2019, and the "Cameroon: Change & Challenges" Conference which was organized at the University of Massachusetts Boston (November 7–8, 2019). While the latter affirmed that the conflict was a decolonization conflict, the outcome of the former was that all the frontline leaders unanimously agreed on complete independence for Ambazonia. The animosity between the two nations is so deep that forcing any kind of union may have dire consequences for the future. The people of *Republique du Cameroun* are very free to hand over their land to the French, work for the French, and grovel before them for crumbs. What they cannot do is try to force the people of Ambazonia to express the same level of stupidity and servility because, as Wirba (2017) pointed out, *the people of Ambazonia are not their slaves, and they did not conquer them in war.*

CONCLUSION

When Ambazonian lawyers and teachers took to the streets in 2016 to stage a peaceful protest against the marginalization of the Anglophone legal and education systems by the nation's predominantly Francophone administration, their requests were very moderate, to say the least. However, given the manner in which the people of Ambazonia have been represented in national discourses over the years, the authorities just did not see any reason why "beggars, dogs, rats, and parasites" should be granted any form of "concession," and besides, they also reckoned that *"Les anglos ne sont jamais satisfaits!"* This probably explains their preference for the military option in any form of discussion. They could not have foreseen the total disaster into which their decision would lead the country. Now, a government that was once egged on by the bulk of the people of *Republique du Cameroun* finds itself increasingly being isolated. Senator Victor Mukete, a stalwart of the ruling Cameroon People's Democratic Party (CPDM), broke rank with his own party and lashed out at the administration for attempting to assimilate Southern Cameroons. His action seemed to have emboldened Senator Kemende of the opposition SDF who also took to the floor of the Senate to express concerns about the ongoing situation. Such acts of apostasy are very rare moments in Cameroon, a country in which members of the Senate and National Assembly only serve as a rubber stamp for the wishes of the head of state. Words do kill, especially when discourses and the regime of truths they propagate are confused with the reality. Unfortunately, government authorities in Cameroon needed a war to learn that!

REFERENCES

Achankeng, F. (2014). *British Southern Cameroons: Nationalism and Conflict in Postcolonial Africa.* Victoria, B.C.: Friesen Press.

Amnesty International. (2018, June 11). Cameroon: Anglophone Regions Gripped by Deadly Violence. *Google Search.*

Anyangwe, C. (2014). A Country Decolonised Becomes a Coloniser: Republique du Cameroun's Colonial Occupation of the Southern Cameroons (Ambazonia). In Fonkem Achankeng (Ed.), *British Southern Cameroons: Nationalism and Conflict in Postcolonial Africa* (pp. 1–12). Victoria, B.C.: Friesen Press.

Ardener, E., Ardener, S., & Warmington, W. A. (1960). *Plantations in Cameroons: Some Economic and Social Studies.* New York: Oxford University Press.

Asante, M. K. (1998). *The Afrocentric Idea.* Philadelphia: Temple University Press.

Atchoyi, D. A. (2017). Entretien avec David Abouem a Tchoyi – Samedi 14 janvier 2017. Presentation: DIPITA TONGO on Spectrum TV.

Awasom, N. F. (2000, Spring). The Reunification Question in Cameroon History: Was the Bride an Enthusiastic of Reluctant One? *Africa Today*, 47(2), 91–119.

Barker, C. (2003). *Cultural Studies Theory and Practices.* London, Thousand Oaks, New Delhi: SAGE Publications.

Bennett Jr., L. (2000). *Before the Mayflower: A History of Black America.* Chicago: Johnson Publishing Company, Inc. (Original Work Published in 1962).

Biya, P. (2010). Paul Biya Speech Bamenda. Bamenda, Northwest Region. *Youtube.*

Butake, B. (2016). Interview With Bola Butake. *Tydskrif Vir Letterkunde*, 53(1).

Cabral, A. (1974). *Selected Speeches.* New York: Monthly Review Press.

Chem-Langhee, B. (1976). *The Kamerun Plebescites 1959–1961: Perception and Strategies* (Unpublished Doctoral Dissertation). Department of History, University of British Columbia.

CIA. (1986). *Cameroon: Challenge Ahead for Biya.* Washington, D.C.: Directorate of Intelligence.

Crowder, M. (1967). *Assimilation in Senegal.* Great Britain: Richard Clay (The Chaucer Press) Ltd.

Cruse, H. (1984). *The Crisis of the Negro Intellectual: A Historical Analysis of the Failure of Leadership.* New York: Quill.

Dallaire, R. (2003). *Shake Hands With the Devil: The Failure of Humanity in Rwanda.* Canada: Vintage.

Deltombe, T., Domergue, M., & Tatsitsa, J. (2011). *Kamerun! Une Guerre Cachée Aux Origines de la Francafrique.* Paris: Edition la Découverte.

Dubrosky, R., & Young, I. (2013 July–September). Iris Young's Five Faces of Oppression Applied to Nursing. *Nursing Forum*, 48(3), 205–10. University of Wisconsin-Milwaukee.

Fanon, F. (1963). *The Wretched of the Earth.* Translated by R. Philcox. New York: Grove Press.

Fonkem, A. (2012). 'Mutual Hurting Stalemates,' 'Ripe Moments' and Third-Party Intervention: Implication for the 'Southern Cameroons' Restoration of Statehood' Conflict. *The Round Table,* 101(1), 53–69.

Fonkem, A. (2014). *British Southern Cameroons: Nationalism and Conflict in Post-colonial Africa*. Victoria, B.C.: Friesen Press.

Foucault, M. (1990). *The History of Sexuality: An Introduction*. The United States of America: Vintage Books Edition.

Foucault, M. (2000). *Power: Essential Works of Michel Foucault 1954–1984*. Vol. 3. Edited by James D. Faubion. United States of America: The New York Press.

Foucault, M. (2010). *The Archeology of Knowledge*. New York: Vintage.

Gorji-Dinka, F. (2017, June 3). Interview With Radio Ghana. *Youtube*.

Hall, S. (1997). Old and New Identities, Old and New Ethnicities. In Anthony D. King (Ed.), *Culture, Globalization, and the World System: Contemporary Conditions for the Representation of Identity*. (pp. 41–68). Minneapolis: University of Minnesota Press.

Hall, S. (2013). *Representation: Cultural Representation and Signifying Practices*. London: SAGE Publication Ltd. (Original Work Published 1997).

Howarth, D., Norval, A. J., & Stavrakakis. (2000). *Discourse Theory and Political Analysis*. Manchester and New York: Manchester University Press.

Hua-Ching, N. (1989). *The Complete Works of Lao Tzu*. Translated and Elucidated From *Tao The Ching* by Taoist Master Ni Hua-Ching. Los Angeles California: The Shrine of the Eternal Breath of Tao.

Johnson, J. W. (1969). *Black Manhattan*. New York: Theneum.

Kamto, M. (2016). 2016 End of Year Message of Maurice KAMTO, National Chairman of the Cameroon Renaissance Movement. *Youtube*.

Kuoh, C. T. (1991). *Une fresque du régime Ahidjo (1970–1982)*. Paris: Karthala.

Kuoh, C. T. (1992). *Le Cameroun de l'apres-Ahidjo (1982–1992)*. Paris: Karthala.

Litumbe, M. N. (2010, November 8). *Mola Njoh Litumbe Interview, Part 1, 2, 3, & 4*. Doula: Equinox TV.

Malcolm, X. (1964). *The Autobiography of Malcolm X*. New York: Grove Press.

Markula, P., & Pringle, R. (2006). *Foucault, Sport and Exercise*. New York: Routledge.

Markula, P., & Silk, M. (2011). *Qualitative Research for Physical Culture*. London: Palgrave Macmillan.

Mentan, I. T. (2014). Stopping War Before It Starts. In *British Southern Cameroons: Nationalism and Conflict in Postcolonial Africa* (pp. 127–162). Victoria, B.C.: Friesen Press.

Mukete, V. E. (2013). *My Odyssey: The Story of Cameroon Unification*. Yaounde: Eagle Publishing.

Mukong, A. (1992). *My Stewardship in the Cameroon Struggle*. Enugu, Nigeria: Chuka Printing Company Limited.

Ndoumbe III, K. (2012). L'Afrique s'annonce la tete haute! *AfricAvenir/Exchange & Dialogue*.

Ngoh, V. J. (1979). *The Political Evolution of Cameroon 1884–1961* (Unpublished Masters Thesis). Department of History, Portland State University.

Niba, W., & Niba, M. N. (2016). Bamenda City. A Luman Communications Production. *Youtube*.

Nkrumah, K. (1974). *Neo-Colonialism: The Last Stage of Imperialism*. London: PANAF.

Ottenberg, S. (1982, Summer). Illusion, communication, and psychology in West African Masquerades. *Ethos*, 10(3), 149–85.

Pratt, M. L. (2004, September). The Anticolonial Past. *Modern Language Quarterly*, 65(3), 443–56.

Rudins, H. R. (2013). *Germans in the Cameroons 1884–1914*. New Delhi, India: ISHA (Original Work Published in 1938).

Said, E. W. (1979). *Orientalism*. New York: Vintage Books Editions.

Saussure, F. (1966) *Course in General Linguistics*. Translated by Wade Baskin. New York City: The Philosophical Library, Inc.

Seignobos, C. (2011). *Biographie succinte d'Eldridge Mohammadou*. Tchad: Reseau Mega-Tchad.

Shay, A. (2006). *Choreographing Identities: Folk Dance, Ethnicity and Festival in the United States and Canada*. Jefferson, NC: McFarland & Company, Inc., Publishers.

Smith, L. T. (1999). *Decolonizing Methodologies*. Dunedin: University of Otago Press.

Soyinka, W. (2012). *Of Africa*. New Haven and London: Yale University Press.

Stokes, J. (2013). *How to Do Media and Cultural Studies*. Thousand Oaks, CA: SAGE Publications, Inc.

Tande, D. (2009). (Memory Lane – May 26, 1990): The Launching of the SDF. *Scribbles From the Den*.

Terretta, M. (2014). *Nation of Outlaws, State of Violence*. Athens, OH: Ohio University Press.

Vissicaro, P. (2004). *Studying Dance Cultures Around the World: An Introduction to Multicultural Dance Education*. Dubuque, Iowa: Kendal/Hunt Publishing Company.

Wancha, T. N. (1998). *Cameroon's Bilingual Civil Servants* (Unpublished Manuscript).

Yang, P. Q. (2000). *Ethnic Studies*. New York: State University of New York Press.

Yeriwaa, J. S. (1998). Official Bilingualism in Cameroon: A Double-Edged Sword. O.R.A.C.L.E. *Google Search*.

Young, R. J. C. (2001). *Postcolonialism: A Historical Introduction*. Oxford, UK: Blackwell Publishers.

Chapter 5

The Anglophone Problem in Cameroon

The Real and Disturbing Dimensions

Peter Stanley Nzefeh

It is an incontestable fact that some part of Cameroon is English-speaking, and it is also a fact that the English-speaking population in Cameroon is a minority. There are numerous minority problems known in history which have precipitated the disintegration of empires, kingdoms, and states. Minority problems, for example, sparked off the 1914--1918 War which ended in the total collapse of the Austro-Hungarian Empire. The French-speaking minority in Canada's Quebec Province has been a thorn in the flesh of that country's body politics since the 18th century. Apprehensions by the Muslim minority caused the partition of the Indian subcontinent in 1947. In the 1990s, the Republic of Niger was in the throes of containing a Tuareg minority uprising so also was Senegal trying to contain the Casamance Separatists.

The Anglophone minority problem in Cameroon exists and is real. Anybody who affirms the contrary, whatever his social and political standing in Cameroon or elsewhere, whatever his national and international reputation, is myopic and is a liar. Though many Francophones pretend there is no Anglophone problem in Cameroon, the fact is Anglophones are a minority in Cameroon and the Francophone majority always treated them as such. The Anglophones, on their part, were united in affirming the existence of a very serious Anglophone problem in Cameroon since 1961. The problem owes its very origin to the so-called "reunification" of the former French Cameroon and the former British Southern Cameroons in 1961. Whereas it started in 1961 only as a problem of the numerical disadvantage of the Anglophones, it has since snowballed to embrace other political, economic, cultural, and psychological dimensions.

The problem, since 1961, hinged on wholesale violation of the rights of the Anglophone minority by the Francophone majority. The crux of the problem is therefore the conflict of two strongly entrenched European cultures, one of which sought to dominate or completely efface the other. To deny the existence of such a problem is a mark of dishonesty and perversion or maybe the dread of having to face the problem. Yet, such denials increasingly became characteristic of the Francophone mentality in Cameroon. Surprisingly, the Francophone Administration in Cameroon tried doing everything since 1961 to make Anglophones in Cameroon see the world through the franconized lens. Verbal denials were therefore always only attempts to mask the reality that stared at them menacingly in the face.

After what was written and taught as reunification of the two Cameroons, the Francophone mentality was carefully nurtured toward denigration and marginalization of the Anglo-Saxon legacy in Cameroon. The objective was to ensure the assimilation of the Anglophone minority to French culture. The first step was to put an end to the autonomy of the Anglophones that was guaranteed by the 1961 Foumban and Yaounde Accords. President Ahmadou Ahidjo of the French Cameroon Republic accomplished this secret objective with the Machiavellian ruse and Gaullist-style authoritarianism. Ahidjo's first target was the West Cameroon Police force and its quasi-military Mobile Police which he disbanded. With this act successfully accomplished, the Anglophones lost their autonomy and the ability to resist any of Ahidjo's other schemes. The Anglophones lost the power to determine their own destiny and since had no bargaining weapon. Increasingly, the Anglophone was given what the Francophone political elite decided s/he should have and invariably that was always the position of an assistant or a deputy to a Francophone. When outwardly an Anglophone was given charge of a department, his/her powers would be apparent rather than real. His/her wings would usually always be clipped by placing under him some powerful francophone assistant with direct links to the power brokers at Unity Palace or the *Champs Elysées*. Some ministries in this country since 1961 were "reserved for 'Francophones' only," and certain positions were given to Anglophones only after a crash assimilation course (*stage*) in Paris. In Cameroon, the loyalty of the Anglophone always came under serious questioning by the Francophone political elite. Anglophones were hardly privy to national secrets, let alone the secrets of political power, most of which were always remote-controlled from the *Elysée* Palace. The only secrets Anglophones were initiated into were those of how to thwart the popular aspirations of the Anglophone populace and deliver the critics, dissidents, and the non-conformists to the sledgehammer of the country's secret police organization known by its French acronym CENER (*Centre d'etudes et recherche*).

The problem got to such a point that no Anglophone in the country could take a decision that would affect the destiny of the Anglophone populace, not to mention the destiny of Cameroon as a whole. The marginalization process, in turn, generated a syndrome of political viciousness within the Anglophone political elite. They schemed and intrigued against each other in order to obtain the least possible sociopolitical self-satisfaction. Once in a key position, an Anglophone thinks more of crushing or blackmailing his potential Anglophone rivals and less of effecting positive change that will benefit the Anglophones of Anglophone Cameroon. Some of them have even embraced the Francomania of speaking only French as a weapon of psychological intimidation against fellow Anglophones. The truth of it all is that the loss of autonomy and the resulting powerlessness of the Anglophone political elite soon after 1961 made it possible for the Ahidjo regime to destroy the West Cameroon economy with psychopathic cruelty. Reunification in 1961 was followed by the deliberate and systematic underdevelopment and the economic strangulation of West Cameroon. The West Cameroon Air Transport Company was closed down; the Tiko International traffic and the Victoria and Tiko Seaports were abandoned for good. The West Cameroon Development Agency, together with its affiliated establishments, was liquidated; the West Cameroon Electricity Corporation (POWERCAM) was scrapped; the West Cameroon State Lottery was confiscated by the Yaounde administration, so also were the West Cameroon Hotels Ltd, Marketing Board, Cameroon Bank, and so on. All the major roads in the West Cameroon were allowed to fall into disrepair, and the economy of Manyu Division was strangled to death with the abandonment of the port on the Cross River in Mamfe. West Cameroon also lost all its Commonwealth preferences because its international trade was redirected to France which was rather reluctant in view of the fact that most of the companies operating in West Cameroon were British companies.

The Anglo-Saxon cultural legacy in West Cameroon also became a major target of a very subtle and insidious assault by the Yaounde administration. It started with the initiation of the West Cameroon political elite and administrative officers into the use of French language and French bureaucratic practices. Thereafter, everything official in Cameroon had to be conceived fist in French before executing it in practices and according to French or franconized norms.

In education, West Cameroon was to gradually and unknowingly adopt a fraconized syllabus. Until very recently, the Anglophone was denied the right to a genuine university education in the true liberal Anglo-Saxon tradition. He was obliged to study at Yaounde University, an institution whose principal language of instruction is French. Major stumbling blocks were placed on the path of Anglophones opting to study away from home by demanding the payment of 350,000 francs deposit before obtaining a passport and visa for traveling. The undeclared aim was to ensure the eventual assimilation of the educated Anglophone elite by making them to study only in the French-dominated institutions. The university of learning in Cameroon offered instruction only in the French language.

All available evidence so far points to the fact the relationship between the Francophones and Anglophones in Cameroon since 1961 has been characterized by the Francophone's attempt to impose the Anglophone minority. The Francophones have developed a disturbing propensity to impose French cultural values on the Anglophones. In the absence of a viable national alternative to the two received cultures, the Francophone majority has sought to make the French legacy a quasi-legitimate national culture at the expense of the Anglophone minority. A fusion of the two colonial cultures not being possible, the only reasonable and common-sense modus vivendi ought to have been the co-existence of the two foreign cultures within their respective culture areas in Cameroon under the federal or confederal structure. That was supposed to be the spirit and understanding of the Foumban and Yaounde agreements of 1961, but the Francophone majority has since demonstrated considerable bad faith and open intolerance vis-à-vis the Anglophones.

Minority problems are generally often handled more satisfactorily by genuine democracies than by dictatorships and authoritarian regimes. Authoritarian regimes and dictatorships, confronted with restless minorities always tend to employ repression, intimidation, outright force, and when desperate, genocide. The regime in Cameroon since independence became a dreadful authoritarian one. In spite of all the denials, the Anglophone minority problem in Cameroon became such a serious threat to French interests in Cameroon and to Biya and the "Beti-cracy" (government by Betis) that it was not going to be long before the regime would resort to desperate measures. Already, assimilation, marginalization, and outright repression had been used without much success and as the Anglophone consciousness persisted and the Cameroon Anglophone Movement and the All Anglophone Conference spirit waxed stronger with the passing of time, the regime would be bound to consider the final solution. The rising Anglophone consciousness already forced the Biya regime to militarize Anglophone Cameroon and the Cameroon-Nigeria border crisis could be used by the regime to further question the loyalty of the Anglophones. It is important to remember that the Francophone politico-administrative hierarchy did not hesitate to refer to Anglophones as Biafrans to accuse Anglophones of singing the Nigerian national anthem and referring to Anglophones as "enemies within."

One cannot help but ask why the Francophone Cameroonians remained so bent on forcing French cultural values down the throat of English-speaking Cameroonians? Why demonstrate such avidity for promoting an alien culture? One could see lurking behind the Francophone attitude to Anglophones in Cameroon the evil hands and insidious fingers of French neo-colonialism in Cameroon.

Chapter 6

Persistent Regression in the Right to Development

Latent Trigger to the Southern Cameroons' Pursuit of Sovereign Statehood

Carol Chi Ngang

In this chapter, I explore the Southern Cameroons' pursuit of sovereign statehood with the purpose to illustrate that although it may not appear apparent, the principal latent trigger that stirred the 2016 "Coffin Revolution" was essentially a deprivation of and regression in the right to development. While the Coffin Revolution inspired by Mancho Bibixy was intended to be peaceful and non-violent, the reaction by the government of La République du Cameroun unavoidably pulled the Southern Cameroons into an asymmetric armed conflict, which eventually radicalized the Southern Cameroons population into an irreversible liberation struggle. Liberation struggles are primarily informed by the fact that all peoples are collectively entitled to self-determination, which guarantees the right to freely determine their political status and to pursue their socioeconomic and cultural development in accordance with the policies they have freely chosen.

In over half a century of (uneasy) co-habitation with La République du Cameroun, it is likely, as reflected in the intention expressed in February 11, 1961, plebiscite, that the people of the Southern Cameroons could have made amends with constructing a political future within the framework of the federal arrangement envisaged in the United Nations (UN) General Assembly Resolution 1608 (XV) if the conditions for creating such a union were adhered to. In making this assumption, I aim to illustrate that the prevailing fratricidal armed conflict could have been averted if the opportunities existed for the exercise and enjoyment of the right to development in the Southern Cameroons. Evidence from other post-independence liberation struggles in Africa that has resulted in the acquisition of statehood like The

Gambia breaking away from Senegal, Namibia breaking away from South Africa, South Sudan breaking away from Sudan, Somaliland breaking away from Somalia, and Eritrea breaking away from Ethiopia (to name just those in Africa) indicates that the Southern Cameroons liberation struggle should have sparked off far much earlier (International Crisis Group 2017, pp. 2–8; Achankeng 2014, p. 2; Ekongtang 1995, p. 9).

While it is unsurprising, given the apparent pent-up frustration and animosity originating from long-standing root causes, that the revolutionary feeling of nationalism has only erupted lately, it is of essence not to ignore the latent trigger of the prevailing conflict that crawled into the fifth year in 2021 and still counting. Suffice to explain that a trigger is some action or event that manifestly or implicitly causes another action or event to happen. Ole Brunn (2013, p. 246) refers to such actions as *"trigger events"* that originate from *"competing rationalities"* and *"cognitive dissonance"* leading to radical shifts in perception and motivations and, in effect, inspiring new forms of protest. The situation in the Southern Cameroons had regressed so much that the strategy in articulating grievances rapidly metamorphosed from the Southern Cameroons National Council liberation slogan of "the force of argument" to the revolutionary exploit that presents in action as "the argument of force" in righteous self-defense against La République du Cameroun's aggression.

A study of the triggers of conflict and the reactions thereto suggests a combination of varying factors including, in particular, "uncertainty about an opponent's desire to cause harm" (Caldara et al. 2017, p. 21). Uncertainty about La République du Cameroun's intentions to cause harm in the form of development injustices among others gave the people of the Southern Cameroons a false hope of belonging and belief in the political indoctrination of a "one-Cameroon" nationalism which, however, is contested on the grounds of a combination of complex historical root causes, explored at length in the literature and commentaries on the subject (Agwanda 2020, pp. 2–3; Anyangwe 2013, pp. 163–184). My purpose in this chapter is to advance the argument that the identity consciousness in asserting Southern Cameroons (Ambazonian) nationalism (Jua & Konings 2017, pp. 609–633) was triggered to life from 2016 owing more to the realities of a persistent regression in the right to development.

To put the argument into a clearer perspective, it is important to refer to the *Endorois* case (2009, para 294) wherein the African Commission held that realization of the right to development entailed non-regression in the enjoyment of existing rights. The right to development, even though it appeared to be a recent progression in the discourse on human rights (classified as a third-generation right), existed long before, implicitly enshrined in International Law (Alston 1988, pp. 5–6; Ware 2010, p. 3) and as Glenn Johnson (1987, p. 36) noted, informed the campaign for the universal recognition of human rights in 1948 as well as the liberation struggles that resulted in the acquisition of sovereign statehood for colonized territories (Özden 2012, p. 1). A regression in the right to development is defined to mean the unjustified limitations and constraints in the enjoyment of all the component socioeconomic and cultural as well as civil and political rights embodied therein.

Taking a step away from regurgitating the facts about the problem and assuming that like many other successful liberation struggles, that of the Southern Cameroons would culminate in the acquisition of statehood, my inquiry in this chapter centers on how a sovereign Southern Cameroons would become different in providing the enabling space for actualizing the right to development. I present a realistic scenario that factors-in the legitimacy of the self-determination claim by looking at the barometers for gauging the right to development, wherein, I describe its component entitlements and how the peoples of the Southern Cameroons have over the decades been deprived thereof. I then proceed to hypothesize how and what it entails for the Southern Cameroons to function and sustain as a sovereign state. I conclude with the argument that it requires a UN-sanctioned referendum and negotiated settlement to be able to effectively redress the fundamental root causes and other underlining factors that triggered the Southern Cameroon's revolution.

BAROMETERS FOR GAUGING THE RIGHT TO DEVELOPMENT

The right to development is listed as one of seven rights-based approaches to development (Marks 2013, p. 12) and therefore presents barometers for gauging development in function of which the situation in the Southern Cameroons is examined. The Declaration on the Right to Development (DRTD) (1986, Article 1(1) and(2)) stipulates that the human right to development entitles every person and all peoples to participate in, contribute to, and enjoy the full realization of all human rights and fundamental freedoms and equally implies the full realization of the right to self-determination and sovereignty over natural resources. This definition obtains three principal components that I proceed to analyze.

Self-Determination and Sovereignty

Dating back to the colonial era, the aspiration for development constituted one of the underlining motivations for decolonization, which manifested in the right to self-determination on the basis of which liberation and independence were achieved for the colonized and Trust Territories in most of Africa. The right to self-determination guaranteed then as much as it does to this present date that all peoples shall enjoy the liberty to seek political freedom and to freely pursue their economic, social, and cultural development. Some scholars have convincingly argued that the right to development derives from the right to self-determination and is of the same nature and purpose (Udombana 2000, pp. 769–770; Ngang 2018, p. 111; Anghie 2013, p. 66; Oloka-Onyango 1999, p. 166).

The African Charter (1981, Articles 19 and 20) recognizes that all peoples, including "[c]olonized and oppressed peoples" (like those in the Southern Cameroons), shall exercise the right to existence, entailing the "unquestionable and inalienable right to self-determination." Read in conjunction with the "freedom and identity" element contained in Article 22 provision on the right to development in the Charter, self-determination obligates the people of the Southern Cameroons to proactively assert a sovereign identity. However, when the Southern Cameroons' quest for self-determination became a matter of litigation in the *Gumne* case (2009, para 179), the African Commission, in an ill-conceived judgment, acknowledged on the one hand that the people of the Southern Cameroons are indeed a distinct people with the right to existence but on the other hand for the sake of protecting the principle of territorial integrity enshrined in the AU Constitutive Act denied the Southern Cameroons entitlement to self-determination and, in effect, also denied that their right to development had been contravened (Ngang & Kamga 2018, pp. 200–201).

According to James Crawford (2010, p. 137), matters of self-determination are not within the domestic jurisdiction of the dominant state, which in effect has no capacity to decide on the claim of the political entity that is asserting the right to self-determination. Against this basic reading of the right to self-determination, La République du Cameroun has in several instances, including before the African Commission in the *Gumne* case (paras 182–191), illegitimately imposed its authority in shaping the decision-making on the Southern Cameroons' self-determination claim, in contravention of International Law that presents self-determination as an inalienable, unquestionable, and unconditional entitlement granted to be achieved without reservation. This guarantee notwithstanding, the Southern Cameroons has since from the times of decolonization unjustly been denied its self-determination claim (Ngang 2021, forthcoming), and by so doing deprived of associated socioeconomic and cultural as well as political development as I proceed to explain.

ECONOMIC, SOCIAL, AND CULTURAL DEVELOPMENT

Central to the conceptual formulation of the right to development in Africa is the guarantee to all peoples to continually strive toward attaining socioeconomic and cultural development. However, none of the instruments that enshrine the right to development provide any additional explanation as to what economic, social, and cultural development actually mean. This lacuna makes the concept relatively fluid and, thus, needs to be attributed contextual meaning based on specific circumstances. The African Charter, for instance, provides in Article 22(1) that "[a]ll peoples shall have the right to their economic, social, and cultural development with due regard to their freedom and identity and in the equal enjoyment of the common heritage of mankind." A closer meaning of socioeconomic and cultural development can, nonetheless, be deduced from the broad concept of the right to development, which as a process of continuous improvement imposes a commitment to equalize opportunities in view of sustaining human well-being and a better life for all peoples. As Arjun Sengupta (2004, p. 185) put it, the right to development creates opportunities for the advancement of human capabilities and the standards for determining well-being.

Even as socioeconomic and cultural development may be understood as a combination of the means and processes that progressively sum up to improved human well-being and better standards of living, it is in reality a question of proportions and competing rationalities given that well-being and standards of living have no homogeneous benchmark. Socioeconomic and cultural development are relative, subjective, and indeed measurable only in function of situational realities, cultural specificities, and the specific ideals of any group of peoples. It is worth admitting in this regard that between the Southern Cameroons and La République du Cameroun with clear ethno-anthropological differences, aspirations for socioeconomic and cultural development can never be imagined to be identical. Unlike in La République du Cameroun with a francophone inclination, socioeconomic and cultural development in the Southern Cameroons with an Anglo-Saxon culture can only be determined by the actual realities on the ground, which glaringly reflect in the curricula and education systems practiced in the two political entities.

Formulated in the African Charter as a composite right, the socioeconomic and cultural aspects of development translate into a legal undertaking to mobilize the requisite resources and value systems into a rights-based process of development wherein peoples can anticipate to rely on and to productively utilize to promote or enhance the potential for self-sufficiency. By virtue of Resolution 1608(XV), which authorized a federal arrangement between the Southern Cameroons and La République du Cameroun as separate political entities, equality of opportunities granted them autonomy in making alternative development choices and for each of the entities to be able to set its own development priorities. In the period prior to 1961 and thereafter up to 1972 when the Southern Cameroons enjoyed (quasi) political autonomy, it self-sufficiently thrived on its flourishing economy, sustained by a broad range of functional state-owned corporations, which unfortunately have either been constrained to shutdown, crippled, and rendered dysfunctional, or completely taken over by the government of La République du Cameroun (Ngang 2021, pp. 300–301; Aka 2002).

In order to ensure sustained improvement in the human well-being, it is noted once more, as highlighted earlier, that the right to development by its nature disallows any regression in the enjoyment of existing rights and accordingly imposes a commitment to eliminate obstacles that may hinder its realization (DRTD 1986, Article 5). This has not been the case for the Southern Cameroons where, for over the decades of entanglement with La République du Cameroun, the level of socioeconomic and cultural development rather increasingly retrogressed to the point where a revolution became inevitable. Looking in lamentation at the *paradise lost* in terms of aspirations for socioeconomic development in the Southern Cameroons in the period covering 1916 to 1972, Nfor Ngala (2020, pp. 35–90) highlights the unwillingness of the people in accepting imported service delivery models but preferred such models to be tailored to their specific needs absent which they increasingly yearned for greater autonomy and sovereignty. For an illustration of some of the contemporary development injustices that triggered the Southern Cameroons' revolution, Happi Cynthia et al. (2020, p. 4) observed that:

There has [. . .] been significant economic disparity when it comes to allocation of investment projects by the State to the two English-speaking regions, compared to the other eight French-speaking regions. According to Cameroon's 2017 public investment budget, the French speaking South Region was allocated far more resources (over 570 projects with over $225 million) than the two English-speaking North West Region (more than 500 projects with over $76 million) and South West Region (over 500 projects with over $77 million).

[. . .] Policies in the education and judicial systems also created a fertile ground for the emergence and violent radicalization of those with grievances. There were 1,265 French speaking magistrates and only 227 English-speaking magistrates in 2016 and out of 514 judicial officers, 499 were Francophone and 15 Anglophone. The current Anglophone crisis is, therefore, a manifestation of frustration arising from both real and perceived discrimination and marginalization of the English-speaking minority.

Political Development

While the right to development is conceived in the African Charter essentially as guaranteeing entitlement to economic, social, and cultural development, it does not obliterate corresponding entitlement to political development.

Paragraph 8 of the preamble to the Charter provides a conceptual understanding of the right to development, which stipulates that civil and political rights cannot be dissociated from socioeconomic and cultural rights and that the realization of the latter provides the context from the enjoyment of the forma. The DRTD (1986, Article 1(1)) and the African Youth Charter (2006, Article 10(1)) are even more explicit; besides guaranteeing entitlement to socioeconomic and cultural development, also make provision for political development. Unlike socioeconomic and cultural development, political development is a bit more elusive and controversial to define in conceptual terms and hence has often been attributed varied and sometimes confusing meanings (Pooja 2017). For Lucien Pye (1965), political development entails equality in the political society, which is defined by the relationship between the structures of power (state authority) and the political process; delineating as Pooja (2017) noted, the "evolution of society from incoherent homogeneity to coherent heterogeneity, with capacity to solve developmental problems."

The 1946 Trusteeship Agreement (Article 46) that entrusted administration of the Southern Cameroons to the British provided, as it concerned, the latter's obligation to ensure political development in the Trust Territory that "the Administering Authority shall promote the development of free political institutions suited to the territory." The British indeed developed functional political institutions and systems, which the people of the Southern Cameroons eventually inherited. With the understanding of development as a continuous process of advancement or simply ensuring constant improvement in human well-being, political development for the Southern Cameroons within the context of the volatile union with La République du Cameroun would have meant a progressive improvement of the institutions inherited from the trusteeship system. It would also have summed up to political maturity in the mutual recognition of the historical diversity between the two entities that emerged from the trusteeship system as was stated in the federal constitution that emerged from the Foumban Constitutional conference in 1961 much more than forging a semblance of homogeneity (false oneness and indivisibility) that has not actually materialized.

Integral to the right to development, political development would imply a context that guarantees genuine liberties to function optimally within the political space, the freedom to participate in the political processes, and the democratic entitlement to contribute without constraints to the policy discourses that define and shape the functioning of a fair and just political dispensation. This is, in summary, the kind of dispensation that the drafters of Resolution 1608(XV) envisaged in Article 5, when the Administering Authority and governments of the Southern Cameroons and of La République du Cameroun were called upon to "initiate urgent discussions with a view to finalizing, [. . .] the arrangements by which the agreed and declared policies of the parties concerned would be implemented." The entity that is presently recognized as La République du Cameroun unfortunately does not represent the federal dispensation that was intended, wherein political development would have been guaranteed to the Southern Cameroons.

The state, which traditionally is recognized in International Law as the guarantor of human rights, including the right to development, has a crucial role to play in laying the bedrock for political development. It entails that the governmental apparatus is sufficiently capacitated to produce optimal development outputs and the capacity to facilitate and orientate development processes toward the ultimate goal of constant improvement in well-being and living standards for the peoples. Article 22(2) of the African Charter delineates the duty of the state, which consists of the obligation to create an enabling environment for the right to development to be actualized. As the entity that exercises the governmental function, La République du Cameroun is, by virtue of the African Charter, which it ratified in June 1989, mandated to adhere to and to comply with Article 22(2) enshrined therein and thus obligated to create the environment conducive for, and to facilitate the processes for, political development to be attained. Its Constitution additionally enshrines the commitment to devote all national efforts in advancing the right to development (Ngang & Kamga 2018, pp. 194–195). The intention of undertaking to advance the right to development, including among others, ensuring political development in the country, cannot be confused.

The above legal undertakings notwithstanding, prospects for political development for the Southern Cameroons since 1961 rather progressively dwindled and disintegrated. Over the five decades of co-habitation with La République du Cameroun, the Southern Cameroons saw its sovereignty as a distinct political entity and its governmental institutions and democratic structures systematically shutdown and bottled up (Fearon & Laitin no date, p. 3; Kofule-Kale 1986, p. 86). Particular reference can be made to the Southern Cameroons (West Cameroon) legitimately constituted parliamentary system of government comprising of a functional executive headed by an elected prime minister, a legislature made up of an upper house of Chiefs and a lower House of Assembly and a common law judiciary system, together with ancillary civil administrative and state security structures, which were increasingly developed in the period between 1954 and 1972. With the advent of the forged unitary state in 1972, the Southern Cameroons government and hence the federal arrangement state were unilaterally dissolved without legitimate consultation to obtain the informed consent of the people of the Southern Cameroons.

Equality of status on the basis of which the two-state federation was established in 1961 meant that the Southern Cameroons retained its autonomy and thus entitled to equitable political representation in the federal government.

However, as time went by, political conversation between the two entities was gradually stifled by the assimilation agenda that was set in motion to obliterate the Southern Cameroons' identity. Contrary to the African Commission's stance in the *Gumne* case (para 195), affirming political representation of the Southern Cameroons in the National Assembly, the core issue that the Commission failed to investigate is the quality of such representation in the facade of a multi-party democracy, which since its inception in 1990 has never witnessed any genuine political development in the country. By genuine political development, I mean the kind of free and open democratic context guided by the rule of law that allows for proportional political representation, meritorious entitlement to opportunities, and equitable access to budgetary allocations for development.

With the understanding of Lucien Pye's (1965) definition of political development highlighted above and looking at the Southern Cameroons' historical journey with La République du Cameroun, it is worth noting that the framework for political development was not only absent but that the forged union was only sustained because of the natural resources that continue to be extracted gratuitously from the Southern Cameroons. It is rightly noted that the Southern Cameroons was never equitably or proportionally represented in the government and institutions of governance of La République du Cameroun (Happi et al. 2020, p. 4). Regression from the level of advancement that the Southern Cameroons had attained in the period prior to 1972 provides reason to zoom into its pursuit of sovereign statehood with keen interest by projecting into the future with an imagination of what a sovereign Southern Cameroons would eventually look like.

IMAGINING A SOVEREIGN SOUTHERN CAMEROONS

A fundamental attribute of the right to development is the fact that it must inevitably lead to the constant improvement of human well-being, which entails eliminating the obstacles and constraints that may hinder its realization (Sengupta 2004, p. 184; DRTD 1986, Article 5). As illustrated in the previous section, co-habitation with La République du Cameroun with its constraining assimilation policies for over half a century fundamentally caused a severe regression in the right to development (socioeconomic and cultural as well as political advancement) in the Southern Cameroons. While the revolution that sparked off in 2016 is intended to eventually remedy the sustained development injustices, the important question that needs exploring at this stage in the pursuit of sovereign statehood is how different a sovereign Southern Cameroons is envisaged to be.

Founding Philosophy[1]

Unlike most African countries, which when they attained independence failed or maybe omitted to conceptualize a founding philosophy to define and shape their proper functioning, the Southern Cameroons has the opportunity, as it strives toward sovereign statehood, to seek to redress that lacuna. Besides the comprehensive Blueprint developed by Millan Atam in 2017, the founding philosophy conceived herein is conceptualized on the basis of actual realities and as pragmatic aspirations anchored on the following precepts that are estimated to define the pathways for advancement in a sovereign Southern Cameroons.

First Priority

One of the anchors on which any state can justifiably become and retain greatness is a strong conviction in the optimal productivity of its people. Of the component elements that constitute a state, the population (people) is indeed central, without which the state will practically not exist. The first priority principle basically corroborates the UNDP's index for measuring development in terms of foregrounding the human potential rather than narrowly focusing on economic growth, which is calculated primarily on the basis of the gross domestic product (GDP) of a country, generally ignoring the peoples who are the principal drivers in the GDP achievable. First priority as it should be understood in this context entails advancing human productive capabilities so that the people can, in turn, effectively contribute to advancing the country's capacity to deliver on its development prerogatives. Reflecting on why states fail, particularly in Africa, it is of essence for the Southern Cameroons, as it looks toward becoming a new state, to consider attributing first priority to its people.

The first priority principle entails that in every facet of government and of governance be it domestic or in terms of external relations, the interests of the people of the Southern Cameroons must at all material times and space be put foremost and above all other considerations. There is no greater asset by which to establish and build a country other than investing in expanding the productive potential of the people of that country. The first priority principle requires that every single person, including the unborn or future generations, be accorded the utmost recognition and protection by virtue of their worth in human potential as the primary architects of the state. The principle is based on the sensible reasoning that an empowered and productive people is an incredible propelling force in animating and sustaining the political economy.

It is true, for example, that the Southern Cameroons is abundantly endowed with a wide range of natural resources. Without the productive capability of the people of the Southern Cameroons to transform those resources into consumable wealth for the sustenance of well-being, the resources would be as good as nothing and probably only serving the rent-seeking interest of foreign stakeholders. To put the first priority principle into actionable measures would require all state and the non-state institutions in a sovereign Southern Cameroons, including the people themselves, to constructively strive to advance human capabilities and the potential to maximize productivity in goods and services for socioeconomic advancement in the country.

The first priority principle is ambitious and maybe quite radical in its formulation but not unattainable if the legitimate interest and political commitment are there and effectively combined to achieve established outcomes. Many nations in Africa upon their birth at independence failed in this respect and rather prioritized the political economy over developing the capabilities of their peoples and thus did not advance in any significant way. South Africa, for example, when it emerged as a new political dispensation born out of the absolutism of apartheid, undertook the constitutional commitment to "improve the quality of life of all citizens and free the potential of each person" (The Constitution of South Africa 1996, preamble). Unfortunately, post-apartheid South Africa quickly abandoned the radical undertaking to give all of its people first priority and hence the present status quo where, despite being the most advanced economy in Africa, South Africa remains the country with the highest poverty configurations with an estimated 41 million impoverished people out of a total population of about 52 million (Ngang 2019a, p. 48). There are a number of other African countries that are economically quite advanced but are among the least developed as per the human development rankings.

With this understanding, it would be of interest for the Southern Cameroons to, in every way, strive to be different in prioritizing the advancement of its people so that they may eventually develop the political economy. The first priority principle requires making a sovereign Southern Cameroons an enabling political safe haven where the right to development can effectively be exercised, and this would entail guaranteeing effective protection of inherent entitlements, cultural diversities, livelihood security, and socioeconomic benefit sharing. In resonance with the argument that Africa is confronted with a systems problem that disallows realization of the right to development (Ngang 2019b, pp. 368–372), to redress that problem, a sovereign Southern Cameroons would be obligated to multiply the drive for an entrepreneurial citizenry, productive and dependable (judicial, education, healthcare, and economic) systems, which should combine into a compelling attraction as an investment destination of choice. First priority would delineate committed patriotism within a constitutional dispensation that promotes expanded freedoms, in relation to which, as I illustrate below, would make a sovereign Southern Cameroons distinctly functional.

Equitable Collective Prosperity

The equitable collective prosperity principle guarantees that a minimum standard of livelihood be established to ensure that no person in the liberated sovereign Southern Cameroons falls below the minimum threshold in living standards. In accordance with the first priority principle explained above, a sovereign Southern Cameroons would have to be established on the platform of equality of opportunities for development and expanded choices in engaging in the development processes to be explored either collectively or individually. The Chinese operate on a similar philosophical grounding, defined as "moderate prosperity" (*xiao-kang*), that reflects aspirations for and the pursuit of a better and happier life, which translates into the broad understanding that equal access to development opportunities and the benefits resulting therefrom are the ideals of every human society (China State Council Information Office 2016). The African Union's (2015, para 6) agenda for development equally makes reference to "shared prosperity" as one of the core elements of the aspiration to elevate living standards for all the peoples of Africa by 2063.

The idea of equitable collective prosperity is conceived from the above illustrations and intended to ensure that poverty and other development setbacks generated by income and structural inequalities are eradicated in a sovereign Southern Cameroons. The Declaration on the Right to Development (1986: Article 5) invoked the commitment to eliminate all obstacles to development, including the "refusal to recognize the fundamental right of peoples to self-determination." The persistent regression in the right to development stems from La République du Cameroun's insistent refusal to recognize that the people of the Southern Cameroons are legitimately entitled to the right to self-determination, which entails asserting the right to existence as a separate and distinct people. The African Commission noted in the *Gumne* case (2009, para 179), "[i]t is up to other external people to recognise such existence, but not to deny it." To deny recognizing the Southern Cameroons as a separate and distinct people with the right to existence as such, not only contravenes the law but also constitutes an obstacle to development, which must be eliminated. The burden is on the liberated Southern Cameroons to do so.

The burden entails ensuring that a sovereign Southern provides an effective right to development dispensation wherein equitable collective prosperity would be guaranteed. It would require establishing mechanisms for (re) distributive justice and equity in regulating the acquisition and accumulation of wealth in a manner that does not disproportionately favor and open up greater opportunities to some persons at the expense of the rest of the population. The equitable collective prosperity principle shall not be interpreted to imply a limitation of rights and freedoms and the extent to which any person in the free and sovereign Southern Cameroons may aspire for greater achievements. It is rather intended to set a level playing field from which great ambitions can be born and nurtured to take off without compromising standard of living and exposure to the horizon of opportunities for the average person.

Visionary Transformative Leadership

Part of the problem that contributed to La République du Cameroun's subjugation of the Southern Cameroons was the lack of a determined visionary leadership capable of foreseeing the pitfalls and impracticability of the forged merger between two culturally distinct peoples with irreconcilable differences (International Crisis Group 2017, pp. 2–8) as Abubakar Balewa (cited in Ngang 2021, p. 301) correctly predicted in 1961. Most present-day great nations including, for example, China and Singapore have only become so by virtue of the political leadership that laid the visionary foundation for their greatness, with remarkable transformation from extremely poor least developed countries to rank among the most flourishing economies in the world. Unlike the leadership model characterized by nepotism that prevails across most of Africa, Singapore's exceptional success, for instance, is constructed on the meritocracy, pragmatism, and honesty (MPH) leadership model, wherein governance is anchored on expertise, conflicting ideologies are synchronized into a functional political economy, and honesty is institutionalized as a guiding principle in combating corruption (VPRO Documentary 2009).

Albeit the Southern Cameroons may be endowed with a wealth of natural resources (much more than Singapore) to be able to sustain a vibrant industrialized economy, it would require visionary transformative leadership in ensuring that the political economy becomes globally competitive. Visionary transformative leadership is not only meant that which exclusively involves the political elite but one that imposes a conscious obligation for sweeping transformation and a culture of justification in the exercise of leadership in everyday operations across the public and private sectors. Given the apparent differences in dynamics, it might not be ideal and, indeed, not sensible to imagine that the Singaporean MPH model for economic transformation could be replicated in the Southern Cameroons with similar accomplishments (Sillah 2020, pp. 1–6). In justification of the revolution and as a starting point, visionary transformative leadership obligates the people of the Southern Cameroons to begin to look beyond the horizon of prevailing odds at the kind of governance model that will be suited to the survival and functioning of a new state within an increasingly competitive global economy that is heavily influenced by dominant political forces.

Governance Model

Right to Development Governance

The right to development governance as a model for development suited to redressing the development contradictions in Africa (Ngang 2018, pp. 114–116; Ngang 2019b, pp. 387–393) guarantees to all peoples exposure to equality of opportunities for socioeconomic and cultural as well as political development, expanded choices and the liberty to explore the full extent of the margins of their potentials, and productive capabilities. It is framed within the understanding of collective advancement, which is conceived in the conceptual formulation of the right to development that guarantees entitlement to *everyone*, literally understood as everyone without distinction or discrimination and thus eventually translates into the global commitment to sustainable development, articulated in the catchphrase "no one is left behind." It posits that no one is more entitled to better standards than others; the contrary of which, in La République du Cameroun, is constructed around the general perception and treatment of the people of the Southern Cameroons as second-class or sub-standard, not deserving of equal opportunities. It shall be to the interest of the Southern Cameroons with regard to prospects for accelerated advancement to correct such a deconstructivist perception by institutionalizing the right to development governance model in ensuring that requisite conditions, systems, and mechanisms are put in place and structured in a coordinated manner to facilitate equitable redistribution of the resources for development as a guarantee of the collective enjoyment of development gains.

The right to development governance is a model that is conceptualized to empower and accordingly commission the people of the Southern Cameroons to actively participate in the processes for shaping the socioeconomic and cultural and the political priorities for nation building. In furtherance of the right to development governance model, a sovereign Southern Cameroons will need to be constructed on the foundation of a solid knowledge economy, designed to expand the acquisition creative potentials and more sophisticated skills needed for conceptualizing transformative solutions to everyday challenges and development exigencies and to transform every sector of the political economy in a manner that will remarkably revive and transform the ailing systems, institutions, structures, and mechanisms that have been destroyed over the decades, including by the on-going conflict. The knowledge economy would need to translate into a right to development policy framework that obliges the pursuit of scientific and systematic methods to problem solving, backed by solid institutional systems and a heavily industrialized market economy.

Unlike with economistic models for development, which generally do not guarantee protection when obligations are contravened, the right to development governance is recommended for a sovereign Southern Cameroons essentially because it is firmly anchored in the law. The importance of doing so is with assurance that when a violation is established, remedy can be sort through legal processes, necessitating for its application a constitutional dispensation that guarantees the rule of law among other acceptable governance practices.

Constitutional Dispensation

As highlighted above, implementation of the right to development governance model would entail an enabling transformative system of government and of governance, requiring the people of the Southern Cameroons, as they navigate through the war for sovereign statehood, to explore contemporary alternatives like adopting a constitutional system, which is beginning to gain greater favor than the predominantly presidential systems that have not recorded much people-centerd development gains on the continent. Conceptually, the right to development obligates every state to establish a development policy dispensation that is suited to their socioeconomic and cultural as well as political realities (DRTD 1986: Articles 2(3) and 10). Reconstruction of the postwar dispensation and laying the foundation for the right to development in a sovereign Southern Cameroons will require a solid constitutional framing that sets the pace for stringent commitment to the rule of law, pluralistic democracy, adherence to human rights, and clearly structured roles and responsibilities with the government operating as a coordinating mechanism.

The constitutional framework would, in addition to relevant enforcement mechanisms and ancillary institutions, have to be grounded on a technically crafted transformative constitution as the core supreme law of the land, which the people of the Southern Cameroons and every organ of state would be obligated to adhere to. To every right and privilege that would have to be enshrined in the constitution, an equivalent responsibility would equally have to be allocated in view of girding the system with regimented patriotism, responsiveness, and a culture of justification for every action or inaction, including by the state. Against the narrative that presents the conflict in the Southern Cameroons as a constitutional problem, making it look like an internal matter to be resolved by the government of La République du Cameroun, I contend that at no point in time has the Southern Cameroons freely ceded its autonomy to La République du Cameroun and so its self-determination claim cannot be considered an internal matter within the purview of La République du Cameroun's decision-making. The dream of a sovereign Southern Cameroons can only be given breath to by the people of the Southern Cameroons.

The element in the right to self-determination that entitles all peoples to freely determine their political future essentially grants the right to craft a constitution as a legal foundation in defining the political future. It thus goes against the basic tenets of the right to self-determination under International Law as James Crawford (2010, p. 137) lucidly expounded on that La Répub-lique du Cameroun should arrogate the authority to make unilateral decisions about the political future of the Southern Cameroons, including by granting it "Special Status" as an integral part of its territory; whereas, the legitimate claim of the people of the Southern Cameroons is for sovereign statehood. Asserting self-determination incorporates the liberty to choose between alter-natives and accordingly equips the people of the Southern Cameroons with the autonomy to frame its political future and clearly define the pathways to a resilient and sustainable socioeconomic and cultural model in a constitutional instrument that guarantees sovereignty and to proceed to religiously profess and defend that sovereignty with unalloyed patriotism and loyalty.

Minimum Threshold in Living Standards

It is noted that "[t]he African conception of the right to development neces-sitates setting a minimum threshold for determining collective well-being through legitimate guarantees of equality of opportunity for socioeconomic and cultural [not excluding political] development to all the peoples of Africa" (Ngang 2019b, p. 390; see also Sengupta 2000, p. 848). This percep-tion is informed by the human development index (HDI), which as concep-tualized in the UN Development Programme (UNDP) 1990 maiden report illustrates that development cannot be measured solely in economic terms by looking a country's growth performance but indeed also, as an alternative, by looking at the level of human well-being and standard of living in every coun-try. For a sovereign Southern Cameroons to become different or thrive where other African countries have not been able to set a benchmark in justification of their sovereignty, it is crucial that from the get-go, a minimum threshold for well-being and livelihood be established as the baseline from where the people of the Southern Cameroons will collectively have the opportunity to launch themselves into greatness and accomplishment.

To ensure sustainable human development and a standard of living propor-tionate with the HDI, the minimum benchmark for the future Southern Cam-eroons should, in accordance with the first priority and equitable collective prosperity principles discussed above, define the basic threshold, which none of its citizens should under any circumstances be allowed to fall underneath. By the established minimum standard, the processes for development in a sovereign Southern Cameroons would have to be measured not by the GDP formula and economic growth rate but by how well and the extent to which life and living standards are sustained beyond the minimum threshold. This is by no means to underrate the importance of GDP contribution in advancing the market economy which, I argue, should rather only be conceived as indis-pensable in sustaining the processes for ensuring that the minimum threshold is retained or elevated to a higher notch. This is estimated to set the pace for the interplay of politics, the market economy, and the sociocultural patterns of life in shaping national development policy priorities in a manner that culminates in the superior purpose of promoting social progress and entitlement to the highest attainable standard of living in a sovereign Southern Cameroons.

CONCLUSION

While the arguments presented in this chapter may seem overambitious given the complexities involved, it does not escape reality that sovereign statehood for the Southern Cameroons is achievable, especially when the historical, legal, and political facts that support the self-determination claim are properly indexed to the existing problem, which unfortunately are ignored or distorted in most accounts on the subject. The best, most likely and worse case scenarios presented by Happi Cynthia et al. (2020, p. 14), for instance, completely obliterate the majority position of the people of the Southern Cameroons, who in two surveys organized by Cardinal Christian Tumi and other religious leaders in September/October 2019 (Crux 2019) and the Coalition for Dialogue and Negotiations in October 2020 (Alan et al. 2020) demonstrated by a response of 69 percent and 86 percent respectively in favor of full independence and separation from La République du Cameroun. These survey results are obviously not official and therefore without binding effect, which in essence necessitates—in accordance with the International Law principle of self-determination—that entitles the people of the Southern Cameroons to freely determine their political future and freely pursue their economic, social, and cultural development.

With respect to the Crawford (2010, p. 137) criteria for qualifying a self-determination claim and the 1933 Montevideo criteria for determining statehood under International Law, it is disingenuous that propositions for resolving the problem, ignore the freely expressed common will of the people of the Southern Cameroons (Ngang 2021, pp. 302–303). The UN's role in the decolonization processes that created the complexities, which the Southern Cameroons is presently confronted with, cannot be ignored. Looking at the odds that persist and continue to conspire against the Southern Cameroons, it will require a UN-sanctioned referendum and negotiated settlement to be able to effectively redress the fundamental root causes and other underlining factors that triggered the intractable conflict against La République du Camerouns' subjugation as Fonkem Achankeng 1 (2018, pp. 1–6) rightly describes it. In light of the legitimacy of the Southern Cameroons liberation struggle, I posit that it would be costly and in effect translate into a tactical mistake to navigate through the war into sovereignty unprepared. This chapter accordingly illustrates how and what it entails in laying the foundation for statehood for the sovereign Ambazonia that is envisaged to be born, wherein the right to development would be guaranteed.

NOTE

1. The founding philosophy described herein is an expansion of an initial document conceptualized by the author of this chapter as self-evidence of the aspirations that motivated the Southern Cameroons' quest for self-determination and revolution in pursuit of sovereign statehood. The ideas draw from and are inspired by development success stories and best practice approaches from around the world in dealing with development challenges that the Southern Cameroons has over the years been confronted with.

REFERENCES

African Charter on Human and Peoples' Rights Adopted by the OAU in Nairobi Kenya on 27 June 1981, OAU Doc CAB/LEG/67/3 rev. 5; 1520 UNTS 217, Arts 19 & 20.
African Union Commission. (2015). "Agenda 2063: The Africa We Want." *African Union.*
African Youth Charter Adopted in Banjul, The Gambia on 2 July 2006.
Agwanda, B., Nyaburi, N. I., & Yasin, A. U. (2020). "Cameroon and the Anglophone Crisis." In *The Palgrave Encyclopedia of Peace and Conflict Studies Publisher.* Cham: Palgrave Macmillan.
Aka, E. (ed: F. Achankeng). (2002). *The British Cameroons 1922–1961: A Study in Colonialism and Underdevelopment.* Nkemnji Global Tech.
Alan, L., Mauro, I., & Fontama, N. V. (2020). "Survey of Southern Cameroonians." *Coalition for Dialogue and Negotiations & 4 Most,* 1 October 2020.
Alston, P. (1988). "Making Space for New Human Rights: The Case of the Right to Development." *Human Rights Yearbook,* 1(3): 1-40.
Anghie, A. (2013). "Whose Utopia?: Human Rights, Development and the Third World." *Qui Parle: Critical Humanities and Social Sciences,* 22(1): 63–80.
Anyangwe, C. (2013). "Manumission From Black-on-Black Colonialism: Sovereign Statehood for the British Southern Cameroons." In S. Ndlovu-Gathsheni & B. Mhlanga (Eds.), *Bondage of Boundaries and Identity Politics in Postcolonial Africa: The Northern Problem and Ethno Futures.* Pretoria: Africa Institute of South Africa, 163–184.
Atam, M. (2017). "The Southern Cameroons (Ambazonia): The Nation's Blueprint." *SCACUF Executive Council.*
Brunn, O. (2013). "Social Movements, Competing Rationalities and Trigger Events: The Complexity of Chinese Popular Mobilizations." *Anthropological Theory,* 13(1): 240–266.
Caldara, M., McBride, M., McCarter, M. W., & Sheremeta, R. (2017). "A Study of the Triggers of Conflict and Emotional Reactions." *Games,* 8(21): 1–12.

Cameroons Under United Kingdom Trusteeship: Trusteeship Agreement Approved by the General Assembly of the United Nations, New York, 13 December 1946, Treaty Series No 27 (1947).

Centre for Minority Rights Development (Kenya) & Minority Rights Group International on Behalf of Endorois Welfare.

China State Council Information Office. (2016). "The Right to Development: China's Philosophy, Practice and Contribution." *People's Republic of China – White Paper on the Right to Development.* english.www.gov.cn/archive/white_paper/2016/12/01/content_281475505407672.htm (accessed: 30 January 2021).

Crawford, J. (2010). "The Creation of States in International Law." *Oxford Scholarship*, 137.

Crux Staff. (2019). "Cameroon's Cardinal: Anglophone Independence Must Be on Agenda." *Crux – Taking the Catholic Pulse.* https://cruxnow.com/church-in-africa/2019/09/cameroons-cardinal-anglophone-independence-must-be-on-agenda/ (accessed: 28 January 2021).

Declaration on the Right to Development Resolution A/RES/41/128 adopted by the UN General Assembly on 4 December 1986.

Ekongtang, E. (1995). "Statement of Presentation of Petition Against the Annexation of the Southern Cameroons by la République du Cameroun." *The Herald No. 238.*

Fearon, J., & Laitin, D. (no date). "Cameroon." *Stanford University.*

Fonkem, A. (2014). "The Southern Cameroons Nationalist Conflict: A Destiny in the Shadows?" *Africa Peace and Conflict Journal*, 5(2): 2.

Fonkem, A. (2018). "Conflicts and Crisis in the Cameroon Anglophone Region." *E-International Relations*, 1–6.

Happi, C.; Chedine, T.; Moussaka, S.; Muluka, S.; Pezu, M.; Tigist, K.F. & Tsion, B. (2020). "Cameroon Conflict Insight." *Institute for Peach and Security – Peace and Security Report.* Vol 1 pp. 1–22.

International Crisis Group. (2017). "Cameroon's Anglophone Crisis at the Crossroads." *Africa Report No 250.*

Johnson, G. M. (1987). "The Contributions of Eleanor and Franklin Roosevelt to the Development of International Protection for Human Rights." *Human Rights Quarterly*, 9(1): 19–48.

Jua, N., & Konings, P. (2017). "Occupation of Public Space Anglophone Nationalism in Cameroon." *Cahiers d'Etudes Africaines*, XLIV(3): 609–633.

Kevin Mgwanga Gumne & Others v Cameroon Comm 266/2003. (2009). AHRLR 9 (ACHPR 2009).

Kofale-Kale, D. (1986). "Ethnicity, Regionalism, and Political Power: A Post-Mortem of Ahidjo's Cameroon." In M. Schatzberg & W. Zartman (Eds.), *The Political Economy of Cameroon.* Westport: Praeger.

Marks, S. (2003). "The Human Rights Framework for Development: Seven Approaches." *François-Xavier Bagnoud Centre for Health and Human Rights*, 1–29.

Nfor, N. N. (2020). *Paradise Lost: A Political History of the British Southern Cameroons From 1916–1972.* Austin, TX: Pan-African University Press.

Ngang, C. C. (2018). "Towards a Right-to-Development Governance in Africa." *Journal of Human Rights*, 17(1): 107–122.

Ngang, C. C. (2019a). "Radical Transformation and a Reading of the Right to Development in the South African Constitutional Order." *South African Journal on Human Rights*, 35(1): 25–49.

Ngang, C. C. (2019b). "Systems Problem and a Pragmatic Insight into the Right to Development Governance for Africa." *African Human Rights Law Journal*, 19(1): 387–393.

Ngang, C. C. (2021). "Self-Determination and the Southern Cameroons Quest for Sovereign Statehood." *African Journal of International and Comparative Law*, 29(2): 288–308.

Ngang, C. C., & Kamga, S. D. (2018). "'O Cameroon, Thou Cradle of Our Fathers…: Land of Promise' and the Right to Development." In C. C. Ngang; S. D. Kamga, & V. Gumede (Eds.), *Perspectives on the Right to Development*. Pretoria: Pretoria University Law Press, 200–201.

Oloka-Onyango, J. (1999). "Heretical Reflections on the Right to Self-Determination: Prospects and Problems for a Democratic Global Future in the New Millennium." *The American University International Law Review*, 15(1): 151–208.

Özden, M., & Golay, C. (2010). "The Right of Peoples to Self-Determination and to Permanent Sovereignty Over Their Natural Resources Seen From a Human Rights Perspective." *CETIM*.

Pooja. (2017). "Political Development: Conceptual Explanation." *Political Science Notes*. https://www.politicalsciencenotes.com/articles/political-development-conceptual-explanation/578 (accessed: 24 January 2021).

Pye, L. (1965). "The Concept of Political Development." *The Annals of the American Academy of Political and Social Science*, 358(1): 1–13.

Sengupta, A. (2000). "Realising the Right to Development." *Development and Change*, 31(3): 553–578.

Sengupta, A. (2004). "The Human Right to Development." *Oxford Development Studies*, 32(2): 179–203.

Sillah, B. M. S. (2020). "Economic Transformation: Can Singaporean Principle of Meritocracy Be Replicated?" *Islamic Development Bank*, 1–9.

The Constitution of the Republic of South Africa, 1996.

Udombana, N. (2000). "The Third World and the Right to Development: Agenda for the Next Millennium." *Human Rights Quarterly*, 22(3), 753–787.

UN Millennium Declaration Resolution A/55/L.2 Adopted by the General Assembly on 8 September 2000, para III (11).

United Nations Development Programme. (1990). *Human Development Report 1990*. New York: Oxford University Press.

United Nations General Assembly Resolution 1608(XV) on the Future of the Trust Territory of the Cameroons under United Kingdom Administration Adopted on 21 April 1961.

VPRO Documentary. (2009). "The Singapore Economic Model." https://www.youtube.com/watch?v=ipQo3b2NU98.

Ware, A. (2010). "Human Rights and the Right to Development: Insights into the Myanmar Government's Response to Rights Allegations." In: *18th Biennial Conference of the Asian Studies Association of Australia*.

Chapter 7

Porcupine in the Throat of a Python

*Perceptions of Ambazonian
Resistance and Activism*

Fonkem Achankeng

This chapter summarizes the findings of a study of the people of ex-British Southern Cameroons who were compelled by the UK (trustee) and the UN (trustor) to lose statehood by achieving "independence by joining" one of her two neighbors (Resolution 1608). The findings are reflected through the perceptions and activism of the people of the territory. The findings demonstrate that the people both in the homeland and in exile not only feel less emancipated than they were at the time of independence in 1960–1961, but they also feel further distanced from the desirable future for which they had hoped. According to the last British Administrator J. O. Field (1958), the territory was looking forward to independence with quiet hope a hundred years after the founding of Victoria and all the people had achieved in the one hundred years. Despite the achievements and the quiet hope that sovereign independence never came. In place of the independence, the people were asked to join a neighbor who turned out to be a new colonizer attempting to swallow them like a python swallows a prey. As one of the study participants pointed out, the people of the ex-British Southern Cameroons consider themselves as "a porcupine stuck in the throat of a python that tried to swallow it." The situation will need a skillful surgeon to get the porcupine out safely for both the python and the porcupine; it cannot be swallowed.

The study resulting in this chapter used the narrative research tradition to collect the data analyzed here. In highlighting the advantages of the narrative research method, Chaitin (2004, p. 11) posited that the method makes it possible for the researcher "to look at the life stories from a number of angles, concepts, and theories" and that it "provided very fertile ground for the postulation of different understandings that come from different disciplines and conceptual frameworks." All the participants in the research interviews, excerpts of which are cited in this chapter, are referred to with pseudonyms because of the sensitivity of the issue under investigation and the safety of the participants.

EXPRESSION OF OUTRAGE AND BITTERNESS

The analysis revealed that the Southern Cameroons' restoration of sovereign statehood conflict is deep-rooted and long-standing. That is the reason most Southern Cameroons' people are outraged with their circumstances of an eternal colonial bondage. This conclusion permeates the story told by Fineman (pseudonym), a founding member of the Southern Cameroons National Council. He conveyed the circumstances that brought three of them together in 1992 within a Constitution Drafting Committee. He explained how they represented very different interest groups, but how each identified the long-standing nationalist needs of ex-British Southern Cameroons from individual lived experiences in *La Republique du Cameroun* (ex-French Cameroon). He also noted how they all worked together to ignite nationalist re-awareness among the people of Southern Cameroons through their call for a return to the 1961 two-state federation, a call which was rebuffed by authorities of *La Republique du Cameroun*. As one of the leaders in the Southern Cameroons exile community, Fineman, explained,

> Some of the people who say the three of us were English-speaking representatives on the constitutional committee do not have the facts right. We were not. It was not like Anglophones and Francophones acting as separate constituencies mandated their respective delegates to the constitutional committee. Sango (pseudonym) got in as a representative of the opposition political parties, Peter (pseudonym) as a representative of the political party in power, and I as a representative of what was called then as "independent personalities." If anything, we were expected to espouse the views of our various interest groups. But it was never to be. Our common lived experience as persons from a polity under ex-French Cameroun annexationist colonization and our sound knowledge of the Francophone mindset bound and impelled us to take a tactical stand on the need to return to the two-state federation which informed the 1961 plebiscite vote for association with ex-French Cameroun. (Interview with the Author, 2015)

The experience of Southern Cameroons in Cameroon Republic since 1961 has been very unsettling in the minds of the people of the territory. Ntumba (pseudonym) in the following excerpt is outraged about his situation in exile, which is caused in turn by the restoration of statehood struggle of his people, who are compelled to live in perpetual colonial subjugation.

> We have written records of everything that happened to us at independence in 1960. Before I finish this interview, I will give you a copy of Resolution 1541 of December 15, 1960. When we were still a trust territory and Cameroon had become a member of the UN in September before December and so Cameroon participated and then came the resolution of April 21, which the UN said the trust mandate would terminate on September 30. Look, Cameroon in fact voted against that resolution led by France. So a lot of French territories with the exception of Mali voted that Cameroon should not have independence and join. Probably that is the reason why we are treated as second-class citizens in Cameroon because Cameroon never accepted the decision of the UN. So we were practically colonized because when Britain left, Ahidjo moved over his security forces and he has been here ever since. Do you understand our situation? The right to self-determination is a continuing right. Every human being the world over has a right to self-determination. Southern or British Cameroon was a separate territory from La Republique du Cameroun. That was the reason why when France granted independence to East Cameroun it did not include us because we were not one country. So, at some point we had to join so that we could become one country. That joining has never taken place. And La Republic du Cameroun represented by Mr. Biya is not prepared to talk so as to arrange matters in accordance with the prescriptions of the UN whose territory we were. So either Mr. Biya agrees to talk to negotiate with a territory that was never part of La Republique du Cameroun, which voluntarily agreed to join but on terms put down by the UN. Those terms have not been respected. How can we not fight for our freedom? (Interview with the Author, 2015)

Most of the Southern Cameroons' people in the study sample were like Ntumba. They can be characterized as "warriors." As a community of people who are not merely a passive and dependent group, but a community whose members are conscious about their political objective to liberate their homeland, they remained adamantly active in the restoration of independence cause. Although Southern Cameroons people in the study did not indicate, through their narratives, that they had an armed section, this definition shows that the people of Southern Cameroons were outraged about the situation of their homeland. Those of them in exile were equally infuriated with exile and wanted a home they could return to and contribute in building a country of their own. While abroad, this outrage served as a catalyst to be actively involved in political activism relating to the conflict in their homeland.

Some of the refugees interviewed were very bitter with Cameroon Republic, a country that has treated them with suspicion since October 1961. Menkeu (pseudonym), a refugee who arrived through Canada, narrated a lengthy story of his experience with a country he had thought was his.

As a young lad of about 22 years old at the time, I was with a group with four others who arrived at Murtala Mohammed International Airport, Lagos one evening in 1981 shortly after a coup d'état had just taken place. We had just completed the Advanced Level examinations and were heading to university full of joy that we were beginning a new stage in our lives. Our flight was routed to Lagos airport from where we had to travel by land to our respective institutions. No sooner did our plane touch down than we learned about the coup. We did not know what to do to be safe because we did not know anyone in Lagos. One of us suggested that the best thing to do was to go the Embassy of Cameroon, our country. We thought the decision was the right one as we did not know how long the emergency situation was going to last. We did not also know how to get to the Embassy or where it was located and how far it was from the airport. Luckily one of us had been smart enough to include the Embassy phone number in his address book. We decided to call the Embassy to inform the authorities there that we, a group of Cameroonian students were at the airport and did not know what to do in the midst of all the confusion and the lack of safety. The person who received the call at the Embassy did not as much as ask for our names, where we were, and where we were supposed to be going. We did not also know who exactly it was who answered the phone. The person simply replied: "We do not know you" in a French accent and dropped the phone. Since that day I have hated myself for being Cameroonian and have never liked to be called Cameroonian. Throughout the four years I spent in the University the main officials of Cameroon at the Embassy in Lagos, Nigeria, were all Francophone who always behaved as if they were not in Nigeria because Cameroonians lived in Nigeria or visited the country. (Interview with the Author, 2015)

From listening to many of the people living in exile talk about their experiences with Cameroon Republic, one infers that they were very contemptuous of their lives in Cameroon and were resentful of the fact that they were perceived as Cameroonians. To them, being perceived as Cameroonian was insulting. They looked forward with hope to that day when they could see a country they recognized as theirs.

TAKING THE PAST ALONG

An appreciation of the past is essential in understanding the perceptions and activism of Southern Cameroons' people in general. Scholars on memory and trauma, like Linstroth (2009, p. 167), have documented the legacy of colonial history and structural violence on people and how they relate to their pasts. Lambek's (2002, p. 238) discussion of the play of the past on the historicity in everyday life of communities in northern Madagascar indicated that people "find themselves shifting between various perspectives to the past in different contexts." This learning is useful when analyzing the perspectives of Southern Cameroons' people on the conflict in their home country and the persistent nature of the conflict.

First, some of the people I interviewed not only had their stories to tell but also had abundant written literature on their struggle. They had archival material on Southern Cameroons from the colonial era, part of Nigeria through the 1960s, then the territory as part of Cameroon. They also had literature on developments following the re-emergence of Southern Cameroons' nationalism within the Cameroon Republic. Regarding the study participants living in exile, I was amazed to discover so much information that the people brought with them and still retained. It was new learning for me to discover that the restoration of statehood struggle remained dear to the hearts of these people and that they were and remained unlikely to let the struggle dissipate.

Second, in view of the numbers and the economic potential of the French Cameroon refugee population in the Southern Cameroons' economy—a population representing about one-third of the workforce in the 1930s (Aka, 2002)—there is no wonder then that the population had so much influence in the local economy and the politics of the territory in the 1950s. And considering that the 1950s were decisive years in the political future of the territory, one can understand how the French Cameroon refugees in the territory at the time influenced the politics and the course of events in the territory and the concerns about independence. Many of the people interviewed considered this French Cameroon refugees as very influential in the life of the territory. Even after 1961, successive regimes in *La Republique du Cameroun* continued to use the population to facilitate the colonization and exploitation of the territory and its native peoples. As one interviewee, Fuabenyong (pseudonym), pointed out,

> They consider themselves as part of us in ordinary circumstances and everyday living, but when the chips are down, they identify only with their people in the ancestral homes; when they die, their bodies are taken back and buried only among their people back in their home villages in French Cameroon. (Interview with the Author, 2015).

This same interviewee, Fuabenyong, asked and answered aloud,

> Where is Ambassador Paul Engo? He is back home in his country. As a Bulu man he is back with his people whereas he was the first Magistrate in Southern Cameroons. He was educated with the tax money from our parents here in British Southern Cameroons. (Interview with the Author, 2015)

Third, the data obtained through the study showed that the people of Southern Cameroons have made extraordinary efforts in strengthening their national liberation struggle through the availability of hi-tech communication devices, including the Internet and cellular phones. These new developments in communication performed a major role in sustaining the conflict; the participants in the study now communicate in many ways that the government of Cameroon Republic could neither sequester nor impede in any way. Further research may be necessary to determine the role of hi-tech communication devices in the evolution and in the escalation of the conflict.

Fourth, an interesting finding in the study was that there are major disagreements over the name used by the different liberation movements for the territory. These names include Southern Cameroons, Ambazonia, and Ambazania. Each group had an argument to back up the respective name it used. However, disagreement retarded the progress of the liberation struggle. The research revealed that one of the liberation movements, the Ambazonia Restoration Council (ARC), had won some court cases on the subject of the territory's liberation both in Cameroon Republic and abroad. These cases included Suit No. HCB 28/92 of May 18, 1992, at Bamenda, in Southern Cameroons territory, in which *La Republique du Cameroun* was found "guilty of aggression by illegally and forcibly occupying the territory of Ambazonia" (former Southern Cameroons). A second case concerning Fon Gorji Dinka, leader of ARC, was said to have been won in the Cameroon Military Tribunal on February 3, 1986. And a third suit was submitted to the Human Rights Committee on behalf of Fongum Gorji Dinka. This suit, Communication No. 1134/2002, was also decided in favor of ARC by the UN Committee on Civil and Political Rights on March 17, 2005, under the Optional Protocol to the International Covenant on Civil and Political Rights. Unfortunately, many of the participants in the study did not appear to have adequately explored the successes in the above-referenced legal victories in the struggle. Two other suits are important in this analysis. They were Communications 266/2003 and 377/2007 brought by Gwang Gumne et al. before the African Commission on Human and People's Rights (ACHPR). The Commission's 2009 verdict on Communication 266/2003 recognized the people of ex-British Southern Cameroons as a people in International Law. The verdict called for dialogue between the peoples of ex-British Southern Cameroons and *La Republique du Cameroun* within 180 days and provided the good offices of the African Union to mediate the dialogue. Regarding Communication 377/2007 praying the African Court to ask *La Republique du Cameroun* to respect Article 4 of the African Union on boundaries inherited at independence, the verdict is still expected.

THE PEOPLE'S ACTIVISM AT HOME AND ABROAD

The data collected for this study from the people both in the homeland and abroad shows ex-British Cameroons' people in the homeland and abroad as very politically active in the restoration of statehood struggle of the homeland. This activism can be understood using the four ideal types of DuFoix's (2008, pp. 62–65) conceptual framework for thinking about the relationship between dispersed populations and their homelands. These four components of the framework are the centroperipheral mode, the enclaved mode, the atopic mode, and the antagonistic mode.

In the centroperipheral mode, the home state is the controlling force, with links extending between home state and collectivities of the people abroad. The country sponsors a students' group, Cameroon Students Association (CAMSA) in the United States; a political party, Cameroon Peoples Democratic Movement (CPDM-USA); and an annual Cameroon Cultural Festival in Washington DC. Put somewhat differently, the link is also about covert efforts to react to the Southern Cameroons' restoration of statehood conflict in the country by creating the impression abroad that Cameroon Republic (*La Republique du Cameroun*) is one and indivisible and at peace with itself. In May 2010, for example, the country had a high-power delegation going from city to city in the United States to address Cameroonians abroad within the framework of transnational political practices. In 2017, after the conflict escalated, Cameroon Republic also sponsored high-powered delegations to the United States, South Africa, the UK, and Belgium to counter the gains Southern Cameroons' exiles were making abroad to inform the world of the plight of ex-British Southern Cameroons. The country equally sent delegations to world capitals in September 2019 just before the start of the Grand National Dialogue of September–October 2019. These several delegations did not seem to have achieved much in terms of convincing anyone. Ostergaard-Nielsen (2003) defined this concept as "various forms of direct cross-border participation by migrants and refugees in the politics of their country of origin by getting involved in the national cause from a distance."

With regard to the enclaved mode, the people of Southern Cameroons at home and in emigrant collectivities draw on a belief in a common origin, but without any corresponding effort directed toward the home state or state intervention directed toward control. The observation among Southern Cameroons refugees in the diaspora as well as in the territory revealed that while some of the people were bought over (International Crisis Group, 2010) a majority did not consider Cameroon Republic as their home country. There was a clear split within the community in regard to common origin.

In terms of the atopic mode, the emigrant collectivities in the diaspora draw on a belief in a common origin. However, the same kind of mutual suspicion among the populations of ex-French Cameroon and ex-British Cameroons in the territory is carried over into the receiving country.

Concerning the antagonistic mode, the emigrant collectivities draw on a belief in a common origin in order to organize against the home state, thus, flows of ideas, people, and resources extend across the emigrant collectivities in order to apply pressure against the home state. DuFoix (2008, p. 82) also considered the maintenance of a clearly defined link with former citizens as a national priority; one that gradually develops as an important asset, especially at the economic level. Cameroon's link with its diaspora gets beyond the economic level. Increasingly the link gets political. As *Nganglebieu* explained, "The government of La Republique du Cameroun is becoming more and more fearful of the statehood restoration struggle. They are not only using their Embassy connections to reach us, they are sending delegations here to meet people privately and publicly." These efforts of the government of Cameroon Republic to control and manage its diasporas are described by DuFoix's (2008, p. 62) "centroperipheral mode" discussed above through the use of official institutions such as Embassy, consulate, cultural center, and educational establishments.

On the basis of the narratives of British Cameroons' exiles living in the diaspora, it may be difficult not to conceptualize the people of ex-British Southern Cameroons living in the diaspora as "people with the understanding, the power, and the will to influence the evolution of conflict in the homeland" (Horst, 2006, p. 16). The Southern Cameroons diaspora understood their experiences within Cameroon Republic, their history, and its context in International Law. This situation puts into question the making of some postcolonial states considering the numerous incompatibilities within the states. To remedy the conflicts arising from such incompatibilities, Malkki (1995, p. 5) suggested the "need to study the modern system of nation-states not just as a political system narrowly understood, but as a powerful regime of order and knowledge."

It was evident in this study that some of the people of the diaspora appeared to hold irreconcilably opposed positions regarding the future of British Cameroons. In order to account for the divisions among the people of ex-British Southern Cameroons living abroad, the data from this study presented a number of mediating variables. These variables, including aspirations, associations, political history, and reason(s) for leaving the homeland, explain the variance in the attitudes and aspirations among the people living abroad from the same homeland, ex-British Cameroons.

The differences between the main groups of Southern Cameroons' people in the diaspora revealed through the mediating variables from the data indicate that there are two major groups of Southern Cameroons' people in the diaspora, many of whom are living on asylum. While the majority of these people looked forward to a freed Southern Cameroons, renamed Ambazonia, some of the people were either aloof or were involved in working against the restoration of statehood struggle.

Although there are no specific figures to support this assertion, this revelation redirected the study toward an explanation for this unexpected finding.

From the names of many of the people in this group, it became obvious that their forebears were themselves refugees in the Southern Cameroons, who had historically been actively involved in efforts to keep the two Cameroons unified during the 1950s. Although most of the people in this group benefitted from the restoration of statehood struggle to gain asylum abroad, their personal stories did not show that they were persecuted in the territory. I did not continue to look for other differences within Southern Cameroons' diaspora. The explanation for any other differences within the group remains to be explored in future research.

The findings indicated that repression was rampant in the home country, that the people active in the restoration of statehood struggle were the target, and that the economy was also quite dire. My challenge was how to explain why Southern Cameroons' people, who sought and got asylum status abroad, had different attitudes toward the restoration of statehood struggle in their homeland. As I began to analyze the interviews some answers began to emerge. As is often the case in qualitative research studies, the data provided new ways to understand theory. In this research, the data led to a different perspective in understanding the experiences of Southern Cameroons' diaspora in relation to the Southern Cameroons' restoration of statehood struggle. I found many similarities among the Southern Cameroons' diaspora in terms of their dislike of what they termed the "marriage of Southern Cameroons and the Republic of Cameroun," the latter generally referenced in the interviews as *La Republique du Cameroun*, and their experiences in the country. However, there were noticeable dissimilarities in their future expectations and their attitudes and commitments toward the restoration of statehood struggle. One difference that did emerge in the study was the overall perception of the restoration of statehood struggle and the future of Southern Cameroons.

Due to the fact that individuals in the Southern Cameroons' diaspora referred to the difficult circumstances they faced in Cameroon because of their Southern Cameroons' origin, I began to alter my focus from the restoration of statehood conflict itself to personality characteristics of the people. The initial intention of explaining the persistence of the conflict in relation to diaspora experience in the homeland and their immigration history became important. This was a consequence of the division among the people living in the diaspora. Those of them who escaped persecution and those who migrated for non-persecution reasons eventually led to the research-generated concept of the quest for freedom, which I refer to as the freedom urge or "imagined human needs." This concept reflects the perceptions of the people wanting to have the homeland free and "a land they could call home" whether or not they would like to return to it. The concept was useful in explaining the stressful circumstances experienced by the refugees in the home country and hence their urge to see the homeland free to determine its own future.

The people in the diaspora who participated in the research affirmed that they arrived in the diaspora mainly after 1992. Most of them (84 percent planned to return to their homeland when it is liberated. Of the 16 percent who had no plans to return to the homeland, about 12 percent were mainly those who took advantage of the liberation struggle to acquire asylum status in the diaspora. These were among the refugees who had not been involved in the struggle in the homeland in the first place and had not been persecuted. They had left the territory for reasons other than political persecution. The data also revealed that many of the refugees in this group were people whose parents had been French Cameroon refugees in ex-British Southern Cameroons before independence. As did their forebears, this group of the refugees has an interest in seeing Southern Cameroons remain part and parcel of a united Cameroon.

While analyzing the narratives of the people in the diaspora, I discovered there were significant similarities in their perceptions of the liberation conflict. In order to determine if these similarities were typical of the views of the people in the territory, I compared the different stories of the study participants in the diaspora with the stories I recorded in the territory beginning from 2008. The narratives about the lives of the activists in the territory and the arbitrary arrests, detentions, and generalized harassment of sympathizers of the Southern Cameroons' liberation cause were consistent with the narratives of the participants recorded in the diaspora. This finding indicated that refugee status of the people in the diaspora did not significantly influence the stories of the people in the homeland; therefore, the perceptions of the people abroad of the liberation conflict in ex-British Southern Cameroons were not a function of political refugee status in the diaspora. For them the liberation struggle appeared to be so deep-rooted that they would continue to struggle wherever they found themselves.

The research equally revealed that some major leaders of the Southern Cameroons' liberation movements were living in the diaspora as political refugees. The implication here is that refugee status, though essential in humanitarian terms, may also have other undertones. When leaders of a liberation struggle are away from the people they are supposed to be leading, the distance may impact the progress of the cause in any number of ways.

Akonde's story reflected the dominant narrative gathered from informal conversations with most citizens of former French Cameroon. Most citizens of former French Cameroon contend that the people of Southern Cameroons voted in 1961 to unify with La Republique du Cameroun and therefore have no reason to complain. The finding in this study is that the *Two Alternatives* imposed on the territory in 1961—choosing between independence by joining Cameroon or Nigeria—constituted an unwanted choice. By contrast, from the narratives of the people, it was never the intention of the people of

Southern Cameroons to have anything short of independence. The narratives of the people indicate that after obtaining self-rule in 1954, the territory was doing very well politically and economically, such that the news of "independence by joining" was bewildering. *Ntieonwoh (pseudonym)* related this experience in Buea, Southern Cameroons, in 1960.

> I went to Buea in 1960 after I completed Primary School in my village. I went to look for work and learned that there was an impending recruitment into the police force. I had relatives in Buea so I was living with them waiting for the recruitment date. While in Buea, we heard that Foncha, the new Prime Minister, and Dr. Endeley, the defeated Prime Minister who was then Leader of the Opposition had gone to the United Nations for the independence of Southern Cameroons. One day the radio announced that Southern Cameroons would not have her own independence but would have to choose to join Nigeria or Cameroon. People in Buea were not happy about that decision. There were lots of protests in the streets. The relatives I was living with did not like the decision. We did not only join many other people in the streets who were angry at that decision, but also spent long hours in the evening talking about the independence everyone was expecting and asking why the United Nations was treating us differently. People wanted independence, not joining a different country. The spontaneous protests went on for many days. (Interview with the Author, 2015)

This excerpt indicated that the people of Southern Cameroons did not like the "independence by joining" idea from the time it was announced. The wishes of the people notwithstanding, Her Britannic Majesty's Government and the UN went ahead to impose "independence by joining" on the UN Trust Territory of Southern Cameroons. Contrary to the dominant narrative of the government and people of La Republique du Cameroun, the idea of "unification" or "reunification" as promoted by the government of Republique du Cameroun was not desired in Southern Cameroons as the UN document mentioned only "'independence by joining" not "unification" or "reunification."

Another revelation of the research was that the Southern Cameroons' people remained very fragmented in the struggle. This fragmentation among the people, both in the homeland and in the diaspora, but mainly in the diaspora became the singular most significant weakness of the struggle. Although most of the people of the territory remained focused on restoration of statehood as the goal, many of the people seemed to belong to different groupings, which had more allegiance to their respective groupings and movements than to the need for unity in liberating the homeland. The participants were quite certain that their people were cheated out of their independence as a fundamental right. They were most determined to take the struggle to any length. However, most of them were not clear on the details of organizing toward achieving the goal of restoring the statehood to the territory. They were equally not adequately organized as a people fighting a common cause and did not seem to agree on the leadership of the struggle and way forward. Nevertheless, despite the apparent confusion within the ranks and the uncertainty about the leadership and the outcome of the struggle, most of the people gave the impression of being focused on the same goal of restoring the independence and sovereignty of Southern Cameroons.

Similarly, the study revealed that the Southern Cameroons' people in exile had not been able to create any durable infrastructure of political, social, economic, or even educational services, neither in the Southern Cameroons homeland nor elsewhere. Although the desire to achieve the restoration of the statehood remained paramount in the minds of many of the people, that desire remained handicapped by many leaders, organizations, and agendas. These setbacks appeared to be of major importance in the persistent nature of the struggle. It would be a considerable advantage in terms of goals and timing if the people worked toward a unified stance. During the fieldwork, I learned of a group working under the umbrella of "The Way Forward" to articulate the strategic advantage in unity of purpose as a way forward in the struggle but by the time this chapter was written that unity was still very illusive.

The Southern Cameroons' people and the restoration of statehood struggle would benefit from recognition, if they learned to work together to convince the government and people of other countries and, in particular, the different host countries, the African Union, and other multinational organizations of the restoration cause. Most of the people continued to dream about the eventual liberation of their homeland and about returning to the country. If the different people who identified with the different liberation movements could work together in mobilizing, organizing, and channeling their efforts and resources toward the goal of liberation, then the presence of thousands of Southern Cameroons' people abroad could be a major force for the restoration of statehood struggle.

The study also found that the political future of British Southern Cameroons in the 1960s was determined to a large extent by exogenous factors. These were the refugees living in Southern Cameroons from French Cameroon mobilized through the French Cameroon Welfare Union and the Unification Movement. This influence was far-reaching and also continued to impact the persistence of the struggle. The group represented by *Akonde* was either dismissive of the Southern Cameroons' national liberation struggle or worked overtly and covertly against the liberation struggle. After fifty years of the struggle, *Akonde* argued that "The union between the British-administered Southern Cameroons and the Republic of Cameroun has not collapsed. From what I last observed in Cameroon it is thriving, mixing, and growing stronger and stronger each passing day."

Akonde and others like him represented an extension of French Cameroon immigrant population in Southern Cameroons from the 1930s, an immigrant population that always worked hard to unify Cameroon and to keep the country united in order to be together with their people in French Cameroon. It was found out that they were simply reproducing the French Cameroon culture and knowledge that had been in Southern Cameroons since the territory hosted the people as refugees from the 1930s to 1940s.

The research equally revealed that the Southern Cameroons' restoration of statehood struggle had a specific uniqueness in that ex-British Southern Cameroons was more than simply a contiguous territory. The territory had an existence in International Law since 1913, and its boundaries were well-known and recognized historically. In addition, the restoration of Southern Cameroons statehood did not infringe on any of its neighboring countries in that the people of this territory neither laid claim to a drop of water nor an inch of land from her neighbors—the Federal Republic of Nigeria, La Republique du Cameroun, and Equatorial Guinea. As the people in the study emphasized, the restoration of statehood struggle was about restoring the statehood of a country, statehood lost in October 1961 as a result of exogenous factors, including the activism of French Cameroonians living as refugees in Southern Cameroons. Among the Western powers, there was a further fear of a perceived communist influence emerging in West Central Africa within the Cold War framework.

Yet another revelation of the research was that the Internet and the cellular phone were new and major forms of empowerment in the restoration of statehood struggle. Not generally intending to remain in the diaspora for the rest of their lives, the people of the territory living abroad were eager to see their homeland liberated so they could return home. Their transnational lives continued to foster the struggle as they could militate safely from the diaspora with the new tools and in the new space. These tools were not only very safe but also readily available to them in the different countries of residence and facilitated contact with activists and fighters in the homeland and around the world. From their narratives, it was evident that these new technologies were also exceptionally helpful to their people in the homeland. There the repressive ability of government forces was virtually overtaken in that it became unable to stall or disrupt Southern Cameroons' groups from planning and organizing meetings. Specifically, hi-tech communication devices presented a unique opportunity for the struggle. These devices helped the people to beat a repressive government in terms of organizing, idea development, and exchange, and meetings without the threat from "*La Republique du Cameroun's colonial agents.*" The Internet and cellular phones therefore became invaluable tools or spaces for political mobilization. Uninhibited, Southern Cameroons' people living in the diaspora were able to exchange ideas with the homeland and other de-territorialized activists engaged in the restoration struggle.

Another interpretation of the narratives collected for the study was that the Southern Cameroons' restoration of statehood conflict had its own unique context compared with other similar conflicts. The Southern Cameroons' restoration of statehood conflict was not a minority conflict in La Republique du Cameroun as some people wanted to depict it. It was not a religious conflict as some other conflicts in other parts of the world. It was also not a conflict over any disputed territory. Unlike many other intractable identity conflicts, the Southern Cameroons' restoration of independence and sovereignty conflict was not even an ideological struggle. Rather, it was singularly about the freedom rights of a people. It was primarily a case of a self-governing people, with recognized international boundaries in history, who felt cheated out of their right to sovereign independence, annexed and colonially occupied by another former UN Class B Trust Territory. The native population was involved in the struggle to restore the statehood and independence of the homeland in accordance with the UN Charter in its Article 76(B), the UN Trusteeship Agreement, and the 1960 UNGA Resolution 1608 on the Declaration on the independence of colonial countries and peoples. It was the case of a people asserting their fundamental right to be masters of their own future, based on their history and based on International Law.

The sovereign independence of any people with territory recognized under International Law is an inherent and inalienable right, not a privilege. The study revealed that this understanding of human rights and the reliance on the concept of human rights established the basis on which the national restoration of statehood struggle was founded; the reality, however, was at considerable variance. The application of that concept in the case of the Southern Cameroons was not what the people had envisioned in the restoration of statehood struggle. This finding appeared to be a major factor in the persistence of the conflict. The people of Southern Cameroons found it difficult to understand why the issue of their "human rights" did not appear to be acknowledged in the West, principally by the UK and the UN. These powerful actors in global affairs did not seem to perceive the restoration of statehood struggle as founded on human rights principles and on the principles of the UN. From a Western perspective, human rights apparently referred mainly to the rights of individuals rather than to groups and peoples.

PERCEPTIONS OF THE STATEHOOD STRUGGLE

The indigenous people of British Southern Cameroons and the descendants of French Cameroon refugees living in the territory of British Southern Cameroons differed drastically in their perceptions of Southern Cameroons and the territory's restoration of statehood struggle. The refugees whose parents were immigrants in Southern Cameroons from French Cameroon viewed the struggle as "secessionist" and as a vain effort that needed to be discouraged or crushed. As most other people of French Cameroon origin, they perceived the Southern Cameroons as part and parcel of a "one and indivisible" Republique du Cameroun and had no qualms with the flag with one star. For them the restoration of statehood struggle was the work of "a handful of disgruntled Anglophones who wanted to go away with the oil wealth in the territory." After the struggle escalated in 2016 and became violent in 2017, the struggle was perceived as "terrorism" and as "the work of bandits who had to be killed for peace and calm to return." This perception resulted in the decades-long denial by the government of Republique du Cameroun of an "Anglophone Problem" in Republique du Cameroun.

On the other hand, the indigenous people of Southern Cameroons in the homeland and in the diaspora, including those who did not think the restoration of statehood project was feasible, viewed the struggle in the light of International Law by a former UN Trust Territory. For them, the struggle was always about the decision of a self-governing people to restore its independence and sovereignty as a right. As Akendong (pseudonym) narrated,

We are only asking La Republique du Cameroun to withdraw to her boundaries at independence in accordance with Article 4 of the Constitutive Act of the African Union. We are asking the world to help us complete the decolonization of our country because the remedy to colonization is decolonization.

One other participant, Fuabenyong, expressed this vision as follows:

We, Children of Ambazonia Republic or Southern Cameroons, have nothing at stake against Biya to demand his removal; the politics of the governance of la Republique du Cameroun do not concern our people; we want Cameroun to pull out of our country and respect our country as their equals as even the status of the Trusteeship Territorial agreement to which we were by far more superior--being a democracy and having changed government peacefully even before the fateful Plebiscite which Cameroun authorities cling on like dying snakes. (Interview with the Author, 2015)

The differences in perception remained consistently present among the people, constituting a major factor in the evolution of the struggle as the differences in perceptions affected the aspiration of the people of the territory. Because of the split among the people, the conflict dragged on in the shadows as it continued to simmer without any end in sight even after the escalation in 2016 and a violent genocidal war from 2017. The believers in the restoration of statehood struggle continued to tenaciously pursue restoration to force La Republique du Cameroun to negotiate.

The people of Southern Cameroons in the diaspora including the descendants of French Cameroon refugees gained asylum status in the diaspora on the basis of the restoration of statehood struggle but viewed the future of Southern Cameroons differently. The majority of the people wanted to see their homeland liberated so that they could determine what happened to their people and how a homeland of their own would be built. Others, mainly the descendants of refugees from French Cameroon, did not view the restoration of the statehood of Southern Cameroons positively. Both groups worked independently in their respective organizations to further their goals. In the United States, for instance, instead of furthering the cause on which they claimed asylum, the descendants of French Cameroon refugees in Southern Cameroons, specifically associated in the United States mainly with other immigrants from their tribal origins in former French Cameroon, such as the *Bassa* Group, the *Nde* Group, the *Bafang* Group, and others. The Bamileke ethnic groups all flocked behind the group referred to as the *anti sardinards (BAS)* which supported presidential candidate Kamto and his ideas about Republique du Cameroun.

EXILES WITH DIFFERENT COMMITMENTS

In looking closely at the narratives of Southern Cameroons' people and their activism toward the Southern Cameroons' restoration of statehood struggle, I noticed changes in their disposition toward restoration and activism in the struggle. Upon arrival in the diaspora, they started out extremely committed to the struggle, especially when they realized that they needed the struggle to obtain asylum status. Many of these individuals began by militating with friends and learning about the struggle. Some were very committed from the outset, like *Nkwarre* and *Tema,* who arrived in the United States via Germany. These two study participants increasingly became more active as they realized the availability of meetings, demonstrations opportunities, and tools like the Internet, which allowed them to interact easily with others. Above all, there was no government surveillance followed by arrests and detentions as were the cases in the homeland.

Over the months of the fieldwork, *Nkwarre* regularly attended meetings with his American girlfriend. Others, like *Ecila,* a resident of Bowie, Maryland, stated that she was committed to the struggle, yet demonstrated little commitment after she obtained asylum status—especially after her husband and child joined her from Cameroon. Two of their children were already in the country as international students. She was easily drawn away from the struggle and rarely attended any meetings. She no longer spoke about the struggle even though she and her family were living in Maryland, which remained the main hub of the struggle in the United States.

Akonde, one other participant in the sample, was one of those who did not demonstrate any significant change in commitment or attitude toward the restoration of statehood struggle. He came to the United States via South Africa to meet his mother and younger brother, who already had asylum status. He was in his early thirties and had been in the country for six years by the time the struggle escalated into a genocidal war. His mother, a descendant of the refugees from French Cameroon who settled in Southern Cameroons in the 1940s, had arrived earlier and had filed for asylum for her children. When *Akonde* and his brother arrived as minors, they did not need to apply for asylum again as they were already included in their mother's file. For that reason he had no reason to be committed to a struggle, which his mother and her people had opposed. He had come to the United States mainly to join his mother and to seek a livelihood. *Akonde* began his American experience by joining the American military, as he had no intention of ever returning to Cameroon.

Contrary to *Akonde, Ecila,* and others like them, most new asylum seekers in the diaspora were committed to the struggle because they (a) wanted to remain active in the struggle that had sent them fleeing from their homeland; (b) they found it was much safer to be involved in the struggle without being harassed, more so with the ready availability of facilities like the Internet; and (c) they realized that in the new country there were ample opportunities to improve their lives.

Unlike *Akonde and Ecila, Ngongmenda* was very aware of and unambiguous about her attitude and commitment to the struggle. As a student in the homeland, she could hardly attend a youth meeting in which the struggle was discussed without risking arrest and detention by the security forces that were everywhere and who scrutinized the movements of students. Back in the home country, the Internet was available but was very costly and very slow. Money was hard to come by, and even when one had a little money, computer availability was sparse, the connections were slow. There were usually long lines of people waiting to access the Internet at different cybercafés in different towns in the territory.

Upon arrival in the United States, *Ngongmenda* noticed that computers were freely available in public libraries. If an asylum seeker enrolled at some academic institution, there was guaranteed access to an abundant supply of computers in good working condition. In addition, she soon recognized it was comparatively easy to earn money abroad if the individual was willing to work hard at any available employment. The cellular phone, another necessity for the struggle, was also affordable. In the homeland there were almost no jobs, even if the individual wanted to work, and so money was scarce. Encouraged by the availability of work, money, phones, and the Internet, and freedom from harassment, *Ngongmenda* became increasingly committed to the restoration of the statehood of Southern Cameroons. These opportunities instilled the incentive to achieve the ultimate goal of the restoration of state-hood of the homeland so she could return to her parents, who were elderly and in declining health.

The narratives of the people and the fieldwork experience in the territory beginning in 2008 indicated that the people had different levels of commit-ment to the Southern Cameroons' restoration of statehood struggle. Most of them fully embraced the struggle, some stayed aloof, and others demonstrated oppositional forms of behavior toward the idea of a separate Southern Camer-oons' existence and the struggle toward that goal. The understanding of peo-ple as subjects with different commitments to the struggle of the homeland departed from most traditional literature in identity studies. The information in this study focused on the conflict context in the homeland and the percep-tions and activism of the people, particularly on the specific circumstances of conflict that forced the exiles to flee. Previous experience in the homeland influenced and reshaped the behavior and activism of the people.

The research results pointed to the interrelationship between the specific circumstances in the restoration of statehood conflict and the activism of the people both in the homeland and in the diaspora. In a departure from past research, rather than focus on the inequities between labor-exporting low-wage countries and labor-importing high-wage countries (Brettell, 2008, p. 119), the research looked at the effects that the homeland environment had on the people's activism both in the homeland and in the diaspora. This perspective differentiated from understanding the people living in the dias-pora as "helpless individuals from countries devastated by war, littered with mines, infested with disease . . . with little infrastructure, and few resources" (Mayotte, 1992, p. 7).

FREEDOM URGE AMONG SOUTHERN CAMEROONS' PEOPLE

The freedom urge has a direct influence on the way subjugated people under-stand the world and behave toward it. This subjective understanding of the world was referred to as the colonial habitus or the urge to be free. I argued in the study that Bourdieu's perspectives on habitus were still relevant in explaining a people's emotions within a subjugated context.

Zolberg (1985, p. 30) referred to national sovereignty and victim groups caught up in nation-state formations. These groups and peoples are viewed as "capable people who struggle for control over their lives" (Mayotte, 1992, p. 5). Nyers (2006, p. xvii) also explained political refugees as human beings who "are everywhere demonstrating agency." By striking out "to reclaim their identity, voice, and presence" as Nyers (2006, p. 35) asserted, subjugated people seek to free themselves and their homeland from the colonizing constraints of the box in which they find themselves.

The concept of freedom urge used in this chapter also covered the mindset and distinct set of values guiding the rejection or resistance prevalent among the subjugated people of British Southern Cameroons. By calling it freedom urge, I emphasized not only the normative aspect of anti-colonialism within the global system, but foremost, the ethical demands embedded in the 1948 Universal Declaration of Human Rights. Other vital UN proclamations, declarations, and resolutions, including Article 76(b) of the UN Charter (the basic objective of the Trusteeship System), and UN General Assembly Resolution 1514 of December 14, 1960, enjoining all imperial and colonial powers to grant independence to colonial peoples reiterate this obligation.

The people of British Southern Cameroons who embraced the urge for freedom and the type of activism indicating a longing to be free from perceived bondage did not only develop those forms of behavior in the homeland but also brought them to the diaspora. Even among those of them still struggling to survive in the different host countries in the Americas, Europe, Asia, and Africa, there was a continued articulation of the need for the homeland to be decolonized. Attending group meetings and taking part in different activities of the liberation movements revealed the urge in the people to liberate the homeland. For those who already had established employment in their respective professions in the United States, Europe, and elsewhere abroad, the data revealed that the majority of these Southern Cameroons' people did not really enjoy being in the respective host countries. The financial compensation for the work they did while in the diaspora was good, but they retained the projection that they would rather be back in the homeland among their own people, advancing a country they knew and called theirs.

The situation of the people of Southern Cameroons living in exile was consistent with and further explained the image of many Africans living abroad. According to Toyin Falola in *USA-Africa Dialogues* (2009, p. 13),

> The vast majority of Sub-Saharan Africans who lived outside of the continent were in exile either self-imposed or forced by the prevailing conditions in the continent. These African immigrants realized that the longer they stayed in exile, the deeper their pain and their agony. They might have big cars and big homes; they might have beautiful wives and successful children; and they might also have investment portfolios that are the envy of most. Yet, most did feel empty.

The concept of the urge for freedom in the people of British Southern Cameroons both in the territory and abroad explained the interrelationship between the homeland context in which they lived or that forced them out and the continuing activism in the desire to liberate their country.

Previous literature, including work by Kottig et al. (2009), focused on the side of individuals content to be in exile. Some authors apparently did not recognize the fact that many people in exile yearn to have a home country of their own where they can live in safety and dignity. This research presented the perspectives of people living in the homeland or abroad who were educated and trained, who came from a homeland with its own resources, and wanted to restore the independence of that homeland. As victims of subjugation caused by external powers and interests, they sought to achieve the liberation of their homeland as a fundamental right, a human need, and a source of the territory's dignity and empowerment. Rather than feel content with life in a homeland annexed and colonially occupied or in forced exile, they remained active in the struggle in the homeland to which the people hoped to return and to call their home.

CONCLUSION

The initial objective of the research leading to this chapter was to develop a broader understanding of the perceptions and activism of the people of British Southern Cameroons—a people who refused to remain in colonial bondage forever. Transferred at independence in 1961 by the UK (Trustee) and the UN (Trustor) to the Republique du Cameroun and France contrary to UNGA Resolution 1514 of 1960 and the provisions of the 1946 UN Trusteeship Agreement, the people refused, after half a century, to remain passive subjects of the political and historical circumstances which they neither sought nor created, and which they understood and wanted to change. For this reason, they are perceived as a porcupine stuck in the throat of a python that tried to swallow it without traces. From understanding the situation of British Southern Cameroons in La Republique du Cameroun and the complex colonial occupation involved through the narratives of the people, the lesson was drawn that the situation would require the services of a very skillful surgeon to save both the porcupine and the python.

From the data collected and analyzed, many of the people considered their homeland a suppressed nation-state. They considered the people of the territory as a subjugated group deprived of its freedom at independence in 1961 by the UK and the UN. They perceived the national struggle as a means of liberating their homeland. For them their conflict case was unique in the world as there was no other country in history whose independence was voted at the UN General Assembly with sixty-four Yes votes, twenty-three No votes, and ten Abstentions that failed to gain complete independence.

The people continued to search for a meaningful explanation for the situation the UN characterized as "Independence by Joining" as a follow up to UN Resolution 1608 of April 1961. At the same time, their belief in freedom and optimism was tempered by several obstacles. In pursuing the freedom goal, they conflicted with a Cameroon Republic national government that did not recognize their struggle even after a war of independence broke out in 2017 and an international community that paid no attention to their petitions and the subsequent genocidal war.

As a community, there also existed many divisions among the people of British Southern Cameroons. While some of the people were outraged about their colonial subjugation and sought total independence in the spirit of Timor, Eritrea, and Namibia, there continued to be a nonchalant attitude prevalent among some within the same community. Despite the divide and conquer strategy of the government in using some of the people to fight the rest, and despite the genocide and the overwhelming suffering of the people in the war especially after 2017, they remained adamant that the restoration of statehood was the only acceptable solution to the conflict.

Throughout the study that resulted in this chapter, I used as theoretical framework a combination of works in peace and conflict studies, human needs theory, and diaspora studies. Some of these research studies by Burton (1984, 1987, 1990), Galtung (1989), Nyers (2006), and Doyal and Gough (1991) contended that all human beings have an inherent right to the optimum satisfaction of their needs. Nyers (2006, p. 99), for example, questioned "whether individuals and collectives forced to flee their home countries were capable of being highly conscious and political rather than just passive and dependent." More importantly, Nyers contended that "these groups are driven by the survival instinct but still remained active." In the analysis of scholars including Doyal and Gough, Burton, and Galtung, the needs of all human beings are fundamentally the same. They argued that basic human needs could be shown to exist, that people have a right to the optimal satisfaction of these needs, and that all human liberation should be measured by assessing the degree to which such satisfaction had occurred.

According to Doyal and Gough (1991, p. 3), there are "universal human goals which people must achieve if they are to optimize their life chances" and "when people express outrage at injustice, somewhere in the background is the belief that basic human needs exist which should have been satisfied but were not." This human need framework remained the basis upon which the people of British Southern Cameroons interpreted events around them both at home and in exile. The human need framework constituted the basis on which we should understand their activism and the resolve in the restoration of statehood war the people fought against the annexation and colonial occupation of the former UN Trust Territory of British Southern Cameroons.

As a suppressed nation and a subjugated people deprived of freedom and statehood, the people of British Southern Cameroons perceived the struggle as a means of their liberation. In contrast to the people of other former colonies, Southern Cameroons' people imagined and fantasized about their freedom based on their understanding of the past experience of life as a self-governing people and territory between 1954 and 1961. Since they saw their forced union with La Republique du Cameroun in 1961 as the source of the occupation and subjugation of their homeland, and as the reason for their forced emigration and refugee status in the diaspora, the struggle for them remained the only alternative. Of the participants interviewed, many based the struggle for an independent Southern Cameroons on International Law and history, and particularly on the UN Charter in Article 76(b), the UN Trusteeship Agreement, and UN General Assembly Resolution 1514 (XV) of 1960. As Tantang (pseudonym) narrated:

> It is not contested that Southern Cameroons is a state recognized as such in International Law. The Southern Cameroons fulfilled the legal criteria of State-hood spelt out in the 1932 Montevideo Convention on Rights and Duties of States. Article 1 of the said Convention states: The State as a person of International Law should possess the following qualifications: a permanent population, a defined territory, a government, and the capacity to enter into relations with other states. That the Southern Cameroons possessed these qualifications is no longer subject of reasonable controversy, regard had to be made to the fact that the UN through its Resolutions affirmed her exercise of the right of self-determination through a well-conceived procedure with full UN participation, that was to commence with a UN organized Plebiscite and ending with an Internationally recognized union treaty with La Republique du Cameroun. That process, we all know, was aborted and so no treaty worthy of recognition and enforcement pursuant to articles 102 and 103 of the UN Charter exists between Southern Cameroons and La Republique du Cameroun. It is therefore futile for anyone to invoke alleged historical or political arguments to justify the existence of any union between the two, without first ascertaining whether the UN-laid down basis for the existence of a legally binding treaty was executed or faithfully implemented pursuant to the Charter responsibilities of all the parties involved. (Interview with the Author, 2015)

One may glean from this excerpt that the Southern Cameroons was a legal entity, prior to the *"annexation"* of her territory in October 1961. Tantang maintained that "The territory had her own executive and legislative organs, conducted foreign relations through her own organs, had her own system of courts and legal system, had her own nationality laws, and above all, had her own constitution." This participant concluded that Southern Cameroons had "internationally recognized boundaries and was the very first nation in Sub-Saharan Africa to organize elections transparently and democratically and to transition administrations peacefully in 1959." The participant was adamant that he did not understand any solution short of achieving the independence of British Southern Cameroons. In this resolve of a Southern Cameroons' statehood restored, the participant imagined Southern Cameroons as "a porcupine that a python tried to swallow. It got stuck in its throat. A careful surgeon will be needed. If not, both the porcupine and the python will not survive because the porcupine cannot be swallowed. There is no other way out" this study participant pointed out with some vigor.

REFERENCES

Aka, E. A. (2002). *The British Southern Cameroons, 1922–1960: A Study in Colonialism and Underdevelopment*. Platteville, WI: Nkemnji Global Tech.

Brettell, C. (2008). Immigrants as Netizens: Political Mobilization in Cyberspace. In Reed-Danahay, D., & Bretell, Caroline B. (Eds.), *Citizenship, Political Engagement, and Belonging: Immigrants in Europe and the United States*. New Brunswick: Rutgers University Press, p. 119.

Burton, J. W. (1984). *Global Conflict: The Domestic Sources of International Crisis*. Brighton, England: Wheatsheaf Books.

Burton, J. W. (1987). *Resolving Deep-Rooted Conflict: A Handbook*. New York: University Press of America.

Burton, J. W. (1990). *Conflict: Human Needs Theory*. New York: St Martin's Press.

Chaitin, J. (2004). My Story, My Life, My Identity. *International Journal of Qualitative Methods* 3(4). University of Alberta.

Doyal, L., & Gough, I. (1991). *A Theory of Human Need*. New York: The Guilford Press.

DuFoix, S. (2008). *Diasporas*. Berkeley: University of California Press.

Falola, T. (2009). *USA-Africa Dialogues Series*. Austin: University of Texas.

Field, J. O. (1958). *Introduction to the Southern Cameroons*. Lagos: Federal Information Service.

Galtung, J. (1989). *Solving Conflicts: A Peace Research Perspective*. Honolulu, HI: University of Hawaii Institute for Peace.

Gwang Gumne, et al. (2009). Mgwanga Gunme v. Cameroon, Comm. 266/2003, 26th ACHPR AAR Annex (December 2008–May 2009).

Horst, H., & Miller, D. (2006). *The Cell Phone: An Anthropology of Communication*. London: Routledge.

International Crisis Group. (2010). *Crise anglophone au Cameroun: comment arriver aux pourparlers.*

Kottig, M., Chaitin, J., Linstroth, J. P., & Rosenthal, G. (2009). Preface: Biography and Ethnicity: Development and Changes in Sense of Socio-Cultural Belonging in Migrant Population in the US and Germany. *Forum: Qualitative Social Research* 10(3). https://doi.org/10.17169/fqs-10.3.1380

Lambek, M. (2002). *The Weight of the Past: Living With History in Mahajanga, Madasgascar*. London: Palgrave Macmillan.

Linstroth J. P. (2009). Mayan Cognition, Memory and Trauma. *History and Anthropology* 20(2): 139–182.

Malkki, L. H. (1995). *Purity and Exile: Violence, Memory, And National Cosmology Among Hutu Refugees in Tanzania*. Chicago: The University of Chicago Press.

Mayotte, J. A. (1992). *Disposable People: The Plight of Refugees*. New York.

Nyers, P. (2006). *Rethinking Refugees: Beyond States of Emergency*. New York: Routledge.

Ostergaard-Nielsen, E. (2003). The Politics of Migrants' Transnational Political Practices. *International Migration Review* 37(3).

Zolberg, A. R. (1985). The Formation of New States as a Refugee-Generating process. *The Annals of the American Academy of Political and Social Science* 467 (May).

Chapter 8

Daily Eaten Alive

A Gruesome Genocide by a Military Occupation of the Southern Cameroons

Rev. Fr. Gerald Jumbam

The context in which we find ourselves here in the midst of the UN Rapporteur on Minority Issues (Dr. Fernand de Varennes) is understood, but it would be difficult to concede to the idea that the Southern Cameroons is a minority. Can we call a territory that in history has had a parliament, prime ministers, and defined international territorial boundaries as a minority? Can we in all sincerity reduce it to just a demographic minority? We are a people, the Southern Cameroon peoples, and therefore self-determination is our business.

A West African proverb says that he who does not know where the rain began to beat him cannot say where he dried his body. The rain of military occupation that beat the Southern Cameroons began sixty years ago. That is counting from October 1, 1961, the day the independence of the territory and its people was stolen through the 1972 dismantling of the two-state federation of equal partners, to President Paul Biya's outright declaration of war on the peace-loving peoples of the Southern Cameroons on November 30, 2017. This sinister declaration that would culminate into a vicious genocide would be the first in our parts of the world since the Biafran civil war to render a defenseless Southern Cameroons people one of the world's endangered oppressed people in postcolonial Africa.

The Southern Cameroons never had an army. Throughout the Mandate and Trusteeship periods before 1961, some Nigerian policemen were deployed mainly in Buea, the capital of the Southern Cameroons renamed Ambazonia. Generally, each community in the Southern Cameroons had its local "police," what was called Native Authority police. In the days of West Cameroon, that is, the period of their federation with French Cameroun, the Buea government established a police force. But it was not armed. The policeman had a whistle and a baton stick. Even when the armed Mobile Wing Police was created, it was a special unit that remained in the barracks and was deployed only on special duty in some trouble spots, especially in border areas with French Cameroun where the "*maquisards*" from there tried to use the West Cameroon (Southern Cameroons) border areas as rear bases. So, our people generally never experienced armed security officials. They were used to civil policing imbued with a high sense of discipline, integrity, and respect for basic human rights. This armless innocent and defenseless nature of these peoples came as a result of their education. During colonial days under the British, it was the missionaries, most especially the Catholics, Baptists, and Presbyterians, who were in charge of education. The British colonial masters never set up even one single college for the people. And so education in the territory was education with a human and spiritual face, Christian education to state it differently. The people of Southern British Cameroons never experienced any incident of violence by security officers.

The policeman in the Southern Cameroons was a peace officer and a friend of the people. The only time the people of the Southern Cameroons saw armed soldiers was when the United Kingdom government deployed a battalion of the British army to ensure security during the plebiscite of February 1961. The British army built and was housed in three camps (built with prefab)—one in Buea, one in Mamfe, and a third in Bamenda. The British army was withdrawn from the Southern Cameroons immediately after the plebiscite.

So, when following the de facto political association with French Cameroun on October 1, 1961, the oppressing government of French Cameroun took three measures within the first week of October 1961. These measures were very traumatic for the people of the Southern Cameroons. First, French Cameroun moved armed troops into the Southern Cameroons and housed them in the very emergency camps British troops had built and vacated. The armed troops from French Cameroun were experienced by the people of the Southern Cameroons up till today as a foreign army of occupation. They spoke and continued to speak only in French even by 2023 (meaning they cannot communicate with the people). What they do is that they rough-handle and mistreat the people on the slightest pretext, and they are armed and ever-present and take pride in intimidating the people. They assume an air of superiority and conduct themselves as an out-and-out army of occupation.

They routinely carry out violent cordon and search operations (for what the people knew not) during which the people are severely abused and treated like prisoners of war. They also set up roadblocks every few kilometers along the highway for checking "*laissez-passer*" and "*carte d'identité*" and other documents as it pleases them to ask. Non-presentation of any document requested is punishable by torture and imprisonment. What I present here is about over half a century-long experience of a defenseless people in the hands of the Cameroun military.

Second, the repressive Yaoundé government decreed a state of emergency over the whole of the Southern Cameroons. The state of emergency was for an indefinite period since it was renewable ad infinitum every six months. The state of emergency decree introduced detention camps called "*les Centres d' Internement Administratif.*" These were detention camps for those declared to be "dangerous to public security." They were not different from Hitler's Gestapo camps.

Third, six months later, in March 1962, Yaoundé decreed a Subversion Ordinance which criminalized a wide range of ill-defined conduct and shielded the regime and its members from any form of criticism whatsoever. In this way, the French Cameroun's system and practice of torture were introduced in the Southern Cameroons. Torture facilities known as BMM centers (brigade mixte mobile centers) were established in Victoria, Kumba, Mamfe, and Bamenda. The favorite torture techniques were the "*balancoire*" and the "*courant*"—a stand sort of device for suspending victims after they have been tied up like animals; they are made to swing on this device as they are subjected to merciless beating; often too, the passage of electrical current through the body of the victim, the points of application being the armpits, the genitalia, the eyelids, and other such very sensitive areas. The emergency decree and the subversion decree were arbitrarily enforced by newly created military tribunals from which there was no appeal.

In May 1972, French Cameroun illegally decreed the federation out of existence and formally annexed the Southern Cameroons. This action was met with continuing protests by the people of the Southern Cameroons. French Cameroun responded by drafting more of its troops to occupy the Southern Cameroons with orders to shoot to kill. From June 1972 to 1989, incidents of military killing of Southern Cameroons' civilians gradually escalated.

Another peak point was the period of the launching of multiparty politics (animated by the political consciousness of the people of Southern Cameroons), that is, after the launching of the Social Democratic Front party in May 1990. In 2016, the people of the Southern Cameroons rose again like one man to protest against repression, occupation, and colonization. The response from French Cameroun was the dispatching of more troops into the Southern Cameroons with orders again to shoot and to kill. Widespread killings by these occupation troops were carried out with impunity. The Yaoundé regime encouraged and glorified these killings by its troops in the occupied territory of the Southern Cameroons.

It was in November 2017 that armed conflict broke out between the Southern Cameroons and French Cameroun when the latter declared war on the former and poured thousands and thousands of troops and war material into the

Southern Cameroons. The occupation was tightened. It entailed more and more widespread killing and destruction and occasioned hundreds of thousands of refugee and Internally Displaced Persons (IDP) flows. I thought of a suitable image to depict the predicament of the people of the Southern Cameroons. What came to my mind, the best metaphor to describe the brutal unbearable nature of military occupation of the French Cameroun over the Southern Cameroons (Ambazonia) as I searched my mind, would be that of *Kinfa'fa'ai*—the poisonous wasp—a notorious predator of the insect family. In the African lore and reality, the sting of a wasp goes with an agonizing, paralyzing bite that lay eggs on the human body, which then proceed to "eat the victim alive." The occupying military forces of French Cameroun have transformed themselves into the personification of *Kinfa'nfa'ai*. Our poor innocent people are daily eaten alive, to say the least, by the Cameroun Republic's military forces. Humanitarian crisis after four years, contrary to the underestimated figures given by international humanitarian institutions and organizations, the real situation of the humanitarian crisis, progressively deteriorated with about:

- ❖ 15,000 deaths
- ❖ 5,000 detainees
- ❖ 400 burned villages
- ❖ 500,000 refugees scattered in various countries, especially Nigeria
- ❖ 2 million internally displaced persons
- ❖ 800,000 children deprived of the right to education.

In four years, the bloody confrontations that broke out in the Southern Cameroons shocked the conscience of the international community, though they refused to become part of the resolution of this problem thus facilitating the despot and oppressor to do his mayhem and go completely free. The silence is deafening especially from international bodies and the media. The affected people must not be scared by the enormity of the task and by the immorality of the present. I call on the international human rights bodies, the African Union and the United Nations Organization (UNO), to play fair. After all the problem at its roots is the failure of the United Kingdom and the UNO to grant full independence to a nation that was supposed to be one.

But the annexation of our people into mental and moral bondage has not augured well for our people. The fear of pain and suffering is no longer the problem, it is the struggle for survival that rules the minds of our people, for this wild and barbaric occupation has been a thing so terrible and despicable that the word "genocide" is only a figure of speech. And this evokes consequences beyond what we have imagined. The genocide has inflicted untold suffering on the people. The explosion of psychosomatic illnesses, violent bouts of anger, literal madness, and depressions of a level little known in the world are only a few consequences. They have been the storybook fatalities of a cultural carnage. Since the biblical story of Cain and Abel history has not inflicted on a people such brotherly betrayal as that in the Southern Cameroons and their so-called brothers of the Cameroon Republic. Indeed, we bear the blisters of brotherhood in an idiotic marriage inflicted on our people by the United Kingdom (trustee) and the United Nations (trustor). I can liken the infamous union only to one between a lamb and a lion.

The moral illness is a weakening of faith in a moral international institution like the United Nations that has let down our people and that has not only passed unnoticed the wounded man in the biblical Good Samaritan parable but that seems to enable and encourage the oppressors of our people. History is our great teacher as Ruanda is still fresh in our minds. Military occupations are an act of moral cowardice on the part of the malignant oppressor, especially in the 21st century where true power is displayed on the dialogue and debate table. For if the government of the French Cameroun knew that its presence in the Southern Cameroons is legitimate, why is the area being militarized? They know very well that the people's hearts had long left Yaoundé.

All that militarization is a clear indication that the annexing power knows that its days are numbered. It is important to underline here that I am deeply involved in this independent struggle because my family has been a victim of the struggle. The example of my biological father has inspired the whole family to choose the painful path of being the awakened conscience of our people—so my whole family is pointedly involved, more because they have been helpless victims of the bestial military occupation. I would betray my conscience if I back down for I am firmly convinced that a true apostle of Christ must embrace, in the manner of Christ himself, the preferential option for the poor, the oppressed, and the vulnerable of this world. Consequently, we are nearly all in exile because of our outspokenness.

My parents are wanted people, wanted by the barbaric political powers of Cameroun Republic, and my life, since 2016, is in the balance, because it has received threats. My father left for Nigeria in 1997 in exile and later joined us in neighboring French Cameroun in Douala for another 15 years of exile. So am in Italy enjoying the freedom I have never had in my entire life. I was already considered dangerous by the Cameroun Government because I was already in newspapers and the radio touching on issues concerning the country's moral soul. There I already had ambitions to be a writer. Since writers name the unnamable, that is, to express what other people fear to say as Salman Rushdie wrote in his novel *The Satanic Verses*, writing became my own weapon against the despicable ethical and political situation of that country.

The Dantean *Inferno*, the hell of the Southern Cameroons today is abysmal. And the betrayal is not only external, but it is deep within the revolution.

The pain is that some people of Southern Cameroons origin have decided to not only want the enjoyment of the fleshpots of Egypt, but they are bent on pooling the suffering people of Southern Cameroons aka Ambazonia back to slavery. They have turned to saboteurs of the revolution. Or like some did recently rely on tainted information of a proud people and withdraw into a life of austere examination in search of masturbatory assistance by resorting, ostrich-like, to material from victims and the oppressed to paint the story of the oppressed people dark and to give victory to the oppressor. It's unfortunate that some chiefs, Fons, imams, and ecclesiastical figures have sadly been victims of such betrayal.

We have discovered painfully that no one can speak for us. And so, our people are ready for anything, to gain their independence. Only those who daily live through the humiliations, the third-class citizenships of the world, in the slaughterhouse of bondage, only we can fully figure out and see the sights of these inconsistencies in a world experiencing such speedy and puzzling changes.

No one can suppress the truth. Colonialism is a crime against humanity, an international evil, and an evil which has been condemned by all nations of the world including the UNO. And when the colonizing power turns out to be one's own brother as it were, it is even more disgraceful. The Southern Cameroons is a territory with well-defined boundaries, and its independence was hijacked or stolen in 1961. As long as the occupying forces of the Republic of Cameroun continue to do what they know is wrong, the people of the Southern Cameroons (Ambazonia) will continue to struggle. As God is always on the side of the truth, I have no doubt whatsoever that the Southern Cameroons would achieve its goal of a fully independent state.

Chapter 9

Blood, Tears, and the Keyboard

Women's Participation in the Southern Cameroons' Conflict

Lilian Lem Atanga

Blood, Tears, and the keyboard have characterized women's participation in the armed struggle in the Southern Cameroons for the past five years. This is a direct consequence of the armed struggle, born of a teachers' and layers' strike that degenerated leaving the people in death and strife, and forcing women's participation in the conflict in multi-varied ways. The multiple killings by the state army, especially the BIR, and the non-state armed groups, the Amba boys, spilling blood on the streets and in homes, left women in tears who then took over their keyboards to denounce the violence and call for peace.

In writing this chapter, as one of these women with personal experiences, I struggled with myself as an Anglophone woman from the Southern Cameroons Ambazonia, officially from the North West Region. Such a description will earn me different appreciations from different groups of people depending on their political orientation either as a black leg to the "Amba boys" or a "terrorist" to the government. Yet I am a woman, like many women in these regions who are caught up in war.

Born in the 1970s, I used these identity words intentionally as one who has lived through the years of the Federal Republic of Cameroon, a then two-state federation born of the Southern Cameroons and the Republic of Cameroon. The Southern Cameroons itself was born of the British Southern Cameroons. These two nations, the former UN Class B Trust Territory and La Republique du Cameroun, were born of the German Kamerun (see Ngoh 1996; Takougang and Amin 2018). And before that my ancestors were Bafut, my *ala'a* (country), Tikars who migrated southward from the Sudanic regions of Africa. In 1972 the "re-unification" renamed the Federal Republic of Cameroon *United Republic of Cameroon*, which was also later renamed by Paul

Biya as La Republique du Cameroun (The Republic of Cameroon) in 1984 (dropping the United and reverting to the French colonial name).

The multiple and multi-layered ascribed, assumed, and (un)contested national and ethnic identities define me. In this chapter, using autoethnography, I seek to deconstruct these layers of identity, including the acquired and the imposed/ascribed identities (Atanga 2010; Thiesmeyer 2003) which characterize many other women of Southern Cameroons.

My memory of my ascribed and largely assumed identity as a "Cameroonian" with the "Southern" dropped was shaped by discourses that circulate around me. These discourses were/are perpetuated by the educational systems—the songs we sang in school, the civic education and history we learned, the form and content of our curriculum, and the social and political structures within my cultural setting. They are also defined by the languages we use for education and the languages we learn as second and third languages. The language policy that de-emphasizes and denigrates our local languages seeks to construct ideal Britishness of language and learning, and a Cameroon as uniquely bilingual. These largely mental and ideological processes shaped not only me as "Cameroonian," but also as a woman of this context, with traditional gender ideologies that construct (my) femininity as silent, not critical, not public. This femininity defined most women in the former British Southern Cameroons who today are officially identified as Cameroonians of the North West and South West regions. For this volume, and based on the study population, and on the basis of the conflict, I would choose to use the name Southern Cameroons to describe how this collection of indigenous people was once formally identified.

The definitions of femininity are not necessarily tradition but constructed within the systems. The women of Southern Cameroons have often challenged these silent femininities. Having gone through different traumatic experiences, these traditions and ideologies no longer were very inhibiting since the start of the armed conflicts in the Southern Cameroons. The conflict started as lawyers and teachers strike (Willis et al. 2020), and on September 22, 2016, women, men, and children came out in large numbers in solidarity to protest against injustices, marginalization, and discrimination. The strikes soon became violent with excessive force from the military of Cameroon resulting in an armed conflict— a war that disrupted the lives of many women (Mbondgulo-Wondieh 2020; Ayuk-Etang 2020).

Women are the most hit by the conflict and bear the brunt of the discrimination of their children. Old mothers over seventy (Ardener 2005) came out in Takumbeng style to protest and demand for justice. These women, together with men and children, came out in thousands across the Southern Cameroons. During these peaceful protests, police and the BIR (French acronym for Rapid Intervention Brigade) will kill several unarmed persons both from the ground and from air using military helicopters. This action sparked anger among an already angry and discriminated population who were severely repressed by the government of Cameroon.

In October 2017, another major protest took place in the Southern Cameroons to mark the Independence Day of the people of Southern Cameroons, again with the military killing dozens of unarmed civilians. Following those killings, Southern Cameroonians resorted to what they called self-defense. On November 30th of the same year, the president of the Republic of Cameroon "declared war" on the "secessionists" marking the beginning of a conflict that would last several years. The BIR burnt many villages, arrested, tortured, and detained many young men, raped and tortured many women and children. The excesses of the military in exacting arbitrary and extrajudicial killings, torture, and rape scared many civilians to escape to Nigeria and many more into the bushes. Many women and children would make bushes and forest their homes with no roof over their heads. Many women would use moss as sanitary towels and some even gave birth in these bushes with no delivery kits. In a nutshell, disease, hunger, absence of water and sanitation facilities, and rape characterized the lives of women in the bushes. These difficulties pushed women-led civil society humanitarian organizations to intervene and mark the beginning of women's protest and activism during the armed conflict.

The violence catalyzed women to participate in the matches and become soldiers (Amba girls), activists, and humanitarian actors although they remain mainly and largely victims. However, as Hedström (2020) observed, women's labor and contribution would become an important factor in sustaining military strategy and warfare (see also Basham and Catignani 2018).

The military and nonmilitary contribution of women in the armed conflict would largely be neglected; and women, as noted by (Ardener 2005), are muted in their contributions. As individuals and as groups, women shape the narrative and the direction of the conflict through their covert and overt actions as citizens of Southern Cameroons. These women would militarily serve as Amba girls, protectors of the Amba boys (and girls), as humanitarians, and as activists doing diplomatic advocacy. Discourses construct warfare as masculine and soldiers as males but hardly ever as females. The mainstream discourse excludes women as key actors. Yet a shift, due to women's persistence and visibility as actors, is beginning to change the narrative.

METHODOLOGY

This chapter drew on an autoethnographic approach (Chang 2016; McCoy 2018) to tell my story and that of women in Southern Cameroons in our contribution to the war effort—our experiences and contributions. Using qualitative approaches, the chapter drew on memoir writing and inventive methods (Lury and Wakeford 2012) to tell the story of women of Southern Cameroons both at home and abroad. Rosenblat and Rober (2015) posited that autoethnography seeks to describe and systemically analyze personal experience (auto) to understand social and cultural phenomena.

In doing autoethnography, I strive to be critically self-reflexive (Fairclough et al. 2011) in my position as a female actor working in the context of armed conflict. Griffin and Griffin (2019) give its defining characteristics and note that it accommodates subjectivity and emotionality. This approach gives the researcher an opportunity to be in the research and tell their history in the larger history of times (Stanley 1993: 43), thus at the same time being a subject of the research.

The chapter focused partly on a memoir writing style, narrative events (sometimes in first person), yet being critical of language use and being self-reflexive of actions and perspectives in the narration. In the sections that follow, I endeavor to show women as sociopolitical actors in the conflict, basing my arguments on personal experiences and those of members of my community of practice. I sometimes use scenario (personal experiences) as data to inform some of my claims. These scenarios draw on the storytelling approach and memoire techniques in autoethnographic studies.

Guns, Tears and Blood: Women and Women's Groups in Armed Conflict

> *Dem leave sorrow, tears, and blood,*
> *dem regula trademark*
> *(Fela Ransom Kuti 1977)*

In many conflicts, women are thought to be silent victims (Baines 2017) with little or no contribution to the outcome of the conflict. The conflict in the Southern Cameroons has uncovered the not-so-hidden contribution of women militarily, politically, and in humanitarian work. These contributions, although less mediatized, are very evident for those who dare to go to the grassroots to observe firsthand. My journey, from the civil strikes to the war, and my involvement as a community member and an activist/advocate peace-builder has given me a unique opportunity to assess women's contributions to the war, as active stakeholders, rather than passive victims or bystanders as constantly portrayed by war literature. The following accounts are mine, first as one who lived the conflict from the start, and as actor in the ensuing events. The scenarios depicted in this chapter are ones of guns, of tears, and of blood. Some are (my) eyewitness accounts, and others are happenings within my context that I recount.

Scenario 1

My phone rings: *"If you have not crossed the town just go back home. It is bad"* and the caller drops. Just then I see many motorbikes speeding with *nkeungs* (peace plants). I make a U-turn and start heading home. I meet a crowd who start banging my car. I raise a fist of power in support, managed to escape them, and branched home. Adrenaline pumping. It was September 22, 2017, the call to strike. One hour later I hear this loud crowd and see on social media the images reporting the crowd met the Fon of Mankon. I change into a pair of Jeans trousers, put on sneakers, my ID card in my pocket, and some money. Go light ready to run. No purse. I go out and meet this crowd of over 10,000 persons (my estimate), and I join in the euphoria. We chanted moving to the City Chemist Roundabout in Bamenda. I melted into the crowd oblivious of my identity as a university professor. At half a kilometer from there, gunshots started. We started running. "They have killed . . . They have killed . . ." people shouted. And we threw away the peace plants and kept running, as the gunshots thundered. I got home battered by fear and tiredness from running, and I am told several protesters were killed.

Scenario 2

May 20, 2019: a ghost town, everyone at home. Baby Martha and her parents were at home as instructed by the Amba boys not knowing it would meet them there. Then they heard the gunshots and the shouting calling on all to run away, that the military is coming. Baby Martha was lying on the chair. The parents had barely time to run away thinking the "human" military could not hurt a baby. They returned to their dead baby shot many times on the chair.

Scenario 3

I am in the office holding a departmental meeting. We hear gunshots on campus sounding not far from the office. We dug under tables and chairs in the tiny, crowded office. Deliberations automatically stop, and each member of the faculty searches for where to hide. Some run to hide in toilets, some scampered to their cars, and the campus is scattered. While all this is happening, I receive a text from my daughter's school. A military man has been shot dead. The military went on the rampage. At the Hospital roundabout in Bamenda, gunshots reverberate. I am at Bambili, and my daughter's school in Bamenda is barely 200 meters away from the roundabout, the battle ground. I braved the odds, dashed to the car, and rushed to Bamenda and could not access her as they are at the center of the shooting. Fast forward, when I picked her up, she told me their teacher got them on the floor, they clambered to another room, more secure. The shooting lasted for three hours. The children cried and confused the teachers, the sounds of the gunshots were terrifying,

These scenarios depict an ethnographic view of women in different situations of the armed conflict. Women at the heart of the conflict experiencing civil and military actions, women and children came face to face with guns, with blood, and tears welled up. Sounds of gunshots, visions of blood, and tears constitute a daily menu for women and children, forcing them to be an integral part of the conflict. In some situations, they serve as soldiers, as caterers, and as spies who alert soldiers of intruders, as those accommodating soldiers, nursing them and feeding them. They supply them with needs. They play the social reproductive roles (Hedström 2020), contributing actively to sustaining the war. But as noted in war literature, the logistics and supply chain are more important than the fighting and field operations (Gruenwald 2015).

They are also victims of violence as they are raped and killed and lose their children and husbands. They pick the bodies, they bury them, they nurse the wounded. The state and non-state armed persons are their children and husbands and brothers. Their ideological alignments in the struggle and their social connections to the conflict and the consequent actions of the soldiers activate their involvement either as soldiers, humanitarians, or activists. As critical actors in the conflict, they are largely backgrounded and sometimes go underground as spies and soldiers, but overtly as activists and humanitarian workers and as victims.

The carnage and the attendant humanitarian needs precipitated women to step in. The excesses of the armed persons especially the military and the "Amba boys"—the brutal killings, the forced disappearances, the school boycott, the ghost towns, and homeless women in the bushes were too much for women to bear. Individual women and groups started offering some form of humanitarian help to communities and individuals especially the internally displaced persons (IDPs) and refugees.

Like many women, I woke up every morning with fear. I had the fear that the young boys under my care could be killed just for being young Southern Cameroons boys. Being a male between fifteen and fifty years and a Southern Cameroons' person was enough for the Republic of Cameroon military to bran you as an "Amba boy" and extrajudicially kill you. No questions were asked. My activism began, and I started using social media to advocate against the violence. WhatsApp became a news station, and I would watch images and read about villages being burned down and women and children forced to live in the bushes. My fears and compassion were not unique to me but to many women of the Southern Cameroons. We would watch the dire abuses and humanitarian needs of these displaced communities. We noted that women were under attack even though they were not carrying guns. They were raped, homeless, and bereaved.

This overwhelming need resulted in women's groups coming together for greater impact. One of such groups of which I am a foundation member is the South West and North West Women's Taskforce (SNWOT). The women would involve themselves in "organizing lamentation campaigns, outreach activities, and serving as host families for internally displaced people, holding public candle vigils, national prayers and fasting" (Mbondgulo-Wondieh 2020: 137). I would mostly participate in the advocacy and the humanitarian aspects of the war, but this would not be all about women's participation.

Many women, in the shadows, would go beyond these reproductive spaces into international advocacy and armed fighting. Coalitions of women's groups were formed and as well as Church groups would work with these coalitions. The first of such coalitions was the SNWOT formed in May 2018 and other movements like Cameroon Women for Peace Movement (CAWOPEM), SOUTH West Women for Peace and Development Movement (SWWOP-DEM), North West Women for Peace Network (NWOPEN), and TAKUM-BENG, Southern Cameroons Women's League (SCAWOL) and Southern Cameroons European Women (SCEW) in the Diaspora. These movements, both national and international, carried out varying and sometimes concerted efforts for ceasefire and humanitarian assistance. The movements also worked in collaboration with international organizations like the UN Office of the Coordination of Humanitarian Affairs (OCHA), The UN Population Fund (UFPA), and the World Food Program. The UN Women also contributed in training peace builders following the UN resolution 1325. Of these women organizations, two stand out, One national—The North West South West Women's Taskforce and the TAKUMBENG at the international front. Other movements like the Coalition for Dialogue and Negotiation (CDN) are co-chaired by a woman. This particular coalition focuses on international advocacy and diplomacy to bring world leaders to contribute to ending the violence in Southern Cameroons through dialogue and negotiation.

WOMEN AND THE WAR: TAKUMBENG, SNWOT, AND THE CDN

The first time I experienced *Takumbeng* was in the 1990s as a young woman. This was when militants of the Social Democratic Front (SDF) took to the streets to protest the results of an election (Tang 2006). My mother and many other menopausal women took to the streets to protest brutal killings by the military. *Takumbeng* as a social practice is an old practice of women mobilizing themselves for social justice (Fonchingong 2005; Tang 2006; Atanga

2010). Although usually the concerns are humanitarian, the origins of crises that rock women to orchestrate Takumbeng are political, and they contest men's actions considered counter life (see Mbondgulo-Wondieh 2020). Following that, Mbondgulo-Wondieh noted that the actions of Takumbeng serve a critical role in catalyzing peace in Southern Cameroons communities. Takumbeng is known by different names in different ethnic groups like the *anlu* of Kom (Atanga 2010). Takumbeng activities, in their traditional form, are women's silent morning protests, including nudity (bodies covered with leaves) while displaying peace symbols. Because women's voices and concerns are usually silenced and ignored, they carry *nkeung* (peace plants) in between the lips symbolizing silence and peace. In addition to being the "traditional weapon," their nudity (Ardener 2005; Goheen 1996) is a composite of sacredness and mysticism, their sexuality and femininity, all no-go zones for men and boys (who in a large part are agents of brutality and violations).

Since 2016, Takumbeng has come out in mutated forms and dislocated contexts, different from the Takumbeng of the 1950s and the1990s. The Takumbeng of the 1950s and 1990s was characterized by sometimes complete nudity or near nudity of menopausal women with leaf blades stuck between their clenched lips and garlands of green leaves, with the *nkeung* in their hands. Post 1990 and contemporary 21st century, Takumbeng is characterized by a fast paced, mediatized era with social media bridging gaps of communication yet exposing bodies beyond traditional norms, and participant populations are younger and largely pre-menopausal women.

The initial tools of power of Takumbeng were nudity, numbers, silence, and the powerful ecological symbolism and motherhood exposed through bare breasts and the ominous curse of the mother. Seeing these nude or near nude mothers on their own was a curse on any man. Yet the Takumbeng protests of 2016 and onward were characterized by modernity and digital mediatization, and thereby impacting on the dress code of the Takumbeng. Takumbeng now became not only a silent and potent group but one that found voice through placards and (social) media in activism and advocacy. Takumbeng migrated to diasporic contexts at international levels both off and online carrying the message of the armed conflict to the international arena.

The Women in the Diaspora overtly naming themselves TAKUMBENG fashioned a dress code to go with the times. They adopt the colors red (for blood) and white (for cleansing) attire and carried green plants for peace and wooden kitchen utensils for African femininity and its values.

Their activities covered street demonstrations in front of international organizations, the US State Department, and the UN in New York. They also carried out social media campaigns denouncing the atrocities of the military of the Republic of Cameroon and notably the BIR. The Diaspora

TAKUMBENG served as an umbrella organization covering other Southern Cameroons women's organizations including the SCEW and the SCAWOL. The current diaspora Takumbeng is made up of over ten different women's organizations, most of which are humanitarian and have contributed largely to actions in refugee camps in Nigeria and Ghana, and in Southern Cameroons on Southern Cameroons Prisoners of Conscience, especially the female prisoners.

The largest local coalition of women remained the SNWOT. SNWOT was a coalition of civil society women-led organizations which had as mission to contribute significantly toward ending the struggle in the Southern Cameroons, while ensuring that women are part of all peace processes and decision-making platforms. It designated itself as apolitical and non-partisan. They adopted these concepts (albeit not to their actions) to be able to navigate the different fighting factions—the Republic of Cameroon military and the Amba boys. Aligning with either party meant being enemies with the other and could hamper their humanitarian mission. It started as a response to the destitution caused by mass migrations of people to refugee camps in Nigeria, the escapes to the bushes, the hunger, the absence of health and sanitation facilities, the homelessness, and the abject plight of women, especially the IDPs.

Scenario 4

We walked to the Bamenda municipal stadium carrying *nkeung*
Carrying *nkeung*, in black and orange
We chose orange, for hope and change
And black to mourn our children, bothers, and husbands
And they came in their green pickups trucks
We told them we don't need protection
We cried, we wailed, and we recounted out pains
We sang dirges and songs of hope
And we read our declaration of the lamentation
We don't want war; we don't want our children killed by the army.
And there the activism began, and SNWOT was
  born. (Written by the chapter Author)

The women organized the first activity termed the *lamentation campaigns.* Dressed in black and orange scarfs, the women went out in the public to lament about the abuses and excesses of armed men. They sat down and wept, singing dirges and songs of pain and sorrow, songs of freedom and liberation, songs of hope, after which written declarations were read.

The women shed tears and cried over the spilling of blood. Fela Ransom Kuti in his song noted "them leave sorrow, tears and blood, their regular trademark" (Fela Kuti 1977). The abuses were to become the new normal of the people of Southern Cameroons. And women were not insensitive to this. The *Lamentation Campaign* thus marked the beginning of many other forms of protest of tears against blood including the #*TalksNotbloodcampaign.*

The SNWOT would grow to over 200 civil society organizations and constitute themselves as police behind armed groups and would focus themselves on fighting against abuses on women and children. This group led several campaigns during the conflict including #*justice for baby Martha* and the #*talksnotblood campaign* together with other national and international organizations.

The CDN, a diasporic movement, was co-chaired by a woman who champions international advocacy through different strategies. This coalition soon emerged as the most credible group advocating for dialogue and negotiation for the resolution of the conflict in Southern Cameroons. With her team, the leader organized an international conference, the first and only (international) conference on the war before the end of 2020 struggle, bringing together national and international stakeholders in the conflict. Using the platform of the conference, they engaged national stakeholders and citizens of Southern Cameroons through survey to gauge which was indicative of the thoughts of the people of the Southern Cameroons. Also, through the conference, they engaged leaders of the struggle and also international actors. This coalition equally engaged the US State Department and congressmen and scored a milestone when they largely contributed to the US Senate Resolution 684. Through the diplomatic offence of this group, many more international missions began to understand the real narrative rather than the distorted version of "terrorists" labels of the government of the Republic of Cameroon.

COMMANDERS, SOLDIERS, SPIES, AND PROTECTORS

Scenario 5

I am going to a funeral of my family member. This was on October 20, 2018. Bafut was no longer a free destination, but now a no-go zone. I had to attend the funeral. I had just returned from an international trip. I managed to get a car that reached *Nsem Bafut.* As we approached, boys popped out of the bushes with guns and stopped us. They told us it was dangerous and that we had to proceed on foot. A journey of 5 km. As we matched on, we met, at every turn of the road "Amba boys" with guns patrolling and very few civilians. About 3 km into the journey, we started seeing young women, carrying guns and patrolling too. They looked fierce. I could not focus on them as this might be suspicious. Some members of my team had the audacity to greet.

One of the young women nodded silently. We moved on. And I wondered why we hear only of Amba boys and never also hear of "Amba girls."

Scenario 6

March 23, 2019, as I was kidnapped and taken to the bush, I thought it would be one real camp in the bush. Indeed, it was an abandoned school building that had grown into a bush. A classroom was used as a cell. However, it was an open cell. Yet it was a cell one could not escape from. While there, a woman was farming the premises of the school, young women were passing up and down. And watched me as if I was a normal sight, yet I was drastically different, and my car did not definitely belong to the bush, yet it seemed a normal sight to the women farming and passing by and exchanging greeting these soldiers. Perhaps their sisters, wives, or mothers. Fast track, I was released on bail to pay as I got home a certain amount of money plus medication and food for the soldiers as my contribution. Upon inquiry, I was told the women and mothers farming by the abandoned school served as spies.

The narrative above depicts women as fighters, as spies, and as ones harboring the "Amba boys." Amba boys as indicated earlier are soldiers in the war in the Southern Cameroons. War discourses represent actors especially soldiers as male. Those who carry the guns and pull the trigger. In the war in the Southern Cameroons, the discourse of *Amba boys* obliterates any female presence. Yet the testimony in the scenario above speaks otherwise and shows there are *Amba girls*. The number of female soldiers may not be many, as there is no data to that effect, yet it does not in any way deny their military action and contribution to the fighting.

However, the government of the Republic of Cameroon has accused women of spying and as those who house and hide the Amba boys. Due to the prevalence of the discourse of women as spies who house and collude with the Amba boys, the government of the Republic of Cameroon has engaged in erasing several villages through fire, killing many women and children as collateral damage in tracking soldiers. It is difficult with the context of the war in Southern Cameroons to say who is an Amba soldier and who is not, and who is a spy and who is not. The foundations of the war are ideological and nearly every boy, man, girl, and woman especially in the indigenous communities subscribe to the struggle. How could you not harbor your son or husband who is fighting for a shared ideology! The dangers of living in "military camps" is high and thus soldiers mostly live at homes as sons, brothers, husbands, and fathers. How can the society then not protect their own, informing each other of the common enemy? Women then, who are mostly domestic as well as being spies and providers of provision for the "army," are also strategists and tacticians. Diaspora women contribute to the war through humanitarian assistance to soldiers financing especially the health and material needs.

Of the many different military commanders and their battalions, there is one female with her army. Ms. Vivian Mbanwie does not hide herself and stands tall as a military leader who has rallied her own army and commands it. Ms. Mbanwie is a key actor in the struggle and unlike many other women and women's groups whose involvement is humanitarian, hers is military. Her military involvement challenges the discourse that women are absent in guerrilla warfare.

THE HUMANITARIANS

The UN High Commission for Human Rights (UNHCR) and Office of the Coordination of Humanitarian Affairs (OCHA) (2020 report) data puts the number of refugees of Southern Cameroons in Nigeria at over 60,000 and the number of IDPs at over 650,000. Over 400 villages have been burned down by the Republic of Cameroon military displacing several persons and forcing them to flee into the bushes. Others from Bamenda fled the violence to neighboring cities and the French-speaking cities of Bafoussam, Mbouda, Douala, and Yaounde. There are also down close to 2000 Southern Cameroons people arrested and locked up in prisons including some of the leaders of the struggle. Even those that have not fled lost livelihoods. Hospitals are burned, schools destroyed and inhabited by armies, and the humanitarian situation is dire. Such a desperate situation invites humanitarian groups to step in. Women's groups are at the forefront of these actions providing from food to non-food items and shelter both to the IDPs and refugees.

Local Women's groups championed by members of the SNWOT coalition are at the forefront of interventions (Mbondguo-Wondie 2020) working alone and sometimes closely with international organizations. Their interventions range from food and non-food items to water, sanitation, and hygiene including economic support. Trainings of survival in conflict situations are also offered. Being at the local contexts, these women face different challenges as they navigate through Republic of Cameroon Military and Southern Cameroons Amba boys, navigating different identities to survive within the context. Their non-partisan approach for providing assistance earned them access to enclaved areas in the bushes. Civil Society organizations like COMAGEND and ReachOut Cameroon are worth mentioning among the groups. Women's groups from different churches have also accommodated many IDPs.

Women's groups in the diaspora with greater financial power have carried out many interventions at refugee camps in Nigeria, some IDPs and among Southern Cameroonian prisoners. These women have constructed homes in the Nigerian refugee camps, bought school materials, food, and provided much more humanitarian assistance. Diaspora women intervene more in refugee camps as they fear repression in Southern Cameroons by the Biya military. Assistance on the ground by these women and women groups is monetized.

THE KEYBOARD SOLDIERS: WOMEN, (SOCIAL) MEDIA, AND THE CONFLICT IN THE SOUTHERN CAMEROONS

The war in the Southern Cameroons has been described as one of the most neglected conflicts in the world. As observed by Jan Egeland General of the Norwegian Refugee Council (NRC)

> The deep crises represented by millions of displaced Africans are yet again the most underfunded, ignored and deprioritized in the world. They are plagued by diplomatic and political paralysis, weak aid operations and little media attention. Despite facing a tornado of emergencies, their SOS calls for help fall on deaf ears.[1]

Little media attention has been given to this conflict. However, women have been at the forefront of mediatizing their plight and the toll the war is taking on the region using social media and other media outlets, including TV and radio. Women have made many campaigns on these different media condemning the violence on women, calling for a ceasefire and for the intervention of the international community.

Of the different media, social media has availed these women a lot of visibility giving them voice beyond the traditional female spaces. Social media as an internet-based tool and service allows users to produce content, consume it, share it, and even search for some of the content. As an interactive computer-mediated technology, it facilitates the creation and/or sharing of information, ideas, career interests, and other forms of expression via virtual communities and networks (Kietzmann et al. 2011). These media offer voice to women who are usually marginal especially in armed conflicts. These women have taken to Twitter especially and Facebook.

The SNWOT launched several social media (Twitter and Facebook) campaigns and used them for the dissemination of their "calls to actions." These campaigns included:

- *#talksnotblood*
- *#pensnotguns*

- *#Ceasefirenow*
- *#Silence the guns*
- *#not our children, put your arms down*
- *#Women peace builders against COVID*
- *#No to war Justice for Ngarbur*
- *#notwarstopthekillings*
- *#A future for our kids, not a cemetery*
- *#End hostilities now*
- *#Justice for Baby Martha*
- *#Protect healthcare*

The campaigns were against different or several kinds of abuses including rape, indiscriminate and targeted killings both by the military and non-state armed persons. Aside their lamentation campaigns, they have had large media campaigns like #pensnotguns campaign. This was a campaign for school resumption in the Southern Cameroons which advocated for evacuation of schools by military and non-state-armed groups and Southern Cameroons leaders and to permit school resumption. When the war started with a teachers' strike, there was a call for school boycott because the teachers contested the curriculum, the teaching methods, and the French teachers imposed on the Anglo-Saxon education system. They advocated for a change in educational system to suit their needs and their culture. This led to an extended suspension of the schools which eventually became used as leverage on the government of the Republic of Cameroon. After three years of no school, advocacy groups, championed by women who bore the brunt of children not going to school, started the #pensnotguns campaign. This campaign was started by SNWOT in 2019 and continued into 2020. In 2020 schools resumed although some state-owned schools in rural communities could not.

The *#Talksnotblood* Campaign was another major campaign to advocate for a ceasefire after the number of deaths both by the Cameroon military and the Southern Cameroons fighters was on the rise. The *#Talksnotblood* Campaign involved two international women's groups and several local women's groups including Church groups like the Christian Women's Fellowship, The Baptist Women, The Methodist Women, The South West Women's Peace and Development Association, and championed by the SNWOT. At the international level, the SCEW and the SCAWOL also joined this campaign. It took the form of webinars, Twitter campaigns, and a concluding statement calling for a ceasefire.

The campaign took colorful posters with texts and images calling for talks and not blood (signifying fighting) and the ensuing statement propagated through Twitter and emails to national and international stakeholders in the war.

The *No war on women's bodies* campaign started as a result of the military raping and killing women for housing or associating with Amba boys or Amba boys claiming they are traitors because they associate with the military of the LRC. The women on the ground, largely victims of these abuses, launched the *No war on our bodies campaign.*

Dislocating the context and form of Takumbeng, these women took Takumbeng to the virtual sphere, on the keyboard, transforming it from a local native practice to a virtual feminist advocacy tool to fight abuses. The exposure of sensitive parts of women, one of the powers of Takumberng, the power of nudity, exposing the sensitive parts of their bodies to men, (which is a cultural taboo), was transposed to the social media space. The exposure of the navel/stomach campaign is a Takumbeng activity, but no longer on the physical space.

The TAKUMBENG women of the Diaspora also used the strategy of transposition of practices from the physical to the virtual spaces. In the diaspora Takumbeng, women used organic kitchen utensils—spoons, spatulas, and so on as symbolic of the center of the family—the kitchen and the hearth that holds the essence of life. This is in protest of the waste of life in the Southern Cameroons.

Although fighting for the same major cause, to end the war in the Southern Cameroons, the focus of the campaigns of the diaspora women, the Takumbeng Campaigns of the women of the diaspora focused a lot more for the liberation of prisoners of conscience and to free Southern Cameroons. Although attacking the conflict from different fronts and facing different realities, these women are all engaged in online Twitter, Facebook, and advocacy campaigns to free the Southern Cameroons.

Juxtaposing the two campaigns above, one can decipher different women and campaign orientations based on ideologies. The women on the ground face violence and their immediate needs are peace, while the Women in the Diaspora face the picture of the conflict which is political freedom.

However, a campaign like *#Talks and not blood* is a rare campaign that unites the diaspora and the home fronts in the struggle with a common objective which is *#Talks and not blood.*

ENGAGEMENT WITH DIPLOMATIC COMMUNITY

Local women engaged in diplomatic advocacy at the level of embassies in Cameroon including the Swiss Mission, the American Embassy, the British High Commission, and the German Embassy including religions bodies and international civil society organizations and the government of the Republic of Cameroon as well. These local women championed by SNWOT sent out statements condemning and calling for the engagement of these missions in the struggle.

Their contribution cannot be minimized. A lot of the data on the ground is collected by these women civil society organizations working on the ground embedded in the heart of the conflict and who lived the reality of the war. A firsthand testimony and their resilience and contribution to sustaining livelihoods get their statements to be given consideration, if not for action but for information on the situation on the ground. Below is a sample except of such statements that legitimates their position as women on the ground who suffer misery and violence.

The engagement of women with the international community and diplomatic missions is increased and substantial. Women's engagement in these circles is enhanced by policies on WPS which warrant women's involvement, and both state and governmental organizations are ensuring this happens, albeit in certain circumstances as tokens. The Swiss Peace, in its many meetings with women-led peacebuilding civil society organizations and other groups have participated in these discussions.

Also, the CDN in their October 2021 Meeting in Toronto termed High Level Leadership Retreat intentionally engaged women stakeholders from the civil society organizations, the armed groups, political groups, and Human rights groups from the Southern Cameroons stakeholders. The participation and contribution of these women was not nominal but substantive as they partook in high level talks, with a side event that resulted in a Women's Position Statement (CDN 2021). Further platforms and activities in international and diplomatic missions are enhanced but we continue to question how these trickle down to marginalized communities like refugee and displaced women. How intentional is the inclusion of these groups of women in international spaces and peace and conflict talk? What access do they have for their voice? These questions however a not the focus of this paper and are thoughts for further research.

CONCLUSION

This chapter highlighted the contribution of women to the war in the Southern Cameroons and catalogued their contributions largely from the standpoint of a woman who lived the war in Cameroon and currently focuses on activism and advocacy in a diasporic context. I argued that women, although largely victims of the war, were also active stakeholders in war situations as soldiers, humanitarians, activists, political leaders who are deeply involved in advocacy, and diplomacy. This involvement is in consonance with Snyder et al. (2011) who argued that the agency of women in conflict and peacebuilding has not been well researched and theorized. This chapter showed the participation of women in Southern Cameroons in the military (as soldiers and spies), in humanitarian activities, as activists, and in advocacy and diplomacy. These are all actions that contribute to mitigating the effects of the war, in communicating the war and resolving the conflict through diplomatic means. To conclude then, the chapter argued that women constitute key actors armed conflicts and not only victims as largely presented by literature.

NOTE

1. https://reliefweb.int/report/cameroon/world-s-most-neglected-displacement -crises

REFERENCES

Ardener, S. (2005). Muted groups: The genesis of an idea and its praxis. *Women and Language* 28(2), 1–5.

Ayuk-Etang, E. N. (2020). Women and social insecurity in Cameroon: A study of selected poems from some Cameroon Anglophone writers. *American Research Journal of Humanities and Social Sciences* 3/12, 23–36.

Baines, E. (2017). *Buried in the Heart: Women, Complex Victimhood and the War in Northern Uganda*. Cambridge: Cambridge University Press.

Chang, H. (2016). *Autoethnography as Method*, Vol. 1. London: Routledge.

Coalition for Dialogue and Negotiations. (2021). *Toronto Declaration*. https://www .facebook.com/CoalitionFDN/photos/pcb.450117513129608/450148529793173.

Fairclough, N., Wodak, R., & Mulderrig, J. (2011). Critical discourse analysis. In *Discourse Studies: A Multidisciplinary Introduction*, 357–378. London: Sage Publications.

Fonchingong, C. C. (2005). Negotiating livelihoods beyond Beijing: the burden of women food vendors in the informal economy of Limbe, Cameroon. *International Social Science Journal* 57/184, 243–253.

Goheen, M. (1996). *Men Own the Fields, Women Own the Crops: Gender and Power in the Cameroon Grassfields*. Wisconsin: University of Wisconsin Press.

Gruenwald, H. (2015). Military logistics efforts during the Vietnam war supply chain management on both sides. *Journal of Social and Development Sciences* 6(2), 57–66.

Hedström, J. (2020). Militarized social reproduction: Women's labour and parastate armed conflict. *Critical Military Studies*, 1–19.

KhosraviNik, M. (2020). Digital meaning-making across content and practice in social media critical discourse studies.

Lury, C., & Wakeford, N. (Eds.). (2012). *Inventive Methods: The Happening of the Social*. London: Routledge.

Mbondgulo-Wondieh, Z. (2020). Women and the anglophone struggle in Cameroon. In *Gender, Protests and Political Change in Africa*, 131–147. Cham: Palgrave Macmillan.

McCoy, S. Z. (2018). The intellectual war zone: An autoethnography of intellectual identity development despite oppressive institutional socialization. *Journal of Diversity in Higher Education* 11/3, 325–346. https://doi.org/10.1037/dhe0000062.

Ngoh, V. J. (1996). *History of Cameroon Since 1800*. Presbook: Limbe.

Rober, P., & Rosenblatt, P. C. (2015). Silence and memories of war: An autoethnographic exploration of family secrecy. *Family Process* 56(1), 250–261.

Stanley, Liz (1993). On auto/biography in sociology. *Sociology* 27(1), 41–52.

Stephens-Griffin, N., & Griffin, N. (2019). A millennial methodology? Autoethnographic research in do-it-yourself (DIY) punk and activist communities. *Forum: Qualitative Social Research* 20(3).

Swift, J. (2017). *African Women and Social Movements in Africa*. Retrieved January 18, 2021.

Takougang, J., & Amin, J. A. (2018). *Post-Colonial Cameroon: Politics, Economy, and Society*. Chicago: Rowman & Littlefield.

Tanga, P. T. (2006). The role of women's secret societies in Cameroon s contemporary politics: The case of takumbeng. *Boleswa Occasional Papers in Theology and Religion* 1, 44–58.

Thiesmeyer, L. J. (Ed.). (2003). *Discourse and Silencing: Representation and the Language of Displacement*, Vol. 5. John Benjamins Publishing.

Willis, R., Angove, J., Mbinkar, C., & McAulay, J. (2020). 'We remain their slaves': Voices from the Cameroon conflict. In *The Cameroon Conflict Research Group, Based in the Faculty of Law, University of Oxford*. Oxford: Oxford University Faculty of Law Working Paper.

Chapter 10

The 2019 Major National Dialogue and the Decentralization Utopia as a Panacea to the Southern Cameroons' Conflict

Some Critical Perspectives

Jean-Claude N. Ashukem

Since the 1970s, institutional reforms in Africa have been marked by trials of various forms of decentralization models often facilitated and influenced by international development partners with the false hope of promoting among other economic growth and poverty alleviation (Ofoulhast-Othamot, 2018; Cheka, 2007).[1] With the increasing but unprecedented poor systems of governance characterizing Africa, most African countries have experienced and are still experiencing myriad waves of decentralization models (with Cameroon recently having a share of its own experience) that are aimed at fundamentally re-designing the political, economic, and social contract between governments and citizens. Whether this form of governance actually benefits international development partners, as in the case of Cameroon, is the subject of another investigation. In the midst of severed governance irregularities, a violent conflict ensued between the Southern Cameroons (now termed North West and South West regions or more colloquially Anglophones regions of Cameroon) clamoring for the formation of an independent state called Ambazonia and the government of a former *La République du Cameroun*, which is resisting this independence struggle with the hope of preserving the controversial notion of a decentralized, united, one and indivisible Cameroon. Whether the territory now called Cameroon is in fact united, decentralized, and indivisible is a question of subjectivity that defies historical and legal rationality. It is important to emphasize that although the origin of the Southern Cameroons' conflict has been traced to and underpinned by sociohistorical and legal factors and the failed decolonization process of the Southern Cameroons (Ashukem, 2021; Ngang, 2021), it metamorphosed from a late 2016 strike by Common Law lawyers and teachers (decrying the forceful assimilation of the Southern Cameroons, while demanding sectoral reforms to rescue the common law and Anglo-Saxon system of education from extinction) to the exercise of the right to self-determination and to restore the independent statehood of the Southern Cameroons—Ambazonia.

Nevertheless, as the armed conflict in the Southern Cameroons raged on, the Yaounde regime is increasingly faced with great uncertainty on how to resolve the conflict. This uncertainty stems from the inability of the Yaounde regime to determine whether to revert to the previous federal system of government or to allow the Southern Cameroons to be independent or to relentlessly preserve its united, decentralized, one and indivisible ideology In alignment with the latter option, the government convened a Major National Dialogue (MND) better known by its French acronym as *Grand Dialogue National*, in 2019, to find peaceful solutions to the Southern Cameroons' conflict (IPSS Peace and Security Report, 2020; Chiatoh, 2019). The MND recommended among others the launching of an effective decentralization reform (which has been stalled for over twenty-three years) and the granting of a (questionable) special status to the Southern Cameroons. It remains to be determined why a government would be interested in resolving the conflict, planning and implementing the MND unilaterally when conflict resolution generally involves two or more parties (Katz & McNulty, 1994; Udezo, n.d.). Would decentralization as proposed by the MND resolve the Southern Cameroons conflict? How genuine would be the government's commitment to ensure effective decentralization?

This chapter considers these questions in the context of the current decentralization reform in Cameroon to determine whether the utopia of decentralization was a viable panacea to the ongoing Southern Cameroons' conflict. I review Cameroon's legal framework on decentralization and question the laxity of the government in implementing the Constitutional mandate to argue that the government lacked the political will to resolve the conflict and only intended to justify the controversial special status granted to the peoples of the North West and South West regions, where power was still exercised and controlled by the central government. The central argument in this chapter is that the rationale behind the decentralization reform was a *déjà vu* which had no practical implication and could therefore be qualified as a window dressing to a serious problem like the Sothern Cameroons' conflict.

The organization of the rest of the chapter is structured into five interrelated parts below. Part 1 is the introduction and part 2 below conceptualizes the theories of decentralization to understand the concept as a model of governance. It further examines the typologies of decentralization as well as some of the benefits and disadvantages of implementing this model of governance. Part 3 examines the theory and practice of decentralization in Cameroon by focusing on Cameroon's legal framework to understand whether and to what extent this approach is viable in resolving the Southern Cameroons conflict. This part also examines the inexplicable gap in implementing the decentralization laws from 1996 to 2019. Part 4 engages a critical discussion of the intricacies and complexities of the MND and the issue of decentralization. The last part provides suggestions on possible ways forward.

DECENTRALIZATION THEORY AS A TOOL FOR GOVERNANCE

It must be noted from the onset that the form and extent of decentralization implemented by states vary from country to country and from region to region (Crawford & Hartmann, 2008). This variation makes it difficult to conceptualize the meaning of decentralization as different authors have viewed it through different and overtly contradictory, analytical perspectives (Bankauskaite & Saltman, 2007). Smoke is of the view that decentralization is not a monolithic concept since it is loosely used to refer to different forms of local governance and is driven either by the state or non-state actors (Smoke). Despite the difficulty in defining decentralization, as it will be evident below, the idea of power transfer seems to be a common element in the array of definitions. However, notwithstanding the perspective from which decentralization is viewed or analyzed, the general theory on decentralization in most developing countries, including Cameroon, is that decentralization is perceived as a strategic policy response for governmental restructuring and vital to promoting and ensuring effective service delivery (Olum, 2014; Kessy, 2013). This need to promote service delivery makes decentralization topical for purposes of governance. The topicality of decentralization therefore warrants determining its driver, rationale, how, and the extent to which its benefits can be maximized by local government and the general public (Jutting et al., 2004). It is for this reason that Kessy (2013, pp. 223–224) advanced socioeconomic and political considerations as justification for any state to initiate and implement decentralization.

Be that as it may, although decentralization could either be fiscal, administrative, or political (Hendricks et al., 2014; Dick-Sagoe, 2020), the general understanding of the concept as posited by some theorists below is that it basically entails the transfer of power from the central government to local government, with the understanding that the transfer of power will augment the decision-making power of local government and their local representatives because their decision is a critical component of effective decentralization plan (Bossert, 1998). In other words, decentralization attempts to shift responsibility from the central government to decentralized units that are responsible for geographically defined areas. The involvement of local authority in decision-making could have a phenomenal impact in helping to ensure and facilitate efficient and cost-effective service delivery. Humes (1991) posits that the rationale for transferring power to local government is because central governments are generally more inclined to distribute some of their power either "areally (sic) or functionally" (Humes, 1991, p. 4), where it is argued that the areal basis requires the distribution of power to regional and local governments, and on the other hand, the functional basis requires that power should be distributed among specialized ministries and other government agencies specialized in related activities. Even though and where either the areal and functional basis or both could be well-suited for decentralization and they complement the process of execution of public duties, it must be emphasized that in developing countries, like Cameroon, some crucial sectors such as education, water, environment, and health are highly centralized and controlled by the central government, tantamounting to what Kessy (2013, p. 217) termed political decentralization. Smith (1985, p. 1) succinctly captured decentralization as "reversing the concentration of administration at a single centre and conferring powers to local government." For Agrawal and Ribot (1999, p. 475), decentralization is "any act in which a central government formally cedes powers to actors and institutions at lowers levels in a political-administrative and territorial hierarchy." From the foregoing, it is therefore a truism that decentralization is a shifting matrix of authority and power from higher to lower levels of government—central government to local government, with the hope of making policy more responsive through measures that improve governance efficiency, promotes national unity, ensures effective service delivery, and enhances the involvement of local government in managing the affairs of the central government (Cabral, 2011; Crawford & Hartmann, 2008). Defined as the

> distribution of responsibility for planning, management and resource raising and allocation from the central government and its agencies to either units of central government such as ministries or agencies, or subordinate units or levels of government or semi-autonomous public authorities or corporations, or area-wide, regional or functional authorities nor non-governmental private or voluntary organisations. (Herath, 2009, p. 159; Kessy, 2013)

decentralization allows for and requires a thorough re-consideration of the place and functioning of local government in governance than just a subset of the functioning or extension of the central government designed to implement its wishes and desires (Hope, 2000).

Beyond definitional issues, the implementation of decentralization has led to a mix of benefits and disadvantages. Generally, decentralization epitomizes a useful institutional reform to strengthen service delivery (Saito, 2001). Thus, it is pursued and envisioned as a form of governance and therefore could supposedly promote good governance through measures that contributes to, and further strengthens democratic values, efficient public administration and good governance (Saito, 2001). Decentralization also has the potential to reduce bureaucratic procedures. Proponents of decentralization hold the view that it is a catalyst for spurring up public service delivery, and it particularly enables the governed to be actively involved in and participate in governmental decision-making process (Dick-Sagoe, 2020). In this way, the activities of local government are opened to more scrutiny and thereby helping to promote and ensure transparency and accountability (Saito, 2001). Consequently, efficient service delivery could increase economic growth as improvement in service delivery in one area could have a snowball effect on other areas. Decentralization also serves to enhance speedy service delivery in part as it has the potential to reduce lengthy and cumbersome bureaucratic procedures (Saito, 2001). As a governance model, decentralization articulates a strategy for ensuring and promoting governance and particularly good governance (Cheema & Rondinelli, 2007). According to Agrawal and Ribot (1999, p. 475), "decentralization is a strategy of governance to facilitate transfers of power closer to those who are most affected by the exercise of power." By shifting some responsibilities to local government, decentralization helps to empower the ability and capacity of local people and to bring decision-making power closer to them through an inclusive participatory approach in decision-making and facilitate their proactive involvement in the management of national affairs (Saito, 2001). In sum, supporters of decentralization considered it as a measure to provide an array of benefits to people such as economic efficiency, effective public administration, political legitimacy, democratization, and poverty alleviation (Saito, 2001).

In contrast, critics of this governance model argue that decentralization can increase government expenditure where the individual units are small leading to duplication of functions (Hendricks et al., 2014). They further claimed that decentralization also fosters both variation of local government functions and responsibilities and local royalty to regional identities than national identities. This contrast increases the autonomy of central government and by implication could compromise national integrity. Relatedly there is also the problem of corruption of local elites which hinders the efficiency and effectiveness of service delivery at the local levels (Hendricks et al., 2014). Also, there is the problem of equity among different localities as more resourceful areas could benefit from the advantages created by decentralization than relatively poor areas (Ibeanusi, 2011).

Typologies and Dynamics of Decentralization

For some weird reasons, whether historical or politico-economic, developing countries seemed to be more centralized than the industrialized counterparts (Olowu, 2001). As an inherent manifestation of a strong system of local governance, decentralization is and must be viewed as a fundamental prerequisite in enhancing and promoting sustainable development and good governance practices. As a form of governance, decentralization has been in practice globally and claimed as a centerpiece of major development policy reforms in Africa. Contrary to the view that decentralization is not a new phenomenon in Africa, the Constitutions of South Africa, Ghana, Ethiopia, Mali, Namibia, Uganda, Kenya Malawi, and Nigeria, as in Cameroon, are underpinned by pro-decentralization tendencies on which basis they are formal recognition of local government, though no single African country is devoid of an operationalized local government (Ribot, 2002).

According to the World Health Organization (World Health Organization, n.d.; Rondinelli, 1983; Kessy, 2013; Hendricks et al., 2014), there are several typologies of decentralization. These typologies include deconcentration, delegation, and devolution. While deconcentration refers to the transfer of specific responsibilities and services from the central to the local government, devolution refers to the transfer to sub-regional levels by the central government, the authority to make decisions and finance control and to enjoy a relatively higher degree of autonomy. On the other hand, delegation is a merger of deconcentration and devolution (Kessy, 2013; World Health Organization, n.d.). However, it is unclear how and the extent to which these different typologies of decentralization or their combination thereof could be translated into realities in any given context in order to promote and ensure proper decentralization, in part, because of the political and bureaucratic resistance from the center (Kessy, 2013; Saito, 2011; Crook, 1994). Whether this is the case in Cameroon is investigated and illustrated below.

THEORY AND PRACTICE OF DECENTRALIZATION IN CAMEROON: OVERVIEW OF CAMEROON'S LEGAL FRAMEWORK

Regarding the theory of decentralization in Cameroon, the World Bank (2012, p. 3) notes that the "design of the decentralization process in Cameroon reflects the normative approaches to decentralization-assuming benign officials and policy makers and stipulating a normative allocation of responsibilities." As the World Bank (World Bank, 2012) further notes a highly politicized economy is at play in Cameroon, with the central government exercising substantial control and influence in virtually all aspects of the government, including the "supposed" local government. Although the theory of decentralization in Cameroon could be traced to the 1972 Federal Constitution, as one that is required to achieve multiple or diverse objectives, it is important to note that decentralization in Cameroon constitutes part of the framework of the national policy on democratization that started in the 1990s (Cheka, 2007). Following the wind of change in Africa, in the 1990s in tandem with international and domestic pressure for change, the government of Cameroon under Law No 96/06 of January 18, 1996, revised the Constitution of June 2, 1972, and adopted a new one—the Constitution of the Republic of Cameroon, 1996 (the Constitution). It is submitted that this Constitution provides for novel ideas and approaches in governance, including an option for a decentralized model of governance overtly encapsulated in Article 2(2) (Ngam et al., 2018). The legal basis for the current decentralization reform in Cameroon is enshrined in the Constitution, which provides an elaborate framework on decentralization considered to be the best in Francophone Africa (Fombad, 2019). Under Part 1 of the Constitution entitled "The State and Sovereignty," Article 2(2) provides that "the Republic of Cameroon shall be a decentralised unitary state." The article further provides that the "government shall be one and indivisible, secular, democratic and dedicated to social service." Article 2(3) provides that "The authorities responsible for the management of the state shall derive their powers from the people through election by either direct or indirect universal suffrage, unless otherwise provided for in this Constitution." This is meant that only elected officials shall have the powers and the mandate to control and manage their respective jurisdictions without any interference. But in reality, this does not seem to be the case since Article 2(3) makes provision for indirect universal suffrage, suggesting the involvement of the central government in this regard. However, Article 55 of the Constitution outlines the mandate of local government within the broader framework of decentralization and provides that:

Decentralised local entities of the Republic shall be regions and councils . . . decentralised local authorities shall be legal entities recognised by public law. They shall enjoy administrative and financial autonomy in the management of local interests. They shall be freely administered by boards elected in accordance with conditions laid down by law.

In furtherance of implementing the decentralization reform and promoting the ideals of one and indivisibility, in 2018, President Paul Biya signed a decree creating the Ministry of Decentralization and Local Development in charge of accelerating the decentralization process through vigorous elaboration, follow up, and putting in place measures to evaluate government policy in matters that relate to decentralization and local development.

In an effort to speed up the process, three bills on decentralization were promulgated into law in July 2004. These laws include: Law NO 2004/017 of July 22, 2004, on the Orientation of Decentralization (Orientation Law), Law No 2004/018 of July 22, 2004, laying down the Rules Applicable to Councils (Law on Councils), Law No 2004/019 of July 22, 2004, laying down Rules Applicable to Regions (Law on Regions). Together, these laws replaced the hitherto 1974 law on local council. Section 2(1) of the Orientation Law reiterate the notion of the transfer of power and considers decentralization as the "devolution by the state of special powers and appropriate resources to regional and local authorities," such that decentralization is perceived as constituting the basic driving force for promoting development, democracy, and good governance (Section 2(2) of the Orientation Law). What essentially entails devolution in the context of decentralization remains unclear. Is it that Cameroonians would not be required to travel to Yaounde again for some official process as stated by the Minister of Public Service and Administrative Reforms (MINFOPRA), when in fact it is the central government that controls the entire process, or it is a strategy to systematically avoid popular agitation against the government? Nonetheless, Section 4 of the Orientation Law reiterates the provision of Article 55 of the Constitution and provide that

> regional and local authorities shall be corporate bodies governed by public law. They shall be endowed with administrative and financial autonomy for the management of regional and local interests. In that capacity, the mission of their councils or boards shall be to promote economic, social, health, education, cultural and sports development in their respective areas of jurisdiction.

Despite this positive move, the process of decentralization was still stalled by the absent of an enabling degree to boost its implementation, until the promulgation of Law No. 2019/024 of December 24, 2019, to institute the General Code of Regional and Local Authorities (Decentralization Code). It is important to understand why this vacuum and its role in the whole decentralization process. In other words, does the vacuum supports the argument that the government lacks any genuine commitment to effectively implement its decentralization reforms?

The Inexplicable Gap, 1996–2019

Since the entrenchment of decentralization in the 1996 Constitution, there has been a blurred legal environment to its implementation characterized, in part, by the lack of an enabling decree as well as complex administrative, institutional, and managerial setback (Cheka, 2007; Agwenjang, 2020). The idea of enacting incomplete laws is not unprecedented in Cameroon (Ashukem, 2017). Perhaps because Constitutional amendment in tandem with other laws are illiberal to the extent that they are always stalled by an implementation decree (Agwenjang, 2020). In the last twenty-three years, twenty-four Constitutional provisions out of a total of sixty-eight have been stalled, pending implementation through a presidential decree (Fombad, 2016; Agwenjang, 2020). For example, Article 46 which envisions the creation of a Constitutional Council is still to be implemented since the Supreme Court continues to act in lieu of the Constitutional Council (Agwenjang, 2020). Such rec-current altitude of the government portrays its lack of political commitment or will, as in the case of the decentralization, to ensure and promote the democratic values of good governance. In the context of decentralization, the government failed to enact a law on decentralization despite its theoretical premise in the Constitution until the adoption of three bills in 2004. Even after their adoption in 2004, the government failed to enact the enabling decree to operationalize the decentralization process until the outbreak of the Southern Cameroons' conflict which facilitated the promulgation of the Decentralization Code in 2019. By this, it is meant that had the Southern Cameroons conflict not occurred in 2016, the government would not have enacted the Decentralization Code or operationalized the decentralization process. The reason for this is that even after the promulgation of the 2004 bills, it is argued that there has not been any positive sign of change that could attest to the level of performance of councils and regions. Yet, the government relied on the MND in conjunction with the Decentralization Code, to hopefully implement the envisage decentralized reform in the Constitution and as a measure to resolve the Southern Cameroons' conflict through the granting of a questionable special status. The foregoing suggests that the government is only providing window dressing solutions to a serious historical and legal problem while attempting to boost the envisage propaganda of a decentralized unitary state in Article 2 of the Constitution. It is therefore unclear why the government would wait this long to operationalize the decentralization if it is truly committed to bringing governance closer to the people and while concomitantly promoting the ideals of good governance. Given this context, the next section of this chapter is devoted to answering the central research on whether and to what extent decentralization is a viable solution to the Southern Cameroon's conflict.

MAJOR NATIONAL DIALOGUE AND THE
CALL FOR DECENTRALIZATION

Despite the reticence of the government for a peaceful resolution of the Southern Cameroons' conflict since its escalation in 2017, international and national pressure precipitated the need for an all-inclusive dialogue to discuss the root causes of the problem. From 30 September to October 4, 2019, an MND was held in Yaounde to deliberate on possible solutions to the ongoing Southern Cameroons' conflict. Even though the MND provided a platform for solution to some of the contemporary governance issues plaguing the country, including the challenge of dual colonial heritage, minority concerns, constitutionalism, ethnic, and tribal tensions, the envisaged decentralization reform was ill-suited to effectively address these challenges (Aime, 2020). Undoubtedly, the MND was a failed strategy, and prima facie, ill-suited to resolve the Southern Cameroons' conflict. Many political activists and religious leaders criticized the MND as a sham and that it was a process that failed on arrival. The entire dialogue and its decision-making were a unilateral process because the government was both a player and an umpire, a fact I argue raised doubt about the credibility and impartiality of the government to resolve the conflict. This begs the question, why the government would initiate and implement the decision of the MND alone when there are always two or more parties to every conflict? The government claimed it does not know who to dialogue with when in fact it abducted and extradited the Southern Cameroons' leaders from Nigeria against the precept of International Law on extradition. Instead, the government hired some unknown individuals to pose as ex-combatants of Ambazonia. It is interesting to know who are those in jail and why they were arrested.

Prior to the MND, Cameroon's Minister of Decentralization and Local Governance stated "We have been instructed by the prime minister to gather the information we have, so that those who are going to come to the national dialogue will find the solutions and the answers they may have concerning decentralization" (Xinhua, 2019).

One of the recommendations of the MND was to accelerate the decentralization process, which the government responded to the promulgation of the Decentralization Code. The MND also recommended the granting of a special status to Southern Cameroons.

Is Decentralization a Solution to the Southern Cameroons' Conflict? Critical Perspectives

In order to determine whether decentralization is a viable solution to the Southern Cameroons' conflict, it is important to provide a synopsis of the origin of the conflict which is rooted in historical and legal considerations. It is important to note that despite the insistence of "one and indivisible Cameroon," in the 1996 Constitution, there are indeed two Cameroons (La République du Cameroun and the Southern Cameroons) which came together in 1961 to experiment a federal form of government. Following the defeat of Germany in First World War, German colonies including the Cameroons were partitioned between the Allied powers. The Cameroons were placed under the League of Nations Mandate under the auspices of Britain and France. With the formation of the UN Organization, the administration of the Cameroons changed from a mandated to the trusteeship system. The general expectation of the trusteeship agreement was that Britain and France were obliged to administer their respective parts of Cameroon, in preparation for independence. While France granted independence to its own part of the territory under the name and style of *La République du Cameroun* on January 1, 1960, the Southern Cameroons was still not yet independent under British administration. On October 1, 1961, the UN granted a questionable independence to the Southern Cameroons with options to either join Nigeria or *La République du Cameroun*. On February 11, 1961, the Southern Cameroons opted for the latter option through a plebiscite to join *La République du Cameroun* with the hope of forming a federal system of government that would preserve the historical, legal, and sociocultural aspects of the two distinct Cameroons, as expressed in Article 47 of the Federal Constitution of 1961. In 1972, President Ahmadou Ahidjo defied the federal Cnstitution and changed the country's name to the United Republic of Cameroon with the adoption of a unitary Constitution the same year. In 1984, barely two years after assuming power, President Biya also unilaterally changed the country's name from the United Republic of Cameroon back to *La République du Cameroun*. The change meant in law and fact the collapse of the federal union between the two Cameroons, as *La République* rekindled the use of her previous independence name. This change also resulted in a change of the national flag from two stars representing the two Cameroons to the one star flag representing and signaling just one Cameroon. Therein lies the problem of the Southern Cameroons overtly expressed in the form of neo-colonization by *La République*, because the change of name was nothing short of a calculated attempt to assimilate the Southern Cameroons into a more centralized French system (Ashukem, 2021). At the Paris Peace Forum in France in November 2019, President Biya admitted that their attempt to assimilate the Southern Cameroons into the larger French-dominated community had not been successful. However, since 1961 this spirit of neo-colonialization was met with stiff resistance from the Southern Cameroons culminating to the recent declaration of the restoration of its independence under the name and style of Ambazonia on October 1, 2017, by Sesseskou Julius Ayuk Tabe, now imprisoned for life in *La République's* dungeon prison in Yaounde.

In response, the central government attempted to frustrate this restoration of independence struggle through the granting of a questionable special status in 2019 and the commitment to spur decentralization reforms as a potential measure to conserve its territorial control and legitimacy over the Southern Cameroons. This much is evident from the provision of Article

2(1) of the 1996 Constitution which as indicated above provides for a decentralized unitary state. By this, it is meant that the territory of the Southern Cameroons (now divided into North West and South West) is viewed as regions of *La République* for which a decentralized form of governance is suited to conserve the one and indivisibility ideology. As a consequence of the frequent and abrupt changes since 1961, it is evident that the agitations from the people of the Southern Cameroons was because they felt that their sociocultural, historical, and legal uniqueness that defined them as a people in International Law and confirmed by the 2009 African Commission of Human and People's Rights decision of *Kevin Mgwanga Gunme and Others Cameroon* (at paragraph 178) have been trounced in the 1961 union, and they are consequently forced to embrace a French culture—an agenda that neo-colonization propagates. As earlier mentioned, in 2016, Common Law lawyers and teachers embarked on a general strike to protest against the adulteration by French-speaking judges of the Common Law system and French-speaking teachers of the Anglo-Saxon culture of education in the Southern Cameroons, which they considered to be a systematic erosion of their unique colonial heritage. This practice is still prevalent today. To be sure, out of 128 magistrates practicing in the North West region, 67 (52.3 percent) are French-speaking with a civil law background; of 97 magistrates in the legal services, 64 (65.9 percent) are Francophones; of 27 magistrates in the legal services in Bamenda, there are 21 Francophones (77.8 percent), and a similar trend is observed in the South West region (Caxton, 2017). Common Law lawyers remained fearful that even in a decentralized state, civil law would continue to dominate, and their concerns would remain unsolved. Dealing with the current impasse would require that the government would re-engage in more comprehensive dialogue and would be more receptive to the problems raised and proposals made.

Against the background of the foregoing, I argue that decentralization is ineffective in resolving the Southern Cameroons' conflict despite its theoretical premise in the Constitution, which is suitable to accommodate the diverse communities of over 240 tribes and 3 ethnic groups—Bantus, Semi-Bantus, and Sudanese (Republic of Cameroon, n.d). Yet, the historical evidence advanced above suggests that the entrenchment of a decentralized form of government only has one objective: to assimilate the Southern Cameroons as regions of Cameroon, if considered that Article 45 of the Constitution even gives the president unfetter powers to do so. Even the Orientation Law gives the president unfetter powers to re-classify and re-group the territory into regions or geographical locations. Section 6(i) and (ii) of the Orientation Law stipulates that the president shall when necessary or deem fit modify the names and geographical boundaries of regions and set up other regions. And in the latter case, he shall name and set their geographical boundaries. Despite the euphoria of decentralization and subsequent attempt to speed up its implementation process, I argue that the current reform process does not represent any genuine commitment by the government to resolve the Southern Cameroons' conflict. Perhaps, Cameroon's decentralization could be well-suited to address governance deficiencies in *La République*. Even there, there are concerns that over twenty years now, no effort has been made to achieve the decentralization prescribed by the Constitution. In 2012, the World Bank (2012) described Cameroon's legal framework on decentralization as "overlapping, cumbersome and contradictory, and in many respects open to different interpretations as decentralized functions are ill-defined and not distinct from 'deconcentrated' operations of the central government." The World Bank also stated that President Biya had not passed a decree of application regarding the format for the implementation of the decentralization process.

In a sense, the current decentralization reform in Cameroon exemplifies the paradox of decentralization as it is not well designed to meaningfully engage with the country's problem. In fact, it befits Fombad's (2019) description of the "anomalies of decentralization with a centralist mindset," because Cameroon's complex history in tandem with its ethnic issues and sociopolitical problems cannot be adequately addressed through decentralization. The decentralization process has, for example, championed representative local government resulting in the creation of many urban councils that are being dominated by councillors from the national political party.

Article 327 of the Decentralization Code merely reduced the Southern Cameroons into a region with the granting of a questionable special status that may empower them to participate in the development of national policies on issues that relate to, for example, the educational and legal sectors of the Southern Cameroons. Although this move could be applauded for being a major step toward resolving the Southern Cameroons' conflict, I argue that the special status lacks the legal justification to resolve the conflict and its reliance is inappropriate in this context. First, a country cannot grant special status to another especially in time of war or conflict. Second, both the Southern Cameroons and *La République du Cameroun* have two distinct and recognizable international boundaries at the UN (Ashukem, 2021) and accordingly, the special status cannot achieve any positive results.

The special status regime under Section 330 of the Decentralization Code provides for a regional assembly and a regional executive council. The regional assembly is to be the deliberative organ of the "two Anglophone" regions and will be constituted of ninety regional councillors, a house of divisional representatives and a house of chiefs, whose duties remain, however, obscure. According to Section 328 of the 2019 Decentralization Code, the special status regime may allow the "Anglophone regions" to participate in the formulation of national policies relating to the Anglophone education system and decide on development projects in both regions and on issues on chiefdoms. However, I concur with Aime (2020) that the use of the conditionality "may" instead of the obligation "shall" in Section 328 of the Decentralization Code suggests a technical measure to refuse the peoples of the Southern Cameroons the right to participate in decision-making on critical and fundamental issues that are vital to their existence.

Reinventing the Wheel of Centralization

Although Cameroon is in the process of implementing its decentralization reforms, the overall intention seems to be different as the government continues to operate centrally with local councils and regions having limited authority or control over their jurisdictions. The fact that decentralization in Cameroon is a devolution of power from the central government to local administrative units and not a relinquishing of power suggests that such devolution is not absolute as the central government can withhold power at any time. Even though Article 115(1) of the Orientation Law empowers locally elected councillors through direct universal suffrage to have control over their councils, their authority is subdued by appointed government officials. This situation puts to question the rationality of the free administration of local councils and contradicts the ideals of decentralization because the "essence of the autonomy of local authorities emanates from the mode of designation of their leaders by direct universal suffrage and the freedom of the deliberating assembly to define norms that bind them; with the provision that they do not conflict with national law" (Cheka, 2007 citing Boudine, 1992, p. 179). Instead of boosting good local governance, the current decentralization reform has thwarted it, since elected councillors are answerable to the chairman of the national/regional councillor who is appointed by the president. Through this approach, the central government still maintains effective control over the management of the councils instead of allowing for independent and impartially elected councillors to govern their respective councils. The appointment of governors to head regional councillors introduces an undisputable twist into the rationality of the autonomy of local authorities. The situation is exacerbated by the introduction of a Regional Council President who together with regional governors heads the regional councils. By making the Regional Council President, the place, duties, or responsibilities of the mayor and government delegate are put in limbo, and they seem to be of no relevance. It is unreasonable to have this multitude of personalities all in the name of decentralization. In practical terms, a council is under an elected executive mayor as in the case of Britain and other parts of the world, and there is no other authority over the mayor in a council. But we see a different and confusing situation in Cameroon, where the government has instituted a centralized system of government in place with influential control at the local government level. The question that runs to mind is why waste state resources and deceive the world and Cameroonians of a commitment to promote effective decentralization when this is not the case either in theory or practice? If the elected local officials only have the powers to execute policies and laws that are formulated by the central government, it means they neither vote for laws nor make useful or critical suggestions for the formulation of laws and policies that benefit their constituencies.

Drawing from the current situation, it is evident that the Cameroon's decentralized reform is still a centralized system where laws and regulations are crafted or enacted by the central government of *La République du Cameroun*. The reason is the central National Assembly is responsible for the enactment of laws that are applicable and enforceable throughout Cameroon. It is logical therefore that the purported decentralized officials are mere instruments to implement the policies and objectives of the central government. In his familiar way of working by decrees, President Biya recently signed Decree No 2021/043 on January 25, 2021, appointing Secretaries-Generals of the regional councils (Presidency of the Republic of Cameroon, n.d; *Journal du Cameroun*, 2021). The new Secretaries-Generals are expected to accompany and strengthen the efforts of the pioneer regional executives in their efforts to ensure vigorous implementation of the special status granted to the Southern Cameroons (Mimi Mefo, 2021). This move shows how and the extent to which the president is back pedalling the decentralization reform and instituting measures that would enable him to have control over the regional councils. In retrospect, this move is analogous to the imposition of government appointees over Southern Cameroons in the 1970s by President Ahmadou Ahidjo to enable him to have total control over the Southern Cameroons. I argue that the current decentralization reform is nothing short of forcibly making and integrating the distinct territory of the Southern Cameroons as regions of *La République du Cameroun*, to justify the questionable provision of Article 2 of the Constitution, on which basis would qualify the struggle for the restoration of the independence of the Southern Cameroons, as a national issue.

The Vagueness of the Decentralization Reform

Theoretically, although local councils may be independent, they are in principle *quasi*-independent since they still have to report to appointed government officials, regional councillors, and governors who oversee their activities. Governors have the duty to monitor the activities of the regional councillors and to ensure that they do not sit four times as expected, but three times a year where a maximum of eight days must be spent for the first three quarters. This implies that elected councillors do not have the capacity to serve on behalf of the people who elected them and cannot implement any developmental policy or objective because a government appointee must give them the go ahead to do so. In other words, an appointed official dictates to those who are elected, the manner in which they are supposed to meet, how and what to do, talk and take decisions regarding the welfare of their people, for example. This creates unnecessary conflict in the management of natural resources and the governance machinery, if decentralization could be viewed from the perspective of principal-agent relationship where the people are the de facto principal and the state the de facto agent, executing the mandate or implementing the wishes of the people. In practice therefore, this relationship has been ironically reversed in Cameroon, where the government instead acts as a principal and the people as agent, a situation which distorts the overall meaning and rationale of decentralization. Within the framework of the current decentralization reform, it remains to be seen whether and to what extent if possible, powers would be devolved to elected local representatives and enhance proactive local community participation in the development process.

WHAT'S THE WAY FORWARD?

The question has been asked over and over again regarding the solution to the Southern Cameroons' conflict. In other words, what is the feasible solution if the envisaged decentralization reform and the special status cannot do the trick? Based on the historical and legal analysis above, I argue that neither a return to federalism nor the struggle to preserve the unitary state disposition of one and indivisible Cameroon would resolve the problem. It was the failed promise of federation that catapulted to the current conflict and accordingly federation or confederation would certainly not yield any result to the peoples of the Southern Cameroons.

Even though the rationale behind decentralization reforms seemed to differ between states, the ability and willingness of any state including the government of La République du Cameroun to carefully design a decentralization model would address the country's dire challenges. Cameroon's decentralization reform as demonstrated above reflects a complete paradox embedded with negative consequences on the country's development, democracy, constitutionalism, human rights, and the rule of law and could be considered a failure. The failure of this governance model is rooted in the misguided conception and rhetoric to protect and conserve the ideal/status quo of Article 2(1) of the Constitution rather than to emphatically implement a decentralized model of governance that would resolve the Southern Cameroons' conflict. In as much as decentralization espoused a shifting matrix of power from the central to the local government, the current utopia of decentralization in Cameroon could be requalified as re-centralization because power is still exercised and controlled by the central government. By focusing power in the hands of the central government through some disguised decentralization reform, I argue that decentralization is ineffective in resolving the Southern Cameroon's crisis which is deeply rooted in history and law. Until the root causes of the problem (neo-colonialism) are discussed and addressed, Southern Cameroons will only be a porcupine in a python's throat.

NOTE

1. I am grateful to Dr. Carol C. Ngang for commenting on an earlier draft of this chapter. All viewpoints and errors are the authors' own.

Chapter 11

Damning Role of Western Powers in the Ambazonian Conflict

Denis Atemnkeng

What is needed to resolve the Ambazonia conflict is justice, truth, and the rule of law, not politics, not sweeping of the facts under the table, not the imposition of Western views, not blindfolding of Africans, and not lording it over the parties. Human rights violations cannot be more important than the illegal occupation and annexation which gave rise to those violations; it would be like condemning Hitler for human rights violations in Austria and refusing to discuss the illegal occupation, or accusing Saddam Hussein of human rights violations in Kuwait while ignoring his invasion.

What is needed is to address the question of who owns the territory of the Ambazonia (the erstwhile Southern Cameroons) and whether the violations will stop. This conflict is entirely a territorial conflict.

Let the West begin to call for justice, truth, and the rule of law in this conflict; let the West call on Cameroon to publish the instruments by which it lays claim to the territory of the Southern Cameroons; let the West call for a UN-organized referendum to settle this conflict conclusively; let the West call on Cameroon not merely to respect human rights but also the people's rights of the people of the Southern Cameroons.

If the West would not talk of justice, truth, and the rule of law in this case, it must know that it is not helping but promoting the conflict! You promote no peace by supporting injustice and open-armed robbery! We can only discover the truth by an examination of the facts; we can only do justice in this conflict by following the principles of the UN Charter, and in this case, those of the African Union Constitutive Act. We invite the West to review its agenda and actions in this conflict and correct them so that at last it may genuinely contribute to lasting peace between Cameroon and Ambazonia.

INTRODUCTION

It is a fact that the Western world has been the only part of the world concerned enough about the conflict raging in Cameroon to the point of some
Western governments talking about it. The African Union and African states,
which in theory were supposed to lead the way, have remained as silent as
the graveyard and shown almost no concern. Credit must be given to Western
powers for this show of concern. At this point, the reasons for their concern
do not matter. All countries in the world have continued to claim that they
all believe in a world without war and in UN principles. It, therefore, beats
the imagination why conflicts such as the one raging in Cameroon should
be ignored by all except the Western powers despite the atrocities, the gross
injustice, the human rights violations, and the purposelessness of the conflict
itself.

While the West has done well to call world attention to the conflict, any
careful person who understands the conflict would wonder what their role in
the conflict is intended to be. On the surface, they have condemned the gross
human rights violations on both sides; have called for dialogue without pre-
conditions; have even partially withdrawn some military aid to Cameroon;
have held various hearings on the matter; sent envoys to Cameroon, purportedly to persuade Paul Biya, president of Cameroon, to accept dialogue;
and the United States together with other countries even initiated an Arria-
Formula hearing on the matter in the UN Security Council.

While the West has done all of the above and seemingly appears to be
working hard to address the conflict or to get the parties in the conflict to dialogue, a careful observer sees clearly that these efforts fall far short of what
is necessary to end the conflict. To say the least, the efforts fuel the conflict
rather than cure it; these efforts all fail to address the key elements necessary
to end the conflict!

WHAT IS THE AMBAZONIA CONFLICT ALL ABOUT?

Do not raise any alarm yet. To see this clearly, it is important to understand
exactly what the conflict is about. The root cause of the conflict is the illegal
occupation and annexation of the British Southern Cameroons (now, Ambazonia) by the Republic of Cameroun, as a consequence of the British failure
to decolonize the Southern Cameroons (Ambazonia) and her illegal transfer
of the territory to the Republic of Cameroon in 1961 at the termination of the
Trusteeship Agreement! As per UNGA Res. 1514 of December 14, 1960,
decolonization could only be said to have taken place if the trust or colonial power transferred the instruments of power to the indigenous peoples

over whom it was ruling. In the case of the Southern Cameroons, there was an elected and functional government in place led by Premier John Ngu Foncha. But the British ignored and bypassed the elected Premier and the House of Assembly and handed the territory to Cameroon as would be seen presently!

MORONIC INDEPENDENCE WITHOUT SOVEREIGNTY

A plebiscite had been conducted in the Southern Cameroons on February 11, 1961, asking the people of the Southern Cameroons whether they wished to achieve independence by joining the Federation of Nigeria or the Republic of Cameroon. No one reading this would understand what to "achieve independence by joining" another country meant, but sadly, those are the very words of UNGA Res. 1352 (XIV) October 16, 1959! Whatever it meant, the vote went in favor of achieving "independence by joining" the Republic of Cameroon.

The UN General Assembly followed up this promise of "independence by joining" by voting overwhelmingly in favor of Southern Cameroons independence on April 21, 1961, and set the date of that independence to be October 1, 1961. The understanding between the two parties for joining was that it was going to be a federation of "two states equal in status." The terms of UNGA Res. 1608(XV) of April 21, 1961, calling for a tripartite conference between the Administering Authority (UK), the government of the Southern Cameroons, and the Republic of Cameroon to urgently work out the terms of union were ignored by the Administering Authority and have never been implemented up till today!

VIOLATION OF UN REQUIREMENT
FOR A UNION TREATY

Without working out any terms of joining and without complying with the critical Res. 1514 of December 14, 1960, dealing with the unconditional independence for trust and non-self-governing territories, Britain on September 30, 1961, invited the president of French Cameroon, Amadou Ahidjo, and handed the instruments of power over the Southern Cameroons to him. This, it is alleged, was in fulfillment of a secret deal between Britain and France since Cameroon was being used merely as a proxy to hand the territory to France. DeGaulle is said to have commented that France received a small gift from the Queen! Ahidjo moved in and occupied the Southern Cameroons, and to fool/deceive the world, amended the constitution of his country,

French Cameroon, into what he called a federal constitution and declared the formation of a federation.

IMPOSITION OF AN UNRATIFIED
FEDERAL CONSTITUTION

The Southern Cameroons House of Assembly never passed any law to form a federation with the Republic of Cameroon because there was no agreement on the terms. From then on, the world was told that the Southern Cameroons and the Republic of Cameroon had entered into a federal union, all of which was a complete hoax! Since there was no agreement, the federation was simply a thin veil to cover the annexation. Article 47 of the so-called federal constitution stated that the federal structure of the country was so holy that no proposal to amend it could ever be accepted; this was again merely a bait to fool the Southern Cameroons.

FRAUDULENT REFERENDUM FOR "UNITARY" STATE

A few years down the road, in 1972, French Cameroon abolished the federation through yet another fraudulent mechanism: by getting the population of French Cameroon, which was four times that of the Southern Cameroons, to participate in a vote to decide whether the federation should be abolished or not! It was so abolished. But how could the population of French Cameroon participate in a vote to abolish the federation when the federation was meant only to protect the people of the Southern Cameroons and when it was the people of the Southern Cameroons alone who had voted to achieve independence in association with French Cameroon?

This, in brief, is the story of the illegal occupation. There is no treaty of union between the two countries; they never achieved independence as one country; there are no terms governing the relationship; there are international boundaries separating the two countries.

CAMEROON'S FRAUD AND OPPRESSION

The history of these two countries is one of unbelievable deceit from French Cameroon. It should be recalled that when the question of the independence of the Southern Cameroons was put to vote on April 21, 1961, at the UN General Assembly, Cameroon was one of those countries that failed to vote for Southern Cameroons' independence! To Cameroon, the UN-organized plebiscite is interpreted as simply a means to make a free gift of the people, territory, and government of the Southern Cameroons to her! Even if contrary to all evidence it is supposed that a union existed, why would the Southern Cameroons be unable to withdraw from it in the same way as Britain is withdrawing from the European Union, for example? And now that Cameroon scrapped the basis of the purported union, on what basis should the Southern Cameroons continue to be bound?

Since the illegal occupation and annexation, the people of the Southern Cameroons have been subjected to the most brutal forms of assimilation and diabolical torments: they are prohibited from all peaceful assembly in their own territory; they cannot form political parties to mobilize and educate their people; they cannot question the basis on which Cameroon is ruling their country; their territory is militarized round the clock; their educational and legal systems are systematically being dismantled; their own language, English, is not even the official language in their territory but they are imposed French; the official language in all professional schools is French; the entire economic infrastructure of the Southern Cameroons has been razed to the ground: banks, airports, wharves, hydro-electrical plants and everything have been dismantled.

CAMEROON'S STRATEGY OF DISTORTING HISTORY

Cameroon has embarked on the diabolic project to delete from the minds of the people of the Southern Cameroons the fact that they are a separate nation and ruled themselves from 1954 to 1961; that it was the country that graciously granted refuge to the hundreds of thousands of citizens of Cameroon escaping the civil war that was ravaging that country in the late 1950s. It was these refugees who first brought the idea of one Cameroon into existence! By 2016, French magistrates and teachers who do not understand a word of English had flooded the Southern Cameroons as an official government policy of assimilation. This is the last straw that broke the Carmel's back, leading to the current revolution.

NAILING IT DOWN: NOT ROOTED IN MARGINALIZATION, BUT A TERRITORIAL CONFLICT

These facts show that the conflict is unmistakably a territorial conflict, not one of marginalization or anything else. Cameroon simply has no jurisdiction within the territory of the Southern Cameroons, and it knows this! If there is one thing that Cameroon seeks from the rest of the world it is this: for the world to assume that Cameroon has jurisdiction over the territory of the Southern Cameroons and thus consider the matter as a domestic affair. All of Cameroon's efforts are geared at preventing the world from ever questioning the basis of its claimed jurisdiction within the Southern Cameroons. Yet, Cameroon cannot cite a single article of the African Union Constitutive Act or the UN Charter or International Law which grants it jurisdiction over the Southern Cameroons/Ambazonia. This is nothing else but territorial armed robbery in the 21st century!

These facts have been repeatedly explained to the whole world, and especially to Western powers. These facts are also independently verifiable, first by consulting the General Secretariat of the UN whether there is a treaty of union between the Southern Cameroons and the Republic of Cameroon in compliance with Article 102 of the UN Charter; second, by consulting the UN Decolonization Committee to provide the instruments of decolonization of the Southern Cameroons, if there are any. These are public sources which will put an end to all disputes.

CONFLICT CANNOT BE RESOLVED WITHOUT ADDRESSING THE TERRITORIAL CAUSE

No one can pretend to try to resolve a conflict without first understanding exactly what the conflict is about. If the conflict is territorial and you think it is one of marginalization, you will never resolve it. In conflict resolution, no sincere broker ignores the facts of the case. The pillars of peace in the world are justice, truth, and the rule of law. Only from this light do we now see clearly what Western powers are doing in this conflict. While claiming in words to be extremely concerned about the gross human rights violations, they have simply refused to examine the causes of those violations; while asking the parties to dialogue without pre-conditions, they, at the same time, permit Cameroon to refuse all dialogue by erroneously and perhaps knowing referring to the territory of the Southern Cameroons as Northwest and Southwest regions of Cameroon.

If Western powers avoid the main cause of the conflict which is territorial and continue to deceive Cameroon that Ambazonia is part of its territory, why would Cameroon accept to dialogue with a part of its country on equal terms?

The West has allowed Cameroon to believe that the Western world sees the conflict as an internal affair. By regarding this conflict as an internal affair, the West virtually ties its own hands and those of the international community and allows Cameroon to do as it wishes! Not once has the West used the words justice, truth, rule of law, or even refer to the facts of the case in this conflict! The West has ignored the facts altogether for an agenda that is yet to be discovered.

Even when the West speaks of human rights violations, it studiously avoids the highest and most fundamental people's rights, which are: external self-determination, the right to own resources, the right to justice, the right to freedom of assembly, the right of association and to form political parties to educate and mobilize its peoples, the right to live free of fear and Cameroon militarization of their territory, the right to use their own inherited language as the only official language in their territory and not to be imposed French, and the right to use their own inherited system of education and law.

The one Cameroon survives only by stifling all debate on its pretended title to the Southern Cameroons. We need not be lawyers or a court of law to use our own common sense and reason on these straightforward matters.

The West has refused to examine the facts and decided to assume, and not verify, whether Cameroon has jurisdiction over the territory of the Southern Cameroons or not. Or perhaps the West is promoting annexation, conflicts, and turmoil in Africa by deliberately choosing to support the illegal territorial acquisition and territorial annexation.

IS THE WEST INTERESTED IN JUSTICE?

Worst still, the West has given Cameroon the impression that it is not interested in justice, truth, and the rule of law; all it is interested in is simply to see an end to the war, whether its causes are addressed or not. What is the consequence? The consequence is that Cameroon has gone all out to commit even more horrific atrocities in the hope of intimidating the people of the Southern Cameroons to surrender, hoping that all it needs is to show the West a military victory for Western concerns to be satisfied! At the same time, the people of the Southern Cameroons are so convinced of the justice of their cause that they would prefer to be all killed than to surrender their territory to Cameroon.

The West cannot fail to see the apartheid it is promoting by tacitly telling the people of the Southern Cameroons that they are good only to obey orders from their superiors from French Cameroon; that they are mere fixtures in their own land or that Cameroon has a right to rule its own territory and cross its boundaries and rule the Southern Cameroons; that even though there are international boundaries separating the two countries, the West would disregard those boundaries. This is to reduce to people of the Southern Cameroons to less than animals, because even animals fight for their territory!

We remind the reader that this war was never started by the peaceful people of Ambazonia; it was declared by the president of French Cameroon against the Ambazonian people, encouraged by Western tacit support of Cameroon's annexation and illegal territorial occupation.

The terrible consequences of supporting the crime of annexation and territorial theft in the 21st century, contrary to all principles of the UN Charter and International Law, are incalculable. How can the West blatantly ignore the provisions of the UN Charter, the African Union Constitutive Act, and International Law to support these crimes at a time when the world has provided itself with all the tools to resolve these issues peacefully? And peacefully, this conflict could be resolved, if the West and the rest of the world had bothered to address Southern Cameroon's peaceful attempts at resolving it since 1961. But true to its creed, without a war, the world will not consider that there is a problem!

Is it so impossible for the West to ask Cameroon to prove its international boundaries? Is it so impossible for the West to request Cameroon to publish the instruments on the basis of which it lays claim to the territory of the Southern Cameroons? Is it easier to publish those instruments or to continue killing innocent civilians in order to impose Cameroon's will on the people of the Southern Cameroons? If the West tacitly supports Cameroon's fraudulent claim over the territory of the Southern Cameroons, why does it continue to think Cameroon will ever accept any dialogue? And what does it expect Cameroon to say in such dialogue, knowing that Cameroon has no proof of jurisdiction over that territory?

The West knows more than anyone else that Cameroon has a case to answer under the International Law principle of intangibility of frontiers in so far as the Southern Cameroons was never part of Cameroon at Cameroon's independence on January 1, 1960.

WHY IS THE WEST CALLING FOR DIALOGUE INSTEAD OF REFERENDUM?

And why is the West calling for dialogue which is a mere political game instead of a UN-organized referendum that can settle the case conclusively? The wishes of the people are at the core of Western systems. In every case where the wishes of the people are in doubt in such matters of overwhelming importance, a referendum has almost always been the final solution.

French Caledonia recently had a referendum to determine its fate; Quebec has had two referenda and can have as many as it likes; Scotland has had its own and is planning another one. The UK joined the European Union and is withdrawing through a referendum. How come the West does not see that an UN-organized referendum is the final and lasting solution in this African case? Instead, some Western powers are even suggesting a return to the federal form of government, which they know Cameroon abolished. But how will the Southern Cameroons force Cameroon to respect a federation which it previously abolished? How do you form a federation between a sheep and a wolf? How do you ask Cameroon to exercise power over a territory in which it has no jurisdiction?

And if theory were not enough, the story of failed federations between different territories is monumental in Africa. By what miracle will such a federation between English and French cultures ever succeed, when no such federations have succeeded in Africa or even in the whole world?

WHAT IS THE INTEREST OF THE WEST?

Some voices have been heard to say that Western attitudes in this case are dictated by the fact that this is an African conflict. They would act very differently if this were happening in Europe. When Hitler tried what Biya is trying with the Southern Cameroons, the West solidly rejected it and waged war against him. There are far more smaller states in Europe than the Southern Cameroons and no one questions that. Is it that the West does not believe that justice and the rule of law should apply to Africans or that Africans can always be fooled to keep killing themselves so that in the end the West can always come in and take what it likes?

The story of peaceful efforts to resolve this long-standing conflict by the people of the Southern Cameroons is long; yet, the unwritten rule has always been that the world will never look in your direction unless blood is being spilled! Can this conflict be resolved by ignoring the facts or by refusing to accept the facts? Can it be resolved by ignoring justice and the rule of law? Can it be resolved by refusing to hear the wishes of the people of the Southern Cameroons and imposing Western views? Neither the West nor Cameroon can cite a single article of the UN Charter or African Union Constitutive Act which gives jurisdiction over the Southern Cameroons to the Republic of Cameroon.

In any conflict, those who do not support justice, truth, and the rule of law are obviously fueling and promoting the conflict, no matter what they say. They are not helping to work for a solution. And this is precisely the case with Western powers in the Ambazonian conflict. By refusing to address the root causes, by refusing to even mention the words justice, truth, and the rule of law, they have made themselves promoters of the conflict and the war in Ambazonia. They can promote these conflicts in Africa as much as they want, partly because the African Union has also woefully failed!

The agenda of the West in this conflict has nothing to do with resolving the conflict! They know very well how to resolve this conflict, but they would not. Rather, they fan the flames of war by giving Cameroon the impression that if Cameroon were to win the war, they would be fully satisfied! They therefore indirectly promote the violations of human rights that they appear to be complaining about! They know that a military victory would not resolve the enduring conflict between these totally incompatible peoples. And for those who do not know, let them know from now on that Ambazonia and Cameroon are two completely incompatible peoples: they do not have the same colonial history, do not have the same state culture; do not speak the same language, do not have the same systems of education and law, and do not have the same outlook to life and virtually disagree on every aspect of running the state.

WHAT THE WEST MUST DO IF IT WANTS TO SOLVE THE AMBAZONIA CONFLICT

What is needed to resolve this conflict is justice, truth, and the rule of law, not politics, not sweeping of the facts under the table, not imposition of Western views, not blindfolding of Africans, and not lording it over the parties. Human rights violations cannot be more important that the illegal occupation and annexation which gave rise to those violations; it would be like condemning Hitler for human rights violations in Austria and refusing to discuss the illegal occupation or accusing Sadam of human rights violations in Kuwait while ignoring his invasion.

What is needed is to address the question of who owns the territory of the Southern Cameroons and whether the violations will stop. Let the West begin to call for justice, truth, and the rule of law in this conflict; let the West call on Cameroon to publish the instruments by which it lays claim to the territory of the Southern Cameroons; let the West call for an UN-organized referendum to settle this conflict conclusively; let the West call on Cameroon not merely to respect human rights but also the people's rights of the people of the Southern Cameroons. If the West would not talk of justice, truth, and the rule of law in this case, it must know that it is not helping but promoting the conflict! You promote no peace by supporting injustice and open-armed robbery! We can only discover the truth by an examination of the facts; we can only do justice by following the principles of the UN Charter, and in this case, those of the African Union Constitutive Act. We invite the West to review its agenda and actions in this conflict and correct them so that at last it may genuinely contribute to lasting peace between Cameroon and Ambazonia.

Chapter 12

Foreign Actors and Foreign Reactions to the Liberation Struggle in Southern Cameroons

John Fobanjong

In response to Southern Cameroonian activists who see the armed persecution in their homeland as an act of interstate war, French Cameroon maintains that the conflict is internal. In maintaining that the conflict is internal, the Cameroonian Government hopes to benefit from the protective shield of the principle of non-intervention. Enshrined in Article 2 (7)[1] of the UN Charter, this International Law principle prohibits foreign intervention in the internal affairs of sovereign states. Four years into the conflict, the principle seems to be holding on, as no foreign actor has made any attempt to intervene kinetically in the conflict. Not all intervention however is kinetic. While foreign actors may have stayed away from intervening physically, they have not been coy about expressing their reactions. In this study, we are going to identify and assess the impact of statements and resolutions made by various foreign actors that have addressed the conflict in Southern Cameroons.

On global policy matters, and particularly on matters relating to peace and security, expectations are for the UN to take action. The UN is at the top of the hierarchy of institutions that make global policy. In the preamble to its Charter, international peace and security is listed as one of its most important goals.[2] In our search for solutions to peace and security in the conflict between the two Cameroons, it is important that we start by examining the actions and reactions that the premier institution for peace and security in the world has directed so far to addressing the conflict.

REACTIONS OF THE UN TO THE WAR
IN SOUTHERN CAMEROONS

Article 1, Section 1 of the UN Charter stipulates that this prestigious world body was founded

> International Law, adjustment or settlement of international disputes or situations which might lead to a breach of the peace.[3]

For victims of persecution and marginalization anywhere in the world, the Charter gives hope and raises expectations. Between the 1970s and the 1980s when the leaders of Southern Cameroons began to sense that their status as a co-equal partner in the de facto federation that was established in 1961 was beginning to be surreptitiously undermined, their immediate thought was to turn to the UN for recourse. The thought was not acted upon until in 1990s when the acts of marginalization had gone from surreptitious to outright blatant and egregious. Following the unilateral abrogation of the constitution to eliminate a provision that provided for the then Southern Cameroons president of the National Assembly to succeed the president in the event of vacancy at the presidency, and following the flagrant theft of the victory of yet another Southern Cameroonian who democratically won the presidency in 1992, it became ostensibly clear that French Cameroon was out to politically emasculate and possibly assimilate English-Cameroon. The Southern Cameroons' National Congress, the founding organization that launched the movement for the restoration of the independence of Southern Cameroons, was obliged to send a delegation to the UN on June 1,1995, to petition the UN to review the UN-proctored process that brought the two former trusteeship territories together in 1961. Led by former rime minister John Ngu Foncha, the delegation invited the UN to step up and prevent French Cameroon from continuing with its annexationist policies. The petition was followed the same year by a signature referendum that produced a 99 percent vote in favor of the restoration of the independence of Southern Cameroons, with 315,000 people voting against.[4]

Soon after the Foncha-led delegation's visit to the UN, a lawyer and traditional ruler from Southern Cameroons, Chief Gorji Dinka sued the government of Cameroon in 2005 at the UN Human Rights Commission. In the suit, the plaintiff, Gorji Dinka, claimed that the government of Cameroon had violated Southern Cameroons' right to self-determination, along with his civil and political rights. In 1984, Gorji Dinka publicly declared independence for the Southern Cameroons, renaming the region the "Republic of Ambazonia" in response to French Cameroons' unilateral change of the country's name from the "United Republic of Cameroon" to the "Republic of Cameroon."[5]

In a ruling that was issued on March 17, 2005, the UN Human Rights Commission argued that under the Optional Protocol on the Covenant of Human Rights, it did not have the competence to consider claims relating violations of the right to self-determination. On the claim for the violation of Gorji Dinka's civil and political rights, however, the Committee ruled for Dinka, declaring that Gorji Dinka was entitled to an effective remedy that was to include compensation and assurance for the enjoyment of his civil and political rights. Pursuant to Article 2 of the Covenant, the government of French Cameroon was asked to take measures to prevent similar violations in the future, including measures that would ensure the rights of all individuals within its territory or subject to its jurisdiction are recognized and protected.[6]

Albeit a private citizen, the ruling in favor of Gorji Dinka was an affirmative acknowledgment of the political marginalization of the people and state of the former UN trusteeship territory of Southern Cameroons. It was a historic ruling. It was the first time a UN organ finally admitted that Southern Cameroonians were victims of marginalization in the *Republique du Cameroun*. As decisive as the ruling was, it provided no enforcement mechanisms and no timeline for the corrective measures. To date, there is no evidence that Gorji Dinka ever received compensation, or that his civil and political rights were ever reinstated. Had French Cameroon taken "measures to prevent similar violations in the future and to ensure that the rights of individuals within its territory are recognized," Cameroon would not be at war today.

The UN has ever since stayed mute on all further pleas for redress by Southern Cameroonians. Prior to an October 27, 2017, visit to Cameroon by the UN Secretary-General Antonio Guterres, there was expectation and anticipation among the Cameroonian English-speaking community at home and abroad that the Secretary-General was hopefully going to address the conflict and possibly begin the process that would lead to its resolution. Guterres visited and left without visiting the English-speaking regions and without publicly addressing the conflict. The only image that lingers of the visit is a photo of the UN Secretary-General receiving a golden statue as a gift from the president of Cameroon.[7]

The gift produced a fallout between the UN and watchdog media organizations in New York. The press credentials of Inner-City Press's Matthew Russel Lee were revoked, and he was permanently banned from the UN for his criticism of the Secretary-General's conduct in Cameroon.[8] While the UN claimed that the de-accreditation and ban was for conduct unbecoming of a journalist, independent observers point out that Lee's ban had to do with corruption and the nitty-gritty way the UN is administered.[9]

In March 2020, the UN Secretary-General congratulated parties to conflicts in eleven countries that answered his call for a COVID-19 ceasefire. Among the parties was the Southern Cameroons Defense Force, SOCADEF—one of the half-dozen liberation forces fighting for the restoration of the independence of the Southern Cameroons region.[10] French Cameroon itself did not heed the UN's call for the ceasefire. It is not known if Secretary-General made a personal request to Paul Biya to honor the ceasefire. One would expect that the personal relationship he developed with Biya when he visited with him in 2017 would probably give him leverage to talk to the Cameroonian president to agree to a ceasefire and begin the process for a ceasefire. Since this did not happen, there is reason to doubt if the UN is interested and/or genuinely committed to carrying out the political heavy lifting that is needed to end the war in Cameroon.

REACTIONS OF THE VATICAN TO THE
WAR IN SOUTHERN CAMEROONS

In the search for pathways to peace and conflict resolution, the Vatican's global influence is second only to that of the UN. In conflicts where the belligerents involved are of the Christian faith, there is the expectation that the Church can be called upon to play a role that would trigger the moral and spiritual sensibilities of the belligerents to agree to end hostilities and seek peace settlement. In the quest for a solution to peace and security in the war in Cameroon therefore, it is important we look at the role the Vatican can play.

Data from the Pew Research Center's Religion and Public Life Project reports that 70.3 percent of Cameroon's population is Christian.[11] The CIA World Fact Book breaks it down to 38.3 percent Catholic, 25.5 percent Protestant, and 6.9 percent other Christian faiths.[12] What this could mean is that a majority of the combatants on both sides of the conflict may be Christians. At the leadership level, it is well documented that the president who declared the war was a seminary student in the early 1950s. Since becoming president, he has visited and met with all three Popes that headed the Vatican at different periods—from John Paul II to Benedict XVI and Francis. In January 2008, he authorized the opening of a Cameroonian Embassy at the Vatican.[13]

On the side of the Southern Cameroons Liberation Movement, as factionalized as it is, it is equally established that the leaders of the various factions are practicing Christians. Despite traveling on a very tight schedule, Julius Ayuk Tabe, Founding President of the Interim Government of Ambazonia, took time off his 2017 tour to the United States to attend Church service at the Good Shepherd Presbyterian Church in Easton, Massachusetts. In many of the speeches given during that tour, he always made sure he called for prayers and made sure he invoked God's guidance to the Southern Cameroons' cause.

Acting Interim President Samuel Sako was, prior to the outbreak of the conflict, pastor of a Church in the United States.

In any conflict where both sides presumably belong to the same faith, there is a good likelihood that they will be predisposed to agreeing to any appeals for peace talks that come from the authority of their faith. That both the leadership and the combatants on both sides of the conflict share the same Christian faith, this should mean that they would be open to agree to any appeal for peace talks that comes from the Vatican. On February 17, 2020, sixteen Bishops from around the world, motivated by their concern for the suffering of unarmed civilians in Southern Cameroons, sent an open letter to President Paul Biya appealing for a negotiated settlement.[14]

Pope Francis has pointedly indicated that resolving the Southern Cameroons' conflict and restoring peace in Cameroon is a major priority for the Vatican. On September 29, one day before the opening of the "Major National Dialogue" in Cameroon, the Pope openly expressed sympathy for "the sufferings and the hopes of the beloved Cameroonian people," inviting worshippers at St. Peter's Square to pray for the dialogue to be "fruitful and lead to peaceful, just and lasting solutions." Citing Cameroon among other countries at his Easter *Urbi et Orbi* address in 2019, Pope Francis called on citizens of the world to end "the roar of arms" in conflict zones and become "builders of bridges, not walls."[15]

In February 2020, the Secretary for Relations with States of the Holy See, British Archbishop Paul Richard Gallagher met with Cameroon's Foreign Minister LeJeune Mbella Mbella and offered to mediate on behalf of the Holy See. One month later, in a follow-up message from Pope Francis to President Biya, the Apostolic Nuncio to Cameroon and Equatorial Guinea, Monseigneur Julio Murat on March 18, 2019, expressed the Pope's desire for a just and peaceful solution to the war and indicated that the Catholic Church was willing to "contribute to the promotion of the common good and to peace in Cameroon."[16] In response to the COVID-19 pandemic, Pope Francis on March 29, 2020, joined the UN Secretary-General in calling for an end to armed conflicts "in all corners of the world," reminding the leaders of nations and armed groups to overcome rivalries and understand that "conflicts are not resolved through war" and that "it is necessary to overcome antagonisms and oppositions through dialogue and a constructive search for peace."[17]

Given the proactive role the Vatican has played so far, there is hope and confidence that the Catholic Church, along with other Christian Churches, can play an instrumental role in influencing the two sides to come together. In the International Crisis Group's 2017 Report, the Crisis Group was confident that "The Catholic Church (one of the country's strongest institutions) could help break the stalemate."[18] And in February 2019, the Vatican did actually offer to serve as a mediator in the conflict.[19]

REACTIONS OF THE AFRICAN UNION TO THE WAR IN SOUTHERN CAMEROONS

The African Union is for the African continent, and the UN is for the global system. On matters of peace and security, it is the go-to institution on the continent of Africa.

> (and) collective sanctions are meant to be triggered should an African state descend into dictatorship.[20]

Its objective as outlined in Article 3(b) of its Constitutive Act is to "defend the sovereignty, territorial integrity and independence of its Member States." The AU has three clearly stated principles that have immediate relevance to the ongoing war in Cameroon: Article 4(b) guarantees "respect of borders existing on achievement of independence"; Article 4(f) prohibits "the use of force or threat to use force among Member States of the Union"; and Article 4(m) calls for "respect for democratic principles, human rights, the rule of law and good governance."

Extra-continentally, policymaking bodies across the Western world—including the British Parliament, the Canadian Parliament, the European Union Commission, and the US Congress—have debated and issued resolutions addressing the war in Cameroon. Even municipalities in Lowell Massachusetts and in Brazil have issued proclamations supporting independence for Southern Cameroons. Meanwhile, there is nowhere on record that the African Union Commission—the body with the immediate jurisdictional competence for conflict resolution in Africa—has ever debated or issued a statement addressing the war in Cameroon. In this section, we are going to take a look at the role the AU has played or failed to play in bringing this agonizing war to an end.

If the African Union Commission has so far not formally committed itself to holding a hearing that would end the conflict in Cameroon, it is not for lack of competence or mandate. By every measure, it has the statutory mandate and the jurisdictional competence. What it seems to lack however is the political will. The African Union provides in Article 4(b) of its own Constitutive Act that the borders of African states remain recognized and inviolable as were obtained at independence. Francophone Cameroon achieved independence on January 1, 1960. Southern Cameroons gained independence on October 1, 1960. These are the grounds on which Southern Cameroonians are fighting. They see it is a "just war." The international boundary between the two states is well demarcated and clearly documented in the archives of the UN, the African Union, and Yaounde. It is for the AU, the UN, or even Yaounde to prove the contrary.

When the facts are this clear and the statutes this clearly defined, policy-making bodies with jurisdictional competence are expected to act proactively. Cameroon would not be at war today had the African Union Commission lived up to its responsibilities. Tensions between Southern Cameroons and Francophone Cameroon have been brewing for decades. The African Union Commission knew it, and long before anyone else, it saw this war coming.

In 2009, the judicial arm of the African Union, the African Commission on Human and Peoples' Rights, held a hearing on a case that was filed by two Southern Cameroons' pro-independence movements—the Southern Camer-oons National Conference (SCNC) and the Southern Cameroons Peoples' Organization (SCAPO). In a decision reached at its 45th Ordinary Session on May 27, 2009, in Communication 266/2003 *Kevin* Mgwanga *Gumne* et al *vs. Cameroon*, the court found that the Republique du Cameroun had violated Articles 1, 2, 4, 5, 6, 7(1), 10, 11, 19, and 26 of the African Union Constitutive Act.[21] The court recognized in its ruling that under International Law, English-speaking Cameroonians identifiably meet the definition of a "people" as "they manifest numerous characteristics and affinities, which include a common history, linguistic tradition, territorial connection, and political outlook."

On the question of whether Southern Cameroons was entitled to the right to independence, the court argued that to invoke independence or self-deter-mination as prescribed by Article 20 of the African Union Constitutive Act, the plaintiff must prove that the two conditions under Article 20(2), namely oppression and domination, have been met. As of the time SCNC and SCAPO filed the suit, the oppression and marginalization of the people of Southern Cameroons was still tactically disguised and subtle, and no way nearly as ruthless as it was in the post-2016 era. As a result, the court argued that the plaintiffs (SCNC and SCAPO) had provided no evidence that would justify a ruling on the right to self-determination. The government of French Camer-oon, in its written argument, implicitly accepted that self-determination could be exercisable by the plaintiffs if massive violations of human rights or denial of participation in public affairs are proven. In its final recommendation, the African Union Court called on the government of Cameroon to enter into constructive dialogue with the plaintiffs to resolve the grievances.

This was more than a decade ago. The government of Cameroon has since not held any dialogue with SCAPO or SCNC. The African Union Com-mission is undoubtedly aware of this. Were dialogue held, the Commission would have known. It funds and oversees the work of the court, and so the proceedings of any dialogue between the government of Cameroon and SCAPO/SCNC would have to be reported to the Commission.

What the African Union Court may have omitted in the *Kevin Mgwanga Gunme et al v. Cameroon* ruling was the stipulation of a timeline. Due diligence requires that when litigants in a case are granted the right to go out and resolve their grievances by dialogue, it is imperative for the court to set a timeline for when the litigants must report back to the court. It is also important for the court to appoint a third-party mediator or broker who would be charged with facilitating the dialogue or mediation. This was a gross failure on the part of the court.

Even after the outbreak of the war, the African Union Commission continued to fail the English-speaking community in Cameroon. An institutional body that was founded and charged with the mission of promoting peace and security is expected to raise an alarm whenever the government of a member state declares punitive war against one of the ethnic or linguistic group. But when Paul Biya declared war against the Southern Cameroons community in 2017, the African Union Commission did not move to question or investigate the decision. Had the Commission demanded an explanation from Biya, this possibly would have avoided the war in Cameroon.

The African Union Commission sees itself as the vanguard for the sonnet "African Solutions to African Problems,"[22] yet, the continental body failed to question or even acknowledge that there was a problem in the Southern Cameroons region in Cameroon. When the Chairman of the African Union Commission, Moussa Faki Mahatmat, visited Cameroon at the height of the war on July 12–13, 2018, he and his host, Paul Biya, were more concerned about making sure the war did not disturb the October 7, 2018, presidential elections.[23] He left without making a public statement to condemn the war. For the Chairman of a continental body whose principal mission is the promotion of peace and security, this behavior was rather unusual.

The only known instance when a statement was made by the Chairman of the African Union Commission acknowledging the conflict in Cameroon was when he visited the country in the company of the Secretary-General of the International Organization of *La Francophonie*, Louise Mushikiwabo, and the Secretary-General of the Commonwealth, Patricia Scotland, in November 2019. On that visit, he endorsed the recommendations of a dialogue that was organized by the government of Cameroon in Yaounde—the "Grand National Dialogue"—in September 2019, describing them as "the only path to peace."[24] The same "Grand National Dialogue" and its recommendations were described by third-party observers as a ruse designed to deflect calls for an inclusive international mediation.

Among the Grand National Dialogue's recommendations was a call for the establishment of a "special status" for the minority English-speaking region and a call for regional "decentralization." The leaders of the Southern Cameroons movement saw the "Grand National Dialogue" and its recommendations as a well-calculated decoy to deflect attention away from the international community's call for ceasefire and for comprehensive dialogue with jailed leaders of the Southern Cameroons' struggle. Thus, what the AU Chairman saw as "the only path to peace," Southern Cameroons' leaders and most international observers saw it as a "non-starter."

REACTIONS BY THE UNITED STATES TO THE WAR IN SOUTHERN CAMEROONS

Reactions from the United States to the war in the Cameroons have included public statements by the US Undersecretary of State for African Affairs, resolutions by the US Congress, termination of Cameroon's preferential trade privileges under the AGOA, and reduction of US Military assistance to Cameroon Republic. Among all of these actors, the Undersecretary of State for African Affairs,Tibor Nagy is the most outspoken and the most passionate American voice on the war. He vociferously defined the United States' position on the war as "support for a unified Cameroon,"[25] and at the same time he has threatened to push for an international hearing if the Cameroonian Government does not act to establish peace. At an interview he gave during a visit to Africa in March 2019, Tibor Nagy bemoaned the suffering of the "Southern Cameroons people."

> My heart breaks for Cameroon. Every day people are dying, and every day people are suffering. . . . those poor people in northwest and southwest . . . are just suffering so, so much. So, we need to be focused on that and maybe take it further to an international forum to look at.[26]

He went on to say in a *Voice of America* radio interview that "What the people in the Southwest and the Northwest want more than anything else is decentralization. They would like to have control over their own lives, their own historical heritage."[27] Describing the "Grand National Dialogue" merely as a symbolic event, Tibor Nagy called on the Cameroon Government to organize a "true dialogue," and citing America's experience with insurgencies elsewhere, he hinted that "The truth is it's not going to be won militarily . . . You can't wipe out a thought militarily."[28]

In May 2019, the US Congress issued a resolution—*H.Res.358*—outlining a list of measures that the Cameroonian Government needed to take to reestablish peace and security in the country. They included, among others, these five critical steps:

- Initiate broad-based dialogue without preconditions and make a credible, full faith effort to work with religious and community leaders in the Southern Cameroons region to address grievances and seek nonviolent solutions to resolve conflict and constitutional reforms that would protect minority concerns, such as reconstituting a Federal system;

- Respect the fundamental rights of all Cameroonian citizens, including political activists and journalists;
- Investigate human rights violations committed in the Southern Cameroons regions and take measures to prevent arbitrary detention, torture, disappearances, deaths in custody, and inhumane prison conditions;
- Release all those detained in the context of the Southern Cameroons crisis, including the Cameroonians forcibly returned from Nigeria;
- Allow unfettered access to humanitarian and health care workers.

On the Southern Cameroons' side, the Resolution made the following demands to the revolutionary leaders:

- Engage with Cameroonian government officials in a dialogue without preconditions to peacefully express grievances and find nonviolent ways to resolve the conflict;
- Stop human rights abuses, including kidnappings, extortion, use of child soldiers and killings of civilians;
- End school boycott; and
- Release all civilians illegally detained or kidnapped in the Southern Cameroons regions.

The Resolution was followed by the visit of its authors to Cameroon. During the visit, Congresswoman Karen Bass head of a seven-person congressional delegation, reiterated America's position on the conflict:

> We especially want to see a peaceful dialogue, a peaceful resolution without conditions. We want to see all sides come to the table. We recently passed a resolution in Congress saying this and we wanted to come and see first-hand what is happening in the country.[29]

In July 2019, just two months after the passage of the first resolution, the US Congress passed a second on the conflict in Cameroon. Sponsored by Senator Benjamin Cardin, the second resolution—S. Res. 292—appealed to all parties in the conflict to:

- Agree to an immediate ceasefire;
- Guarantee unfettered humanitarian assistance;
- Exercise restraint and ensure that protests remain peaceful; and
- Engage in inclusive dialogue with civil society to get to a political solution that respects the rights and freedoms of the people of Cameroon.

One year later, on September 8, 2020, the US Senate issued yet another resolution—S.Res.684—addressing the conflict in Cameroon. Sponsored by Senator Risch James, the Resolution condemned

> abuses committed by state security forces and armed groups in the Northwest and Southwest regions of Cameroon, and it affirmed that the United States continued to hold Cameroon responsible for safeguarding the security and constitutional rights of all of its citizens, regardless of their region, religion, or political views. Further, it urged all parties to the conflict in Cameroon, the government of Cameroon, U.S. foreign relations entities, and members of the international community to take specified steps toward resolving the ongoing civil conflict in Cameroon.[30]

The Executive Branch of the US Government also passed policies in direct response to the conflict in Cameroon. On October 31, 2019, president of the United States signed an order terminating Cameroon's eligibility for trade privileges with the United States under the African Growth and Opportunity Act (AGOA), citing Cameroon's failure to address concerns over "persistent gross violations of internationally recognized human rights, including torture and extrajudicial killings, by its security forces in the Southern Cameroons region of the country."[31]

The termination of the trade privileges was extended to include reduction in military assistance to the Cameroonian Government, translating to a loss of $17 million in security assistance. It also resulted in the withdrawal of Cameroon's membership in the State Partnership Program, which pairs nations with various US National Guard units for training.[32]

REACTIONS OF THE EUROPEAN UNION TO THE WAR IN SOUTHERN CAMEROONS

In reaction to the war in Cameroon, the European Parliament in 2019 issued a resolution (RSP/2019/2691) calling on the Cameroonian Government to end human rights abuses and its culture of impunity in the Southern Cameroons region. It appealed to the government to organize an inclusive political dialogue to resolve the conflict, offering that the international community was ready to play a mediating role. The EU Resolution actually went further to propose a roadmap for the peace talks. It suggested the talks would start with hearings at the AU and the Economic Community of the Central African States (ECCAS), with the EU on standby to support the process. In the event that the conflict is not resolved at this level, the talks would then be moved to the UN Security Council.[33] In addition to the proposed use of the

AU, ECCAS, and the UN Security Council as possible institutional venues for mediation, the European Union in June 2019 joined the US and the UN to endorse a Swiss-led mediation initiative proposed by the Swiss Federal Department of Foreign Affairs.[34]

THE ELUSIVE QUEST FOR PEACE AND SECURITY IN CAMEROON

In our study, we conceptualized peace and security as two sides of the same coin. You cannot have peace without security, and you cannot have security without peace. An end to the reign of war in Cameroon will not by itself produce a reign of peace and security in the country. War or no war, peace, and security are values that we must constantly cultivate and nurture.

This means therefore that sustainable peace and security require sustainable investments in peace-building initiatives. It demands the creation of conditions where the will and aspirations of the people are expressed and reflected in the politics and policies that govern them. This means redefining and restructuring governance to allow power to go from the bottom-up, rather than from the top-down. When this is done, the masses are empowered; and when the masses are empowered, it gives them "buy-in" in the system. When the people are allowed to have a stake or "buy-in" in the policies and politics that govern them, they are less likely to become disruptive or rebellious. Nobody would want to be party to a call to help drown a boat that s/he has contributed to building.

The current structure of power in Cameroon is one that goes from the top-down. This was one of the reasons why the 2017 negotiations between the government and the consortium of teachers, lawyers and civil society organizations failed; and it is the principal reason why there is war in the country today. For sustainable peace and security to return to Cameroon, this structure would need to be flipped upside down—and sovereignty returned to the people. The authority that governs Cameroonians would need to come from the bottom-up, and not from the top-down. This will demand that at all levels of government, from city councilors to mayors, governors, and president, people are allowed the freedom to choose their leaders from an electoral list that is established by them, and not by Yaounde. Divisional officers, or prefects and sub-prefects, are relics of colonial administrators. In a democratically restructured Cameroon, there should be no place for appointed divisional or sub-divisional officers. The functions these officers exercise are functions that inherently belong to elected mayors and elected city councilors.

Sustainable peace and security reigns in an environment of transparency and accountability. Accountability is achieved by establishing conditions that allow for alternation in power. Alternation here implies term limits. No one, from the city councilor to the mayor to the governor and president, should be allowed to stay in office past two terms. Nobody has the monopoly of knowledge or wisdom. No matter the knowledge and wisdom a leader may have, that knowledge and wisdom would with time go stale, and complacency would kick in if allowed to stay in power for too long. It is through the constant recycling of political leadership that new ideas and new visions can be injected in government.

RIPE FOR SETTLEMENT

The war in Cameroon has lasted for as long as the First World War lasted. If nothing is done to stop it, by next year and the year after, it would have lasted for as long as the Second World War. This was a war the government of Cameroon thought was going to take just weeks. It is obvious that the government grossly underestimated the will and determination of the Southern Cameroons population. By now, after four years of fighting, the regime in Yaounde may have finally come to the realization that this is an unwinnable war. Early on in the war it was forewarned of this eventuality by international observers. But for reasons that may have had to do with sovereign self-pride, it refused to yield to calls for dialogue. War is a costly venture. There are no weapons industries in Cameroon. This means that all the weapons that are used in prosecuting the current war in Cameroon—from boots to uniforms to armory—have to be imported. With the country's economy running at half-throttle (the war forced country's largest private sector employer, the CDC, to shut down three years ago), it is obvious that the weapons are purchased with borrowed money. In addition to the financial toll, the war is also costing the regime the lives of its soldiers. When you add this to the opportunity costs that the regime has to suffer as the result of failed or abandoned investments in other sectors of the economy, it would be easy to sense "war fatigue." The "war fatigue" may actually be on both sides; and if it is determined to be on both sides, then this can lead us to conclude that the war is ripe for settlement.

On the side of the Southern Cameroons, two factors have contributed to the "war fatigue"—factionalism and school closure. Differences that appear irreconcilable have led to factionalism, and factionalism has led to organizational infighting. Energy and resources are directed at fighting rival factions than at fighting the common enemy. This has made the development of a common front and a common war strategy impossible. There is no known case in history where a divided army ever won a war. When you add this gloomy picture to the school closure that has lasted for four years, one can see that psychologically there is mounting pressure for the war to end. All things considered, any rational person can readily see that the war is ripe for settlement.

FINDING A FACE-SAVING STRATEGY

That a war is ripe for settlement does not necessarily mean that both sides will, at the first beckon, willingly drop down their weapons and go in for peace talks. This is a war in which both sides went in fully determined to obtain battlefield victory. As the government stuck to its "one and indivisible Cameroon" clarion call, the Southern Cameroons people stuck to their "Independence or resistance forever"[35] battlefield pledge. To have them break or give up these strongly worded pledges and settle for something less than total victory, there needs to be some face-saver for them. They both will need some face-saving excuse that they can take back to their constituencies to explain why they are now agreeing to go in for a negotiated settlement. The collective challenge for facilitators of the peace process will be to come up with a face-saver that will be convincing and acceptable to both sides.

ADDRESSING THE CONFIDENCE DEFICIT

Prior to the outbreak of the conflict, there was a serious confidence deficit between Southern Cameroons and the government of Cameroon. Even between themselves, Francophone Cameroonians have no trust or confidence in their government. This is how ominous the confidence deficit is.

Going back to 1961, betrayal after betrayal has caused Southern Cameroonians to lose all trust in the government of Cameroon. In addition, Southern Cameroonians are profoundly suspicious of Francophones. They live in constant fear of Francophone hegemony; and of a likely hidden agenda to assimilate or dissolve them into what Joseph Wirba describes as "two cubes of sugar in a bowl of water." The president of French Cameroon confirmed this agenda at a Peace Forum moderated by Mo Ibrahim in November 2019.[36] Under these circumstances, any efforts directed at bringing the parties together for peace talks without first of all taking time to address the confidence or trust deficit may not yield the desired outcome.

PAVING THE WAY FOR A NEGOTIATED
PEACE SETTLEMENT—RECOMMENDATIONS
AND PRACTICAL PROPOSALS

Conduct A Public Opinion Survey To Find Out Peoples' Preferences On Whether the War Should End or Continue.

After establishing here above that both sides to the conflict may be "fatigued" by the war, I think it would be proper to test that hypothesis. The best way to test it would be to organize the conduct of two public opinion surveys—one in the Southern Cameroons and one in the French Cameroon. The respondents to the survey will be asked to say whether they would like to see the war end or whether they would like it to continue. In the event where a majority on both sides say they would like the war to end, the results could be used to help save the faces of leaders on both sides of the conflict. It would be seen as a greenlight from their constituencies to participate in a negotiated peace settlement.

Cardinal Tumi did one such survey two years ago, so we know that it is doable. We however recommend that this survey be done by a neutral party—preferably a foreign NGO—in order to avoid any bias or semblance of suspicion.

Identify Countries That Have Leverage on Both Sides and Have Them Put Pressure on Their Clients to Go in for a Negotiated Peace Settlement

France, Israel, China, and Chad seem to have leverage on the government of Cameroon. Anyone of them will be invited to talk to the Cameroonian Government into agreeing to participate in the peace talks. The US, Ghana, Bosnia, and the Dominican Republic have at one time or another openly expressed sympathy to the Southern Cameroonian side. Any one of them too will be invited to talk to Southern Cameroonians into participating in the peace talks.

Secure Prior Commitment of Good Faith and Enforcement Guarantees

To reassure the parties that any agreement concluded at the peace talks will be honored and implemented, it would be necessary to secure written commitments from both sides before the commencement of the negotiations. It would also be necessary to obtain enforcement guarantees after the agreements are signed. Signatories to the guarantees will include the litigants, along with multilateral stakeholders such as the UN, the AU, ECOWAS, and ECCAS.

There have been cases in the past of one-party reneging on a negotiated agreement and re-engaging in combat. This was the case of the Jonas Savimbi in Angola, who after signing and agreeing to a UN-mediated peace agreement that ended the war in Angola and ushered in democratic elections, he later reneged on the agreement after losing elections and decided to return to war even after he was offered the position of vice president.

Bring the US Institute of Peace on Board as a Consultant/Facilitator

The US Institute of Peace has extensive experience in peace negotiations and peace facilitation in a wide range of conflicts in different parts of the world.

Among the technological applications the Peace Institute can put to the service of the mediator(s) is the Shared Studios portal,[37] a social medial tool that can and has been used in other experiments to virtually bring together participants in Germany, Afghanistan, Iraq, and Mexico to connect and interact with fellow peacebuilders.

Identify a Mediation Team That Has the Trust by Both Sides

Such a mediation team may include representatives from the World Council of Churches, the Catholic Church, Germany, Canada, Rwanda, and Gambia. Besides the likelihood that they are going to be trusted by both parties, these countries and organizations also come with very unique qualities and experiences: (1) The Catholic Church is respected and revered by both parties to the conflict—the Southern Cameroons and French Cameroon. This means that both sides will be happy to have the Church in the team of mediators; (2) Germany's colonial ties with both sides predate British and French colonial ties. Southern Cameroons and Francophones continue to hold Germany in very high regard, and thus will be happy to have Germany on the team. (3) Canada's successful experience in the management of a linguistic divide that is similar to the divide in Cameroon will make her an asset on the mediation team. (4) Rwanda's astounding recovery from the 1994 genocidal war may have produced useful experiences that would be shared with the mediation team. (5) Gambia came out politically unscathed from a short-lived federal experiment it had with its larger neighbor, Senegal, in the early 1980s. The experience gained from that experiment will definitely be of benefit to the mediation process.

Amnesty and Prisoner Release

Prior to the start of the negotiations, the Cameroonian Government should be invited to release and grant general amnesty to all prisoners, including activists at home and in the diaspora, as a show of goodwill. Amnesty and prisoner release were among the goodwill gestures the Nigerian Government made, when it offered to hold peace talks with the Movement for the Emancipation of the Niger Delta. The Talks succeeded in ending that decades-long insurgency.

Guarantees of Postwar Economic Opportunities for Combatants

Any party going into peace talks must know a priori that concessions are part of negotiated peace agreements. To elicit such concessions, the carrot-and-stick approach is a tested and proven strategy. To get the fighters in upcoming peace talks to make concessions and agree to the compromises that will lead to a successful outcome in the negotiations, a carrot will need to be dangled. In this light, it should be recommended that integration in the civil service and/or in the security forces be considered as a possible carrot. The Southern Cameroons/Ambazonian fighters will have the option to join the Ambazonian civil service or national army, and militia groups that were trained and funded by French Cameroon will be given the option to be integrated in the French Cameroon military or civil service.

Following the disintegration of the Soviet Union in 1990, troops and civil servants from constituent Soviet bloc states who were under the service of the Soviet Union were allowed to be reintegrated in the respective militaries and civil services of the former bloc states of the USSR. Similar re-integrations took place following the separation of Czechoslovakia and following the disintegration of Yugoslavia. If it worked for these other countries, it should work for Ambazonia and for La Republique du Cameroun.

CONCLUSION AND SUMMARY REMARKS

Many governmental and nongovernmental actors have reacted in various ways to the ongoing conflict in Southern Cameroons. We cannot analyze all of those reactions here. It will take volumes of pages to research and analyze what organizations such as Amnesty International, Human Rights Watch, Doctors without Borders, the Crisis Group, and hundreds of other NGOs (national and international) have done in response to the war in Southern Cameroons. This is not the direction this research wanted to take. What this research set out to do is to focus on the actions and reactions of actors that have the potential to influence international policy. Almost every organization or institution whose policies are examined in this study has the potential to play a role either as an observer or as an influencer whenever the conflict in Cameroon comes up for mediation. If any of the actors studied here are going to be sitting in the room where the negotiations between Southern Cameroons and French Cameroon are going to take place, then knowing what their stance or policy positions are before the start of negotiations can only but benefit the parties to the negotiations.

For all of the reactions analyzed in this study, the one recurrent theme that rings across nearly all of them is the call for a "political solution" through a "negotiate settlement." The theme was most strongly stated by US Undersecretary of State Tibor Nagy at a press conference and by US Senator Benjamin Cardin in Senate Resolution *S.Res.292*.

Like all wars, the war in Cameroon shall inevitably come up for mediation and negotiations. Just as it is important to know ahead of time what the
actors who will be attending the peace conference as either observers or as
influencers have in the back of their minds, it is equally important to know
the principles, facts, or statutory points of references that each party to the
negotiations would likely use as arguments to support their contention. In
table 1.1, we have listed statutory facts that we think both sides in the conflict
are likely going to invoke to buttress their case.TABLE 12.1

Looking cross-comparatively at the above statutory instruments, there is
no doubt which side would have an advantage in drawing from the legal
and historical facts that are on record to justify their claim. But then we
must be mindful here that we are dealing with an existential crisis. Any
crisis that impugns on the national sovereignty and territorial integrity of
a member state of the UN is by all historical measures an existential crisis.
Statutory instruments alone are not enough to resolve such a crisis. The
day the Southern Cameroons' conflict will come up for negotiations, other
instruments—such as instruments of *power politics*—are unavoidably going
to come to play. And in a face-off between statutory instruments and the
instruments of power politics, there is no doubt who the winner will be. In
the history of existential conflicts, there are no known cases where claims that
were grounded on statutory instruments have prevailed over claims that were
grounded on power politics.

Thus, as the Southern Cameroons' leaders and the government of French
Cameroon prepare to go in for negotiations, they must know that in the conference room the negotiations are going to be silently driven by two levels of
pressure—one subtle, one forceful. The subtle pressure will come from the
actors whose views and predispositions we have analyzed in this study. The
forceful pressure will come from the Southern Cameroons' delegation who
will cite international statutes, forcefully making their point that "the law says
so; the UN Charter says so." Eventually, the outcome will be determined not
by statutes, but by the interplay of statutes and power politics.

A presage to the subtle pressure that will be brought to bear on the
negotiations are passive comments that have come from two of America's
famous statesmen on African affairs, Tibor Nagy and Herman Cohen. Current Undersecretary of State Tibor Nagy has publicly indicated that America
does not want another mini-state in Africa, stating emphatically that "We
support a unified Cameroon! We support a unified Cameroon, because the
last thing America needs is another ministate that will be full of poverty and
suffering and needing billions of dollars foreign assistance to make it."[38] At
the same time, former Undersecretary of State Hermann Cohen has repeatedly cautioned Southern Cameroonians that they will likely lose access
to the oil resources in Cameroon, should they break away from French

Table 12.1   Litigation Points of Reference

Anticipated Points of Reference for the Southern Cameroons Side	Anticipated Points of References for the La Republique du Cameroun's Side
• UN Resolution 1541 establishing the principles for decolonization and the granting of independence to colonized territories. • United Nations Resolutions 1608 of April 21, 1961, authorizing independence for the British Southern Cameroons. • Article 1(1) of the United Nations Charter that calls for effective collective action in the suppression of acts of aggression or other breaches of the peace. • Article 2(3) of the United Nations Charter that calls for all members to settle their international disputes by peaceful means. • The flawed and manipulative organization of the 1972 Referendum. • Abrogation of Section 47 of the Federal Constitution that brought British Southern Cameroons and French Cameroon together. • The unilateral abrogation of the Union in 1984. • The 2009 *Kevin Mgwanga Gumne et al vs. Cameroon.* • Article 4(b) of the Constitutive Act of the African Union for respect of borders achieved at independence. • Article 3(f) of the Constitutive Act of the African Union that promotes peace and security on the continent. • Article 4(f) of the Constitutive Act of the AU prohibiting the use of force. • Article 3(h) of the Constitutive Act of the African Union that promotes and protects human and peoples' rights. • Article 4(h) of the Constitutive Act of the African Union that gives the AU the right to intervene in a member state to prevent war crimes, genocide, and crimes against humanity. • Article 4(m) of the Constitutive Act of the AU on respect for democratic principles, human rights, the rule of law, and good governance. • Article 4(0) of the Constitutive Act of the AU on respect for the sanctity of human life, condemnation, and rejection of impunity.	• Article 3(b) of the Constitutive Act of the AU that protects sovereignty and territorial integrity. • Article 4(g) of the Constitutive Act on non-interference by any Member State in the internal affairs of another. • Article 2(7) of the United Nations Charter which prohibits the United Nations from intervening in matters which are essentially within the domestic jurisdiction of any state.

Source: Created by the chapter author.

Cameroon.[39] This is a foretelling of the role power politics is going to play at the negotiations.

Southern Cameroons have since the launching of their campaign for independence hoped to achieve it by counting on the rule of law. This belief in the rule of law was reflected in the slogan "the force of argument; not the argument of force." The statutory documents listed here above were what they were hoping (and still hoping) to use to validate their "force of argument." It is an argument that would work if we lived in an idealist world. But the reality is that we live in the realist world of power politics. It is a world in which idealism has never yielded to realism.

The three key actors that influence political outcomes in Africa are the state, civil society, and foreign interests. On domestic political matters, the state is hegemonic. On domestic economic matters, it works in tandem with foreign interests. For this reason, it would be correct to say that the state (including the state of Cameroon) is in partnership with foreign interests. Meanwhile, not only is civil society non-hegemonic, it has no partner. This is actually the case with the Southern Cameroons Restoration Movement. As part of the Cameroon civil society, it is not hegemonic, and it has no partners. So, going into any future negotiations with the government of Cameroon, this is what the negotiation team needs to bear in mind. While the statutory instruments may be stacked up in their favor, hegemonic forces are stacked up in favor of their nemesis.

NOTES

1. United Nations Charter, Article 2(7).

2. https://www.un.org/en/sections/un-charter/preamble/

3. United Nations Charter, Article 1(1).

4. Southern Cameroons Peoples Organisation website Archived 2007-09-27 at the Wayback Machine.

5. https://www.dw.com/en/will-ambazonia-become-africas-newest-country/a-40780904 (Accessed 07/12/2020).

6. Fongum Gorji-Dinka v. Cameroon, Communication No. 1134/2002, U.N. Doc. CCPR/C/83/D/1134/2002 (2005).

7. William Munji, How'd Dag Hammarskjöld's COVID-19 Ceasefire Call Sounded Like? https://medium.com/@wbam/dag-hammarskj%C3%B6lds-covid-19-cease-fire-call-9f950bf51b8b (Accessed 09/93/2020).

8. Jacqueline Thomsen, United Nations bans independent reporter for failing to meet "professional standards," https://thehill.com/homenews/media/402480-united-nations-bans-independent-reporter-for-failing-to-meet-professional (Accessed 10/10/20).

9. Simon Ateba, "I was banned from U.N. today because of my tough questions on corruption and Cameroon, journalist says," August 17, 2018, https://todaynews-africa.com/i-was-banned-from-u-n-today-because-of-my-tough-questions-on-corruption-and-cameroon-journalist-says/ (Accessed 10/02/2020).

10. Edith M. Lederer, UN chief: Cease-fire appeal backed by parties in eleven nations, https://abcnews.go.com/US/wireStory/chief-cease-fire-appeal-backed-parties-11-nations-69961494 (Accessed 10/10/20).

11. http://www.globalreligiousfutures.org/countries/cameroon#/?affiliations _religion_id=0&affiliations_year=2010&region_name=All%20Countries (Accessed 10/10/2020).

12. https://www.cia.gov/library/publications/the-world-factbook/geos/cm.html (Accessed 10/10/2020).

13. Cameroon and the Vatican a long and warm history, https://newafricanmagazine.com/4023/ (Accessed 10/10/2020).

14. Fr. John Waters, Catholic Bishops urge Cameroon to start talks with separatists, https://www.vaticannews.va/en/church/news/2020-02/cameroon-catholic-bishops-urge-peace-talks.html (Accessed 10/10/20).

15. Crux, "Pope, UN Chief press for solution to Southern Cameroons problem in Cameroon," May 10, 2020, https://cruxnow.com/church-in-africa/2020/05/pope-un -chief-press-for-solution-to-Southern Cameroons-problem-in-cameroon/ (Accessed 10/10/20).

16. ibid.

17. Gerard O'Connell, "Pope Francis calls for a global cease-fire, attention to overcrowded prisons in response to coronavirus," March 29, 2020, https://www .americamagazine.org/faith/2020/03/29/pope-francis-calls-global-cease-fire-attention -overcrowded-prisons-response (Accessed 10/10/2020).

18. The International Crisis Group, "Cameroon: Proposed Southern Cameroons General Conference Deserves National and International Support," https://www.crisisgroup.org/africa/central-africa/cameroon/cameroun-la-conference-generale-Southern Cameroons-merite-un-soutien-national-et-international (Accessed 10/10/20).

19. Cameroon: Vatican wants to mediate to solve Southern Cameroons crisis, Journal du Cameroun, Feb 26, 2019. (Accessed 10/10/2020).

20. Alex Thomson, African Politics, Routledge Publishers, New York, 4th Edition, New York, 2016, p. 280.

21. "The Banjul Verdict," *Google Docs*. Retrieved 8 October 10, 2020.

22. Communique of the 797th meeting of the PSC on the State of Peace and Security in Africa and the Initiatives and Steps for Promoting African Solutions to African Problems, http://www.peaceau.org/en/article/communique-of-the-797th-meeting -of-the-psc-on-the-state-of-peace-and-security-in-africa-and-the-initiatives-and-steps -for-promoting-african-solutions-to-african-problems (Accessed 10/10/20).

23. Taarifa, Patrick Bigabo, African Union Intervenes In Cameroon Crisis https:// taarifa.rw/african-union-intervenes-in-cameroon-crisis/ (Accessed 10/10/20).

24. The Commonwealth, African Union, and International Organization of La Francophonie delegation Voice of America, https://www.voanews.com/africa/commonwealth-au-oif-call-peace-and-unity-cameroon (Accessed 10/10/20).

25. https://www.youtube.com/watch?v=k3hj0XlIwWY (Accessed 10/10/20).

26. AllAfrica.com, https://allafrica.com/stories/201903140502.html (Accessed 10/10/2020). Associated Press, Top US diplomat suggests taking Cameroon to global forum, March 12, 2019, https://apnews.com/article/151d430054284b33aac 5fe5fc7582c53 (Accessed 10/10/20).

27. Voice of America, https://www.voanews.com/africa/us-diplomats-remarks -stir-controversy-cameroon (Accessed 10/10/20).

28. Journal du Cameroon.com, Cameroon: US calls for "true dialogue" to end Southern Cameroons crisis, https://www.journalducameroun.com/en/cameroon-us -calls-for-true-dialogue-to-end-Southern Cameroons-crisis/ (Accessed 10/10/20).

29. Voice of America, https://www.voanews.com/africa/us-congress-delegation -calls-talks-rebels-cameroon (Accessed 10/10/20).

30. https://www.congress.gov/bill/116th-congress/senate-resolution/684 (Accessed 10/10/20).

31. https://ustr.gov/about-us/policy-offices/press-office/press-releases/2019/octo-ber/president-trump-terminates-trade, The Washington Post, https://www.wash-ingtonpost.com/politics/2019/11/29/trump-wants-pull-cameroons-preferential-trade -status-heres-what-you-need-know/ (Accessed 10/10/20).

32. The New York Times, U.S. Reduces Military Aid to Cameroon Over Human Rights Abuses, https://www.nytimes.com/2019/02/07/world/africa/cameroon-mili-tary-abuses-united-states-aid.html (Accessed 10/10/20).

33. https://www.europarl.europa.eu/doceo/document/RC-8-2019-0245_EN.html (Accessed 10/10/20).

34. https://newsdaycameroon.wordpress.com/2019/06/29/uneu-and-the-us-bless -swiss-led-mediation-on-cameroon-imbroglio-au-stays-silent/ (Accessed 10/10/20).

35. https://www.journalducameroun.com/en/we-remain-committed-to-total-inde-pendence-or-resistance-forever-sisiku-ayuk-tabe/ (Accessed 11/12/2020).

36. Pan African Visions, Cameroon, From Biya , A Mea Culpa on the Anglophone Crisis In Paris, https://panafricanvisions.com/2019/11/cameroon-from-biya-a-mea -culpa-on-the-anglophone-crisis-in-paris/ , Accessed 12/12/2020.

37. https://www.sharedstudios.com/

38. https://www.youtube.com/watch?v=k3hj0XlIwWY (Accessed 10/10/20).

39. Secretary Herman Cohen made this statement at an video conference he give to the Cameroonian community in Boston on October 5, 2019 at the Holiday Inn Hotel,

REFERENCES

Ateba, S. (2018, August 17). *"I was banned from U.N. today because of my tough questions on corruption and Cameroon, journalist says,"* Retrieved May 12, 2022, from Today Newa Africa: https://todaynewsafrica.com/i-was-banned-from-u-n -today-because-of-my-tough-questions-on-corruption-and-cameroon-journ.

Cameroon and the Vatican a long and warm history,. (n.d.). Retrieved October 10, 2020, from New Africa Magazine: https://newafricanmagazine.com/4023/.

Cameroon Overview. (n.d.). Retrieved October 10, 2020, from Pew Templeton Global Religious Futures Project: http://www.globalreligiousfutures.org/countries/cameroon#/?affiliations_religion_id=0&affiliations_year=2010&region_name=All %20Countries.

Cameroon: Paul Biya Mea Culpa. (n.d.). Retrieved December 12, 2020, from Pan African Visions: https://panafricanvisions.com/2019/11/cameroon-from-biya-a -mea-culpa-on-the-anglophone-crisis-in-paris/.

Cameroon: Proposed Southern Cameroons General Conference Deserves National and International Support. (n.d.). Retrieved October 10, 2020, from The International Crisis Group,: https://www.crisisgroup.org/africa/central-africa/cameroon/ cameroun-la-conference-generale-Southern Cameroons-merite-unsoutien-national -et-international.

Cameroon: Top U.S. Official Reveals Behind the Scenes Talks on Anglophone Crisis. (n.d.). Retrieved October 10, 2020, from AllAfrica.com: https://allafrica.com/sto-ries/201903140502.html.

Cameroon: US Calls for "True Dialogue" to End Southern Cameroons Crisis. (n.d.). Retrieved October 10, 2020, from Journal du Cameroun: https://www .journalducameroun.com/en/cameroon-us-calls-for-true-dialogue-to-end-Southern Cameroons-crisis/.

Cameroon: Vatican Wants to Mediate to Solve Southern Cameroons Crisis. (2020, January 26). Retrieved October 10, 2020, from Journal du Cameroun.

Communique of the 797th Meeting of the PSC on the State of Peace and Security in Africa and the Initiatives and Steps for Promoting African Solutions to African Problems. (n.d.). Retrieved October 10, 2020, from Peace and Security Council: http://www.peaceau.org/en/article/communique-of-the-797th-meeting-of-the-psc -on-the-state-of-peace-and-security-in-africa-and-the-initiatives-and-steps-for-pro-moting-african-solutions-to-african-problems.

Fongum Gorji-Dinka v. Cameroon, Communication No. 1134/2002, U.N. Doc. CCPR/C/83/D/1134/2002. (2005).

Joint Motion for a Resolution on Cameroon. (n.d.). Retrieved October 10, 2020, from European Parliament: https://www.europarl.europa.eu/doceo/document/RC -8-2019-0245_EN.html.

Lederer, E. M. (n.d.). *UN Chief: Cease-Fire Appeal Backed by Parties in 11 Nations.* Retrieved October 10, 2020, from ABC News: https://abcnews.go.com/US/wire-Story/chief-cease-fire-appeal-backed-parties-11-nations-69961494.

Munji, W. (n.d.). *How'd Dag Hammarskjöld's COVID-19 Ceasefire Call Sounded Like?* Retrieved September 13, 2020, from https://medium.com/@wbam/dag-ham-marskj%C3%B6lds-covid-19-cease-fire-call-9f950bf51b8b.

O'Connel, G. (2020, March 29). *Pope Francis Calls for a Global Cease-Fire, Atten-tion to Overcrowded Prisons in Response to Coronavirus.* Retrieved October 10, 2020, from American Magazine: https://www.americamagazine.org/faith/2020/03 /29/pope-francis-calls-global-cease-fire-attention-overcrowded-prison.

Pope, UN Chief Press for solution to Southern Cameroons Problem in Cameroon. (2020, May 10). Retrieved October 10, 2022, from Crux News: https://cruxnow

.com/church-in-africa/2020/05/pope-un-chief-press-for-solution-to-Southern Cameroons-problem-in-cameroon/.

President Trump Terminates Trade Preference Program Eligibility for Cameroon. (n.d.). Retrieved October 10, 2020, from Office of the US Trade Representative: https://ustr.gov/about-us/policy-offices/press-office/press-releases/2019/october/ president-trump-terminates-trade.

S.Res.684 - A Resolution Calling on the Government of Cameroon . (n.d.). Retrieved October 10, 2020, from https://www.congress.gov/bill/116th-congress/senate-resolution/684.

Southern Cameroons Peoples Organisation website Archived . (2007, September 27). Retrieved July 12, 2020, from The Wayback Machine: https://www.dw.com/en/ will-ambazonia-become-africas-newest-country/a-40780904 (

Taarifa, P. B. (n.d.). *African Union Intervenes in Cameroon Crisis.* Retrieved October 10, 2020, from Tarrifa.Rw: https://taarifa.rw/african-union-intervenes-in-cameroon-crisis/.

The Banjul Verdict. (2018, October 10). Retrieved from Google Docs.

The Commonwealth, African Union, and International Organization of La Francophonie delegation Voice of America. (n.d.). Retrieved October 10, 2020, from VOA News: https://www.voanews.com/africa/commonwealth-au-oif-call-peace -and-unity-cameroon.

The World Fact Book . (n.d.). Retrieved October 10, 2020, from US CIA: https://www .cia.gov/library/publications/the-world-factbook/geos/cm.html.

Thomsen, J. (2020, October 10). *United Nations Bans Independent Reporter for Failing to Meet 'Professional Standards'.* Retrieved from The Hill: https://thehill.com /homenews/media/402480-united-nations-bans-independent-reporter-for-failing-to -meet-professional.

Thomson, A. (2016). *African Politics.* New York: Routledge Publishers.

Top US Diplomat Suggests Taking Cameroon to Global Forum. (2019, March 12). Retrieved October 10, 2020, from Associated Press: https://apnews.com/article /151d430054284b33aac5fe5fc7582c53.

Ttrump Want Pull Cameroons Preferential Trade Status . (n.d.). Retrieved October 10, 2020, from The Washington Post: https://www.washingtonpost.com/politics/2019/11/29/trump-wants-pull-cameroons-preferential-trade-status-heres-what -you-need-know/.

UN,EU and the US Bless Swiss Led Mediation on Cameroon Imbroglio, AU Stays Silent. (n.d.). Retrieved October 10, 2020, from News Day Cameroon: https:// newsdaycameroon.wordpress.com/2019/06/29/uneu-and-the-us-bless-swiss-led -mediation-on-cameroon-imbroglio-au-stays-silent/.

United Nations Charter, Article 2 (7). (n.d.). Retrieved from https://www.un.org/en/ sections/un-charter/preamble/.

US Congress Delegation Calls for Talks With Rebels in Cameroon. (n.d.). Retrieved October 10, 2020, from Voice of America: https://www.voanews.com/africa/us -congress-delegation-calls-talks-rebels-cameroon.

US Diplomat's Remarks Stir Controversy in Cameroon. (n.d.). Retrieved October 10, 2020, from Voice of America: https://www.voanews.com/africa/us-diplomats -remarks-stir-controversy-cameroon.

US Reduces Military Aid to Cameroon Over Human Rights Abuses. (n.d.). Retrieved October 10, 2020, from The New York Times: https://www.nytimes.com/2019/02 /07/world/africa/cameroon-military-abuses-united-states-aid.html.

Waters, F. J. (n.d.). *Catholic Bishops Urge Cameroon to Start Talks With Separatists.* Retrieved October 10, 2020, from Vatican News: https://www.vaticannews.va/en/ church/news/2020-02/cameroon-catholic-bishops-urge-peace-talks.html.

We Remain Committed to Total Independence or Resistance Forever - Sisiku Ayuk Tabe. (n.d.). Retrieved November 12, 2020, from Journal du Cameroun: https:// www.journalducameroun.com/en/we-remain-committed-to-total-independence-or -resistance-forever-sisiku-ayuk-tabe/.

We Support a Unified Cameroon. (2020, April 3). Retrieved October 10, 2020, from Youtube: https://www.youtube.com/watch?v=k3hj0XlIwWY.

Chapter 13

From the Anger of Despair to Resistance and Self-Defense

The Trajectory of 21st-Century Genocide in Cameroon

Tatah Mentan

From what used to be known as a "Heaven of Peace" in the turbulent Central African region, the situation in Cameroon is gradually becoming another story of carnage and bloodshed as the world stays silent. As the massacre continues, it is fast becoming another episode of the international community failing to uphold the right to protect human beings from brutal treatment by oppressive regimes. In the meantime, the Anglophone regions of Cameroon, otherwise known as Southern Cameroons, have become the epicenter of a policy orchestrated by the pro-Francophone regime.

Thousands of military men and women, including those still undergoing training at various military facilities, have been sent to put out any uprising orchestrated by members of the Anglophone community. The policy has entailed mass arrests and arbitrary killings, which have grown to the extent where many have been reported missing for months now. It also involves the burning down of villages to the extent that some villages have been almost completely annihilated. In some cases, the elderly, who are unable to run into the bushes as is the tradition now, are being roasted alive. In the meantime, thousands have taken refuge in forests, sleeping in the open and living on wild food, while more than 50,000 people according to UNHCR have successfully crossed into Nigeria as refugees. In some situations, even the houses of priests and pastors have been burnt—like the case of the pastor of the Presbyterian Church Kwa-Kwa (in the South West of the country) and the Roman Catholic priest in the same area.

In one of these gruesome acts, Chiabah Samuel, popularly known as Sam Soya, was beheaded by security forces who suspected him of conniving with

Anglophone separatists. Even those who have been arrested have been taken from Anglophone regions to Francophone regions further away from their families, where medical attention has been denied to them in most cases. At least an Anglophone detainee was reported dead in the Yaounde maximum security prison in March because he was forced to leave the hospital bed to a prison cell (even against his doctor's protest). In the ensuing development, the international community has remained very silent, and very little is said about the situation on the global media, which is why the problem persists.

THE INABILITY TO UPHOLD THE "NEVER AGAIN" CAMPAIGN

The situation in the Southern Cameroons has been dragging on now for close to two years and with the passing of time, it is getting worse. From a peaceful protest by members of the Anglophone communities demanding more rights in a Francophone-dominated country and government, it has mutated over time to an outright violent struggle as Anglophone groups are being born every day with the objective of facing government troops in a violent showdown. The protracted struggle has been informed by the intransigence of the government to open rooms for dialogue despite incessant calls made by Anglophone groups and even the country's National Human Rights Commission.

In addition, the silence of the international community has paved the way for more human rights abuses to be committed. The UN and friendly countries have not shown enough support for the Southern Cameroons' case, which is why most inhabitants in the area feel they have been abandoned. The "Never Again" campaign, which was born out of the negligence of the international community to prevent the 1994 genocide, has not been upheld, as atrocities similar to that of Rwanda are being committed daily. "Never Again" was a pledge by the international community to never allow what happened to Rwanda—or similar situations—to repeat themselves.

However, the reality on the ground seems different.

It is this lack of protection and upholding of justice and the "Never Again" campaign by the international community which has pushed many to pick up arms as a last resort to defend their communities against government forces. Very little or no pressure has been brought on the government of President Biya by the international community. The UN has failed to condemn the situation, and the country's former colonial masters, including France and Britain, have more or less been very silent, treating the matter as an internal affair. In their latest communications, they have instead warned their nationals to refrain from traveling to Southern Cameroon. The United States of

America, in its usual role of "police of the world," has also not policed the Southern Cameroons' case. The US government has, like the other governments, instead warned its nationals from taking to the volatile areas. None of these countries has pleaded for the case at any international instance, which is why it has not been mentioned at the level of the UN General Assembly or the UN Security Council despite the high level of violence and brutality ongoing.

The visit of the Commonwealth Secretary-General in December 2017 was seen as the eminent panacea to heal wounds. But the Right Hon Patricia Scotland came and left, and months after, nothing has been heard of the Commonwealth. Most especially, the international media has been very silent. All focus is on conflicts in Syria, Iraq, Yemen, Libya, Congo DR, and so on. Meanwhile, a similar situation is unfolding in Cameroon. Many villages, including *Guneku, Belo, Batibo, Kwakwa, Nake, Bole, Boa Bakundu, Matoh, Mufako Bekondo, Kembong, Kendem*, have almost been completely razed down with fingers pointing at state security officers. Southern Cameroonian separatist groups which target only security officers have also killed tens of these men and women in uniform. While the carnage continues, the international media that serves as acheck and balance at the international level has not projected these images. The story of the suffering masses has not also been told, and even the refugee situation in Nigeria which is appalling according to the UNHCR has also been eclipsed.

UNDERSTANDING ANGER AND RESISTANCE: A THEORETICAL PERSPECTIVE

Understanding the relationship between emotion and human behavior has long fascinated those who endeavor to contribute to a broader knowledge of human nature. Great classical philosophers such as Plato, Aristotle, Spinoza, Descartes, Hobbes, and Hume all had identifiable theories of emotion. It was Cicero, for instance, who reminded orators of his day of the power of emotion when attempting to persuade an audience. In particular, he encouraged the use of pathos (the appeal to emotion), because it is by drawing on emotion, he argued, that opinion can be swayed most effectively. Here I have in mind Cicero's *De Oratore*, particularly book I, chapter V.

Conveying anger to one's listeners is epistemically valuable in two respects: first, it can direct listeners' attention to elusive morally relevant features of the situation; second, it enables them to register injustices that their existing evaluative categories are not yet suited to capturing. Thus, when employed skillfully, angry speech promotes a greater understanding of existing injustices. This epistemic role is indispensable in highly divided societies, where the injustices endured by some groups are often invisible to, or misunderstood by, other groups.

Although people commonly tend to think of anger as a troublesome, negative emotion, Aristotle wisely noted how: "Anyone can get angry—that is easy; however, to be angry at the right person, to the proper extent, at the proper moment, with the right motive, and in the right way, that is not so easy" (350 BCE/1925). The motivation for all human action, according to Aristotle, can be assigned to one of seven causes: chance, nature, compulsion, habit, reasoning, anger, and appetite. Anger he referred to as an expression of passion and pain, for which humans have both an appetite and a fear. In this view, anger is not simply a negative emotion to be shunned and avoided, it is also a source of passion that may be concentrated and directed toward the pursuit of important goals.

In a similar sense, anger can play a dual role within the process of social influence in general, and persuasive message design in particular. As it concerns health communication, anger may be either a curse or a blessing—either an obstacle to be avoided or a vehicle to be driven and finessed. In the pages that follow, the functions and consequences of this powerful emotion are reviewed with a mind toward identifying the direct and indirect roles anger can play in motivation, decision making, judgment, choice, and behavior. The goal is to explore how anger may be employed as a message feature with application across a broad range of health communication contexts.

As it concerns health message design, anger may be usefully focused on the harmful effects of disease, substance abuse, health risks in general, and the companies profiting through products harmful to public health. On the other hand, anger may be unintentionally generated and misdirected toward policymakers and health campaigns perceived as unjustly limiting hedonically relevant personal freedoms (Miller, 2016). In either case, the effects of message-generated anger on pertinent health behaviors can be quite powerful, whether directed against risky and harmful outcomes, or rebounding in resistance to well-intentioned health promotion campaigns.

Defining Anger

Anger may be defined as a primary, event-related negative emotion (Ortony et al., 1988), and although it need not be directed at an agent in the same sense as an attribution-related emotion, such as resentment, contempt, or indignation, anger can be particularly intense in response to negative outcomes associated with the agency and actions of other people. Within a social–emotional context, anger is expressed and experienced as an interpersonal event that may often damage relationships by reducing intimacy, spawning discord, intensifying negative feelings, and escalating mutual hostility (Fehr

& Baldwin, 1996). Conversely, anger may also lead to a number of positive outcomes, including the redress of grievances, shared understanding, emotional closeness, and the reduction of tension and anxiety through emotional ventilation and catharsis (Tavris, 1984).

In general, the subjective experience of anger is negatively valenced and aversively arousing, although some people may find it less aversive than others (Harmon-Jones, 2004: 18, 337–361). Because of anger's potential for intense arousal, some individuals may experience a reinforcing, self-stimulation effect felt to be energizing and invigorating, although conducive to aggression (Berkowitz, 1970: 1–7; Bushman et al., 1999: 367–374). At input, the elicitation of anger depends on perceptions of goal-relevant, situational disruptions (Ortony et al., 1988); whereas at output, anger affects cognitive processing strategies (Nabi, 2002: 204–216; Schwarz, 1990: 522–561), risk assessment (Lerner & Keltner, 2000: 473–493), and judgments bearing on goal-directed behavior (Clore et al., 1993; Schwarz & Clore, 1983). Though the occurrence of anger can be cognitively disruptive and affectively unpleasant, it can also have powerful effects on concentration, determination, and focus (Nabi, 2002, 2003: 199–223), particularly when aimed at approaching, engaging, and removing goal-hindering obstructions.

Relative to sad or neutral emotion states, anger may also cause people to be more influenced by heuristic cues, especially source-relevant information. Bodenhausen, Sheppard, and Kramer (1994: 45–62) argued that anger may induce a lack of analytic processing resulting in greater source derogation due to reduced motivation to actively analyze judgment-relevant information. According to Bodenhausen and colleagues, anger may reduce people's ability to engage in thoughtful analysis. It seems likely that the high levels of physiological arousal that often accompany anger serve to reduce cognitive capacity and discourage analytical thinking. Regardless of the cause, increased reliance on heuristic cues is likely a result of limited information processing, and most anger theorists agree that angry people generally do not process information systematically (Moons & Mackie, 2007: 706–720).

In essence, anger is a subjective feeling tied to perceived wrongdoing and a tendency to counter or redress that wrongdoing in ways that may range from resistance to retaliation (Fernandez, 2008). Like sadness and fear, the feeling of anger can take the form of emotion, mood, or temperament. Many psychological tests of anger present a list of anger-provoking scenarios, as in the Reaction Inventory, the Multidimensional Anger Inventory, and the Novaco Provocation Inventory (Novaco, 1975). Some of the items on these inventories are highly specific. In general, research shows that wrongdoing is perceived not merely in the instance when one is physically assaulted. Wrongdoing also falls within several psychosocial categories: (i) insults or affronts, (ii) insensitivity or indifference, (iii) deception and betrayal, (iv) abandonment and rejection, (v) breach of agreement or promise, (vi) ingratitude, and (vii) exploitation.

Ways of reacting to such angering pain are multiple. One of them is learned helplessness. Learned helplessness is a phenomenon observed in both humans and other animals when they have been conditioned to expect pain, suffering, or discomfort without a way to escape it (Thomas, 2016). Eventually, after enough conditioning, the animal will stop trying to avoid the pain at all—even if there is an opportunity to truly escape it! When human or other animals come to understand (or believe) that they have no control over what happens to them, they begin to think, feel, and act as if they are helpless. This phenomenon is called learned helplessness because it is not an innate trait; no one is born believing that they have absolutely no control over what happens to them and that it is fruitless to even try to gain control. It is a learned behavior, conditioned through experiences in which the subject either truly has no control over his circumstances or believes that he has no control over his circumstances.

Violent Resistance as a Duty?

Every living being on this planet has experienced injustice and oppression at some point or another and in some form or another. As humans, our lives are shaped by blatantly violent and subtly coercive forces that compel us to act in certain ways and to not act in other ways. It is, unfortunately, an unavoidable part of the very fabric of our everyday lives, whether we realize it or not. For some, this oppression is obvious and terrible, as they regularly experience assault, rape, arrest, murder, starvation, and theft in their families and communities. Others experience it to a slightly lesser degree as they are openly mocked, discriminated against, and treated with lesser value than other members of their culture due to their gender, sexual orientation, age, health, class, or race. Still others might not see these forces in their lives at all, as their experience with oppression is on the receiving end when they receive wealth and power at the expense of those underneath them on the pyramid of social inequality.

There is a reason why it is normal and acceptable for living creatures to treat each other with hatred and disrespect. The reason is that a lot of people believe in certain ideas. There are many ideas out there, but unfortunately the most popular ideas are also the most destructive ones. For example, there is a very popular idea out there that if you take the sexual organs of a cotton plant, flatten it into a piece of paper, dye it green, and make figures and pictures of dead royalty on it, you can then use this piece of paper to have power and control over other living creatures. If someone has a lot of these pieces of paper, they can purchase whatever they want and kill billions of humans, cows, fish, forests, streams, or whatever else they can come up with. The question of whether somebody *should* do these things is never brought into question, because the fact of the matter is that they *can*. This is a very bad idea.

Another popular idea is that certain humans can own other animals and areas of our planet. When certain humans are allowed to own other animals, human or otherwise, they often do very bad things to them. When certain humans own parts of our planet, they often like to create imaginary lines called borders and kill other people who also want to live in that part of the Earth, as well as doing great damage to the Earth as they take trees, water, plants, minerals, and other parts of the Earth away in order to make lots of money. Someone who owns another animal or a part of the Earth can do almost whatever they want to them, even very horrible things, just because they *can*. This is also a very bad idea.

There is also the idea that certain people have less value because of their skin color, their gender, their sexual orientation, their age, their education, their religion, their cultural values, how much green paper their family has acquired through the generations, or various other reasons. This is another very bad idea that has caused incalculable levels of suffering in our world and continues to do so every day.

There are also some good ideas, though. There is an idea that all living creatures should be treated with respect and dignity. There is an idea that all humans are of equal value and that nobody should be able to hurt or oppress someone else regardless of how much money or power they have. There is an idea that everybody should have the freedom to live how they choose as long as they don't hurt or oppress anybody else. These ideas are often called "radical," "revolutionary," and "dangerous," because they are a threat to those who have a lot of green paper and imaginary lines on the Earth. These radical ideas, although they seem like good ideas to most people who take the time to think about them, are unfortunately not the ideas that run the world. Therefore, those who believe these radical, dangerous ideas and believe that they are worth fighting for must resist the dominant and powerful bad ideas and those who enforce them. This is called "resistance."

Those who engage in resistance have acquired a very large arsenal of tactics and strategies for engaging in resistance over the past several thousand years, and resistors today have a wealth of knowledge to draw upon. On the other hand, many resistors are also struggling with the challenges of living in a new era. The old ideas don't always work in this age of expanding technology, Orwellian surveillance, and increasingly militarized police forces.

Within the world of resistance, there are many different ideas for what ideas we should be fighting for and how we should fight. How should we resist? When someone asks the question, "How should we resist?" there are two big ideas that immediately jump up and loudly answer, "Resist this way!" Idea one says that you should resist using violent tactics, and idea two says that you should use nonviolent tactics. Both of these ideas have their heroes, success stories, philosophies, and various arguments for their legitimacy and supremacy. Both of these ideas have a long history of successful resistance, and both ideas have produced many incredible thinkers, writers, activists, radicals, and revolutionaries who have left a legacy that is admirable and inspirational.

Here there is a problem. Amid the shouting match between these two big ideas of violence and nonviolence, there is also an idea that I think has not received much attention, yet it is very important. This idea says that both methods of resistance are good ideas. This idea says that there are not just two main ways of resisting, but rather there is one bigger idea that includes both of the other ideas within it. This idea attempts to dissolve the rigidly polarized worlds of violent and nonviolent resistance by introducing a model that, by introducing a concept called colonization into the dialogue, encompasses the whole spectrum of resistance. This idea honors the experiences and beliefs of all people so that any individual or group of people can effectively resist bad ideas until they no longer exist.

Resistance against various power relations is the result of interpretations of the aim and discourses of the organized resistance, and how those resisting recognize themselves in relation to those interpretations. This, in turn, creates particular conceptions of the self, which allow people to move outside the boundaries of the resisting organization and make their own everyday resistance. In the end, self-reflection becomes the very base for an individual's decision to practice everyday resistance against the violent tyrannies of all sorts.

Violence: Violence is any physical, emotional, verbal, institutional, structural, or spiritual behavior, attitude, policy, or condition that diminishes, dominates, or destroys others and ourselves. Violence consists of actions, words, attitudes, structures, or systems that cause physical, psychological, social, or environmental damage and/or prevent people from reaching their full human potential. Johan Galtung (1969), one of the founders of Peace and Conflict Studies and creator of the Violence Triangle, posited that violence generally falls into three categories: direct violence, structural violence, and cultural violence.

Direct violence can take many forms, but its most obvious form involves the use of physical force, as in assault, rape, murder, mugging, and so on. Verbal violence is also a form of direct violence, as in hateful and derogatory speech intended to do harm to another.

Structural violence exists when some groups, classes, genders, nationalities, and so on are assumed to have, and in fact do have, more access to goods, resources, and opportunities than other groups, classes, genders, nationalities, and so forth, and this unequal advantage is built into the very social, political, and economic systems that govern societies, states, and the world. These tendencies may be overt such as Apartheid or more subtle such as traditions or tendency to award some groups privileges over another.

Cultural violence is the prevailing attitudes and beliefs that we have been taught since childhood and that surround us in daily life regarding power and the necessity of violence. We can consider, for example, dominant narratives of history which glorify genocide, rape, and theft and present them as necessary evils in the face of cultural progression. Almost all cultures recognize that killing a person is murder, but killing tens, hundreds, or thousands during a declared conflict is called "war" or "colonizing a country," and the casual killing of civilians by the state is declared "collateral damage."

It is important to realize that there is interplay between the components of the triangle. *Cultural* and *Structural Violence* cause *Direct Violence*, while *Direct Violence* reinforces *Structural* and *Cultural Violence*. *Direct Violence* is visible as behavior in the triangle; however, this violence does not come out of nowhere; its roots are *Cultural* and *Structural*. For the purposes of this book, property destruction is not considered violent unless it directly jeopardizes another living creature's ability to support and sustain their existence (Bobichand, 2012).

The State: By the state, I mean any hierarchical political organization which holds a monopoly on violence within its defined territorial boundaries and serves to "legitimize" the use of violence on other states, on its own citizens, and on the Earth with the purpose of increasing the wealth, power, and oppressive capacity of the ruling class of that state.

Pacifism: Pacifism is a broad ideology which encompasses many schools of thought and attitudes of resistance. There are two beliefs which unite all pacifists—being anti-war and against oppressive violence. Within that spectrum are many approaches to resistance, ranging from nonresistance to active resistance. For the purposes of this book, I need to create an ideological distinction between ineffective, disengaged, nonresistance and active, engaged, effective resistance, and although the term *pacifism* is not completely accurate, it will serve the purposes of this book. Therefore, I will use the term *pacifism* to denote nonresistance and *active nonviolence* to denote resistance, although not all who identify as pacifists are nonresistors. I realize this may be a troubling choice of definitions to some, but due to the poverty of language I could not find a better way to distinguish the two ideologies. Thus, when I use the term *pacifism,* I am describing an ideology of nonviolent nonresistance; a philosophy which forbids an individual to engage in direct oppressive violence but does not allow for effective resistance to oppressive violence. The writings of Martin Buber, Leo Tolstoy, John Howard Yoder,

Adin Ballou, The Buddha, and Greg Boyd are good examples of pacifist ideology.

Active Nonviolence: Also known as *Satyagraha, the third way, nonviolent resistance,* and *nonviolent direct action,* this philosophy distinguishes itself from pacifism in many important and often misunderstood ways. Active nonviolence posits that through offensive, yet loving and creative action, violence can be overthrown with a dedication to and willingness to suffer for one's cause. Adherents to this philosophy often put themselves in physical danger and engage in direct action, property destruction, and civil disobedience to the state, but their actions are carefully planned as to never harm or assault another living being. Active nonviolence as a form of resistance has gained great popularity in social change movements over the past century. The writings/actions of Mohandas Gandhi, MLK Jr., Dorothy Day, Shane Claiborne, Walter Wink, Yeshua, and many others are representative of *active nonviolence.*

Violent Resistance: Any action taken that intentionally harms another living beings life, health, or well-being for the purpose of resisting oppression will be understood to be *violent resistance* or *violent direct action.* Advocates of violent resistance believe that violence is a powerful, effective weapon that the state uses to legitimize itself every day, and those that resist the state are therefore entitled to also use violence to defend themselves against oppression. Almost all revolutions and resistance movements throughout human history have been violent, and many nonviolent movements have been bolstered by their violent counterparts, as we'll explore later on in the book. Advocates of violent resistance include Huey Newton, Malcolm X, Ernesto Guevara, Derrick Jensen, Ward Churchill, Peter Gelderloos, Ted Kaczynski, John Brown, Johann Most, Luigi Galleani, Emma Goldman, Victor Serge, Severino Di Giovanni, and Naomi Jaffe.

Colonization: Colonization is the illegitimate economic exploitation and political domination of a people by a violent oppressor, as well as the separation of colonized peoples from their individuality and culture. Frantz Fanon, one of the greatest theorists of colonization and decolonization, has explored this concept exhaustively, and we will borrow heavily from his writings as we continue throughout this book. Fanon believed that the rich history, culture, and wisdom of oppressed peoples are physically and symbolically destroyed, and in their place the colonizer creates a people who deserve only to be ruled and exploited. The colonizer reconstructs colonized peoples as "lazy" and "unproductive," thereby justifying low wages or coercive systems of labor. He also reconstructs them as "stupid," thereby justifying the imposition of the colonial power's institutions and practices—boarding schools, religious training centers, and plantations/factories. Finally, he constructs them as "savage" and "dangerous," thereby justifying military conquest, police repression, and coercive forms of social control (Fanon, 1969). The result is a people "in whose soul an inferiority complex has been created by the death and burial of its local cultural originality" (Fanon, 1952). Fanon (1965) believed it was important to realize that colonialism

> hardly ever exploits the whole of a country. It contents itself with bringing to light the natural resources, which it extracts, and exports to meet the needs of the mother country's industries, thereby allowing certain sectors of the colony to become relatively rich. But the rest of the colony follows its path of underdevelopment and poverty, or at all events sinks into it more deeply.

Decolonization: Decolonization is both the act of physically freeing a territory from the external control of settlers and the psychological act of freeing the consciousness of the native from the effects of colonization: the states of alienation and dehumanization. Fanon posits three premises in his theory of decolonization:

the act of colonization is never legitimate, as it is rooted in exploitation and oppressive violence;
due to the illegitimacy of colonization, the oppressed (the colonized) are entitled to two actions: the reclamation of physical liberation and sovereignty as well reclamation from the psychological suffering of colonization;
almost no nonviolent options are available which serve the ends of both physical and psychological liberation.

Due to this reasoning, Fanon concludes that violent resistance is not only justified but required in order for the oppressed to fully decolonize themselves and resist oppressive violence. While there are some critiques of Fanon's theory (1974), I believe it a helpful model to help us understand the complexities of and requirements for effective decolonization.

The path to the decolonization stage is for individuals or organizations that have engaged in some activity—whether it is explicitly violent or not— that has broken their former view of themselves as weak and subservient and has empowered them to "stand up for themselves," regardless of the consequences. This shift may or may not necessitate physical violence, as many individuals may be able to transit to a state of empowerment by simply realizing and accepting the truth that they are not victims, but for the vast majority of people it will require some sort of physical violence. The transition to this stage requires a full and complete decolonization of fear from the oppressed psyche, a rooting out of the mentality of subordination and domination and replacing it with a clarity of truth—a truth that destroys the former illusions of fear and understands that no human has the right to oppress/kill/rape/extort/intimidate another form of life.

Most of the time this stage will be accompanied with violence, as Fanon (1961) stated, "At the level of individuals, violence is a cleansing force. It frees the native from his inferiority complex and from his despair and inaction, it makes him fearless and restores his self-respect." This stage may be seen as a "reaction" to the oppression and disempowerment felt during the previous stage, and thus many individuals and groups may remain in this stage for a very long time, enjoying their newfound freedoms and savoring their liberation of their bodies, hearts, and minds.

It will follow as a general rule that the amount of oppressive violence that an individual or culture has been subjected to is directly proportionate to the amount of violence they will need to exert on their oppressors in order to effectively decolonize themselves. Fanon repeated this assertion many times, and Gandhi (1942) understood this as well, when he famously said, "Nonviolence cannot be taught to a person who fears to die and has no power of resistance."

The failure to properly define the functions of violence or nonviolence presents a false dichotomy. Therefore, it is important to dissect the terms nonviolence and violence. Nonviolence is traditionally understood as being a way of life, or a moral philosophy. This moral view of nonviolence is often given a religious overtone. Another way to understand nonviolence is as a tactical political philosophy, for example, nonviolent direct action. In this case, one actually uses their body to effect political or moral change. Violence, on the other hand, is understood as a reactionary, political tool. Indeed, violence may generally be understood in relation to the term revolution. Violence, then, is understood as killing, murder, death, and tyrannical. In addition, violence can and should be understood in a more complex manner. For example, one could argue that violence can be physical, psychological, emotional, rhetorical, or epistemic. Thus, the use of retaliatory physical violence becomes a matter of one's moral taste, which in some sense could prove apolitical.

What both of these terms have in common is the desire to change some form of systematic oppression, both of which can be physical or psychological, but is violent, nevertheless. The major difference between nonviolence and violence is the means or the method in how this change in power comes about. To be sure, power is at the heart of nonviolence and violence as political, moral, or ideological change. However, as the historical record indicates, there was no real contradiction between the use of nonviolence or armed self-defense as a political tactic if they work in tandem. Morality became an issue for Black folk under the constant strain of violent white supremacy when someone came along and said nonviolence was a way of life.

BACKGROUND TO CAMEROON COLONIAL HISTORY

The crisis in Southern Cameroons, which has resulted in a violent confrontation between armed pro-independence groups and the Cameroonian forces over the last two years, is not giving any sign of moving toward a solution—rather the contrary is true. Since the date of the symbolic declaration of Southern Cameroonian independence of 1 October, at least hundreds have been killed in a conflict that has been dragging on since the 1960s and has a lot to see with the centralization of power at the hands of the Cameroonian state.

The Republic of Cameroon could be said to have a complicated and an unfortunate history, perhaps, more than a vast majority of the other African states. The Portuguese were the first Europeans to get to the area now known as the Republic of Cameroon in the 15th century. They established a sugarcane plantation in the 16th and subsequent centuries, up to the early 19th century. Portuguese and Dutch slave traders dominated the slave trade in the area until slavery was abolished. Sometime in the 19th century, nomadic Fulanis arrived in Northern Cameroon and settled.

Germany eventually gained possession of the area and established Cameroon as a Protectorate in 1884, thereby, making the country a colony. German colonial authorities ruled the colony until 1916 when a combined French, British, and Belgian military force drove out the Germans during the First World War. After the First World War, Cameroon was taken away from Germany as part of the armistice that ended "the war to end all wars" in 1919. It was divided into two and shared by two of the victorious allied powers (Britain and France). As a result, Britain administered Northwestern and Southwestern Cameroon under the Mandate of the League of Nations while France administered four-fifth of the total territory. (*The Commonwealth*, 2017, October 5; Caxton, 2017, July 21). Obviously, France had a much bigger territorial area under its control than Britain. After the Second War, both countries continued to administer the territory under the Trusteeship of the UN.

While still under the trusteeship of the UN and administered by France and Britain, indigenous African political parties emerged and began to agitate for Cameroonian independence. For instance, the Union of the Peoples of Cameroon (UPC), led by Ruben Um Nyobe, demanded that the two parts (English-speaking and French-speaking) should be amalgamated to form an independent country. Due to its proactive role in agitating for independence, the UPC was banned in the 1950s by the colonial powers. The ban resulted in a massive rebellion in which a considerable number of people were killed, including the leader of the party Mr. Nyobe (Ibid).

In any case, partial self-rule was granted to the colony. Eventually, Cameroon gained full independence on January 1, 1960. A UN plebiscite was held in 1961 in which Northwestern Cameroon decided to join Nigeria while Southwestern Cameroon joined French Cameroon, following the feeling that it was ignored, discriminated, and marginalized by Britain, while being ruled as part of Nigeria. Due to the nature of the country, a federal system of government was established with both language zones (English-speaking and French-speaking) having their own parliaments. The prime minister of the English-speaking Cameroon became the deputy president of the country while the leader of the French-speaking regions served as the president (Morse, 2017, June 2).

However, the federal system was illegally dissolved in 1972 by President Ahmadou Ahidjo and replaced by a unitary system of government, resulting in the concentration of power at the national level. As a result, the name was changed from the Federal Republic of Cameroon to the United Republic of Cameroon. In 1984, the name was changed again, and the country became the Republic of Cameroon (Republique du Cameroun), the name at independence in 1960.

Cameroon, unlike its Nigerian neighbor, which has had fifteen heads of state since independence in October 1, 1960, has had only two since independence in January 1960. Ahmadou Ahidjo first ruled as the president from 1960 to 1982, then President Paul Biya took over in the same year and has continued to rule the country to the present. Both political leaders originate from the French-speaking regions. This means that no English-speaking Cameroonian has had the opportunity to serve as a head of state of the country. All policies and decisions seem to originate from the strategic interests and calculations of the French-speaking regions. Even Cameroon's foreign policy is greatly aligned with that of France. This accounts for why President Paul Biya visits France regularly and is strongly aligned with France. On the other hand, Britain has had little or no influence on the English-speaking regions, thereby, leaving those regions to feign for themselves.

An interesting aspect of Cameroon's politics is that the military attempted four unsuccessful military coups in 1979, 1983, and February and April 1984. The last two attempted coups were alleged to have been staged by military officers who were loyal or sympathetic to former President Ahidjo. As a result, the former head of state was tried for instigating the coups in absentia and found guilty. This means that unlike many other African countries, Cameroon has never had a military regime in power. Nonetheless, the country tilted toward a unitary system of government because the power-wielding elite opted to centralize political authority at the center to reduce divisiveness. They did so by merging two governing political parties and some opposition groups in 1966. Similarly, the ruling party was reconstituted as the Cameroon National Union (Union of National Camerounaise), otherwise known as the UNC. Then, it was renamed as the Reassemblement Democratique de people Camerounais (Cameroon's Peoples Democratic Movement (CPDM) or RDPC).

In sum, Cameroon started as a German colony, then was taken over by the British and French following the end of the First World War, under Mandate of the League of Nations and UN trusteeship. The French (Francophone) and British (Anglophone) regions were amalgamated. The majority (four-fifth or about 80 percent) of the regions of the country is French-speaking while a smaller portion (about 20 percent) of the regions is English-speaking. (International Crisis Group, 2017, August 2). Perhaps, due to this factor, the French regions (see map below) have dominated the country so much so that the English-speaking region feel marginalized and discriminated against in almost every aspect of the country's life.

The Trouble with Cameroon

The government of La Republique du Cameroun thrives on falsehood and tells a lot of lies and seems to truly believe its lies. The country can never stand because it is built on lies and maintained by a desperate and very costly attempt to sustain the falsehood at all costs. The history of the country has been thoroughly falsified. Everybody seems to overlook the impact of the falsehood, and it will never triumph over truth. The history of the country has been falsified to the extent that even legal minds tend to believe that there was a valid and subsisting federation in the Cameroons between 1961 and 1972 whereas what was obtained was a gigantic fraud orchestrated by the government of President Ahmadou Ahidjo against the gullible and unsuspecting leaders of the Southern Cameroons under Premier John Ngu Foncha in 1961. Ahidjo and La Republique du Cameroun carefully put in place an undeclared hidden agenda to systematically annex and assimilate the Southern Cameroons over time. This is what happened:

When the Second World War ended, the United Nations Organization (UNO) was created to take over the role hitherto played by the League of Nations to safeguard world peace and stability in the comity of nations. The Mandates System of the League of Nations under which former German colonies were administered by members of the League of Nations came to an end in October 1947 when the UN Trusteeship Council was created as an organ of the UNO to oversee the various European powers administer and prepare the said former colonies for independence. As part of the said trusteeship system, France was given the UN Trust Territory of French Cameroons while Britain was Given the UN Trust Territory of British Cameroons.

The British Cameroons was divided for administrative convenience into two territories (British Northern Cameroons which was administered from Kaduna as part of the Northern Region of Nigeria and British Southern

Cameroons which was administered from Enugu as part of the Eastern Region of Nigeria).

In 1954, there was a crisis in the Eastern House of Assembly at Enugu that caused the representatives of the Southern Cameroons in the said Eastern House of Assembly to withdraw from there and come home to Buea where they set up the Southern Cameroons House of Assembly. Britain, the administrative authority, quickly gave its blessings to their plight and a parliamentary system of government with a bi-camera assembly akin to what obtained in Great Britain was put in place with an elected prime minister who was Head of Government business and a cabinet of ministers appointed from the House of Representatives by the Queen of England who handled issues of sovereignty like foreign affairs, defense, police, and currency. There was a Constitution for the territory known as The Southern Cameroons Constitution Orders in Council. Sovereignty was then still vested with the Queen (administrative authority). Dr. EML Endeley was the first prime minister from 1954 to – 1958 when he was defeated in a free and fair elections by John Ngu Foncha to whom he handed power gracefully and sat in House of Assembly as leader of the opposition.

In October 1959 the UNO General Assembly passed Resolution 1541 setting a dateline for immediate independence of all colonial territories under trusteeship in 1960. The British ironically complained that the British Southern Cameroons was not ready for independence having been administered from Nigeria with most of the civil service, police, and other staff coming from Nigeria and so with their mafia, the UN Resolution got modified and the notion of independence by joining either Nigeria or former French Cameroons that had just obtained independence on January 1, 1960, was crafted. Meanwhile, French Cameroons got its independence on January 1, 1960, and was admitted into the UNO as a member in 1960 with its territory clearly mapped out, frozen, and her flag, Coat of Arms, and articles of state which did not include the territory of Southern Cameroons which though quasi-autonomous with bi-camera parliament and government under an elected prime minister was still a Trust Territory of the UNO under Britain.

Meantime campaigns raged in British Cameroons as to independence by joining either independent Nigeria or La Republique du Cameroun. The third option spearheaded by PM Kale with the support of scholars like Fr. Paul Verdzekov (then Curate in Catholic Mission Bota) who had just returned from studies in Ireland and Soborne in France was unpopular and muzzled out. Hence the plebiscite was organized on February 11, 1961, under the auspices of the UNO with the publication of the pamphlet entitled "The Two Alternatives" which clearly spelled out the terms of either eventual union. Voting was done separately in Northern Cameroons and Southern Cameroons and as was secretly planned by the British, Northern Cameroons voted to join

Nigeria while Southern Cameroons voted for union with La Republique du Cameroun.

To give meaning to and settle the issues of the plebiscite results, the UNO General Assembly passed Resolution 1608 of April 21, 1961, which further clarified the conditions under which the respective federations would be constituted on the basis of equality. Thereafter, Northern Cameroons pursuant to the same Resolution got independence by joining Nigeria on June 22, 1961, while the Southern Cameroons was to have its own independence from Britain on October 1, 1961. It must be underlined here that the Northern Cameroons that went to Nigeria got partitioned into two regions within the Nigerian federation and never acceded to self-government with an elected Premier and House of Assembly like the Southern Cameroons from 1954 when they rioted and left the Eastern House of Assembly at Enugu and consequently has undergone a peculiar political evolution and development as part of Nigeria.

As soon as the territory was thus partitioned by the UNO that created the trusteeship system, President Ahmadou Ahidjo of La Republique conceived his fraudulent, grand plan to systematically annex and assimilate the British Southern Cameroons which he announced at the UNC (CNU) Party Congress in Ebolowa in 1961 how part of their territory which was estranged had come back to the motherland.

June 22, 1961—British Northern Cameroons obtains independence and becomes part of the independent Federal Republic of Nigeria while British Southern Cameroons is still under UN Trusteeship waiting for midnight 30th September when trusteeship would end so she becomes independent and joins La Republique du Cameroun in a UN-sponsored federation *". . . equal in status" as per UNGA Resolution 1608 of 21/04/1961.*

July 1961—La Republique du Cameroun conceives draft Bill to change the name of the country to "Republique Federale du Cameroun" and allegedly smuggles the bill to John Ngu Foncha who does not reveal same to Southern Cameroons' House of Representatives nor government that he headed.

July 1961—Ahidjo organizes Foumban Constitutional Conference where the draft Bill for federal Constitution was to be debated but unfortunately the conference ends in disarray without any Resolution.

August 24–25, 1961—the draft Bill for Federal Republic of Cameroun is debated and adopted in the parliament of La Republique du Cameroun only. Neither House of Representatives, House of Chiefs nor Government of The Southern Cameroons who had voted to join them were consulted.

September 1, 1961—President Ahmadou Ahidjo by virtue of powers granted him by the Constitution of La Republique du Cameroun promulgates the adopted draft Bill into Law No L/F/01 of 01/09/1961 on the Constitution of the Federal Republic of Cameroun which immediately goes operational in his country while the Southern Cameroons is still under UN Trusteeship with

The Southern Cameroons Constitution Orders in Council as our own governing law under the British Crown and Union Jack.

September 30, 1961—at the Tiko international Airport in the afternoon, while Southern Cameroons was still under UN Trusteeship that was to expire at midnight for the territory to achieve independence and join La Republique du Cameroon, Ahidjo comes for official visit, the Union Jack is lowered, and the Two Stars Flag of La Republique du Cameroun is hoisted, Ahidjo inspects Guard of Honour mounted by the remaining British soldiers and Ikeja trained police, Ahidjo is thus handed the Southern Cameroons illegally and prematurely by J. O. Fields (last Commissioner) who waves good bye, enters the plane, and goes off to England.

October 1, 1961—Ahmadou Ahidjo, Head of State of the Federal Republic of Cameroon and Commander in Chief of Armed Forces:

had already sent his troops to occupy Buea and Bamenda.

appointed John Ngu Foncha an elected prime minister as vice president of the Federal Republic with office and fabulous salary/allowances in Yaounde.

appoints J. C. Ngoh as Federal Inspector of Administration answerable to the president and with more powers than the elected prime minister of West Cameroon.

Signed Decree in 1962 extending Terrorism Law of La Republique du Cameroun to West Cameroon to give legal cover to arrest and incarcerate political opponents like Nde Tumazah, Albert Mukong, Peter Banfogha, and so on of the UPC and One Kamerun party stock who were still enjoying liberties in West Cameroon.

1966—One-party system was rammed down throats of Southern Cameroonians who had managed a vibrant multiparty system with multiple free and fair elections since 1954.

1968—Augustine Ngom Jua another elected prime minister of West Cameroon (never appointed vice president of Federation) was sacked ignominiously while addressing parliament in Buea and replaced with S. T. Muna

1970—S. T. Muna was appointed Federal vice president while J. N. Foncha was appointed Grand chancellor of National Orders (whatever that means).

May 20, 1972—hoax of Referendum was organized to create United Republic of Cameroon, sovereignty is vested with the president who creates seven provinces dividing West Cameroon into South West and North West provinces respectively making sure that seeds of division are sowed, watered, and nurtured between them and sponsoring VIKUMA (Victoria, Kumba, Mamfe alliance against the NW).

February 1, 1984—Paul Biya signed decree resurrecting the erstwhile Republique du Cameroun which had only gone into abeyance with the illegal imposition of the federal Constitution on the UN Trust Territory of the Southern Cameroons.

1992—High Court of Bamenda in Judgment No HCB/28/92 per Justice FOMBE Richard, between The State of Southern Cameroons alias Ambazonia & 2 Ors Vs La Republique Du Cameroun & 1Or declared the administration of La Republique du Cameroun illegal over the Southern Cameroons territory (Judge was subsequently killed and Case File disappeared).

May 2009—Notwithstanding the existing illegality, the African Commission on Human and People's Rights *in Communication 266/2003 dated 27/05/2009* between *Kevin Ngwang Gumne, SCNC & SCAPO Vs Cameroon* wherein the special tribunal of the African Union held that Southern Cameroonians are a distinct people different from citizens of La Republique du Cameroun and recommended constructive dialogue between La Republique du Cameroun and the peoples of the Southern Cameroons. In fact when the leader of the Cameroon delegation (Dr. Joseph Dione Ngute) raised the issue of them being tried in the military tribunal because they were terrorists, the court asked him whether terrorists go to court, and he was dumbfounded. In fact this same recognition was made by the United Nations Human Rights Committee (UNHRC) in *Communication 1134/2002 dated 17/03/2005* between *Fon Fongum Gorji Dinka Vs Cameroon* as well as in the very recent *Communication 1813/2003 dated December 2014* between *Ebenezer Derek Mbongo Akwanga Vs Cameroon* wherein the UNHRC went ahead to award damages in the sum of US$3.445.904 against the defendants.

– The recommendations for constructive dialogue between the two peoples of La Republique du Cameroun and the Southern Cameroons (Ambazonia) by both the African Union and the UNO Secretary-General, Koffi A Annan, had been roundly frustrated with impunity and utmost disdain by Paul Biya's La Republique du Cameroun and everybody seems so helpless!!

– It must also be underlined here that while it was legal and legitimate for the draft Bill for the Constitution of the Federal Republic of Cameroun to be debated only in the parliament of La Republique du Cameroun and then promulgated into law by their President Ahmadou Ahidjo and implemented in their territory, it remains a gigantic fraud and illegality for that federal Constitution and ALL OTHER SUBSEQUENT LEGISLATION and practice deriving from it to be implemented in the territory of the Southern Cameroons (Ambazonia). A law that was adopted and promulgated without the consent of Ambazonians should not be implemented on them. This happens to be one of the principal causes of the American War of Independence, the principle of NO TAXATION WITHOUT REPRESENTATION. How can a law adopted in Parliament of Nigeria be implemented in Cameroon?

– By the same argument should Southern Cameroons continue to pay taxes and sponsor a government that rather than build roads, schools, and hospitals sends armed policemen, gendarmes, and military to torture, maim, rape, loot, and even kill innocent unarmed school children? Do parents suffer with children like this only for them to reach university and be tortured, maimed, raped, and killed by armed troops of La Republique du Cameroun? Why the carnage as if Southern Cameroonians were conquered in war? This is the source of the anger of Ambazonians-separate, annexed, and excluded (see the two maps below). What were the two maps that the UN representative handed to Biya in Yaounde on May 20, 2010? According to live reports from CRTV, the UN representative, Dr. Ali Triki, who was the president of the 64th General Assembly of the UN, in handing the two maps to Cameroun's Head of State, declared *"Voici les cartes de Cameroon Britannique . . . histoire en a decidee (Here are the maps of British Cameroons . . . history had so decided."* According to another state-owned media, Cameroon Tribune of Tuesday, May 25, 2010, on pages 1 and 3, carrying the pictures of the two maps in the presence of Paul Biya and Jean Victor Nkolo, who is of the Information Department at the UN, the two maps were well framed, large enough for Biya to understand even from twenty meters away.

The first and very gigantic one is the Map of La Republique du Cameroun as of January 1, 1960! It shows clearly the red line and green line separating British Cameroons from La Republique du Cameroun. LRC is no more a triangle with British Cameroons as Biya and Yaounde claim. What Dr. Ali Triki was presenting through this first big map was the map showing LRC as far as the UN is concerned. That is LRC as per January 1, 1960. The second map is also very clear and well framed, clearly separated from the first. It shows the Map of British Southern Cameroons as of October 1, 1961.

What does this entail? It means one and one thing only. The UN cannot suffer itself to print and frame very large maps of one's country to come and present it as birthday gifts just like that. Imagine that on your birthday, someone comes up with framed pictures of yours when you were born. Or, in another circumstance, imagine that you are celebrating the 50th anniversary of your marriage, someone comes with two framed pictures of you, and your wife, separately, when she was a maiden and you a bachelor. More so, he refers to her as Miss. The message is simple! That the man, say, the court magistrate or mayor, is reminding you that your stay together is still not regularized as per International Law.

ABORTED DEMANDS FOR POLITICAL DECENTRALIZATION, EQUITY, AND FAIRNESS IN GOVERNANCE

During the 1990s, there were a series of protests and demonstrations against one-party rule since it tended to concentrate political power at the center. This led to the multiplication of political parties. Despite the multiplication of political parties, the incumbent president, Mr. Paul Biya, was able to win various presidential elections handily, including those of 1992, 1997, 2004, and

2011 (*The Commonwealth*, 2017, October 5). It should be noted that in 2008, President Biya abolished term limits, thereby enabling him to run for office as the president without any constitutional restriction (Morse, 2017, June 2).

Even though Cameroon joined the British Commonwealth in 1995 as a result of the fact that it has an English-speaking population, nevertheless, Cameroon has operated as if it is a wholly French-speaking country, to the detriment of the Anglophone region. Feeling neglected, marginalized, and deprived, English-speaking Cameroonians started clamoring for a change or a restructuring of the country. In particular, they insisted upon the equitable sharing of the oil wealth, which presently is lopsidedly in favor of the country's majority French-speaking regions. They also insisted upon changing the judicial system which is currently based on French language and legal traditions while ignoring English language and legal traditions (*Vanguard*, 2017, October 1). They are particularly irked by the fact that Anglophone Cameroon courts are sometimes operated by French-trained judges who have no understanding of British common law. In addition, English-speaking students decry the fact that they are not given opportunity to take examinations in English (Morse, 2017, June 2). They also decry the fact that there are too many French-speaking teachers in the Anglophone region that are not proficient in English. The employment environment is very stifling to English-speaking Cameroonians who find it difficult to gain employment and to join professional associations (Caxton, 2017, July 21). This makes English-speaking citizens feel like foreigners in their own country. To solve some of the problems, the English-speaking citizens called upon the government to redeploy the French-speaking teachers and encourage more English-speaking teachers to be deployed in English-language schools. In particular, the Anglophone Cameroonians want the reintroduction of a federation rather than a unitary system (Ibid.).

Like in many other African countries, Anglophone Cameroonian's demand for restructuring of the country has been ignored or rejected by the political leadership and the French-speaking majority which assume that they have the political and military wherewithal to stop or prevent any major rebellion on the part of the English-speaking people from taking place. Hence, protests have been met with harsh security measures. The harsh security measures simply added fuel to the anger and the desire to restructure the country or separate the two parts. Hence, starting in late 2016, the crisis in the English-speaking regions escalated as the people demanded a restructuring or a rearrangement of the country. Consequently, thousands of English-speaking Cameroonians, including students, teachers, lawyers, and civil society organizations, mounted demonstrations and strikes against discrimination (Morse, 2017, June 2). Due to the confrontations, the casualty rate was increasing. For instance, four protesters were killed in December 2016. In another protest, 100 people were arrested and detained. On October 1, 2017, a mass protest in the English-speaking Northwest and Southwest regions resulted in the death of seventeen protesters as security forces used live bullets to disperse the pro-testers (Unh & Ojeme, 2018, February 2). In the effort to curtail rebellion in the English-speaking regions, the government went as far as banning internet communication for three months and proscribing two organizations. It even arrested and charged the leaders of the two banned organizations with crimes bordering on terrorism. It also instituted a temporary restriction on travel in both the Northwest and Southwest regions of the English-speaking zone (*Nigerian Tribune*, 2017, October 12).

As the conflict escalated, certain elements decided to opt for secession and are now demanding the separation of the English-speaking region from the French-speaking regions. They call their region Ambazonia. The demand for independence has increased confrontations between security forces and the separatists, thereby, resulting in armed resistance. The violent clashes have forced more than 40,000 English-speaking Cameroonians to flee their country and seek refuge in Nigeria. Apparently, there are thousands of Cameroonians who are now in refugee camps in Nigeria. In early January 2018, Sisiku Ayuk Tabe, the leader of the separatists, and other important members of the Southern Cameroon National Council (SCNC) were arrested in Abuja, the capital of Nigeria, by Nigeria's Department of State Service while they were organizing a meeting to find ways of taking care of the thousands of English-speaking Cameroonians who left Cameroon to seek refuge in Nigeria (BBC, 2018, January 8). The arrests prompted human rights lawyers and advocates in Nigeria to demand the release of the individuals since they have a right to express their political opinions. Similarly, the Amnesty International warned against repatriating the separatist leaders back to Cameroon by reminding Nigeria of its obligation to adhere to international law regarding human rights (*Premium Times*, 2018, January 12). Sadly, Nigeria secretly repatriated the separatist leaders back to Cameroon, thereby, putting their lives in great danger.

Thus, the country has incrementally edged toward an uncontrollable civil war as an increasing number of English-speaking Cameroonians have joined the call for total separation from French-speaking Cameroons. As a conse-quence, the major cities in the English zone are now occupied by military and police forces. Buea, the major city in Southwest Cameroon, became a ghost town when separatists decided to symbolically declare independence on October 1, 2017. This date was chosen for the symbolic declaration since it was the day that both the French-speaking and English-speaking regions amalgamated in 1961 (*Vanguard*, 2017, October 1). It should be noted that Nigeria got its independence on October 1, 1960. As the conflict spreads, even rural areas in the English-speaking zone are feeling the impact of the escalating conflict. In many rural communities, people are running into the bushes to hide from Cameroon's security forces that are desperately trying to stop the rebellion.

President Paul Biya, despite his old age, seems to have a total grip on power like a dictator. He rules Cameroon as a personal estate. Strongly backed by the French-speaking Cameroonians, he holds cabinet meetings infrequently. As a result, cabinet meetings are held two or three years apart. Just in passing, a cabinet meeting took place in March 2018 and the previous one was held in October 2015. The cabinet meetings generally last for very short durations and the minutes of the meetings are rarely published (*Premium Times,* 2018, March 15). Indeed, Cameroon operates like a personal colony of President Paul Biya and his ardent supporters. He is free to do whatever he wants and whenever he wants without any political oversight. He takes vacations regularly in Switzerland. In an attempt to appease the aggrieved English-speaking population, he appoints individuals among them to sinecure positions as prime minister and hopes that this would dampen the agitation for separation (Ibid.).

THE RESPONSIBILITY TO PROTECT AND THE INTERNATIONAL MEDIA SILENCE

The double face of the international community has once more been unveiled in the situation in Ambazonia. Many in Ambazonia have pondered about how a social movement in Iran, which led to the death of about twenty-one people, would lead to an urgent session of the UN Security Council, while a struggle lasting close to two years in an African country, with tens of deaths recorded, many missing, thousands arbitrarily arrested, civilians without arms tried in military courts, patients dragged out of hospital beds and taken to unknown destinations, villages burnt and entire communities displaced, an appalling refugee situation, has not received a similar treatment. Despite the numerous appeals in person and in writing, protest marches organized by South Cameroonians at the various international organizations especially the UN, the situation is yet to be heard at the General Assembly, or the more powerful and influential Security Council. This goes to support the thesis that "black lives do not matter" to the international community. Even the Commonwealth, which preaches the upholding of human rights as its key value, is still to promote these rights in one of its member states.

The overbearing influence of France in the UN in general, and Security Council in particular, has also become a deterring factor to the hearing of the Southern Cameroons' case. France is the former colonial master of Francophone Cameroon, and since the reunification of Anglophone and Francophone Cameroon in 1961 it has kept its gripping effect over the country, controlling its economy and resources—most of which come from Southern Cameroons or Anglophone regions.

However, for the UN to uphold its integrity which is fast dwindling, it has to uphold its famous policy of the "responsibility to protect," which was endorsed in 2005 by all members of the UN who pledged to prevent genocide, war crimes, ethnic cleansing, and crimes against humanity. It was invoked in the Libyan case in 2011. According to the UN, the responsibility to protect ensures that when a state fails to protect its own citizens who are vulnerable, the international community is empowered to take necessary actions to protect the vulnerable population. This was upheld in Resolution 1973 when the UN Security Council empowered NATO countries to stage an incursion into the country as a means of protecting the Libyan people who it was reported could no longer be protected by their government. Moreover, other related organizations including Commonwealth and La Francophonie (to which Cameroon is a member) can also uphold their own integrity by imposing their might on the situation.

The imposition of violence as a solution to the problem is a clear indication that the government of Cameroon has run out of options and needs urgent assistance. Cameroon has a serious problem unfolding in the area called Southern Cameroons (Anglophone Cameroon) where Anglophone separatists are fighting for the creation of their own state called Ambazonia Republic where they believe they would be fairly represented. This is an occasion for the international community to help the government and people of Cameroon come out of this quagmire. In the present situation where both parties have lost faith in each other, the international community could provide good offices as well as mediate in the conflict.

In the present lackluster situation, pressure on the international community can only be imposed by the media power. In his book *The Power of News*, Michael Schudson argues that the media has a central role to play in the choices people make in politics. The power of the media in Cameroon is not underestimated as it is usually called the fourth power, meaning it can bring pressure and effectuate changes in any situation. Presently, the eclipse of the situation is such that even Francophones do not have a clear picture of the real situation in Southern Cameroons as the state media has never mentioned the story of the suffering masses and the refugees in Nigeria. Most private media houses in Cameroon have also shunned images from Southern Cameroons and rather prefer to uphold the thesis of politicians who are exploiting the situation to make gains.

The refugee crisis in Libya only received attention after *CNN* exposed the sale of African migrants into slavery. Immediately, countries and organizations weighed in and within months thousands of migrants were rescued and repatriated to their countries of origin. A similar media exposure of the

Southern Cameroons' case especially at the international level would also expose the real issue in context and the carnage ongoing (see map of Southern Cameroons).

ANGER, RESISTANCE, AND SELF-DEFENSE

As a matter of common sense, guns lethalize anger, domestic disputes, mental illness, and despair. A gun in the home makes the likelihood of homicide three times higher, suicide three to five times higher, and accidental death four times higher. The pro-gun lobby has created the fantasy of a gun as a homeowner's perfect protection against a mythical intruder. In reality, each time a gun in the home injures or kills in self-defense, there are four unintentional shooting deaths or injuries, seven criminal assaults and homicides with a gun, and many completed or attempted gun suicides.

The pogroms unleashed against Ambazonians by the Biya regime, especially from November 30, 2017, when the president declared war, created interest in violent self-defense. In fact, the extermination of Ambazonians, rather than emerging fully formed from President Paul Biya's long-term plans, was a piecemeal process driven to a large extent, "from below," by initiatives from rival power centers within the highly fragmented Cameroonian bureaucracy. To say this is not to absolve Biya of responsibility for the genocide in Ambazonia. The annihilation of Ambazonians in Cameroon was frequently cited by both Biya and his subordinates as they sought to fulfill his prediction in the fraudulent "One and Invisible" Cameroon. Mass murder came to seem to Biya officials as the only way out of what they experienced as a managerial political nightmare. Every revolution is accompanied by anger. Anger does not necessarily make one blind. It is also active and temporary. When anger breaks out, one still has time to reflect—*sine ira cum studio*—otherwise one would be tainted by that so easily corruptible hate.

Self-defense is defined as the right to prevent suffering force or violence through the use of a sufficient level of counteracting force or violence. This definition is simple enough on its face, but it raises many questions when applied to actual situations. For instance, what is a sufficient level of force or violence when defending oneself? What goes beyond that level? What if the intended victim provoked the attack? Do victims have to retreat from the violence if possible? What happens when victims reasonably perceive a threat even if the threat doesn't actually exist? What about when the victim's apprehension is subjectively genuine but objectively unreasonable?

Defensive violence against actions from groups or nations is a justified form of violence. Defensive violence can be defined as forceful or violent acts against a group who makes the initial violent acts. Throughout the history of wars in the world, including First and Second World War , when a country would attack another using violence, the victim country would generally respond by defensively using violence to protect themselves and forcing the attacker to flee. There are many other examples that surface today and in recent events, as well as other events that have occurred throughout history to show justified defensive violence.

The UN Charter is the one authoritative source of International Law regulating the use of force. Since the 9/11 attacks that inaugurated the "war on terror," scholars and countries such as the United States have sought to develop a new legal framework that would essentially justify an expanded version of self-defense. The UN Charter is the one authoritative source of International Law regulating the use of force. The 9/11 attacks that inaugurated the "war on terror" prompted the claim that the law of the Charter was obsolete because it was intended to deal with conflicts between states, the principal actors in the international system, and not non-state actors such as Al Qaeda. A novel situation has arisen; the old law of the UN must be appropriately adapted to deal with these new threats, or else, a new legal framework must be established: this in general is the argument made, not only by scholars but powerful countries such as the United States which, through successive administrations, has sought to develop new doctrines that would essentially justify its approach to the "war on terror."

The resulting framework—I present a tentative version here because debates as to its character are ongoing—is based on the paramount importance of self-defense; it profoundly challenges a body of law, relating to sovereignty, self-defense, human rights, and the use of force that has been carefully and laboriously constructed over the past decades through the auspices of the UN and various other related institutions. In this chapter I examine this new framework first, in terms of how it seeks to amend or reinterpret existing principles restricting the use of force; second, its underlying vision of war and violence; and third, I suggest ways in which this framework serves to reproduce certain colonial structures which appear to be deeply embedded in both International Law and international relations.

SELF-DEFENSE, STATES' SILENCE, AND THE SECURITY COUNCIL: EXAMINING ACQUIESCENCE CONCERNS AND UN ARTICLE 51 REPORTS

When is silence juridically relevant in International Law? When is it pertinent to measures of self-defense? Under what circumstances does a state—or the UN Security Council—tacitly consent to another state's conduct by not speaking out against it? Where do states and where does the UN Security

Council have an obligation to publicly denounce unlawful conduct lest they acquiesce in the violative conduct and, possibly, in a revised interpretation or modification of the legal provision corresponding to that violative conduct?

The basic contours of the relevance of silence in International Law are not new. They have resurfaced over centuries and across a range of contexts, touching on such matters as the attribution of territorial title, change of a land boundary, and derogation of a treaty. The (Draft) Articles on the Responsibility of States for Internationally Wrongful Acts (2001) recognized, for example, the loss of the right to invoke responsibility where the injured state is considered, by reason of its conduct, to have validly acquiesced in the lapse of the claim.

More recently, silence and inaction have been raised—in draft conclusions of the International Law Commission (ILC)—regarding two topics that pertain to (re)interpreting, or perhaps even modifying, legal provisions. One topic concerns treaties and the other relates to customary International Law. Both topics are under active consideration by the ILC in conjunction with UN Member States, and both may be relevant to self-defense. That is because the legal parameters concerning self-defense measures pertain not only to the UN Charter but also to customary International Law.

The first ILC topic is the establishment of the agreement of parties to a treaty through subsequent practice. According to the ILC's most recent draft conclusions[1] regarding that topic, silence on the part of one or more parties can constitute acceptance of the subsequent practice *when the circumstances call for some reaction*. (Those draft conclusions also state that silence by a party shall not be presumed to constitute subsequent practice under Article 31(3)(b) of the Vienna Convention on the Law of Treaties accepting an interpretation of a treaty as expressed in a pronouncement of an expert treaty body.) The second ILC topic is the identification of a rule of customary International Law. According to the most recent ILC's draft conclusions concerning that topic, relevant practice may, under certain circumstances, include *inaction*, and failure to react over time to a practice may serve as evidence of acceptance as law (*opinio juris*), provided that states *were in a position to react* and the circumstances *called for some reaction*.

The status of the norms and the corresponding treaty provisions and customary rules at issue—in particular, those concerning the prohibition of the use of force in international relations—may further complicate the legal analysis. That is because certain norms, including those recognized as reflecting obligations *erga omnes* or *jus cogens*, give rise to additional considerations. Those considerations might, for example, implicate a potential obligation of third states to cooperate to bring the breach to an end and to not recognize as lawful any situation created by the breach, as well as modalities through which the relevant norm may, or may not, be modified.

Today, foundational questions concerning the juridical relevance of silence resonate perhaps most significantly with respect to extraterritorial state military attacks that are (purportedly) conducted on a self-defense basis, that are directed against non-state armed groups, and that are undertaken (at least seemingly) without the consent of the territorial state. Such attacks directed against ISIS in Syria make up one prominent set of examples. But they are far from the only instances.

An ongoing debate among international lawyers concerns aspects of the legality of such resorts to force under the UN Charter and under customary International Law. One subset of that debate concerns whether—and, if so, under what conditions—the international legal regime governing self-defense permits a state, without UN Security Council authorization, to resort to force by directing an attack against a terrorist group in circumstances where that group is neither directed nor controlled by but operates in and emanates cross-border threats from another state and where the attacking state does not have the consent of the territorial state. A related strand of debate relates to what, if any, legal effects may arise in the face of those resorts to force from silence—whether it is the silence of states other than the attacking state(s) or the territorial state(s) or the silence of the UN Security Council itself.

Against the backdrop of those debates, this project seeks to deepen and widen our understanding of the role, if any, of silence or inaction in discerning whether armed action directed against non-state armed groups in the identified circumstances fits within the existing international legal order. Of the array of potential concerns in this thematic area, this project will focus on two linked sets of issues.

The first set of issues that this project will explore concerns the legal relevance, if any, of states' silence or inaction in relation to the resorts to the use of force (purportedly) in self-defense raised above. Among the relevant stakes are whether—by not publicly protesting or otherwise denouncing resorts to force in the form of military attacks directed against non-state armed groups (seemingly) without the territorial state's consent—certain states (perhaps especially states other than the attacking state and territorial state) and/or the UN Security Council may be considered to have tacitly consented to the validity of those resorts to force and/or of the legal rationales underlying them. We will explore normative parameters in light of subsequent practice of parties to the UN Charter and of state practice and *opinio juris*, as well as jurisprudence of international courts.

The second set of issues that this project will examine concerns so-called "Article 51 reports." Article 51 of the UN Charter lays down that: Nothing in the present Charter shall impair the inherent right of individual or collective self-defense if an armed attack occurs against a Member of the UN, until the Security Council has taken measures necessary to maintain international peace and security. Measures taken by members in the exercise of this right of self-defense shall be immediately reported to the Security Council and shall not in any way affect the authority and responsibility of the Security Council under the present Charter to take at any time such action as it deems necessary in order to maintain or restore international peace and security.

We will explore the role of Article 51 reports within the normative regime as well as international legal aspects concerning the UN Security Council's responses, or lack of responses, to those reports. In doing so, we will consider such issues as the accessibility of and transparency concerning those reports; trends and trajectories regarding the content (including legal arguments), form, and other substantive and procedural aspects pertaining to those reports; and the UN Security Council's responses to those reports and/or its own silence or other forms of inaction regarding them.

SELF-DEFENSE AND DEFENSE OF
VULNERABLE AMBAZONIAN OTHERS

Self-defense and defense of vulnerable others are two criminal defenses that can be used when a criminal defendant commits a criminal act but believes that he or she was justified in doing so. Although our legal system generally discourages the use of force or violence against others, courts have recognized that all individuals have the right to protect themselves from harm and may use reasonable force in order to do so. Likewise, the defense of others also recognizes the right to use reasonable force in defense of others who are threatened.

Today, some 300 homes have been burnt to ashes; 1,000 children drifting around with neither food to eat nor any knowledge of the whereabouts of their parents; at least one million internally displaced people. In the meantime, thousands have taken refuge in forests, sleeping in the open and living on wild food, while more than 50,000 people according to UNHCR have successfully crossed into Nigeria as refugees. In some situations, even houses of priests and pastors have been burnt—like the case of the pastor of the Presbyterian Church Kwa-Kwa (in the Southwest of the country) and the Roman Catholic priest in the same area. It is therefore not a surprise to hear Professor Fonkem Achankeng wonder whether with such carnage "we (Ambazonians) are winning."

Perhaps the easiest way to understand why French Cameroon barbaric colonialism is so horrific to Ambazonians and the international community is to imagine it happening in your own country now. It is invaded, conquered, and occupied by a senile and savage foreign power. Existing governing institutions are dismantled and replaced by absolute rule of the colonizers. A strict hierarchy separates the colonized and the colonizer; you are treated as an inconvenient subhuman who can be abused at will. The colonists commit crimes with impunity against your people. Efforts at resistance are met with brutal reprisal, sometimes massacre. The more vividly and accurately you manage to conjure what this scenario would actually look like, the more horrified you will be by the very idea of colonialism.

When the colonizers sense that the jig is up, they co-opt the local elite—the intellectuals, priests or preachers, movers and shakers in the political class. These people are so deeply colonized that they collaborate with colonizers to keep a lid on things. They do so because their colonization conditions them to see revolution as a threat to values like dignity, equality, individualism, and reasonableness.

The reason is that the colonized elites prefer reform to revolution. They get a seat at the table of reasonableness and get to negotiate the terms of reform with the colonizers, terms that will, no doubt, help to cement their own power and privilege. But trying to find reasonable compromises with the colonizers, the colonized elites become "oh so reasonable" instruments of the colonizers. In the end, reform promises no fundamental change at all, at least not for the masses. That's why it's always the Ambazonian masses and not the co-opted elites who are the leading edge of revolution. And that's why nonviolent reform is for sell-outs, who are blind to their own colonization and complicit in not just their own oppression, but the oppression of the masses.

SELF-DEFENSE AND THE UN CHARTER

The UN Charter is the one authoritative source of International Law regulating the use of force. Under the UN Charter, force is permitted only in two circumstances: first, when the use of force has been authorized by the Security Council acting under Chapter VII; and second, under section 51 of the Charter a state which has been the victim of an "armed attack" may respond by using force in self-defense. These basic principles are supported and complemented by a number of other customary rules. For instance, the use of force must be proportional to the injury suffered. Further, territorial restrictions are imposed on the use of force: it is impermissible under International Law to wage war in the territory of a state which is not strictly party to the conflict for that would violate the sovereignty of the attacked state. Finally, a relatively clear boundary existed between "peace" and "war"; wars were usually brought to an end by some sort of treaty, peace was restored, and this enabled the different legal regimes of peace and war to operate with clarity.

The UN Charter recognizes the fundamental, indeed primordial, character of self-defense by stating that "nothing in the present Charter impairs the inherent right of self-defense." Crucial to this framework is the question of the scope of the right of self-defense. The right, in other words, precedes the Charter, even if the Charter attempts to limit the circumstances in which that right is exercised. The potency and primacy of the right of self-defense is suggested by the fact that the International Court of Justice left open the possibility that a state could use nuclear weapons in self-defense—this despite the catastrophic global consequences that would most likely follow. It is notable further that both the Non-proliferation Treaty and the Chemical Weapons Convention explicitly permit a member state to withdraw from the treaty if "extraordinary events" occur and upon giving due notice-as North Korea did with the Non-Proliferation treaty. One way to understand this apparently anomalous provision is that it recognizes that the inherent right of self-defense possessed by all states will only be meaningful if they have a concurrent right to develop and use whatever weapons are available for that purpose.

CONCLUSION

A broad consideration of French Cameroon colonialism of Ambazonia suggests that this senile system of domination entails contest of reality in three worlds: *the world of things*, of *people*, and *of meaning*. Driven firstly by economic motives, French Cameroon colonizers attacked the world of Ambazonian things to obtain natural resources for its French overlords and markets for manufactured French goods. To obtain cheap or free labor, they not only occupied the land but also assaulted the world of people to force submission militarily and politically. Once they subdued Ambazonian people and occupied their land with savage security outfits and evil administrators, they assaulted the world of meaning because no system of oppression lasts without occupation of the mind and ontology of the oppressed.

In short and in conclusion, French Cameroon colonialism is today more entrenched objectively and subjectively than it was in the past in Ambazonia. Effective and sustainable change to decolonize Ambazonia can come only when those within the center of the metacolonized world and those in its peripheries work together both to *deconstruct* metacoloniality in its different forms and jointly *reconstruct* a more just Ambazonian world on the ruins of the brutally imposed old French Cameroon colonialism. The call for collaboration is not a mere appeal for sympathy or generosity from the United States of America, UN, African Union, or European Union; those at the centers of metacolonialism also pay heavy but hidden costs for injustice and dehumanization of Ambazonian others. I therefore see the project of decolonizing psychology in Ambazonia (using bottom-up rather than top-down approach

to decolonization) as a means toward broad-based critical thinking and collaboration on what to *deconstruct* and how to *reconstruct* for the benefit of
all.

The reason for this bottom-up approach lies in the logic that social and
political systems seldom die or dismantle easily; they often reinvent themselves for three chief reasons. First, the economic and political interests they
served in the past continue to prevail in subsequent generations. Second, the
institutions—schools, law enforcement agencies, courts, and others—that
served those interests do not readily change. Third, those who grow up under
these systems——beneficiaries as well as victims——get so indoctrinated
through childhood socialization, schooling, and adult experiences that they
do not seek or accept alternative ways of looking at the world. Turned into
true believers or acting as programmed robots, they defend the oppressive
structures as if life would be impossible without them. In fact, they would
(and often do) sacrifice life to defend and perpetuate these systems, however
unjust.

NOTE

1. https://legal.un.org/docs/?symbol=A/CN.4/L.872.

REFERENCES

*Amnesty International Warns Against Extradition of Cameroon Separatist Leaders
Arrested in Nigeria*. (2018, January 12). *Premium Times*. Retrieved January 16,
2018.
Berkowitz, L. (1970). Experimental investigations of hostility catharsis. *Journal of
Consulting and Clinical Psychology*, 35, 1–7.
Bobichand, R. (2012). *"Understanding Violence Triangle and Structural Violence"* –
Rajkumar Bobichand (2012).
Bodenhausen, G. V., Sheppard, L. A., & Kramer, G. P. (1994). Negative affect and
social judgment: The differential impact of anger and sadness. *European Journal
of Social Psychology*, 24, 45–62.
Bushman, B., Baumeister, R., Stack, A., & Kruglanski, A. W. (1999). Catharsis,
aggression, and persuasive influence: Self-fulfilling or self-defeating prophecies?
Journal of Personality and Social Psychology, 76, 367–376.
Cameroon City Deserted Ahead Independence Declaration. (2017, October 1). *Van-
guard*. Retrieved October 4, 2017, from https://www.vanguardngr.com/2017/10/
cameroon-city-deserted-independence-declaration/.
Cameroon's Aging Biya Holds First Cabinet Meeting Since 2015. (2018, March 15).
Premium Times. Retrieved March 22, 2018, from https://www.premiumtimesng

.com/foreign/west-africa-foreign/261929-cameroons-aging-biya-holds-first-cabinet-meeting-since-2015.html.

Cameroon's Anglophone Crisis at the Crossroads. (2017, August 2). International Crisis Group. Retrieved October 6, 2017, from https://reliefweb.int/report/cameroon-s-anglophone-crisis-crossroads.

Caxton, A. (2017, July 21). The Anglophone Dilemma in Cameroon. *Accord.* Retrieved April 3, 2018, from www.accord.org.zo/conflict-trends/anglophone-dillema-cameroon/.

English Speakers Take to the Streets. (2017, September 22). *MNews24.* Retrieved September 23/17, from m.news24.com/news24/Africa/News/English-speakers-take-to-the-streets-in-cameroon.20170.

Fanon, F. (1967). *Black Skin, White Masks.* New York, NY: Grove Press.

Fanon, F. (1968). *The Wretched of the Earth.* New York, NY: Grove Press.

Fanon, F. (1969). *"Towards the African Revolution"* – Frantz Fanon (1969).

Fehr, B., & Baldwin, M. W. (1996). Prototype and script analyses of laypeople's knowledge of anger. In J. Fitness & G. Fletcher (Eds.), *Knowledge Structures and Interaction in Close Relations: A Social Psychological Approach* (pp. 219–245). Hillsdale, NJ: Lawrence Erlbaum Associates.

Fernandez, E. (2008). The angry personality: A representation on six dimensions of anger expression. In G. J. Boyle, D. Matthews, & D. Saklofske (Eds.), *International Handbook of Personality Theory and Testing: Vol. 2: Personality Measurement and Assessment* (pp. 402–419). London: Sage.

Galtung, J. (1969). *"Galtung's Violence Triangle"* – Johan Galtung (1969).

Gandhi, M. (1942). *"Nonviolence in Peace and War, Volume I"* – M.K. Gandhi (1942).

Harmon-Jones, E. (2004). On the relationship of anterior brain activity and anger: Examining the role of attitude toward anger. *Cognition and Emotion*, 18, 337–361.

Lerner, J. S., & Keltner, D. (2000). Beyond valence: Toward a model of emotion-specific influences on judgment and choice. *Cognition & Emotion*, 14, 473–493.

Moons, W. G., & Mackie, D. M. (2007). Thinking straight while seeing red: The influence of anger on information processing. *Personality and Social Psychology Bulletin*, 33, 706–720.

Morse, Y. L. (2017, June 2). Cameroon has been in crisis for six months. Here's is what you need to know. *The Washington Post.* www.vanguardngr.com/2017/03/46-killed-96-wounded-ife-yoruba-hausa-clas-police/.

Nabi, R. L. (2002). Anger, fear, uncertainty, and attitudes: A test of the cognitive-functional model. *Communication Monographs*, 69, 204–216.

Novaco, R. (1975). *Anger Control: The Development and Evaluation of an Experimental Treatment.* Lexington, MA: Heath.

Ortony, A., Clore, G. L., & Collins, A. (1988). *The Cognitive Structure of Emotions.* New York: Cambridge University Press.

Our Member Countries - Cameroon History. (2017, October 5). The Commonwealth. Retrieved October 5, 2017, from https://the commonwealth.org/our-member-countries/Cameroon/history.

Schwarz, N. (1990). Feelings as information: Informational and motivational functions of affective states. In E. T. Higgins & R. Sorrentino (Eds.), *Handbook of Motivation and Cognition: Foundations of Social Behavior* (Vol. 2, pp. 527–561). New York: Guilford.

Siebert, R. (1974). *"Frantz Fanon: Colonialism and Alienation: Concerning Frantz Fanon's Political Theory"* – Renate Siebert (1974).

Tavris, C. (1984). *Anger: The Misunderstood Emotion.* New York: Simon & Schuster.

The Crackdown on Southern Cameroonians. (2017, October 12). Nigerian Tribune. Retrieved October 20, 2017, from https://odili.net/news/source/2017/oct/12/602 .html.

Thomas, D. (2016). *Channeling the River: Using Positive Psychology to Prevent Cultural Helplessness, as Applied to African-American Law Students.* MAPP Capstone.

Unh, E., & Ojeme, V. (2018, February 2). Cameroun Boils: From Separatist Fighters to Refugees II. *Vanguard.* Retrieved February 3, 2018, from https://www.vanguardngr.com/2018/02/cameroun-boils-separatist-fighters-refugees-ii.

Whittington, K. E., Kelemen, R. D., & Caldeira, G. A. (Eds.). (2010). *The Oxford Handbook of Law and Politics.* London: Oxford University Press.

Wilson, J. (1896). *The Works of James Wilson.* Edited by J. DeWitt Andrews, 2 Vols. Chicago: Callaghan.

Chapter 14

Cameroon's Anti-Terrorism Law and the Trials of Ex-British Southern Cameroons' Activists in a Military Tribunal

Patrick Agejoh

The concept of terrorism has been defined as the unlawful use of violence and intimidation, especially against civilians, in the pursuit of political aims or goals (The Dictionary.com., n.d.). This unlawful use of violence has serious implications locally and internationally, especially if they involve an increase in state control over the flows of information, commodities, capital, and people, as this might affect the international observance of human rights. Terrorism activities influence international politics and shape the role of hegemony in the world system (Stemplowski, 2002). Dictatorial regimes adopt terrorism as a means to suppress and dominate their opponents or any opposition.

State counter-terrorism measures both in form and function are alternative to reinforce state political legitimacy. Counter-terrorism entails the adoption of more and more aggressive provisions such as torture, extrajudicial executions, military campaigns, and acts of extreme violence to justify their actions as "necessary." The human rights framework demands the right to life and property which places a correlative duty on the government to ensure that these rights are not violated (Donohue, 2012). Can anti-terrorism policies comply with human rights standards without impinging on liberal democracy and the rule of law? According to Conte, state policy to counter-terrorism may be draconian and utilized as an excuse to extend state powers on the part of conservatives who might argue that there is little or no place for human rights considerations in the context of security and the combating of terrorism (Conte, 2006).

In the case of Cameroon, the ex-British Southern Cameroons' human rights complaints against widespread annexation and colonial occupation in various areas of public life pointed to the existence of a huge problem including the disregard of constitutional provisions by the powerful state. The questioning of this injustice by activists led to the state invoking terrorism as the reason for the trials in a military tribunal.

Within the framework of human rights, it is important to understand whether or not Cameroun anti-terrorism law is the best option or useful tool to address grievances against the state. This and many more questions linger in one's mind, and the answers may not be given in this chapter, which serves to remind state actors of their *"obligatio erga omnes."*

According to Amnesty International 2017/2018 Report on Cameroon, the organization pointed out that security forces in their campaign to fight against terrorism continued to arbitrarily arrest individuals accused of supporting terrorism, often with little or no evidence and sometimes using unnecessary or excessive force (Amnesty International Organisation, p. 2021). Those arrested were frequently detained in inhumane, life-threatening conditions. At least 101 people were detained incommunicado between March 2013 and March 2017 in a series of military bases run by the Rapid Intervention Battalion (BIR) unit and facilities run by the Intelligence Agency of the Cameroon Armed Forces. They were subjected to torture and other ill-treatment (Amnesty International Organisation, 2021).

The case of ex-British Southern Cameroons human rights activists may be understood from the fact that Cameroon is a collage of two former League of Nations Mandate Territories and the United Nations (UN) Trusteeship Territories that were handed to Britain and France to administer following the collapse [sic] of Second World War (Trusteeship Council, 2020). On January 1, 1960, French Cameroun became independent and one year nine months later, British Southern Cameroons also gained independence by joining French Cameroun on October 1, 1961, to form a federation of two equal states. Inequalities and human rights abuses emanating from the two entities coming together to form one state have been the situation since 1961.

The UN General Assembly Resolution 1352 (xiv) on the British Southern Cameroons' plebiscite of 1961 ruled out the separate independence of British Southern Cameroons but rather a union between British Southern Cameroons and La Republique du Cameroun. It is also believed that the Government of Great Britain tactfully blocked every chance of the people of British Southern Cameroonians voting for independence as a separate entity, convincing the UN that Southern Cameroons was not economically viable and could only survive by leaning on Nigeria or La Republique du Cameroun and recklessly steering the Mamfe All Party Conference of August 1959 to ensure that the parties did not achieve consensus (Bamenda Provincial Episcopal Conference [BAPEC] Memorandum to the Head of State, 2017).

The failure of successive Governments of Cameroon, since 1961, to respect and implement the articles of the Constitution that uphold and safeguard what British Southern Cameroons brought along to the Union in 1961 led activists to push against these failures (Banseka, 2006). The flagrant disregard of the provisions of the federal Constitution, demonstrated by the dissolution of political parties and the formation of one political party system in 1966, and other such acts judged by the people of British Southern Cameroons to be unconstitutional and undemocratic to them (Loi N°2014/028 Portant Répression des Actes de Terrorisme (2014), Sect. 2(1) (a)(b), 2014).

THE FIGHT AGAINST TERRORISM IN CAMEROON

Before the adoption of the recent law on terrorism, a series of decrees were signed that dealt with *locus standi* of some civil authorities before military courts and another sought better organization of military tribunals.

Section 2(1) (a) & (b) of Law No. 2014/028 of Cameroon relating to the suppression of acts of terrorism considers acts likely to cause death, endanger physical integrity, bodily injury or material damage, destruction of natural resources and the environment with the intent to provoke a situation of terror as acts of terrorism punishable by a death penalty (Loi N°2014/028 Portant Répression des Actes de Terrorisme (2014), Sect. 2(1)(a)(b), 2014).

This section of the law is used by the government to suppress public demonstrations by any group of civilians against public services. Scared of the fact that some of the protests may lead to violence, this law becomes the major weapon to suppress public demonstrations contrary to the citizens' constitutional rights to protest. The trials of Southern Cameroons or so-called "Anglophone" activists in military tribunal were on the ground that these activists committed acts of terrorism which included secession, hostility against the state, rebellion, civil war, destruction of property, killing, and non-possession of identity cards during public demonstrations (Africanews, 2018).

The 1996 Constitution of Cameroon provides in its Preamble that:

> every person has a right to life, to physical and moral integrity and humane treatment in all circumstances. Under no circumstances shall any person be subjected to torture, to cruel, inhumane or degrading treatment. The freedom of communication, of expression, of the press, of assembly, of association, and of trade unionism, as well as the right to strike, shall be guaranteed under the conditions fixed by law. (Cameroon Law No. 96-06 of January 18, 1996, to amend the Constitution of June 2, 1972, 1996)

The anti-terrorism law of Cameroon seems to contradict the highest law of the country (the Constitution). The framers of this Constitution stated in Article 65 that "the preamble shall be part and parcel of this Constitution" (Cameroon Law No. 96-06 of January 18, 1996, to amend the Constitution of June 2, 1972, art. 65, 1996). This provision in the 1996 Constitution of Cameroon is a replica of articles 6(1) and 7 of the International Covenant on Civil and Political Rights 1966 (UN International Covenant on Civil and Political Rights (1966), art. 6(1) & 7, 1966). The preamble guarantees freedom of communication, expression, and strike. One is unable to understand the extent to which this freedom of communication and expression can take place. As a dictatorial regime, the government sees terrorism only on the side of those they consider as enemies of the state. Given that the French legal system is inquisitorial with the active involvement of the *Juge d'Instruction* in the prosecution of suspects accounted to the contravention of human rights standards and contrary to the Common Law adversarial practices. This justifies what the US Permanent Representative to the UN, H. E. Clement Zabloiski, said on October 6, 1959. He said

> The USA congratulates the people of Southern Cameroons for their accession to auto determination as it constitutes the will of the population who want to run its affairs democratically as opposed to a hurried idea of unification (unification with La Republique de Cameroun). The result of a hurried choice imposed on the population of the British trust territory would be catastrophic for their political future. (Ayim, 2008)

French Cameroun's concept of terrorism is opposed to the Anglo-Saxon concept of human rights and the rule of law.

Meanwhile, the Code of Military Justice provides in Section 4(1) of Law No. 2017/012 that the Yaounde military tribunal may under such exceptional circumstances hold hearings of any matter that seriously threatens public order and state security or act of terrorism as well as exercise nationwide jurisdiction (Law No. 2017/012 of July 12, 2017, to lay down the Code of Military Justice, Sect. 4(1)). Curiously, the Suppression of Acts of Terrorism Law of Cameroon abrogates habeas corpus rights by stating in Section 11 that "the duration of remand in custody shall be 15 days renewable upon the authorisation of the State Prosecutor" (Law 028 on the Suppression of Acts of Terrorism in Cameroon (2014), Sect. 11). The period for this "15 days renewable" is not specified thereby implying the authority has the liberty to extend it as long as he/she wishes it to be.

Section 8 (b)(c) of the Code of Military Justice gives the Military Tribunal exclusive jurisdiction or competence to hear and determine crimes against humanity and genocide as well as offenses relating to acts of terrorism and state security (Law No. 2017/012 of July 12, 2017, to lay down the Code of Military Justice, Sect. 8(b)(c)).

The Law on the Suppression of Acts of Terrorism in Cameroon in more than three sections mentioned the death penalty for individuals who are engaged in terrorist activities. Sections 2(1) (d), 2(2), 4(b), and 5(1) all reiterated punishment with the death penalty (Law 028 on the Suppression of Acts of Terrorism in Cameroon (2014), Sect. 2(1d), (2d), 4(b), and 5(1)..

These provisions of the law made it very difficult to differentiate between civil protests and acts of terrorism. Any democratic protest that leads to violence is likely to be classified as a terrorist action according to the anti-terrorism law. The use of military force to arbitrarily arrest and torture demonstrators, exact extrajudicial killings, and inhumane detention or imprison people is usually applied as a means to implement the anti-terrorism law.

Amnesty International 2017/2018 Report on Cameroon also quoted unfair trials in related cases where ex-British Southern Cameroons' journalists Tsi Conrad and Mancho Bibixy were arrested in Bamenda in January 2017, transferred to Yaounde, and slammed fifteen years imprisonment each by the Cameroun Military Tribunal (Amnesty, 2018). Reporters Without Borders (RSF) in June 2020 reported the disappearance of Cameroon Anglophone Pidgin news reporter Samuel Ebuwe Ajiekah (aka Samuel Wazizi) who was arrested in August 2019 and nine months after was reported that he died in military detention without trial. The corpse was never seen or handed to his family (RSF refers Cameroonian journalist's death to UN rapporteurs, 2020).

Incommunicado detention became a norm in Cameroun to treat suspected terrorists. An example was the recent abduction of forty-seven ex-British Southern Cameroons asylum seekers from Abuja, Nigeria, to Cameroon and held incommunicado. It is assumed that incommunicado torture is a process of compliance and submission, humiliation, and psychological breakdown, and psychological torture more targeted often to achieve the desired effect in a shorter time (PP Sale, 2016). Incommunicado detention of Anglophone activists was conducted such that the detainees were denied access to family, friends, and lawyers. In early 2018, the forty-seven Southern Cameroons (Anglophone) who were abducted and detained in Nigeria and then refouled to Cameroon were subjected to incommunicado detention for at least three months. They were denied access to lawyers and were not charged with any offense. The location of their facility was unknown (The Centre for Human Rights and Democracy in Africa (CHRDA) and The Raoul Wallenberg Centre for Human Rights (RWCHR) "Cameroon's Unfolding Catastrophe" report of June 2019 at 53, 2019). The CHRDA Report highlighted that Human Rights Watch had between January 2018 and January 2019 documented twenty-six cases of incommunicado detention and enforced disappearance at Gendarmerie National Secretariat (SED) detention sites, the headquarters of the National Gendarmerie, including fourteen cases of torture (CHRDA & RWCHR "Cameroon's Unfolding Catastrophe" report of June 2019 at 53, 2019). These human rights violations contravened the intended adoption of the anti-terrorism law in Cameroon thereby raising concerns to repeal this law.

Cameroon anti-terrorism law must be read along with the provisions of the country's Penal Code (Law 007 of 2016 Relating to Penal Code, 2016).[1] Some of the ingredients of terrorism as mentioned above in the law include hostilities against the state which is a crime in the Cameroun Penal Code. In Section 102 (a)(b) of the Penal Code, "any citizen taking part in hostilities against the Republic of Cameroon or assisting or offering to assist the said hostilities shall be guilty of treason and punished with death." Meanwhile, Section 111(1) of the Penal Code provides that "whoever undertakes in whatever manner to infringe the territorial integrity of the Republic shall be punished with imprisonment for life" which is considered as a secession offense. These provisions of the Penal Code and the anti-terrorism law were used in the trials of Anglophone Human Rights activists as terrorism against the state thereby giving the military tribunal in the nation's capital, Yaounde, jurisdiction to try these individuals. The crafting of these legislations has been interpreted by rights activists and historians as intended to suppress any question relating to former Southern Cameroons' independence by joining La Republique du Cameroun.

The punishment for the acclamation of acts of terrorism as stated in Section 8 of the law on the suppression of acts of terrorism is imprisonment from fifteen to twenty years or a fine of twenty-five million francs (25,000,000) to fifty million francs (50,000,000) (Law 028 on the Suppression of Acts of Terrorism in Cameroon (2014), Sect. 8). The language of "acclamation of acts of terrorism" in this provision is not clear as to whether a criminal act can be acclaimed by an individual.

The Cameroon Penal Code in Section 21(1) classified the highest "offence punishable with death or with loss of liberty for more than 10 (ten) years and fine where so provided." Section 22(1) states that "every sentence of death shall be submitted to the president of the Republic for his decision on commutation" (Law 007 of 2016 Relating to Penal Code (2016), Sect. 21(1) & 22(1)). Legal pundits continue to wonder whether civil courts in Cameroon do not have jurisdiction to try civilians accused of crimes of capital punishment. The African Commission on Human and Peoples' Rights Principles and Guidelines on the Right to a Fair Trial and Legal Assistance in Africa states that:

> Military or other special tribunals that do not use the duly established procedure of the legal process shall not be created to displace the jurisdiction belonging

to the ordinary judicial bodies (African Commission on Human and Peoples' Rights "Principles and Guidelines on The Right to a Fair Trial and Legal Assistance in Africa" (2013), Sect. 2(1) (e)).

The use of a military tribunal may not be fair for the trial of ex-British Southern Cameroons activists on the ground that the trial is against African Commission Guidelines and other international human rights instruments.

Before the adoption of the Law on Suppression of Acts of Terrorism in 2014 and the 2016 revision of Cameroon Penal Code, the country had been practicing the death penalty from the days of former president Amadou Ahidjo. In 1984, former president Ahidjo and two former aides were tried in February on charges of conspiracy to assassinate President Paul Biya and to overthrow the government. All three were found guilty (Amadou Ahidjo in absentia) and sentenced to death, but the sentences were later commuted to life imprisonment (Cameroon "Annual Human Rights Reports Submitted to Congress by the U.S. Department of State 9," (1984) at 49–58).

Tande has stated in his article to Cameroon's Human Rights Commission and the United Nations High Commission for Human Rights as well as the Cameroon Bar Council to the Government of Cameroon to abolish the death penalty (Tande, 2016). Application or maintaining the death penalty is contrary to Cameroon's international treaty obligations (UNGA, 1989).

The Cameroon Constitution prohibits torture, and Law N°2005 of July 27, 2005, on the Cameroon Criminal Procedure Code in Section 122 (2) prohibits the use of torture during police custody. In addition, Section 132 (1) of the Penal Code prohibits public servants from using force against any person. However, there were credible reports during 1984 of ill-treatment, such as beatings, during police interrogation and imprisonment of captured persons suspected of treason against the state. Amnesty International has also reported allegations of harsh prison conditions and ill-treatment of detainees.

In addressing the issue of terrorism, it is pivotal to note whether the war against terrorism will allow human rights regime to recover its balance in the face of the current control technique (Fitzpatrick, 2003). Since the outbreak in 2016 of an armed conflict in the Southern Cameroons (Anglophone region), pre-trial detention appears to have become the norm, sometimes for months at a time. the people of ex-British Southern Cameroons were called with derogatory names likes "dogs and rats," and the military was reportedly breaking into homes either shooting young men on their legs or arresting others even from places of worship (Fonkem, 2018). In response to military brutality, young people began arming themselves in self-defense as they could not sit by and watch the military to kill, maim, rape, torture them, and burn down their villages with impunity (Fonkem, 2018). Human Rights Watch alleged that the government engaged in a continued practice of "forced disappearances" where individuals were arrested and held incommunicado without any formal charges being laid against them or their families/legal representatives being informed of their whereabouts. There are also a number of reports that lawyers have been denied access to their clients during the pre-trial and then trial process, and sometimes face threats and physical violence if they insist on upholding their clients' legal rights (Oxford University, 2019).

According to a German newspaper report on August 31, 2018, the trials of ex-British Southern Cameroons activists in a military court was an unfortunate government's reaction to a civil protest or unrest in the region based on Cameroon's unique history. The government's reaction involved the crackdown on ex-British Southern Cameroons (aka Anglophone region), shutdown of internet connections for three months (ninety-three days) (DWNews, 2017). By a deliberate refusal to grant sovereign independence to the territory, the British forced a plebiscite on the people of British Southern Cameroons, asking them whether they wished to achieve independence by joining the Federal Republic of Nigeria or the Republic of Cameroun. The vote went in favor of achieving independence by joining La Republique du Cameroun. The UN General Assembly followed up the vote to pass the Resolution 1608(XV) of April 21, 1961, to grant the British Southern Cameroons independence in association with French Cameroun (Fonkem, 2018, p. 3). The region has since suffered discrimination and other human rights violations from the majority of French-speaking Cameroon (Fonkem, 2018, p. 3).

An important question in this narrative is whether the quest for self-determination includes a form of terrorism. According to Article 1(2) of the UN Charter, to maintain international peace and security, the principle of equal rights and self-determination of a people must be strengthened against acts of aggression that breach universal peace. This is reiterated in Article 20(1) of the African Charter on Human and Peoples' Rights which says that:

> All peoples shall have the right to existence. They shall have the unquestionable and inalienable right to self-determination. They shall freely determine their political status and shall pursue their economic and social development according to the policy they have freely chosen. (African Charter on Human and Peoples' Rights (1981), art. 20(1))

Governments have been unable to agree on a definition of terrorism, where political disagreements are supposed to be fairly easy to resolve, but rather turned to the choice of morally inexcusable tactics to sacrifice innocent bystanders as terrorists (M Scheinin & M Vermeulen, 2013).

Some of the temptations confronting states in the fight against terrorism are where the states ignore procedural principles and rights safeguards which might have counter-productive consequences. Such moves eventually increase rather than reduce levels of violence and alienate or radicalize groups while reducing the state's moral authority and its ability to rely on the legitimacy of public institutions (Ford, 2013).

The misuse of the term "terrorism" in Cameroon anti-terrorism law has aggravated the potential risk for unintended human rights abuses. The use of the term "terrorism" without a clear definition of it can result in the international legitimization of conducts undertaken by oppressive regimes by delivering the message that the international community wants strong action against terrorism (M Scheinin & M Vermeulen, 2013, pp. 22–23). In Spain, the anti-terrorist laws allow for incommunicado detention for up to five days, which can be extended to thirteen days, during which the right to communicate with family members and have access to lawyers or doctors of the detainee's choice is denied (PP Sale, 2016, p. 22). Human rights groups continue to denounce the abusive use of the term "terrorism" as contrary to International Law.

Although counter-terrorism and security threats are legitimate, how a state responds to terrorist threats tells a good deal about the quality of its wider commitment to constitutionalism. This may be contrary to a situation where a state will treat ordinary criminals and political challenges or opponents as terrorists (Ford, 2013, p. 3). One of the important factors worthy of note is when it comes to the respect of human rights activists or partners seeking to persuade governments of the merits of demilitarizing their domestic counter-terrorism approaches. In the case of the trials of ex-British Southern Cameroons activists in the military court, a lot of pressure was mounted on Cameroon to drop charges of terrorism against these activists and seek for an alternative democratic solution to their actions than the use of the 2014 Law on Suppression of Acts of Terrorism (Ford, 2013, p. 3). The insistence by Republique du Cameroun on using terrorism has primarily been to win international favor and to proceed with their annexation agenda. It is an escape route and a rationalization of state terror on the people and leaders of ex-British Southern Cameroons. Second, insistence on terrorism regarding the Southern Cameroons' conflict is a conflict approach known as avoidance. Government's desire to avoid the conflict makes her use the fight against "terrorists" as a strategic response to the conflict. This is a tactic in conflict studies (International Crisis Group, Report N. 250 August 01, 2017).

Angela Quinta of the South African *Sunday Times* newspaper reported that Cameroon's anti-terrorism law is a powerful tool of fear, to opposition parties, the media, trade unions, and civil society and human rights organizations. The law is criticized as overly broad with easy potential for abuse of political opponents and the right to freedom of expression. The law has a maximum sentence of the death penalty and allows authorities to detain indefinitely those accused of terrorism. It also provides for prosecution in military court, contravening Article 10 of the Universal Declaration of Human Rights (hereinafter

UDHR), which guarantees individuals a fair, independent, and public hearing of any criminal charges against them, and the African Charter on Human and Peoples' Rights, which Cameroon ratified in 1989 (A Quinta, 2017).

There have been several international and regional calls to repeal the Law on Suppression of Acts of Terrorism in Cameroon (UN Universal Periodic Review, 2017). Local and international media and rights groups have protested Cameroon's use of the anti-terrorism law to target critics. Some media groups like the Northwest Chapter of the Cameroon Association of English-speaking Journalists (CAMASEJ) and the Independent Cameroon Journalists' Trade Union called for a repeal of this law because the government uses the law to target also their colleagues (CAESJ, 2017). At the World Editors Forum in Durban, South Africa, in June 2017, the World Association of Newspapers and News Publishers adopted a resolution about the lack of press freedom in Cameroon. This law like many other laws of the state is to replicate international prescriptions or regulatory mechanisms in the fight against this phenomenon.

INTERNATIONAL CAMPAIGN ON COUNTER-TERRORISM AND HUMAN RIGHTS

Although human rights standards have not changed since the September 11, 2001, attack on the World Trade Centre in the United States, the political atmosphere has palpably been altered leaving the human rights regime menaced by potentially dramatic alterations in the rules on the use of force in international relations and in norms of humanitarian law. Not surprisingly, repressive governments have become empowered to pursue their own business as usual, with less fear of critical scrutiny by the UN Charter-based bodies. Little has been achieved to address the root causes of terrorism within the UN System (Fitzpatrick, 2003). The UN Resolution 2178 of 2014 has provided that states shall ensure that their domestic laws and regulations establish serious criminal offenses sufficient to provide the ability to prosecute and to penalize in a manner duly reflecting the seriousness of the offense (United Nations Assembly, 2014).

The human rights imperative of preventing harm to civilians, many foresaw the damaging effect that a global counter-terrorist narrative might have on African authorities' respect for human rights and due process, and the potential to abuse it for domestic political purposes. Another form of counter-terrorism as suggested in the UN Resolution is by promoting political and religious tolerance, economic development, and social cohesion and inclusiveness, ending and resolving armed conflicts, and facilitating reintegration and rehabilitation (United Nations Assembly, 2014, p. 2).

Military involvements in law enforcement are not an innovation in counter-terrorism but in some cases have aggravated the violence (Fitzpatrick, 2003, p. 244). This is evident with Cameroon's military expedition in the fight against armed restorationists in the ex-British Southern Cameroons through the application of brute force or excess force, extrajudicial killings, and maiming of civilians. Military aggressions continue to be reported in the Anglophone region of Cameroon under the pretext of fighting against terrorism.

One of the challenges concerning the applicability of human rights principles in the counter-terrorism context is the argument that human rights obligations are territorial in scope, limited to a state's own territory where it exercises jurisdiction (M Scheinin & M Vermeulen, 2013, p. 37). While this argument has some support in the wording of Article 2(1) of the International Covenant on Civil and Political Rights (ICCPR) 1966 which states that "each State Party to the Covenant undertakes to respect and ensure to all individuals within its territory and subject to its jurisdiction the rights recognised in the Covenant," the government of Cameroon may have violated the same treaty it ratified. This provision demonstrates also that states must comply with the Covenant wherever they exercise powers that affect the enjoyment of the rights enshrined in the Covenant. State terror and the use of military power in the supposed fight against terrorism continue to cause untold suffering on the population of the affected area. Nevertheless, the international campaign in the fight against terrorism dates back to the League of Nations aimed at preventing dangerous activities such as assassinations, hostage-taking, and other forms of terrorism which posed a great social danger and were declared an international crime (M Kovacevic, 2012).

United Nations International Action against Terrorism

Since 1937, the League of Nations drafted the Convention for the Prevention and Punishment for Terrorism and the international community from 1963 developed twelve universal legal instruments to prevent terrorist acts. The UN Security Council adopted the Security Council Resolution 1373 in 2001 (hereinafter UNSC Resolution 1373) following the September 11, 2001, terrorist attack in the United States (UNO, 2006). The Resolution has among others also established the Counter-Terrorism Committee (CTC) comprising all fifteen members of the Security Council. The job of the CTC is to motivate and monitor the implementation of Resolution 1373 and to facilitate technical assistance to the Member States who lack the capacity to comply with their obligations under the Resolution and all other terrorism-related conventions and protocols (United Nations Security Council, 2001). The government of Cameroon's use of its anti-terrorism law for the trial of ex-British Southern

Cameroons activists and other brutal campaigns cannot benefit from this Resolution.

Recent actions between Cameroon and Nigeria (UN Member States) which violated the principles of non-refoulement had brought to light the controversy in relation to the UNSC Resolution 1373. The 1951 UN Convention relating to the status of refugees as provided for in Article 33(1) that:

> No Contracting State shall expel or return ('refouler') a refugee in any manner whatsoever to the frontiers of territories where his life or freedom would be threatened on account of his race, religion, nationality, membership of a particular social group or political opinion. (United Nations Res. 429 (V) on Convention Relating to the Status of Refugees (1951), art. 3(1))

Article 1(1) of the Protocol to the Convention stipulates that "The States Parties to the present Protocol undertake to apply articles 2 to 34 inclusive of the Convention to refugees as hereinafter defined."

The United Nations High Commission for Refugees (UNHCR) in February 2018 condemned the action taken by Nigeria on January 5, 2018, that forcefully returned to Cameroon ex-British Southern Cameroons asylum seekers or refugees in Nigeria who according to Cameroon were suspected terrorists trying to destabilize the country (UN Refugee Agency, 2018). A press statement from UNHCR office in Nigeria on February 1, 2018, stated that

> The UN Refugee Agency has learned with great concern of the forced return by Nigeria of 47 Cameroonians, who were handed over to the Cameroonian authorities on 26 January 2018. Most of the individuals in question had submitted asylum claims. Their forcible return is in violation of the principle of non-refoulement, which constitutes the cornerstone of the United Nations Convention relating to the Status of Refugees 1951.

The justification behind this action was international cooperation in the fight against terrorism. The two states also abrogated the provision under International Convention against Torture in which its Article 3(1) says that: "No State Party shall expel, return (refouler) or extradite a person to another State where there are substantial grounds for believing that he would be in danger of being subjected to torture" (Convention against Torture and Other Cruel, Inhuman or Degrading Treatment or Punishment, (1984), art. 3(1)).

Lack of a uniform or universal definition of the term "terrorism" potentially undermines possibilities for extradition or other forms of judicial cooperation which traditionally require double criminality or only acts which are criminal in both the requesting and requested states as extraditable offenses (M Scheinin & M Vermeulen, 2013, p. 23). The UN General Assembly Resolution 16/158 of 2005 enjoined all Member States to ensure that any measures taken to combat terrorism comply with their obligations under International Law, in particular human rights law, refugee law, and international humanitarian law.

Convention against Torture and Other Cruel, Inhuman, or Degrading Treatment or Punishment 1984

The Preamble of the Convention states that "recognition of the equal and inalienable rights of all members of the human family is the foundation of freedom, justice and peace in the world" (UN Convention against Torture and Others, 1984). The trials of ex-British Southern Cameroons' activist in a military tribunal in Cameroon probably violated or undermined the provision of Article 1(1) of this international instrument which Cameroon ratified to respect and uphold. The 1996 Constitution of Cameroon also stated in Article 45 that "duly approved or ratified treaties and international agreements shall, following their publication, override national laws, provided the other party implements the said treaty or agreement" (Law No. 96-6 of January 18, 1996, to amend the Constitution of June 2, 1972, art. 45). Unfortunately, the trial of ex-British Southern Cameroons activists in a military tribunal seemed to have had no regard to this supreme law of the state thereby relying only on the Law of Suppression of Acts of Terrorism as a means of fighting terrorism.

The prohibition of torture also appears from the fact that in several conventions, the article which prescribes this prohibition is one of the few articles where no derogation may be made in a time of war or in other public upheavals, for example, the International Convention against Torture and Other Cruel, Inhuman, or Degrading Treatment or Punishment, Article 2(2). An individual right not to be exposed to torture is a natural ingredient of any human rights instrument of a general character (H Danelius, 1989). According to Article 5 of the Universal Declaration of Human Rights 1948, "no one shall be subjected to torture or to cruel, inhuman or degrading treatment or punishment." Such prohibition is also provided in the African Charter on Human and Peoples' Rights 1981 in its Article 5 that:

> Every individual shall have the right to the respect of the dignity inherent in a human being and to the recognition of his legal status. All forms of exploitation and degradation of man particularly slavery, slave trade, torture, cruel, inhuman or degrading punishment and treatment shall be prohibited. (African Charter on Human and Peoples' Rights, OAU Doc. CAB/LEG/67/3 rev. 5, 21 I.L.M. 58 (1982), art. 5)

The analysis of these provisions against torture highlights the fact that in the fight against terrorism, state actors must pay serious attention to human rights principles and other related instruments. The disregard of these instruments may lead to a state of anarchy and degrading treatment of suspected "terrorists." Article 3 of the Declaration on the Protection of All Persons from Being Subjected to Torture and Other Cruel, Inhuman, or Degrading Treatment or Punishment 1975 has also reiterated the fact that no state should invoke any justification of torture or a form of degrading treatment based on war or threat of war, internal political instability, or any public emergency.

Torture, inhumane treatment, and unfair trials are instances for state excuses when granted a license to kill suspected enemies of the state which cannot be appealing to anyone sensitive to human rights and abuse of power. The disparity in such attitude through targeted killings and unfair trials reveals a fundamental disagreement not only with regard to their morality or legality but also on the issue of the legal regime by which that legality is judged (D Kretzmer, 2013).

According to Kretzmer, the real threat to the fight against terrorism as a threat to the present situation lies in over-reaction to terror by governments and adoption of measures that are incompatible with both human rights standards and rules of humanitarian law (D Kretzmer, 2013, p. 326).

The issue of fair trial and military excesses is a continual concern for the Cameroon justice system. The paramilitary or penitentiary administrators routinely beat or torture to death prisoners throughout the country; in several instances, they beat and abused opposition party activists to intimidate and repress political activity (Anonymous, 1994).

The crisis in ex-British Southern Cameroons region of Cameroon has deepened a pre-existing culture of censorship, with several civil society organizations that represent the interests of journalists arguing that the regime in Yaounde has instigated a climate of fear that has led to reporters self-censoring to avoid persecution. The US State Department's report in 2019 on the situation in Cameroon noted that several journalists had been arrested by police for investigating human rights abuses within the Anglophone region (Oxford University, 2019, p. 25).

The court system is highly controlled by the executive organ of the state, such that the Judges are subject to the government orders or directives, especially in political cases. Magistrates are instructed to render decisions in political cases in favor of the government and failure to do so may lead to their transfer to less desirable positions (Anonymous, 1994, p. 31). The 1996 Constitution of Cameroon provides for freedom of assembly and association, but such freedoms are highly restricted in practice. The Penal Code prohibits public meetings, demonstrations, or processions without prior government approval. The government severely hindered the ability of opposition parties to operate, generally by refusing them permission to hold meetings on the basis of various technicalities (Anonymous, 1994, p. 33). Any movement formed to protect the Southern Cameroons identity has been outlawed by the government of Cameroon. For example, the Southern Cameroons' National Council formed in 1993 was banned as a "rebel movement," and in 2017 the Cameroon Anglophone Civil Society Consortium was banned, and its leaders were arrested and jailed for eight months with trumped charges of terrorism and insurrection against the state. The use of government apparatus often-times results in torture or unfair trials of the individual(s).

SUBSTANTIVE NORMS UNDER THE AFRICAN CHARTER ON HUMAN AND PEOPLES' RIGHTS

The African Charter on Human and Peoples' Rights (1981) guarantees the life and integrity of the human person. Several provisions in the Charter pro-hibit torture. The obligations in Article 5 of the Charter emphasize the right to dignity and state responsibility to ensure "all forms of exploitation and deg-radation of man, particularly slavery, slave trade, torture, cruel, inhuman or degrading punishment and treatment shall be prohibited when fighting against terrorism, and to uphold human rights principles." This provision is reiterated in the African Commission on Human and Peoples Rights Principles and Guidelines on Fair Trial that "States must ensure that no person, lawfully deprived of his or her liberty is subjected to torture or to cruel, inhuman or degrading treatment or punishment." The emphasis is without guarantee to equal protection of the law, right to life, fair trial, and due process (F Vil-joen & C Odinkalu, 2006, pp. 36–37).

The African Commission on Human and Peoples' Rights in addressing African States approach to counter-terrorism has taken the view that "detain-ing individuals without allowing them to contact with their families and refusing to inform their families of the fact and place of the detention of the individual(s) amounts to inhuman treatment both of the detainees and their families" (F Viljoen& C Odinkalu, 2006, p. 38).

Some of the human rights conditions concerning counter-terrorism cam-paign have to do with pre-trial detention and incarceration of captured activists. This has to do with system nature that pertains to physical or psy-chological conditions. The notion of terrorism in Cameroon, therefore, means that terrorism charges against citizens who exercise their fundamental human rights are a serious threat to the enjoyment of these rights. The reason is that the application of any section of the law, in the form it has been in recent years, would have a concurrently disproportionate impact on civil rights and liberties guaranteed in the *Constitution of the Republic of Cameroon*, 1996 (the Constitution) (JCN Ashukem, 2020). Although some of these fundamen-tal rights expressions through public protests do turn violent disrupting public tranquility, they may not amount to acts of terrorism in its definition.

CONCLUSION

The use of the anti-terrorism law that provides for capital punishment led to a lot of military excesses among which are summary executions or extrajudicial killings, rapes, maiming, and many other related human rights abuses within the framework of fighting against terrorism. The Cameroon anti-terrorism law has confused the judicial system in understanding which jurisdiction has competence in the trials of human rights activists.

Tolerated torture or ill-treatment of human rights activists is still very much prevalent in many African countries despite the very extensive norm-setting work that has been carried out by African Union member countries and the UN Organization.

The Law on Suppression of Acts of Terrorism in Cameroon has stifled any public demonstration in the country that touches on the non-respect of the rule of law, violations of human rights, national discrimination, political exclusion, socioeconomic marginalization, and lack of good governance, without recognizing that none of these conditions can excuse or justify acts of terrorism. It has become complex to determine who is a "terrorist" and who is a "human rights activist" in the application of this law against terrorism.

Over the years, the government of Cameroon has denied political criticisms, and the anti-terrorism law poses potential threats to fundamental human rights and freedoms. Instead, the government has argued that the death penalty targets terrorist groups. Contrarily, since the enactment of the anti-terrorism law, there has been a widespread disruption of the exercise and enjoyment of fundamental human rights and freedoms, to the extent that people have been tagged, judged, and imprisoned as terrorists by the Yaounde Military Tribunal.

The trials of ex-British Southern Cameroons Activists in a military tribunal in Cameroon have been condemned as contravening international and domestic laws. The use of a repressive law in the trials of human rights activists may be interpreted as a weapon to deal with those considered as enemies of repressive or dictatorial regimes. A review of this law may without gainsay institute proper administration of justice and the respect of human dignity.

It can be true that terrorism has adverse impacts on human rights and the functioning of civil society and the international community as a whole (Conte, 2006, p. 281). State's obligations to counter-terrorism must be in a manner that is consistent with human rights, although the respect for human rights is not an absolute blind position. Such measures taken to combat terrorism must comply with human rights standards. The measures must remember that human rights standards themselves allow for limitations (Conte, 2006, p. 282).

REFERENCES

A Quinta. (2017). *In Cameroon, Anti-Terror Law is Used to Silence Critics, Suppress Dissent.* Sunday Times Newspaper, https://www.timeslive.co.za/ideas/2017-09-20 -in-cameroon-anti-terror-law-is-used-to-silence-critics-suppress-dissent/.

African Charter on Human and Peoples' Rights (1981), art. 20(1).

African Charter on Human and Peoples' Rights, OAU Doc. CAB/LEG/67/3 rev. 5, 21 I.L.M. 58 (1982), art. 5.

African Commission on Human and Peoples' Rights 'Principles and Guidelines on The Right to a Fair Trial and Legal Assistance in Africa' (2013), Sect. 2(1) (e).

Africanews. (2018). *Cameroon Military Tribunal Jails Seven Anglophone Activists - Local Media.* www.africanews.com/.../cameroon-military-tribunal-jails-seven -anglophone-activists-l.

Amnesty International Organisation. (2018, January). https://www.amnesty.org/en/ countries/africa/cameroon/report-cameroon/.

Amnesty International Organisation. (2021). https://www.amnesty.org/en/countries/ africa/cameroon/report-cameroon/.

Amnesty International Organisation. (2018). *Cameroon 2017/2018 Annual Report.* Amnesty International Organisation. https://www.amnesty.org/en/countries/africa /cameroon/report-cameroon/.

Anonymous. (1994). Cameroon. *Annual Human Rights Reports Submitted to Congress by the U.S. Department of State*, 29–37.

Ayim, M. (2008). *Former British Southern Cameroons Journey Towards Complete Decolonization, Independence, and Sovereignty: A Comprehensive Compilation of Efforts.* Vol. 2. Bloomington, IN, 208.

Bamenda Provincial Episcopal Conference [BAPEC] Memorandum to the Head of State . (2017). https://mission-universelle.catholique.fr/wp-content/uploads/sites/7 /2017/01/Bamenda-Provincial-Episcopal-Conference.Pdf.

Banseka, C. (2006). The Anglophone Problem in Cameroon: A Conflict Resolution Perspective: Cameroon. *African Renaissance*, 94–104.

CAESJ. (2017). *Cameroon Association of English Speaking Journalists Condemns Government Crackdown on Southern Cameroons Media' Cameroon Intelligence Report 11 February 2017.*

CAESJ. (n.d.). *Cameroon 'Annual Human Rights Reports Submitted to Congress by the U.S. Department of State 9', (1984) at 49-58.*

Cameroon Law No. 96-06 of 18 January 1996 to amend the Constitution of 2 June 1972. . (1996, Januray 18). http://confinder.richmond.edu/admin/docs/Cameroon .pdf.

Cameroon Law No. 96-06 of 18 January 1996 to amend the Constitution of 2 June 1972. art.65. (1996, January 18).

CHRDA. (2019a, June). *The Centre for Human Rights and Democracy in Africa (CHRDA) & The Raoul Wallenberg Centre for Human Rights (RWCHR) "Cameroon's Unfolding Catastrophe" Report of June 2019 at 53.* https://static1.square-space.com/static/5ab13c5c620b859944157bc7/.

CHRDA. (2019b). *The Centre for Human Rights and Democracy in Africa (CHRDA) & The Raoul Wallenberg Centre for Human Rights (RWCHR) "Cameroon's Unfolding Catastrophe" Report of June 2019 at 53.*

Conte, A. (2006). Anti-Terrorism, the Charter, and International Law. *Review of Constitutional Studies*, 281–316.

Convention against Torture and Other Cruel, Inhuman or Degrading Treatment or Punishment, (1984), art. 3(1). (n.d.).

Danelius, H. (1989). Torture and Cruel, Inhuman or Degrading Treatment or Punishment. *Nordic Journal of International Law*, 172–184.

Donohue, L. (2012). Terrorism and the Counter-Terrorism Discourse . In V. R. Al, *Global Anti-Terrorism Law and Policy* (p. 23). New York: Cambridge University Press.

DWNews. (2017). *DW.COM 'Cameroon Drops 'Terror' Case Against Anglophone Activists.* https://www.dw.com/en/cameroon-drops-terror-case-against-anglophone -activists/a-40306919.

Fitzpatrick, J. (2003). Speaking Law to Power: The War Against Terrorism and Human Rights. *European Journal of International Law*, 241–264.

Fonkem, A. (2018). Conflicts and Crisis in the Cameroon Anglophone Region. *E-International Relations*, 1.

Ford, J. (2013). Counter-Terrorism, Human Rights and the Rule of Law in Africa. *Institute for Security Studies Papers*, 3.

International Crisis Group. (Report N. 250 August 1, 2017). *Cameroon's Anglophone Crisis at the Crossroads.* https://www.crisisgroup.org/africa/central-africa/camer-oon/250-cameroons-anglophone-crisis-crossroads.

JCN Ashukem. (2020). To Give a Dog a Bad Name to Kill It–Cameroon's Anti-Terrorism Law as a Strategic Framework for Human Rights' Violations. *Journal of Contemporary African Studies*, 123.

Kovacevic, M. (2012). Harmonization of Legislation Fighting Against International Terrorism. *International Journal of Economics and Law*, 49–54.

Kretzmer, D. (2013). Target Killing of Suspected Terrorists: Extra-Judicial Executions or Legitimate Means of Defence? (2005) 16:2 *European Journal of International Law* 171–212. In M. Scheinin, *Terrorism and Human Rights* (p. 326). Cheltenham, UK: An Elgar Research Collection.

Law 007 of 2016 Relating to Penal Code. (2016a).

Law 007 of 2016 Relating to Penal Code (2016b), Sect. 21(1) & 22(1). (n.d.).

Law 028 on the Suppression of Acts of Terrorism in Cameroon (2014), Sect. 11. (n.d.a).

Law 028 on the Suppression of Acts of Terrorism in Cameroon (2014), Sect. 2(1d), (2d), 4(b) and 5(1). (n.d.b).

Law 028 on the Suppression of Acts of Terrorism in Cameroon (2014), Sect. 8. (n.d.c).

Law No. 96-6 of 18 January 1996 to amend the Constitution of 2 June, (1972), art. 45. (n.d.).

Law No. 2017/012 of 12 July 2017 to lay down the Code of Military Justice, Sect. 4(1). (n.d.).

Law No. 2017/012 of 12 July 2017 to lay down the Code of Military Justice, Sect. 8(b)(c). (n.d.).

Loi No. 2014/028 Portant Répression des Actes de Terrorisme (2014), Sect. 2(1)(a)(b). (2014). Cameroon.

Loi No. 2014/028 Portant Répression des Actes de Terrorisme (2014), Sect. 2(1)(a)(b). (2014).

Oxford University, F. O. (2019). *Faculty of Law, University of Oxford Report 'Human Rights Abuses in the Cameroon Anglophone Crisis' Submitted to UK Parliament (30 October 2019) 23.* London: Oxford University.

PP Sale, E. A. (2016). Incommunicado Detention and Torture in Spain, Part III: 'Five Days is Enough': The Concept of Torturing Environments. *Quarterly Journal on Rehabilitation of Torture Victims and Prevention of Torture*, 23.

RSF Refers Cameroonian Journalist's Death to UN Rapporteurs. (2020). https://rsf .org/en/news/rsf-refers-cameroonian-journalists-death-un-rapporteurs.

Scheinin, M., & Vermeulen, M. (2013). Unilateral Exceptions to International Law: Systematic Legal Analysis and Critiques that Seek to Deny or Reduce the Application of Human Rights Norms in the Fight against Terrorism. In M. Scheinin, *Terrorism and Human Rights* (pp. 21–22). William Pratt House, UK: Edward Elgar Publisher. Stemplowski, R. (2002). Anti-Terrorism and Hegemony. *Polish Foreign Affairs Digest*, 37–48.

Tande, D. (2016). *An Overview and Full Text (English) of the New Cameroon Penal Code.* http://www.dibussi.com/2016/07/cameroon-penal-code.html.

The Dictionary.com. (n.d.). https://www.dictionary.com/.

Trusteeship Council. (2020). https://www.britannica.com/topic/Trusteeship-Council.

UN Convention Against Torture and Others. (1984). *The Preamble of Convention Against Torture and Other Cruel, Inhuman or Degrading Treatment or Punishment.* https://www.ohchr.org/en/professionalinterest/pages/cat.aspx.

UN Refugee Agency. (2018, February 20). *UNHCR Condemns Forced Returns of Cameroon Asylum-Seekers From Nigeria.* http://www.unhcr.org/afr/news/press /2018/2/5a731fcf4/unhcr-condemns-forced-returns-cameroon-asylum-seekers -nigeria.html?query=nig.

UN Universal Periodic Review. (2017). *Republic of Cameroon Joint Submission to the UN Universal Periodic Review 30th Session of the UPR Working Group.* https://www.civicus.org/documents/CameroonUPRSubmission2017.pdf.

UNGA. (1989). *United Nations General Assembly Resolution 44/128 of 15 December 1989 Relating to Second Optional Protocol to the International Covenant on Civil and Political Rights, Aiming at the Abolition of the Death Penalty.* https://www .ohchr.org/EN/Pro/ProfessionalInterest/Pages/2ndOPCCPR.aspx.

United Nations Assembly. (2014). *72nd Meeting of United Nations Security Council Resolution 2178.* http://www.un.org/en/ga/search/view_doc.asp?symbol=S/RES /2178%20%282014%29.

United Nations International Covenant on Civil and Political Rights (1966), art. 6(1) & 7. (1966). https://www.ohchr.org/en/professionalinterest/pages/ccpr.aspx.

United Nations Res. 429 (V) on Convention Relating to the Status of Refugees (1951), art. 3(1). (n.d.).

United Nations Security Council. (2001). *United Nations Security Council Resolution 1373.* United Nations Organisation. https://www.un.org/sc/ctc/resources/databases /recommended-international-practices-codes-and-standards/united-nations-secu-rity-council-resolution-1373-2001/.

UNO. (2006). *United Nations International Action Against Terrorism.* https:// documents-dds-ny.un.org/doc/UNDOC/GEN/N05/504/88/PDF/N0550488.pdf ?OpenElement.

Viljoen, F., & Odinkalu, C. (2006). *The Prohibition of Torture and Ill-Treatment in the African Human Rights System: A Handbook for Victims and Their Advocates.* Geneva: World Organisation Against Torture, Vieux-Billard.

Chapter 15

Invincible People of Ambazonia

Carlson Anyangwe

The colonial occupation and brutal oppression of Ambazonia by Cameroon Republic is now close to sixty long years. Cameroon Republic is daily plundering and looting the resources of Ambazonia, violently imposing on Ambazonians, humiliating them, and terrorizing them.[1]

The die was cast three years ago. We took one giant step to end our shameful status as a colonized people. Like all slaves, we revolted. The colonial oppressor then demonstrated its determination to exterminate us and steal our Homeland. It unleashed an unjust war on us. Since then, we have been in the throes of an existential armed threat. In fact, since August 1961 to this day, Cameroon Republic has routinely been killing Ambazonians, year in and year out without any let up. Consider the following random examples: raid in Bamenda in August 1961 by Cameroon Republic troops causing an unspecified number of deaths, the Ebubu massacre in September 1961, Tombel massacre 1966, Bamenda massacre 1990, Ndu massacre 1992, Kumbo massacre 1996, yearly massacres every 1st October when the people come out to commemorate that date which is one of ending of trusteeship and achievement of independence, and massacres periodically perpetrated since the beginning of Ambazonia's War of Resistance in 2017. These killings evince a clear intention to exterminate the people of Ambazonia. We therefore do not use the term genocide or "Ambacide" lightly.

We are fighting for survival as a people. We are literally fighting with bear hands, apparently with no expertise in the art of war. But against all odds, we continue to resist the mighty onslaught of a well-resourced Cameroon Republic army backed by mercenaries and well-known foreign governments.

That notwithstanding, we remain defiant and undaunted. We shall fight on for 100 years, if need be. We shall fight on until our Homeland is totally liberated. We shall fight on until we are free. We shall fight on until we unfetter the shameful shackles around our necks and feet, like those of slaves of old. We shall fight on until we defeat the enemy. We do not doubt success and final victory.

Let the world know and bear witness that we are fighting for the decolonization of Ambazonia. That territory is historically, culturally, and legally our Homeland. It has been ours from time immemorial. It belongs to us and to none other. Sovereignty over it lies with us, the people of Ambazonia. No other people can possibly assert a superior title to that land.

It is our right and duty to institute a government on that territory, laying its foundation on such principles, and organizing its powers in such form, as to us seems most likely to secure our national interest, our safety, our welfare, and our happiness. No one, no country, and no organization should presume to do so for us or to deflect us from doing so.

In the past:

- We allowed the UN to impose on us an unwarranted and choice-less plebiscite that took place on February 11, 1961;
- We attended a purposeless and agenda-less charade in Fumban in July 1961;
- We submitted to an annexationist document unilaterally framed and adopted by Cameroon Republic on September 1, 1961, and dressed up as a so-called federal constitution; whereas, it was a mere framework for the cannibalization of Ambazonia;
- We submitted on September 30, 1961, to the British transfer of powers not to the Government of Ambazonia as ought to have been the case but to a foreign country, namely, Cameroon Republic, resulting in the re-colonization, rather than the decolonization, of Ambazonia;
- We submitted on October 1, 1961, to occupation by Cameroon Republic forces and to rule by a Cameroon Republic pro-consul deceptively presented as "inspector of administration";
- We allowed in 1962 French Cameroon to extend to Ambazonia its torture outfits and its draconian Subversion Ordinance that sanctioned the trial of our people by military tribunals for a number of ill-defined crimes and, in effect, made every Ambazonian a prisoner in the closed society imposed on us by French Cameroon, practically converting our space of existence into an open prison system:
- We submitted in 1962 to Cameroon Republic imposition of its French colonial currency, its metric system, its system of driving on the right-hand side of the road, and of the French language as the language of governance;
- We allowed in 1966 French Cameroon to impose on us its one-party despotic rule;

- We failed in 1972 to oppose the odious plot and historical swindle of a so-called referendum which purported to have given a veneer of suspect legality to the continuing cannibalization of Ambazonia;
- We failed in February 1984 to confront President Biya when he purported to have completed the cannibalization of Ambazonia by resurrecting extinct *République du Cameroon* as a legal, territorial, and political expression, while at the same time asserting an unsubstantiated territorial aggrandizement claim to the territory of Ambazonia;
- We failed in 1990 and 1992 to reject the poisonous and conditioning fake "peace" discourse of Cameroon Republic;
- We failed in 1994 at the tripartite to reject and denounce Cameroon's continuing perfidy and efforts to get us to accept its brutal colonial rule and oppression;
- We allowed ourselves in 2010 to be manipulated by Cameroon's deceptive and aggressive use of the term "reunification" to think that the independence of French Cameroon involved us and that our Homeland is part of the territory of Cameroon Republic;
- We allowed ourselves to be hoodwinked in 2016 to agree to "dialogue" with the devil, a "dialogue" which ended with the kidnapping and incarceration of our then leadership.

All this nonsense is now over. Never again shall we give ear to and act on anything other than what we, as a sovereign people, have decided. Cameroon Republic, like an invalid, has used Ambazonia as footstool for decades. It has got free lunch from Ambazonia for over five decades. It must now grow up, get rid of its mentality of an invalid, start living on its own, and begin to cater for itself. The era of Santa Claus is over.

On this auspicious occasion, I pay tribute to the memory of our valorous soldiers who have gained honorable death in battle. I pay tribute to all those, including babies and the elderly, who have been cowardly murdered by enemy forces. I commiserate with all those who have been raped or maimed. I salute all our valiant people, our brave refugees and internally displaced persons. I salute our gallant and resourceful freedom fighters. We stand together until the end.

I salute our friends who continue to stand by us in various ways in this our hour of great tribulation, the darkest hour of our history as a people. Our life of sorrow will not last long. May our enemy be put to eternal shame! May our merciful Lord hasten the advent of our redemption!

Darkness tarries only for a while before dawn. The dawn of national liberation, the dawn of a free people, is about to break.

Long live the invincible people of Ambazonia!

Long live Ambazonia!

NOTE

1. This chapter is a copy of the address given by the author on the occasion of Ambazonia's 2019 Independence Day Celebration in Soweto, Republic of South Africa, October 1, 2019.

Appendix A

Important Dates in the Historical Development of the British Southern Cameroons Nation

Nfor Ngala Nfor

The incontrovertible fact that must be reaffirmed here is that the nation called Southern Cameroons is like all other modern African nations, a creation of European colonial interest. This was done without seeking the consent of the owners of the land. In carving out their early spheres of influence which later became colonies, they amalgamated hitherto separate autonomous kingdoms and chiefdoms together into larger political and legal entities to which new names were given. Hitherto, these separate autonomous kingdoms and chiefdoms were sovereign nations in their own rights and exercised varied functions of statehood. Contact with the west leading to the formal establishment of colonial rule started as follows:

1. In about 500 BC Carthaginian Mariners visited the Bight of Biafra and awed by the majesty of Mount Fako named it "the Chariot of the Gods." Many other European sailors, explorers, and traders visited the coast of Guinea, but nothing significant took place until the 19th century.
2. In 1848, Baptist Missionaries from Jamaica set up a Missionary Station in Bimbia. Joseph Merrick who returned to his routes in Africa to evangelize his African brothers and sisters led these Missionaries. This was the first Christian Mission Station in Southern Cameroons.
3. In 1858, Rev. Alfred Saker, an English Baptist Missionary, who had been forced out of Fernando Po, crossed over to the mainland and bought a piece of land from the Bakweri and Isubu Chiefs and founded the Sea Port town of Victoria. Rev. Alfred Saker named it Victoria in honor of the British Monarch H. M. Queen Victoria. Here we see the marriage of imperial politics and Christianity.
4. In 1884, Consul Hewett hoisted the British Flag and proclaimed Victoria a British Protectorate. To east of the River Mongo, Dr. Nachtigal, a

German Imperial consul general, concluded treaties with the Chiefs of the Douala area and declared the area German Protectorate.

With the British on west of the Mongo River and the Germans on the east, this marks the initial birth of the two Cameroons.

5. In 1884/1885, European powers held the Berlin Conference at which the African continent was partitioned among themselves for direct control and naked exploitation. This marks the birth of colonialism in Africa.

6. In 1886, the British withdrew their claim over Victoria, and it was ceded to the Germans. This means that from 1848 to 1886 (almost forty years), it was unchallenged British influence that was spreading in present-day Southern Cameroons.

7. Because the peoples cherished British rule over that of the Germans, they (the Germans) did not find it easy taking over and establishing their own system of administration. Up to 1905, the Germans were still held down in battles to subdue the natives. For record purposes, the Germans were in Southern Cameroons for less than three decades, that is, from 1886 to 1915 including period of the war.

8. In 1914, the First World War broke out and British and French combined forces under General Charles Dubel (British), defeated, and chased away German troops from German Kamerun in 1916. Failing to set up a joint administration (condominium) due to internal hostility and distrust, German Kamerun was provisionally partitioned into French Cameroun and British Cameroons. What initially was German Kamerun became French Cameroun while the British simply recovered their territory lost consequent upon Nachtigal's German-led coup of 1884.

9. In the spring of 1919 Viscount Milner, Secretary of State of the British Empire, and the French Colonial Minister Henry Simon on behalf of their respective Imperial Governments reached a permanent agreement on the British Cameroons and French Cameroun boundary. This is known in history as the Milner-Simon Agreement in honor of the two Colonial Ministers.

10. In 1922, the League of Nations ratified the partition and placed the two Cameroons under Mandate System. While British Cameroons was a Mandated Territory of the United Kingdom, French Cameroun was that of the French. Article 22 of the League of Nations Covenant constitutes the first international legal instrument on the existence of two Cameroons. No one in his sound mind can recognize the partition of Africa at the Berlin Conference and fail to give due legal meaning to the partition of German Kamerun, into two distinct Cameroons, that was ratified by

the Versailles Peace Treaty that gave birth to the League of Nations, the forerunner of the UN.

11. On June 26, 1923, pursuant to a British Order in Council, British Cameroons, for administrative convenience, was divided into British Southern Cameroons and British Northern Cameroons. While British Southern Cameroons constituted a separate province within Nigeria's group of Southern provinces, British Northern Cameroons was further split with a small part administered with Benue Province and two large chunks as parts of Adamawa and Bornu Provinces of Northern Nigeria.

12. The Second World War (1939–1945) ended with the founding of the United Nations Organization. On December 13, 1946, the United Kingdom signed the Trusteeship Agreement with the UN assuming responsibility as the Administering Authority over British Cameroons. British Cameroons, as all other Mandated Territories of the defunct League of Nations, became Trust Territories under the Trusteeship Council of the UN System. British Cameroons and French Cameroun were equal and were respectively registered as class "B" Trust Territories.

13. In November 1948, the UN General Assembly adopted Resolution 224(III) protecting each Trust Territory from annexation by either the Administering Authority or any other state.

14. The Trusteeship Council in discharging its obligations in respect of Art. 76(b) of the UN Charter sent out Visiting Missions to the Trust Territories. British Southern Cameroons received four Visiting Missions, the first being in 1949. The Visiting Missions assessed the political, economic, and sociocultural development of the territory toward independence and reported to the Trusteeship Council.

15. In 1953, Southern Cameroonian Members of Houses of Assembly (Regional House, Enugu, and Federal House, Lagos) declared "Benevolent Neutrality" in Nigerian politics and gave up all their rights and privileges to fight for the autonomy of Southern Cameroons. They convened the first political national conference in Mamfe with representatives from all over British Southern Cameroons. At this national conference a petition addressed to Her Majesty the Queen was adopted requesting for a separate Region for Southern Cameroons with its own House of Assembly and Government. Dr. E. M. L. Endeley led the delegation to London.

16. On October 26, 1954, Brigadier E. J. Gibbons, Commissioner, as President of the Southern Cameroons House of Assembly, inaugurated the House of Assembly. Dr. Endeley formed the first government of Southern Cameroons. By a Motion from Hon. J. T. Ndze of Nkambe, the House after due debate adopted October 26 as Southern Cameroons

National Day replacing Empire Day, May 24. This was in honor of this historic achievement of regional status and self-government. From this time on Southern Cameroons sent six representatives to the Federal House in Lagos. The Southern Cameroons House of Assembly consisted of (1) the Commissioner, who, as direct representative of H. M. the Queen, was the president of the House, (2) three ex-Officio Members, (3) thirteen elected members, (4) six Native Authority members, and (5) two special members.

17. In 1957 following the adoption of a new constitution, that is, Lyttleton Constitution, two important landmarks in the political development of Southern Cameroons were achieved. First, ministerial form of government was approved for Southern Cameroons effective in 1958. Second, a House of Chiefs was created in addition to the House of Assembly. It was in 1957 that French Cameroun had its first government under Mr. Mbida as the Premier.

18. In 1958, the Commissioner J.O Field declared, "A modern state is in the making, and today, one hundred years after the founding of Victoria, the Cameroons can look back with pride at its achievements *and look forward to its rapidly approaching independence with quiet confidence*" (emphasis mine).

19. On December 5, 1958, by Resolution 1282(X111) the UN General Assembly took judicial note of the statement made by the representative of the UK Government to the effect that, as compared with Nigeria, the Southern Cameroons had not been delayed in political evolution and that it was expected to achieve in 1960 the objectives set out in Art. 76(b) of the UN Charter, namely, "self-government or independence." This UK Government statement was contained in Memorandum T. 1393 of June 27, 1958, submitted to the UN.

May I further add:

a) That the UK Representative to the UN made this pledge before the UN in 1960 adopted Resolution 1514 on the mandatory granting of unconditional independence to all colonies and Trust Territories as the necessary instrument for the enjoyment of complete freedom and development by all peoples.

b) That the UK Representative here subscribed to the distinctiveness of British Southern Cameroons in international politics and law and her duty, as the Administering Authority, to respect her obligations as enshrined in the UN Charter and the Trusteeship Agreement—the treaty she signed with the UN on behalf of the Southern Cameroonian people.

20. In January 1959, general elections were held in which J. N. Foncha's KNDP that had been in opposition since 1955 narrowly defeated Endeley's CPNC. As democracy had become the culture of the Southern Cameroonian, Dr. Endeley, the first Premier, acknowledged defeat and peacefully handed over to J. N. Foncha. Foncha became the second prime minister of Southern Cameroons while Endeley became the Constitutional Opposition Leader in the House.

21. On March 13, 1959, the UN General Assembly adopted Resolution 1350(X111) recommending the holding of a plebiscite in British Southern Cameroons to ascertain the true wishes of the Southern Cameroonian people.

    From this UN Resolution it is conclusive that the conduct of a plebiscite would have been uncalled for had Southern Cameroons been an integral part of French Cameroun, which became La Republique du Cameroun on attainment of independence on January 1, 1960.

22. In 1959, the Mamfe Conference was held to decide on the political future of the Southern Cameroons. It was at this conference that Fon Achirimbi of Bafut, speaking on behalf of the Natural Rulers, made the following famous statement "We rejected Endeley because he wanted to take us to Nigeria. If Mr Foncha tries to take us to French Cameroun, we shall also run away from him. To me French Cameroun is *fire* and Nigeria is *water*. Sir, I support secession without unification."

23. On September 24, 1959, the Premier of the Southern Cameroons, J. N. Foncha, addressing the 4th Committee of the UN General Assembly, declared: "Any attempt to force us gain independence in a way that does not accord with our wishes would tantamount to a breach of the UN Charter and a violation of our fundamental human rights."

24. On October 6, 1959, the US Permanent Representative to the UN, H. E. Clement J. Zabloiski, contributing to the debate on the political future of the Trust Territory of British Southern Cameroons said: "The USA congratulates the people of the Southern Cameroons for their accession to auto determination as it constitutes the will of the population who wants to run its affairs democratically." Opposed to the idea of unification, he predicted "The results of a hurried choice imposed on the population of the Trust territory would be catastrophic for their political future."

25. On October 16, 1959, the UN General Assembly respecting the status and territorial integrity of Southern Cameroons adopted Resolution 1352(XIV) separating the former from Nigeria before the latter attains independence on October 1, 1960.

26. On May 31, 1960, the UN Trusteeship Council adopted Resolution 2013(XXV1) by which the UK Government, as the Administering

Authority, was requested "to take appropriate steps, in consultation with the authorities concerned, to ensure that the people of the territory are fully informed, before the plebiscite, of the constitutional arrangements that would have to be made, at the appropriate time, for the implementation of the decision taken at the plebiscite."

27. On October 1, 1960, the Southern Cameroons House of Assembly adopted a new (Constitution) Order in Council, 1960 S./1960.No./1654. This was the instrument to lead Southern Cameroons to independence. Southern Cameroons, as a distinct state, existed as a separate political and legal entity, independent of Nigeria and La Republique du Cameroun.

28. In October 1960, the UK Colonial Secretary of State for the Colonies, Mr. Iain Macleod, in interpreting the options before the Southern Cameroonian people as concerns the second plebiscite question, said:

> "A vote for attaining independence by joining the Republique would mean that . . . the Southern Cameroons and the Cameroun Republic would unite in a Federal United Cameroon Republic. The arrangements would be worked out after the plebiscite by a conference consisting of representative delegations of equal status from the Republic and the Southern Cameroons. The United Nations and the United Kingdom would also be associated with this conference."

The two nations to be partners in the new free association of two independent states respectively endorsed this formula, as it was clear that the UN was to be the sole umpire. By giving a new name, "Federal United Cameroon Republic" emphasis was here being laid on the equality of the two components and that even within the larger nation, each maintained, as it is legally binding in all unions of equals, its inherent identity.

29. In a plebiscite message to the Southern Cameroons' people, Dr. E. M. L. Endeley, like a prophet of old, predicted the fall of Southern Cameroons from a status of a distinct people in international politics and law, respected by the international community, to a colonized and enslaved people if they voted to join La Republique du Cameroun. Like the predictions of US Representative to the UN, Clement J. Zabloiski and Fon Achirimbi of Bafut, all Endeley's ten predictions (prophesies), came to pass.

In his 8th prediction he declared: "If you vote for Cameroun Republic, you will forever fail to secure independence for the Southern Cameroons because Cameroun Republic is still a COLONY of France." He reiterated, "it is no use for Southern Cameroons to move from the British COLONY system to the French COLONY system."

30. On February 11, 1961, a UN-sponsored plebiscite was held in Southern Cameroons, which according to UN plan was to enable Southern Cameroonians choose the nation (Nigeria or La Republique du Cameroun) with which to enjoy independence. The results favored La Republique du Cameroun.

31. On April 19, 1961, the powerful (political) 4th Committee of the UN General Assembly by fifty "YES," two "NO," and twelve abstentions overwhelmingly voted for the independence of Southern Cameroons. October 1, 1961, was declared Independence Day. Some of the fifty nations that voted "YES" are UK, USA, USSR, Australia, New Zealand, Canada, Sweden, Denmark, Norway, Japan, Mexico, Chile, Venezuela, Cuba, Japan, Iran, Iraq, Pakistan, Nigeria, Ghana, Sudan, Ethiopia, South Africa, Mali, Tunisia, Libya, among others.

32. On April 21, 1961, the UN General Assembly adopted Resolution 1608(XV) prescribing the holding of a post-plebiscite conference to adopt modalities for the formation of the Federal United Cameroon Republic by the two former UN Trust Territories of Southern Cameroons and La Republique du Cameroun. It was to be a federation of two states of EQUAL STATUS. The post-plebiscite conference was to be attended by the government of Southern Cameroons, the government of La Republique du Cameroun, the UK government, as the Administering Authority, and the UN. Though no date was fixed but being a UN agenda, indisputably, the UN was the legal authority to convene and preside at the conference. This post-plebiscite conference was never held.

33. On July 17–21, 1961, delegates of Southern Cameroons and those from La Republique du Cameroun met in Foumban. This was the first official contact of the representatives of the two states to discuss the constitution that should constitute the instrument for the formation of the federal union of two equal states. This meeting which could only have been preparatory to the UN programmed post-plebiscite conference adjourned to be reconvened in August. It never did.

34. On August 1, 1961, Hon. G. M. Thomson (MP Dundee East), now Lord Thomson, addressing the British House of Commons on the bungled decolonization process in British Southern Cameroons after reminding the British Government of its legal and moral responsibility, said:

> "The problem these two territories would in any event be difficult. There are two territories of completely different cultures, with different political systems . . . there are extremely complex problems in bringing these two countries together within one national state" (emphasis mine).

35. From the British Declassified Documents, it is eloquently stated: In order that people of Southern Cameroons may achieve independence by joining the Republic of Cameroun it is necessary that the Federation should come into existence at midnight of 1ˢᵗ October. At one and the same moment there will born the independent State of Southern Cameroons and the Federation of the United Kamerun Republic. The Federation would be a free association of independent and equal states. (emphasis mine)

36. The annexation, colonization, foreign occupation, and imposition of alien rule of Southern Cameroons by La Republique du Cameroun as of October 1961 are direct consequences of non-implementation of Art. 76(b) of the UN Charter and Resolution 1514 of December 14, 1960, on the unconditional granting of independence to all dependent territories. This situation was further complicated by the imposition of "independence by joining" and the failure to implement Resolution 1608 by the UN. This failure facilitated annexation and imposition of alien rule by expansionist La Republique du Cameroun.

37. On April 2–3, 1993, the holding of the All-Anglophone Conference (AAC I) in Buea to carry out a political autopsy of Southern Cameroonians under La Republique du Cameroun domination and adopt a road map for their destiny. Among many other things, the Buea Declaration vehemently condemned the subjection of Southern Cameroonians to second-class status and called for the building of a genuine federal system of the two states based on UN recommendation as enshrined in Resolution 1608.

38. In May 1994, AAC II was held in Bamenda amid an imposed military siege, after Yaounde failed in all its diabolic plans to sabotage the AAC II Conference. The Bamenda Proclamation, unambiguously, called on La Republique du Cameroun to dialogue with Southern Cameroonian leaders within a "reasonable time." But if this timely and legitimate call was not respected, Southern Cameroonians, within the ambit of their inalienable right to self-determination as provided for and protected by international law, will restore the statehood and sovereign independence of Southern Cameroons.

39. In June 1995, the SCNC sent a nine-man delegation to the UN to petition against the annexation of Southern Cameroons by La Republique du Cameroun. While in London, they issued the London Communiqué.

40. In September 1995, the SCNC conducted a signature referendum in which an absolute majority, 99 percent, voted for the peaceful restoration of the statehood and sovereign independence of Southern Cameroons. Many were arrested, tortured, and detained, but the people's will triumphed.

41. On the night of December 30, 1999, Justice Frederick A. Ebong by tape-recorded broadcast proclaimed the restoration of the statehood and sovereign independence of Southern Cameroons.

42. On January 8, 2000, Justice Ebong, Chief Ayamba E.O, James Sabum, and three others were arrested, and after four days of detention in Buea, they were whisked off to Yaounde, where they spent fourteen months in an underground detention cell. In the end, the secession charge against them was dropped, and they were released.

43. In May 2000, a Constituent Assembly was held in Bamenda in conformity with Articles 6 and 7 of the Bamenda Proclamation of 1994. At this Constituent Assembly state symbols for the nation, namely, Flag, Anthem, Coat of Arms, and Seal were adopted. It was also resolved that Southern Cameroons was to be a federation, the name, FEDERAL REPUBLIC OF SOUTHERN CAMEROONS was adopted. For a genuine federation, effective devolution of powers to the Local Government Areas and Counties, as the lower tiers of government will be known, was also approved.

A presidential system of government was adopted for the New Southern Cameroons. To put a firm foundation for constitutional democracy, after the gruesome dark age of annexation, a thirty-six-month Transitional Period was approved, and within this period the Southern Cameroons Constitution of 1960, *muta'tis mutan'dis*, will be the governing instrument until a new constitution is adopted by the people in a referendum.

44. In May 2000, the UN Secretary-General H. E. Kofi Annan paid his maiden visit to Yaounde, Cameroun, and called for "meaningful dialogue" between the stakeholders. The SCNC welcome his call for "meaningful dialogue" but made it clear that for this to be effective the UN should preside and Justice Ebong and all other SCNC leaders incarcerated in torture chambers of La Republique du Cameroun should be released.

45. In October 2001, historic celebration of 40th Independence Anniversary of the Federal Republic of Southern Cameroons took place. The UN Secretary-General, the Commonwealth, the AU, the Heads of States of the fifty nations that voted for Southern Cameroons independence in 1961, the Diplomatic Corps in Yaounde, La Republique du Cameroun, as a neighbor, and other important personalities including Lord G.M. Thomson were invited to witness the historic celebration. Treating this as an affront, the Yaounde expansionist regime put its troops on red alert and ordered troop reinforcements into Southern Cameroons as from mid-September. Bamenda, the center of the celebration was exceptionally militarized. In spite of the heavy presence of the

repressive forces, the celebrations went ahead. Many were arrested, brutalized, and detained, and in Kumbo three were short dead, many wounded and hospitalized of which one died later.

46. In November 2001, the nineteen SCNC leaders who were arrested and detained in Bamenda Central Prison since October 1 Independence Day celebration were forced out of prison at night. The Yaounde Proconsul in Bamenda had ignored court judgments and appeals granting bail with impunity. But with international pressure, Yaounde had to bow.

47. Twelve Southern Cameroonians in their names and on behalf of the Southern Cameroonian people in February 2002 filed a suit in the Abuja Federal High Court against the Federal Government of Nigeria for conniving with La Republique du Cameroun to seal its grand design to annex, colonize, and occupy Southern Cameroons.

On March 5, 2002, the court ruled recognizing Southern Cameroons as existed as of October 1, 1960, and compelled the Federal Government of Nigeria to table the right of Southern Cameroonians for self-determination at the UN, ICJ, and any other international body.

48. Firmly committed to peaceful resolution of the annexation, colonization, and foreign occupation of Southern Cameroons, these twelve patriots, reinforced by six other Southern Cameroonians, in conformity with the African Charter on Human and Peoples' Rights sued La Republique du Cameroun in the African Commission, Banjul, The Gambia on January 9, 2003. By "Banjul Decision on Admissibility," issued by the Secretariat of the Commission and signed on its behalf by Commissioner Professor Dankwa dated March 30, 2005, Southern Cameroonians won on ADMISSIBILITY. Final verdict comes up in May/June 2006.

49. In November 2004, Southern Cameroons, under the SCNC, was granted membership in the UNPO, at The Hague, The Netherlands. During the UNPO General Assembly of June 2005, the Southern Cameroons National Team SC 13 won Third Prize and National Vice Chairman; Nfor Ngala Nfor was elected into the Ten-Man Presidency (Governing Body) of the UNPO.

50. In March/April 2005, the Southern Cameroons' question for the first time, after forty-four years, was eloquently raised on the floor of the UN Commission on Human Rights in Geneva on the platform of the IFPERLM by Nfor Ngala Nfor. The response of La Republique du Cameroun's Ambassador, the following day, March 31, 2005, only confirmed the fact that in Africa there are two distinct Cameroons, namely, Southern Cameroons (Anglo-Saxon) and La Republique du Cameroun (Francophonie) and that the latter has annexed, colonized, and occupied the former in violation of International Law. The Written Statement submitted earlier on the annexation of Southern Cameroons

by La Republique du Cameroun and calling for urgent effective decolonization to avoid a blood bath was approved and forwarded to the UN
Secretary-General. This is the first time, since April 1961, that an organ
of the UN System officially handled the Southern Cameroons matter.

51. Following the arrest and their detention incommunicado of Nfor, Ngala
Nfor, Stephen Kongnso, and a foreign journalist, Mr. Andrew Mueller
(later released after two days to avoid a diplomatic row) in November
2005, the UNPO on December 1, 2005, organized a massive demonstration at The Hague, The Netherlands, calling on the Yaounde regime
to release the detainees and all other Southern Cameroonian prisoners of conscience. Above all, they pledged their SOLIDARITY with
the Southern Cameroonian in their legitimate and pacific struggle for
FREEDOM and INDEPENDENCE.

Appendix B

Some Compelling Documentary Evidence Corroborative of Cameroon's Colonization and Annexation of Ambazonia

Carlson Anyangwe

Ambassador Kosciuko-Morizet, France, April 1961: "In the space of a few weeks, after reading a report submitted in the last minute, which most of its members had not had time to examine seriously, the [Decolonization] Committee pronounced, in haste, on the question concerning the future of a people ... We hope that today's vote will not entail dramatic consequences, though we fear that a disguised annexation is being perpetrated, under the label of the United Nations, against the will of the people. We hope that all those who, in good faith, felt it their duty to vote in favour of this resolution will not some-day have cause to regret their somewhat hasty pronouncement."

George M. Thomson, MP for Dundee East, UK, speaking on August 1, 1961: "If anything goes wrong in the Southern Cameroons on or after 1st October ... the British government and the British people will get the blame for it."

Dag Hammarskjold, UNSG (1953–1961): "Uniting the Southern Cameroons to the Cameroon Republic is like forcing a balloon under the sea. One day, it will come out."

Pierre Messmer, the last colonial governor of French Cameroon, states authoritatively that on October 1, 1961, Ahidjo effected the annexation of the Southern Cameroons to Cameroon Republic. He points out that the so-called federal constitution provided merely for "a sham federation, which was, except in appearance, an annexation of the Southern Cameroons." "President Ahidjo came up with a draft deceptive federal constitution carefully written for him by his French lawyers. Ngu Foncha ... accepted without discussions what was, except in appearance, an annexation" (*Les blancs s'en vont—Recit de Decolonisation*, Paris, 1998, pp. 134–135).

Philippe Gaillard states that there was no union on October 1, 1961, and that what took place was a mere border adjustment, presumably, so it seems, enabling the Cameroon Republic to adjust its south-western border some 400 km westward to the point where it shares a common border with Nigeria (*Ahmadou Ahidjo: Patriote et Despote, Batisseur de l'Etat Cameroonais*, Paris, 1994, p. 123).

Stark argues that a federation in the sense of a voluntary relationship between political units did not exist. He points out that there was no true and genuine federation and that in reality the Southern Cameroons was incorporated into Cameroon Republic ("Federalism in Cameroon: The Shadow and the Reality," *Canadian Journal of African Studies*, vol. x, no.3, 1976, p. 441).

In the *Northern Cameroons case* it was opined that "on 1 October 1961 . . . the Southern Cameroons joined the Republic of Cameroon within which it then became incorporated" (ICJ Reports, 1963, at p. 22).

J. Vanderlinden concludes that the federation was merely a smoke screen meant to enable the Southern Cameroons to swallow the bitter pill of its annexation by Cameroon Republic, as in the case of Eritrea annexed by Ethiopia ("L'Etat Federal, Etat Africain de l'An 2000?" in *L'Etat Moderne Horizon 2000*, LGDJ, Paris, 1985, p. 307).

J. Crawford cites the Southern Cameroons as one of a number of former colonial territories "integrated in a state" ("State Practice and International Law in relation to Unilateral Secession," Report 1997, para 21).

Jacques Benjamin asserts that there was a creeping annexation of the Southern Cameroons by Cameroon Republic (*Les Cameroonais Occidentaux—La Minorité dans un Etat Bi-communautaire*, Montreal, 1972).

Deltombe et al. make the following point: "Ahidjo effected the political asphyxiation of the Anglophone newcomers. He did so . . . at the Foumban 'constitutional conference' where his French advisers devised a water-tight plan which, under the pretext of an egalitarian federation, consisted in reality in the annexation of the Southern Cameroons to the centralized and authoritarian system already in force in Yaoundé since the previous year. . . . In the purest of French traditions Ahidjo annexed the Southern Cameroons . . . thanks to the help of his clever French advisers. He then quickly embarked on a policy of forcible cultural assimilation with the help of '*la Coopération Française*,' as always. . . . Noting the effects of this enforced political and cultural assimilation, Bernard Fonlon, a native of the annexed country, quickly sounded the following alarm: 'In two or three generations, we shall be French'" (*Kamerun! Une Guerre Cachée aux Origines de la Françafrique 1948–1971*, Paris, 2011, pp. 483–485).

The overwhelming view of even authors who are not citizens of the Southern Cameroons and who have examined the evidence is that the Southern Cameroons was indeed annexed by Cameroon Republic.

Aboya Endong Manasse writes, "A federal constitution adopted on 1 September 1961 . . . established a very centralized system in which the Southern

Cameroons saw its autonomy gradually whittled away up to the point of total annexation. . . . The exploitation of . . . oil marked the beginning of the acceleration of the process of enforced franconisation" ("Ménaces sécessionistes sur l'Etat Cameroonais," *Le Monde Diplomatique*, Décembre 2002, no. 585, p. 12).

Luc Sindjoun another citizen of Cameroon Republic also points out that the "federation" was a mere make-belief strategy by Cameroon Republic designed to hoodwink the United Nations and the Southern Cameroons. It was "a federalism of absorption of the Southern Cameroons by Cameroon Republic . . . a phagocytosis strategy" and it "was used to procure the enlargement of Cameroon Republic." He also writes that on September 30, 1961, at Buea the Government of the United Kingdom solemnly transferred sovereignty over the Southern Cameroons to Ahidjo (*L'Etat Ailleur. Entre noyau dur et case vide*, Paris, 2002, pp. 127–129, 171).

Exactly the same conclusion was arrived at by other citizens of Cameroon Republic such as Lekene Donfack and François Mbome ("Les expériences de la révision constitutionnelle au Cameroon,'" *Pénant*, no. 808, janvier—avril 1992, p. 20).

Index

About the Contributors

Fonkem Achankeng, PhD, Hubert H. Humphrey International Fellow, and a conflict scientist, is a full professor at the University of Wisconsin Oshkosh. Prior to joining the faculty at the University of Wisconsin Oshkosh, Dr. Fonkem taught at Marian University (2002–2006), University of Wisconsin Parkside (2005–2006), and the University of Wisconsin Fox Valley (1999–2004). He also served for a decade and a half as a senior official in the Ministry of Foreign Affairs of Cameroon and was the founder and executive director of the Association for Nonviolence in Cameroon (1993–1998). Dr. Fonkem also earned his B.A. (summa cum laude) from the University of Benin, Benin City Nigeria, a master's degree from the University of Buea, and another master's from Antioch University, Yellow Springs, Ohio. His research interests encompass peace and conflict studies; postcolonial nationalism and conflict; nonviolence; identity, culture, and conflict; human and people's rights; international mediation; and crisis intervention. In addition to over twenty-six peer-reviewed articles and book chapters, Dr. Fonkem's recent books include *After the Rain Began*, Babcock University Press, 2023; *Crime, Second Chances*, and *Human Services: Creating a Pathway to Ordinary Life for the Convicted*, Lexington Books, 2019; *Nationalism & Intra-State Conflicts in the Postcolonial World*, Lexington Books, 2015; *British Southern Cameroons: Nationalism & Conflict in Postcolonial Africa*, Friesen Press, 2014; *Lefua in Lebialem: Decline or Transformation*, Nkemnji Global Tech, 2006. Dr. Fonkem is currently a member of the Executive Council of the Wisconsin Institute for Peace & Conflict Studies (WIPCS) representing the University of Wisconsin Oshkosh. He also serves on the Global Education & Research Team of the Dignity & Humiliation Studies (DHS) and on the Leadership & Scientific Committee of the Transnational Education & Learning Society (TELS).

Patrick Agejoh, LLD, also earned his LLB degree from the University of Yaounde 2, Soa; diploma in cyber laws at the Asian School of Cyber Laws, Pune, India; LLM degree from the Department of Law, University of Pune, India; and before his LLD from the University of Pretoria, South Africa. His research interests are in Intellectual Property Law, Human Rights, and International Trade Law. Dr. Agejoh has four years of teaching experience in law and has supervised Master's Degree candidates and mentored several Honors Degree candidates. He has published in international peer-reviewed journals and has one book in the market. He is a member of the American Society of International Law (ASIL) where he served as Co-Chair of the Africa Interest Group of ASIL for three years. Dr. Agejoh is also a member of the international network of Prison Fellowship International.

Carlson Anyangwe, LLB, LLM, PhD (Law, London University), is a professor of International and Human Rights Law. He has taught in universities in Cameroon and Southern Africa. He has also served in various senior management positions in the academia, including those of Executive Dean of Laws and of Rector. Professor Anyangwe brings nearly four decades of struggle credentials to the epic struggle of the people of Ambazonia, the former United Nations Trust Territory of the Southern Cameroons under the United Kingdom Administration. He provides strategic counsel to the various Ambazonian liberation movements. He has litigated in the African Commission on Human and Peoples' Rights the question of self-determination for the people of Ambazonia and gross human rights abuses against them. He has written extensively on the legal and historical aspects of the Ambazonian Sovereignty Question and continues to do so. He has spoken on this issue at various forums in America, Britain, and South Africa and is always available when called upon to do so.

He is a member, since 2007, of the Working Group of Experts on Death Penalty, Extra-Judicial, Summary or Arbitrary Killings and Enforced Disappearances in Africa. This Working Group is a special mechanism of the African Commission on Human and Peoples' Rights. Rated in 2013 as a C2 researcher by the National Research Foundation of South Africa, he has over a hundred publications to his credit, including half a dozen law textbooks. Recognitions include the Distinguished Leadership Award by the ABI (1994), Ambassador of the State of Arkansas (1992), Honorary Citizen of the City of Monticello in Arkansas (1992), USIA International Visitor Fellowship (1992), and Research Fellow of the Max Planck Institute in Hamburg (1983).

Jean-Claude Ashukem, PhD, is an independent researcher and an expert in environmental law and natural resource governance. His other interests include environmental comparison, environmental procedural rights, human rights, aspects of constitutional law, land grabbing, and climate change impact of investment activities, from an African perspective. He has published extensively on these issues in scholarly journals as well as book chapters. Prior to being an independent researcher, Dr. Ashukem was a postdoctoral research fellow at the University of the Free State, Bloemfontein, South Africa, and the North-West University, Potchefstroom, South Africa, and a visiting research fellow at the University of Gissen, Germany, in 2013.

Lilian Lem Atanga, PhD, is an associate professor at the University of Bamenda, Cameroon, and a visiting researcher with the University of Free State, Bloemfontein, South Africa. She is a gender and discourse scholar, focusing on women, media, and politics. She recently completed her Fulbright program as a visiting scholar at the University of Florida and has published severally including her book on *Language and Gender in Sub-Saharan Africa: Tradition, Struggle and Change.*

Denis Atemnkeng, MA, has a background in law, economics, and translation. He is a retired official of the African Union Commission. He has spent decades investigating the root causes of the conflict between the Republic of Cameroon and the Southern Cameroons, both from the historical and legal perspectives. With the strong legal background he has, he has spearheaded many legal actions, including the Banjul case, Communication 266, which was initiated by him before being turned over to the main liberation movements. He has written hundreds of articles on different aspects of the struggle.

John Fobanjong, PhD, is a professor of Political Science at the University of Boston, Dartmouth.

Thomas Ayeh Jing earned his PhD in Education from the University of Regina in Saskatchewan, Canada.

Tatah Mentan is a pacifist and peace activist, Theodore Lentz Peace and Security Studies Scholar, and professor of Political Science.

Carol Chi Ngang, LLD, LLM, IDHA, SUSTLAW, and LLB, is a senior lecturer in Law at the National University of Lesotho and a research associate at the Free State Centre for Human Rights, University of the Free State, South Africa. His areas of expertise include Public International Law, International Human Rights Law, Sustainable Development Law, and Constitutional Law. His research interest combines human rights and development, with a niche focus on the right to development, and socioeconomic and cultural rights. He is a South African National Research Foundation (NRF) category C2-rated researcher with an extensive range of publications, including journal articles in peer-reviewed accredited local and international journals as well as books and book chapters by prominent book publishers. He has also previously accumulated a rich career profile as a development practitioner within the NGO sector, with experiences working in Cameroon and South Africa.

Nfor Ngala Nfor is a product of the Political Science Department of Ahmadu Bello University (ABU), Zaria, Nigeria. He is a Pan-Africanist and a lover of humanity. Her hates injustice and racism to the core and any acts that impose discrimination, no matter how thinly veiled. Nurtured in African core values and trained in mission schools with great emphasis on the fear of an omniscient and omnipotent Creator, he is a strong advocate and defender of truth and a crusader for human freedom, justice, equality, and dignity, and right of all peoples to be master of their destiny. He served for decades as the National Chair of the Southern Cameroons National Council (SCNC), a position in which he was severely persecuted by the government of Republique du Cameroun. At the time of publishing this book, Nfor Ngala Nfor was serving a life sentence in Yaounde as one of the leaders of British Southern Cameroons renamed The Republic of Ambazonia. His books include *Paradise Lost? A Political History of British Southern Cameroons from 1916 to 1972*, Pan-African University Press, 2020; *Died Not Dead*, Langaa RPCIG Publishing House, 2016; *Urgency of a Dawn: Prison Thoughts and Reflections*, Langaa RPCIG Publishing House, 2016; *In Chains for My Country: Crusading for British Southern Cameroons*, Langaa RPCIG Publishing House, 2014; *The Two Cameroons: Southern Cameroons for Southern Cameroonians*, Bamenda: Neba Publishers, 2010; *The Southern Cameroons: The Truth of the Matter*, Bamenda: Unique Publishers, 2002; *To Cameroon Patriots*, Zaria: Ramsel Publishing Corporation, 1985.

Gerald Nyuykongmo Jumbam is a Roman Catholic priest and a professor of theology in Rome.

Peter Stanley Nzefeh, PhD, is the author of two books. He taught History for many years at the Cameroun College of Arts and Science, Kumba.

Milton Keynes UK
Ingram Content Group UK Ltd.
UKHW041835220923
429235UK00003B/51